W9-ABQ-093

The History of Civilization
Edited by C. K. OGDEN, M.A.

The Roman Spirit

The History of Civilization

In the Section of this Series devoted to PRE-HISTORY AND ANTIQUITY *are included the following volumes:—*

I. *Introductory and Pre-History*

II. *The Early Empires*

III. *Greece*

IV. *Rome*

* An asterisk indicates that the volume does not form part of the French collection "L'Evolution de l'Humanité" (of which the present work is No. 17 of the First Section) published under the direction of M. Henri Berr, editor of the "Revue de Synthèse Historique."

A full list of the SERIES *will be found at the end of this volume.*

PLATE I

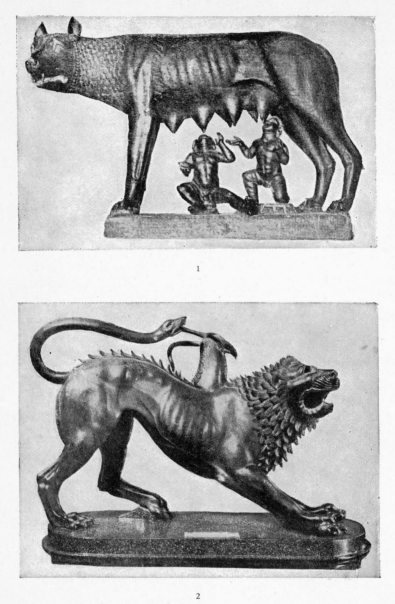

1

2

1. The Wolf of the Capitol. (Rome, Conservatori)
2. The Chimæra of Arezzo. (Florence, Archæological Museum)

[*front.*

The Roman Spirit

in Religion, Thought, and Art

By

ALBERT GRENIER

*Sometime Member of the French School in Rome and Professor at the Faculté
des Lettres of the University of Strasburg*

*WITH SIXTEEN ILLUSTRATIONS IN THE TEXT
AND SIXTEEN PLATES*

LONDON
KEGAN PAUL, TRENCH, TRUBNER & CO., LTD.
NEW YORK: ALFRED A. KNOPF
1926

Translated by

M. R. DOBIE

PRINTED IN GREAT BRITAIN BY
THE EDINBURGH PRESS, 9 AND 11 YOUNG STREET, EDINBURGH

CONTENTS

CONTENTS

PART II

ROME AS A MEDITERRANEAN CAPITAL.

CONTENTS

PART III

THE AGE OF AUGUSTUS.

CONTENTS

Conclusion

LIST OF ILLUSTRATIONS

ILLUSTRATIONS IN THE TEXT

PLATES

FOREWORD

ROME AND GREECE

ROME AND GREECE—*this was originally to have been the title of this volume. On consideration it seemed preferable to adopt as title the sub-title, slightly modified :* The Roman Spirit in Religion, Thought, and Art.[1]

It is true that when we study the life of the mind in Rome we encounter Greece. But Greek influence is at once more diffused and less dominant than is often supposed. For many years it filtered in, through the intermediacy of Etruria, and later of Campania and Sicily. When, afterwards, defeated Greece seemed to have " conquered her conqueror," the seductions of Asia and Egypt were perhaps more potent than hers.

For this Foreword the title Rome and Greece *presents no such disadvantage. In it I shall take up a traditional problem, the solution of which is, indeed, furnished by the illuminating inquiry of M. Grenier. If the whole book had borne this title, it would have been reduced to this single problem. Now, the object of our collaborator is very much wider—namely, to determine, from its first very humble manifestations, a psychical germ—itself, no doubt, the result of ethnical mixtures and certain conditions of life, but appearing at a given moment in history and essential if one is to speak of a " Roman spirit "—and then to follow this spirit of the people in its evolution. The special interest and the great merit of this work are that, without any preconceived idea, without philosophic theory, without belief in a* Volksgeist, *it constitutes a penetrating study in historical psychology. In other volumes of the same section the character of the Roman people is studied implicitly in its political life and the social organization which it created ; in this volume it is studied explicitly in the works of the mind. M. Grenier's work is an important contribution to* collective ethology.

I have tried elsewhere to show [2]—*and I believe that* L'Évolution de l'humanité *will prove—that research in collective ethology, which is concerned with what may be called " psychological races," has a greater range for the purpose of historical explanation than anthropology can have, seeking as it does to discover zoological races. I have defined the various forms of this branch of knowledge—descriptive, comparative, and genetic. The present study is genetic, as it should be. M. Grenier says emphatically that " the Roman spirit never was ; it gradually grew " ;* [3] *or at least*

---

[1] This volume corresponds to three in the Greek section of this series, viz. *The Religious Thought of Greece, The Art of Greece,* and *Greek Thought and the Scientific Spirit.* On the other hand, the Roman section has two volumes on institutions, as against one in the Greek section. This seems to be in accordance with the nature of things.

[2] *La Synthèse en histoire,* pp. 84-7.

[3] See pp. 114, 387.

xi

it developed, not merely at the dictate of circumstances, but through the exercise of the " marvellous power of assimilation " which was characteristic of the Roman from the intellectual point of view.

As we have previously seen,[1] the dominant features here are practical sense and will-power. The Greek is inclined to speculation and the play of art and literature ; the Roman acts. For a long time active, outdoor life—work in the fields, civic duties, and the conduct or preparation of war—seem to him the only occupations worthy of a free man. A full life is passed out of doors, in luce. Umbra, umbratilis secessus, *life indoors, retirement, is good for women, at the most, or for sick men. What makes life interesting is business,* negotium. *All forms of physical and civic inactivity,* otium, *however studious, cast some discredit on the individual who indulges in them. Hard peasants, who have led a hard life, who have known " long poverty," sustained constant struggles, and grown great and prosperous through their strict discipline and sense of realities—that is what M. Grenier first shows us in a summary full of vigour ; and in the striking portrait of Cato he sums up the moral physiognomy of early Rome.[2]*

One part of this book makes us see how the life of the mind—religion, thought, and art—originally bore the stamp of this pragmatism, how speculative interest in religion and aesthetic interest in all its forms were here reduced to the minimum.

The reader may be referred to the Foreword of the volume on the Religious Thought of Greece *for the study of the nature of religions and their rôle in human life. Of course, in Italy as elsewhere, the human being, by religion, interpreted the external world, in order to bind himself to it. We may compare the Roman of the earliest times to the primitive man whom the sociologist studies.[3] But we must be on our guard against a too schematic and absolute conception of this " primitive man." Even among the " lower " peoples of to-day, and therefore still more among early peoples which had made some progress and had therefore the impetus to carry them further, one cannot conceive of the famous " prelogical mentality " as being impermeable to experience.[4] Life is only consolidated by a certain foresight, by a certain power over things, which are based on a certain knowledge. The so-called prelogical mentality is all the more marked as a society crystallizes, as the minds in it become interconnected—as is noted in the case of the so-called primitive men who are in reality outcasts of civilization, isolated and degenerate.*

In some excellent chapters M. Grenier brings out the very special character of the religion of the Romans. Lacking imagination, poetic, plastic, or metaphysical, they had, corresponding to the real world, an infinity of powers, numina, *clearly defined in their function but ill-defined in their nature, forms, and relations.*

---

[1] Foreword to *Primitive Italy ;* cf. Foreword to *Rome the Law-Giver ;* both in this series.
[2] See pp. 144 ff.   [3] See pp. 85-6.
[4] See Forewords to *Language* and *From Tribe to Empire.*

" *The instinct which personifies concepts,*" Renouvier says in his Introduction à la philosophie analytique de l'histoire, " *is here carried as far as possible, and to the point of creating more deities than were known even to the fertile Greeks. But once these gods were created, they remained without history, without legends. Their devotees entered into relations of worship with them, and were more concerned to make them propitious and to interpret their will than to learn about their private affairs. As for the attributes which determine the divine, they were taken sometimes from natural phenomena and more often from the endless series of the customs, conditions, and accidents of human life.*" [1]

If he lacked the creative faculty to produce a theogony, the Roman applied to the religious practices in which his whole activity, private and public, was wrapped up that legal spirit which was one of his dominant characteristics. Worship was the performance of a contract—do ut des. *The ritual was minutely regulated and the formalism absolute ; neither too little nor too much must be done ; too much was* superstitio. *The priests were the* Jurisconsulti *of religion, the* Pontifices *were its* Prudentes. *There was no ardent aspiration, and no emotion—except that of fear, when one had not paid one's due.*

If the Romans were religious, if it was they who actually invented the word, it was because the original meaning of the term was not at all mystical, but legal and social. Relligio, *as Renouvier says, " is all that holds and fetters the soul.*" [2]

This religion, devoid of system and wholly practical, was necessarily hospitable to foreign gods. It took in the Etruscan and Greek gods in order to make them into higher gods and to establish some organization and some order of rank in the host of numina, *it welcomed many others in the interest of the* res publica, *and it annexed the Emperors, in order to deify the Empire. Rome " made religion serve her own aggrandizement " and " she was as eager to conquer gods as cities.*" [3] *The catholicity, which was later to unite all peoples in the worship of the same God, at that time united the worships of all gods in one same religion.*

Although, as we know,[4] *religion answers an individual, not a social need, it becomes an institution everywhere. In Rome this process was so thorough that the inner life was stifled by the casing. There were a few living beliefs only in the countryside, and a few religious questionings among a cultured few who asked Greek philosophy to satisfy their reason. But on various occasions an invasion of ecstatic, orgiastic cults, of the Oriental mysticism which was so contrary to Roman formalism, showed that there was a void in men's souls to be filled.*

From the primitive character of Roman religion it is evident that knowledge did not interest the Romans for its own sake. They cultivated neither philosophy nor science spontaneously. Not only were they indifferent " to the purely disinterested specula-

[1] P. 378.   [2] Op. cit., p. 382.
[3] Fustel de Coulanges, *La Cité antique*, p. 431 (14th ed.).
[4] See *The Earth before History*, in this series, General Introduction, pp. ix-x.

tive virtue which Pythagoreans and Platonists exalted in mathe-matical research," but they " despised " pure science, and " Cicero praises them because, by the grace of the gods, they are not as the Greeks, and are able to confine the study of mathematics to the domain of useful applications (Tusc., i. 5)." [1] *Whether they con-sider nature or man, they only attend to what will be useful for practical life ; there never was and never could be a scientific circle in Rome. Man, however, interested them more than nature, and in psychology and morals they acquired knowledge which made them the creators of the " humanities." And that is why they stand, not only as organizers of social life, but, with the Greeks, as teachers of the human race.*

In Rome, of necessity, even literature and art had to be closely attached to practical considerations, and this is what M. Grenier shows forcibly. The realist spirit of the Romans caused them to produce at an early date, in legislation, eloquence, and history, works which, by their qualities of exactness, vigour, and even utility—perfect utility—take on a character of beauty, but are militant, and do not make beauty their object. I may refer to the capital distinction which I have drawn [2] *between what aims at aesthetic pleasure and what procures it without seeking it—or at least without having as its special object the procuring of pleasure.* [3]

We must, however, recognize in satire and the dialogue the humble germs of literary art. These products of the soil, born in the rude merry-making of various festivals, reveal Roman realism in the spirit of observation, the tendency to sarcasm, manifested in the abundance of nicknames, and the aptitude for repartee. What would have come of this promise, if Greek influence had not come in, we can only conjecture.

Lastly, we must note that on the fine arts, inspired by the Etruscans, the Romans placed their mark at the beginning. Here, too, was realism in scenes from life and portraiture, the practical desire to record history and its heroes, to form a testimony of the past which should be useful to the present.

In Greece the useful was beautiful ; in Italy even the beautiful was useful.

Now we come to the other side of the picture. All through his book M. Grenier shows forcibly that this practical sense was too wise, and even too curious, to reject everything which might come from outside, and that independently of sudden actions and diffused influences there was a conscious, deliberate assimilation of intellectual elements borrowed from abroad—chiefly from Greece and the East.

Nowhere, in previous history, has it been possible to study in such a precise and instructive manner the phenomenon which we call reception. *We have observed that the logical principle*

[1] Arnold Reymond, *Histoire des sciences exactes et naturelles dans l'antiquité gréco-romaine*, preface by L. Brunschvicg, 1924, pp. vii, 91.

[2] See *The Art of Greece* in this series, Foreword.

[3] *Artes quae efficiant ut civitati usui simus*, that is what the Roman should learn (Cic., *Rep.*, i. 4). *Poesis* is a Greek word.

which founds a society and explains its internal transformations also presides over the relations of societies and explains various phenomena in them. Reception, renaissance, and co-operation answer in different ways to a " will to culture " which, for peoples, is one form of the need to be more.[1]

The crisis which transformed the Roman people occurred, or rather the crises commenced, when Greek civilization, instead of filtering in, penetrated direct, and, as it were, in mass, and affected even the education of the young. What Greece introduced into Rome was play.[2] The whole activity of the Roman was utilitarian; painfully, seriously, he did his duty as a pater-familias, a citizen, and a soldier; his joys were rare and austere; he found them chiefly in duty done and material success. He now learned to taste the life of pleasure. Art, literature, and speculation offered him all their delights at once. What had been diversion—in the Christian sense of the word—distraction from duty, idleness, became a necessity.

But the origin of the crisis must not be sought simply in the importation of all that the Greek genius had created. The causes were manifold. The general circumstances of Roman life had altered. Political and economic changes were the result of these transformations of the social structure—the empire constantly extending its bounds and the populace of the city constantly growing more numerous and more heterogeneous. M. Grenier lays stress in his earlier chapters on the contribution of the Latin peasant, on the virtues and the narrownesses which Rome owed to the soil, and shows that, in spite of the usual supremacy of the towns in all ancient history, the country played the first part here. Now we must see the rôle of the great city which Rome had become, the importance of the urban plebs and, through trade, of the foreign element, the hostis whom the country masses were disposed to mistrust or to hate. In the enlarged city human interests came into conflict with civic interests. The arts inspired by Greece and the East were a cause of moral evolution; but the spirit in which this inspiration was received was also the effect of the new circumstances. With great subtlety M. Grenier has disentangled these complex relations and interactions of works and morals in the process of growth, making clear the part played by the masses and the intellectual few, the thinkers, the artists, and women, in this psychological evolution.

It was a period of intense life, in which Rome was receiving things from every side and assimilating them, before reacting with a back-stroke of her pragmatism. In Italy, as in the whole of the Mediterranean basin, the fine arts became Hellenized. The reception of Greek things killed Italian art, just as the Renascence of antiquity was to kill Gothic art. But the peculiar feature in the case of Rome, as M. Grenier very justly observes, was the possession, without effort, of foreign beauty. The wealth of the Romans gave birth to a love of antiquities and to a magnificence in

[1] See *The Earth before History*, General Introduction, pp. xi-xii.
[2] See Foreword to *The Art of Greece*.

collections which, while it developed the aesthetic sense, fostered eclecticism and did not strengthen the creative spirit. On certain works, however—statues, coins, and historical scenes—Rome continued to place her own decided stamp.

On literature this reception had less negative effects. Filtering in through Italy, the great art of Greece, tragedy and the epic, in which Rome was able to find inspirations sufficiently in agreement with her ideal of moral force, was the first to penetrate. Later, as a result of direct contact, the Romans were attracted by all that was most subtle in Greek art in its refined decadence, acquiring from it qualities of elegance and ingenuity which were foreign to them. But in the Alexandrian form they often expressed passionate feeling. Art for art's sake, pure dilettantism, was repugnant to the Roman soul. Although by patient efforts a language which was originally poor and stiff grew richer and more pliant, Latin still obtained its happiest effects from its conciseness and strength, and its triumph was to be in the imperative brevity of the sententia. Moreover, there came a time when a happy alloy was created of Greek qualities and Roman tendencies. It was seen that play might serve the most serious and the noblest ends. Augustus raised all the arts by using them for the grandeur of Rome. With him, the Empire attained full consciousness of its past and its mission ; what inspired masterpieces was the Imperial City, and the land, gods, and men which had made it.

But within the city, now open to the world which it ruled, in the medley of races, appetites, and ideas, individual sensibility developed. Restless in the intellectual class, coarse and violent in the masses, it was soon to seek and find its pleasures and its beliefs, more and more, outside the Roman tradition, and outside the Greek ideal. In spite of the strong fabric of the State and the State religion, the moral crisis of the ancient world was preparing.

So there was a long predominance of practical reason, of mental adaptability combined with moral strictness and energy of will. Then sensibility, imagination, and taste developed. Then an equilibrium of faculties was established, and soon broken down in favour of sensibility. This is what M. Grenier shows in his study of the graduations of the Roman spirit.

The problems clearly set forth at the beginning—of the formation of that spirit, of its transformations, of the internal and external factors which produced them—are treated with remarkable sureness. In solving them our collaborator combines historical knowledge proper with the " specialities " of which the " pure " historian is often ignorant or neglectful. One feels that he is anxious not to make history too simple and not to forget, when considering abstract problems, the complexity of living reality. He gives us penetrating analyses and striking portraits. History is a science, it cannot be repeated too often. History is not an art. But the most scientific historian may be an artist.

HENRI BERR.

2 ROME AND ITALIAN CIVILIZATIONS

PART I

THE CITY OF ROME AND THE ITALIAN CIVILIZATIONS

CHAPTER I

THE FOUNDATION OF THE CITY

As I commence this work, I have not the least idea what the Roman Spirit may be, and I propose to do no more than consider certain of the successive aspects of the religious, intellectual, and artistic life of the Roman people. This survey will perforce be very incomplete; in particular, it will not touch upon all that legal activity which is treated in a separate volume in this series.[1] But perhaps in the end some general ideas will emerge, which may in a measure justify the title of this book. The reader must not, however, expect a systematic theory of the qualities, nor even of the development, of the Romans. Not in the abstract, but in the living reality of men and their works, following a strictly historical plan, we shall look for the Spirit of Rome.

For details of fact I may refer the reader to the volume which precedes mine.[2] Nevertheless, without fear of repetition, I have decided to take up my subject with the day of the very foundation of Rome. Before describing the flowering of Roman civilization, it seems right to consider the roots which fed it, and to ascertain, as far as possible, the deep layers of soil from which it drew its sap.

From its beginning, the Roman people lacked unity. It was not a race, nor even a natural association. We see it forming from the fusion of diverse ethnical elements, arti-

[1] J. Declareuil, *Rome et l'organisation du droit* (*L'Évolution de l'humanité*). A translation will appear in the series *The History of Civilization* under the title *Rome the Law-Giver.*
[2] Homo, **LXXXVI.**

ficially combined on a political and religious formula which is alien to them. The substance of which it was composed was chiefly Latin and Sabine. But the Etruscans gave it its form and truly created the people.

I

LATIUM AND THE LATINS

Round Rome, to-day, the desolate waste of the Campagna stretches as far as eye can see. The scanty grass, soon burnt up by the sun, gives the whole landscape a greyish tint, broken here and there by the black blot of an umbrella pine. The long lines of the aqueducts, thorn-bushes growing over buried ruins, an occasional *osteria* or a group of houses with their arbours and a few fields, a light cart travelling along a straight, white road—these alone give life to the solitude.[1] Man's neglect has allowed a desert to form at the gates of a capital.

Yet the countless ruins of the Roman Campagna bear witness that this land was once populous and flourishing.[2] Outside the walls of the city there were, first, the lines of tombs along the roads. Most of these monuments are now destroyed; hardly any survive but such as could be used as fortresses in the Middle Ages, like the celebrated mausoleum of Caecilia Metella, on the Appian Way. Then came the villas of the Roman aristocracy, surrounded by parks with fine orchards and shady groves. Farther on, we find the ruins of small towns, such as Gabii, a great relic of early times, once almost a rival of Rome, and later a modest suburban municipium. Thus at every step, along the ancient ways, there rises a witness of the intense life which, in Imperial times, made the Campagna into a vast garden at the gates of the city.[3] Still earlier, until about the Ist century before our era, these tracts, barren to-day, were the fields which fed the Roman people.

[1] For the geography of Italy, and of Latium in particular, cf. Fischer, **LXXIV,** and Nissen, **CXV,** i, pp. 254 ff.; ii, 2 (1902), pp. 555 ff.
[2] Tomasetti, **CLXI.**
[3] T. Ashby, "The Classical Topography of the Roman Campagna," in **XIX,** i ff.

For the land in this region cannot do without the labour of man. Only by intense, stubborn work and constant effort can nature be made to bring forth. The soil is a friable volcanic tufa, the surface of which, decomposed by atmospheric agents, affords a thin layer of humus. The arable layer is made by the plough. The earth is really created by man.

To one who looks at the whole district from a distance, the Roman Campagna appears almost completely flat and uniform. South of the Anio, there is no stream of any size to dig a valley. The rises, crowned by tufts of trees, are few and unassuming. Yet the ground is extremely broken. Where it has not been levelled by the work of man, there is a succession of swellings and hollows. There are frequent rents in the tufa, laying bare the rusty colour of the subsoil. In this chaos, the water finds no natural outflow. It lies in pools in the hollows, and, above all, it drips everywhere from the side of tiny cliffs. Even to-day the district is unhealthy.[1] It defends itself with fever against attempts at colonization, though these are gradually breaking in upon its sterility. To make life possible there in old times, and to make the land productive, a fairly numerous population had to struggle doggedly and without rest, controlling the water by digging channels for the very smallest rivulets and draining the whole surface.

Under the domination of man, this land of unkindly appearance is becoming pleasant. The human settlements which venture into this desert soon take on the aspect of oases. One may quote as an example the abbey of Tre Fontane, a mile or so to the south of the Porta S. Paolo. Magnificent eucalyptuses, which absorb the moisture of the soil and drive away the fever-carrying mosquitoes, overhang the abbey walls, behind which there is a glimpse of rich, deep orchards. Work is gaining ground on hostile nature.

Before it could become a land of plenty for which men fought, the Roman Campagna had to have the benefit of the efforts of many generations to colonize it. The first occupants

---

[1] Yet malaria does not seem to have existed in Italy before the IIIrd century B.C. Probably it came from Africa, and was introduced by Hannibal's men. This disease may have been one cause of the general depression of the mob in Imperial Rome and its fits of mischievousness. Cf. Stuart Jones, Ross, and Ellet, **CLIII**.

had to conquer it from itself. Their successors, through all antiquity, found themselves obliged to continue their work of hard control without remission.

One of the most surprising archaeological discoveries of the end of the XIXth century was that of a whole system of drainage developed beneath the surface, all over the Campagna and most of Latium as far as the Pontine Marshes. As a matter of fact, these channels had always been known. Many of them are to-day open to the sky, the vault having fallen in. All appear to have been dug as tunnels, at least in the middle and upper part of their course ; many still run underground, either entirely, or in stretches of various length, and the sight of them inspires the peasants with curiosity mingled with fear. Scholars had already examined them, and engineers had drawn plans of some, but their object remained uncertain. Then a member of the French School in Rome, de la Blanchère, saw that it was a work of canalization, certainly ancient, which had been carried on during the Roman epoch, but seemed to have been commenced long before historical times. These drainage operations were apparently undertaken by the earliest occupants of Latin soil.[1]

These strange galleries, about 5 feet high and 2 or 3 feet wide, vaulted, but without masonry, cut in the tufa itself, descend in some places 50 feet under the earth. They never follow the bottom of a valley, but always run along one of its slopes, often crossing from one to the other, because the people who dug them strove to follow the veins of water on the side where they were most abundant. Altogether, these drains, crossing each other, sometimes superimposed in two storeys, ramified like the venous system of a mammal, embrace the whole district of the Latin tufa, the lower basin of the Tiber, that of the Anio, and all the lower slopes of the Alban Hills to the Pontine Marshes. " It has all been done," de la Blanchère observes, " with a unity of plan, a certainty of conception, and a rightness of execution which make this great achievement like the instinctive, perfect work of a colony of beavers or a republic of ants. . . . And I would remark that such a work cannot have been the product of individual efforts ; everything is interrelated, everything

---

[1] De la Blanchère, " La Malaria de Rome et le drainage antique," in **X**, ii (1882), pp. 94 ff. ; **XXXII**.

shows one combined plan. It is a work which can only have been done all at once for each general basin."

Being destitute of any natural system of drainage, the Latin country was not originally inhabitable. This great work was done to make it so. It was this which, in ancient times, sanified the Campagna and kept it in a condition of fertility and healthiness which, if not remarkable, was at least sufficient. It was this work, too, which necessarily caused the earliest inhabitants to remain in the place, the men who had undertaken it and, in virtue of hereditary experience, were able to keep it up and continue it. The Latin lowlands remained, and probably always had been, the property of the autochthons who had made them fertile. This perpetual fight with nature, carried on through millenniums, formed the race, hard, patient, alert, ever on the watch for the hidden danger, recommencing the work destroyed by storm or accident without a feeling of discouragement, and obedient, because the interest and the life of everyone depended on it, to the discipline of the social group. Man made his land ; the land, too, made the character of its men.

But the plain which fed Latium did not command it. It was dominated by the mountains. On the east, from every point in the Campagna, the mass of the Alban Hills can be seen closing the horizon. On these heights the Latin peoples had their political and religious centre. The Mount of Alba was their Ida. Jupiter dwelt there. Every year the representatives of the thirty peoples of the plain proceeded to his sanctuary on the high place to hold the feast of the league, and, in sign of communion, received part of the flesh of the victims. The national god had given supremacy over the whole people to the city nearest to him. Alba Longa was for a long time the capital of Latium. It has left no material trace. But in the memory of men its name has outlived its fall.

There is a profound contrast between the austere nakedness of the plain and the appearance of the mountains. The Alban Hills are extinct volcanoes, and have all the natural fertility of lands which were once burnt. Their sides are covered with vegetation ; the white villages are framed in fruit-trees, olives, and vines. Wide meadows and woods stretch over their tops. Great lakes, those of Albano and

Nemi, lie in old craters, the one bright and open, the other darkened by the forests which hem it round. The water flows freely over the surface of the ground, leaping from the springs in fresh rivulets. Nature, so severe at the foot of the hills, is all smiles as soon as one reaches them. The mountains represent the pleasant country of Latium.

When, from the top of the Alban Hills, one looks over the land stretching towards the sea, one understands the true significance of the information preserved by Dionysius of Halicarnassus on the population of the country.

"In the most distant times within the memory of men, the territory of Rome was occupied by the *Siculi*, a barbarous, autochthonous race. But later, after long wars, the Siculi were driven out by the *Aborigines*, who took possession of all the land between the Tiber and the Liris. They established posts at the strongest points, and have always remained there, without ever being driven out by others. They have only changed their name. Under King Latinus, about the time of the Trojan War, the Aborigines began to call themselves Latins. Sixteen generations later, when Romulus had founded Rome, they took the name of Romans."[1]

The strongest and most attractive parts, the Alban Hills, were the acropolis from which these invading Aborigines commanded the autochthons of the plain.

While the people of the lowlands were patient tillers of the soil, the conquerors, Dionysius adds, were chiefly herds-men and brigands. The population of early Latium was the result of the fusion of these two elements. Each needed the other. The ploughmen of the plain were alone capable of keeping it fertile ; the lords of the mountains could alone protect the workers. The two regions complemented one another. So we find in the Latin people a combination of the patience of the peasant and the adventurous, violent spirit of the warlike herdsman.

One of these herdsmen of the Alban Hills was, according to legend, the founder of Rome. Outlawed by his own people, Romulus collected other fugitives, and, on the borders of Latium, by the Tiber, established himself with them on one of the summits of the Palatine. This hill had, no doubt, long been used as a grazing-ground, at least in winter, by the beasts of Alba ; it owes its name to the god or goddess of flocks and herds, Pales. One day it became the seat of a

[1] i. 9.

village, a modest colony of the federal capital of the Latin nation.

II

THE SABINES

North and east of the Alban massif, from which they are separated by the road which leads to southern Italy, lie the mountains of the Sabina. The heights of Tivoli continue on the east the ring which closes the horizon of Rome. Then comes the summit of Palombara Sabina; and lastly, due north of Rome, rises the imposing crag of Soracte. At the foot of these mountains and behind them extends the Sabina, a country of broken hills and cool valleys, a splendid agricultural district which has always bred a strong race of peasants.

Like the Latins, the Sabines belonged to the great family of Indo-European invaders. Whether they had, like the Latins themselves, mingled more or less with autochthons, whether they were in more or less continuous relations with the peoples of the Adriatic coast, and, through them, were contaminated by Balkan influences, does not greatly matter.[1] What we know of their speech makes them cousins of the Latins and brothers of the Samnites, who, moreover, bear the same name as they—*Safini*. The dialect of all these peoples, whom the Greeks of Campania designated by the common and improper name of *Oscans*, stands half-way between Latin, apparently the oldest of the Italic dialects of the peninsula, and Umbrian, the most recent.[2]

Like the herdsmen of Alba, those of the Sabina were compelled to come down to the plain in winter to seek pastures for their beasts. Tradition speaks of inhabitants of Cures in the Sabina who had a settlement on one of the hills by the Tiber, the Quirinal, so named in memory of their home. The Sabines thus found themselves next door to the Latins on the Palatine. They were separated by a swampy depres-

---

[1] On the Sabines, cf. Piganiol, **CXXX**, especially pp 33 ff. M. Piganiol ascribes to the Sabines an Illyrian origin, which does not seem to be confirmed by what is known of their language.

[2] Cf. J Vendryes, "La Place du latin parmi les langues indo-européennes," in **XXIV**, ii, pp. 90-103.

sion with a rivulet in the centre ; this was what afterwards became the Forum. The Lacus Curtius there preserved the memory of the original swamp. The stream was enclosed later in the Cloaca Maxima, a drainage channel similar to those all over the Campagna. It is here that legend places the epic combats between the Romans of Romulus and the Sabines of Tatius. These were, very probably, nothing more than scrimmages of herdsmen over stolen cattle, or some seizure of women.

Compared with the Latins on the Palatine, the Sabines on the Quirinal seem to represent an element of law and order. The former were nothing but fugitives, a rabble of outlaws who had severed all ties with their people, and had no tradition but what they made for themselves. The latter brought to the Quirinal the memory and the worships of their Sabine home. They were the *populus Quiritium*, the worshippers of Sabine Mars. They had their customs and their laws. This contrast is symbolized in the opposition between Romulus and Numa, the warrior pure and simple and the priest of the gods, inspired by Egeria, the wise law-giver of the people. Under him, it seems, the two villages of different origin were united on an equal basis. The neighbours became brothers.

But villages, even when fraternally united, do not make a city.[1] Between the establishment of Romulus on the Palatine, the union with the Sabines of Tatius, and the existence of Rome, we must suppose a series of other events which have left only a vague memory in legend, but seem to correspond to the occupation of the site of Rome by the Etruscans and the foundation of the city in accordance with the rites of Etruria. This foundation is the real beginning of Rome.

III

THE ETRUSCANS

Round Rome, we find the Etruscans established by the VIIIth century at Caere (Cervetri), a busy and ancient port, founded long ago, it was said, by the Pelasgians, and Veii, between the Tiber and the sea. A little to the north, over-

---

[1] On the site of the ancient Roman villages, see Homo, **LXXXVI**, ch. ii, § 2.

looking the Tiber, they occupied Falerii and Narne. East of Rome, on the edge of the Sabine hills, Praeneste (Palestrina) seems to have been under their influence. In the Alban Hills, Tusculum, as its name shows, was an Etruscan foundation, and so was Velletri, south of the mountains. At the end of the VIIIth century Etruria pressed upon Latium on every side, and, on the Janiculum, touched Rome.

At Rome itself the road connecting central with southern Italy crossed the Tiber.[1] The relations of the Etruscans with southern Italy soon created on this crossing a traffic which grew more and more intense. The sea-route along the coast was, without any doubt, that first used. It continued to be taken by heavy goods. The ores, metal ingots, and corn of Etruria always had to travel by water ; boats could bring, as return cargo, the great vases filled with wine or oil which came in abundance to Caere from the beginning of the VIIth century. But for articles of small weight and great value, laminated bronzes, jewels, etc., there was every advantage in avoiding the many and various risks of the sea.[2] Many Etruscan caravans, therefore, must have gone overland and presented themselves at the Tiber bridge.

The Sublician Bridge, the first, and for long the only bridge of Rome, thus came to play a highly important part in Italian life. We know the sacred character which it retained in classical times. Built of wood, it might contain no iron nail, and no metal tool could be used even to repair it. These survivals of very early times seem to show that it was older than Rome and the Etruscans themselves. But its importance dates from the period in which trade developed. Round it, on the left bank of the river, a kind of station must have grown up, with caravanserais, warehouses, and all the minor forms of trade and industry which live on the traffic of men and goods. The site of Rome thus became a commercial bridge-head of Etruria.

From their villages perched on the Roman hills, the natives, whether husbandmen or herdsmen, must gradually have become interested in all this movement which was

[1] For the importance of the Tiber bridge all through the history of Rome down to modern times, the reader is referred to the brilliant article by V. Bérard, " Rome intangible," in the *Revue de Paris*, Oct., 1903, especially pp. 887-8.
[2] The pirates of Antium had a bad name for a long time. Cape Circeo has always kept it.

going on at their feet, and might help to make them richer. Then, as commercial life grew more intense, it assumed the ascendancy even among them. From the banks of the river, Etruscan influence gradually reached the heights. A day came when the foreign element felt strong enough to command. The Etruscans transformed the chance collections of men formed on the hills into an ordered town, subject to their authority. They created a city on the exact pattern of their own cities.

IV

THE SYNOECISM OF ROME

In ancient civilization, the foundation of cities marks a turning-point. The city dominated the whole social and political life, and to a certain extent, one may say, the intellectual and moral life of antiquity. Its civilization was an urban civilization. The classical age begins when the cities appear, the ancient world dies when the barbarian invasions destroy them and give greater importance to the countryside.

A city, in antiquity, is not a collection of men formed by chance or determined solely by topographical and material conditions. It is created, in one day, by a definite act of will, by a thought which is both political and religious. This thought determines its form, governs all the features of its organization, and exercises strong and continual influence on the inhabitants. The life of the city is their life, its power makes their prosperity, and this idea is impressed on them in the smallest details of existence. The citizen holds all his rights from the city and its gods, and in return he owes them his whole life. As the city raises its acropolis above the country, as it is separated by its walls from the surrounding territory, so the citizen is separate from non-citizens and above them. Nowhere is this feeling seen in greater force then in Rome; in the Roman's soul it occupies a supreme place, and makes the ardour but also the pride and the narrowness of his patriotism.

Whence does he get this very peculiar conception of political and social organization ?

The Greeks also had the city system. Fustel de Coulanges

has described the normal process of its formation.[1] At the beginning, he says, most cities consisted of separate villages, and some of them, Sparta and Delphi, for example, always remained at this primitive stage. But others, like Athens, took pains to collect the patron deities of the old villages in a common acropolis, and to make this citadel the centre of a community of a new type. Round the common sanctuary, the villages, once independent, became merely quarters of a single whole obeying the same law. The act which thus created the city was called the *synoecism*.

On the coasts of Sicily and southern Italy, the Greek colonies introduced the city form from the end of the VIIIth century onwards, and especially during the VIIth. But at the same time, perhaps even a little before, and in any case outside the circle of their influence, we see cities forming in central Italy under the Etruscans. Most of these seem to be the result of the grouping of old villages round a new acropolis and within a common circuit wall.[2] Is this an Italic type of settlement, the first examples of which should be recognized, as early as the Bronze age, in the pile villages built on dry land in the valley of the Po ? It is not at all likely. Since Roman tradition, which preserved the old rites for the foundation of cities intact until Imperial times, declared that they were taken from the Etruscans, we prefer to see in the city form the very type of the civilization brought into Italy by the Etruscans.[3] In that case, these survivors from the old Oriental empires of Nearer Asia and the Greeks of the Ionian period would, independently of one another and with notable variants, have taken the idea of the city from Asiatic traditions. Certainly Rome was founded according to the Etruscan rite.

Let us follow the account which, drawing upon Dionysius of Halicarnassus and Plutarch, Fustel de Coulanges gives of the ceremony.[4]

After purifying the people by making it leap over the

[1] **LXXVIII**, iii, 3, p. 157.
[2] The early cemeteries belonging to these villages are sometimes found dispersed at a fair distance from the later centre. The topography of Tarquinii (Corneto) and its cemeteries is typical in this respect. Cf. Von Duhn, **CLXXII**, pp. 310-12.
[3] Nissen, **CXVI**, pp. 79-108 ; Thulin, **CLVIII**, iii, pp. 3-41 ; Grenier, **LXXXI**, pp. 91 ff.
[4] **LXXVIII**, iii, 4, pp. 151 ff.

slight flame of a brushwood fire, the hero founder, clad in the heavy embroidered cope which the Etruscan paintings show us, and holding in his hand the *lituus*, a curved, crosier-like staff, the emblem of his priestly function, consults the gods. Standing on the top of one of the hills, he observes the flight of the birds. The auguries are favourable—the gods approve his intention. Amid the religious silence of his companions, he makes sacrifice to the gods of the sky, to those of the earth and the water, and to those of the underworld, consecrating the acropolis where the patron deities of the city will hence-forward reside. In Rome this acropolis is neither the Latin hill of the Palatine nor the Sabine hill of the Quirinal; it is the Capitol. The gods who reign there are neither the Latin gods nor the Sabine gods, but the Etruscan trias, Jupiter enthroned between Juno and Minerva. The Etruscans, tradition tells us, did not consider a city properly founded if it did not possess the three temples of Jupiter, Juno, and Minerva.[1] So the Capitol, with its temple of three dwellings, is certainly an Etruscan acropolis.

From the height of their acropolis the gods to whom the keeping of the city is entrusted must be able to view their whole domain, the sacred circuit of the ramparts, the river at the bottom of the valley, and the plain as far as the mountains.[2] Under the eye of the gods, therefore, the founder proceeds to define the perimeter of the city and to separate its soil absolutely from alien land. He yokes a white cow and bull, with the cow towards the interior of the city, to the plough with a bronze share, and, with his head veiled, reciting formulas, followed by his silent companions, he drives the primordial furrow. As the ploughshare turns up the sods, they are carefully thrown inside the circuit, that no piece of this sacred earth may remain outside the *pomoerium*. The furrow is interrupted at the places marked for the gates, for none must dare to cross it, and none will be able to touch the walls which will be built upon it; in order to repair them, expiatory sacrifices and the express permission of the gods will be needed.

The founder takes possession, in the name of the gods, of the site thus delimited. He consecrates it, aligning the chief

---

[1] Serv., *ad Aen.*, i. 422. Cf. Mueller, **CXIV**, ii, p. 150.
[2] Vitruv., *De Arch.*, i. 7; iv. 5.

streets of the future city on the cardinal points. With this object he sets up near the central point the staff whose first shadow at sunrise will give the exact direction of the east-and-west way, the *decumanus*. With the *lituus* he draws on the ground a line parallel to the sun's course, and then one perpendicular to it, which gives the *cardinal* line, parallel to the north-and-south axis of the firmament. The recent discovery of a member of the French School in Rome, Monsieur A. Piganiol, has revealed in the Forum, among the chaos of superimposed foundations, the traces of the old *decumanus* and *cardo*. The *decumanus* started, on the west, from the Temple of Saturn at the foot of the Capitol; crossing the Basilica of Constantine, it ended, on the east, at the Tigillum Sororium, the arch of legendary expiation under which Horatius was said to have passed when he had defeated the Curiatii but had murdered his sister. The *cardo* began, on the north, at the Porta Janualis, near the Forum of Nerva, and ended at the Porta Romanula, at the foot of the Palatine. The two ways crossed at the point marked later by the mysterious Puteal Libonis, hard by the Temple of Vesta.[1] It was here that the founder's staff of orientation had been set up. The three gates are quite in accordance with the number laid down in Etruscan ritual.[2]

The consecration of the soil by orientation represents a specifically Etruscan idea, parallel to that which underlies *haruspicina*, that is, the reading of the will of the gods in the entrails of sacrificed beasts. The substance of this idea is as follows.

Consecration in general is supposed to leave a material stamp of the divine thought on the thing consecrated. Thus the victim, at the moment of sacrifice, bears on the most sensitive part of its body, the inwards, and particularly the liver, the order and, as it were, the figure of the universe. Therefore the *haruspex* who can perceive it is able, from the state of the organs, to discover the will of the gods and to give men useful advice. So, too, the city, the abode of the gods and the portion of earth consecrated to them, should

---

[1] Piganiol, "Les Origines du Forum," in **X**, xxxviii (1908), pp. 233-82; cf. **CXXX**, p. 298.

[2] Serv., *ad Aen.*, i. 422. Cf. Mueller, **CXIV**, ii, p. 43. The Etruscans required in a properly founded city three temples and three gates.

reproduce in its essential features the divine plan of the world.[1]

This plan is clearly revealed to the eyes of men in the course of the sun and the four cardinal points. So the consecrated earth, the abode of the gods, like the sky, must also be divided in four regions. All these doctrines, both orientation and *haruspicina*, come to the Etruscans from the most ancient East. We know the Babylonian formula which emphatically expresses the power of the sovereign : " King of the Four Regions." Babylon, according to Herodotos' description, was divided into four regions by two great streets at right angles.[2] In Imperial times the worship of the Four Winds was introduced from Oriental religions. In Etruria orientation on the cardinal points can be seen, at least in the new cities entirely built by the Etruscans ;[3] in the others it must be there, hidden, as it was in Rome, in some particular part of the city. In classical times the establishment of the *decumanus*, a main road running east and west across the city and its territory, and the *cardo*, running north and south, remains the principle of all surveying ; it is the first act of the establishment of a military camp or a colony.[4]

Another rite of Etruscan and Oriental origin is also mentioned in connexion with the foundation of Rome—the arrangement of the *mundus*. Romulus, says Fustel de Coulanges, digs a small circular ditch, and throws into it a sod of earth which he has brought from the city of Alba. Following him, each of his companions throws in a little earth from his place of origin, " that each might say, pointing to the new place adopted by the founder, ' This is still the land of my fathers (*terra patrum, patria*) ; here is my home, for here are the ghosts of my family.' " The *mundus* is really a mouth of hell, a way of communication between the upper earth, the abode of the living, and the subterranean world, the dwelling of the dead. As he opens it, the founder calls upon all the ancestral ghosts and all the spirits, whatever they may be, which dwell below the earth, to recognize the new city, asking for their approval and their goodwill for his creation. Afterwards the *mundus* is opened every year on certain days. *Mundus patet*—these are *dies nefasti*, during

[1] Blecher, **XXXIII** ; Thulin, **CLX** and **CLVIII**.
[2] Hdt., i. 180.   [3] Grenier, **LXXXI**, pp. 95, 112.   [4] Nissen, **CXVI**.

which the invisible ghosts of the men who once lived go about among the living.   The house-doors must stand open, that they may be able to come in and warm themselves at the hearth.   Care must be taken not to irritate them.   Then, at the end of the day, the dead return to their underground abode and the *mundus* is closed again.[1]

Certain paintings on Etruscan tombs [2] and many painted vases from the same source give us representations of the *mundus*.   It is a pit from which we sometimes see rising a human form, with a wolf's head and claw-like hands, the figure of the Etruscan god of death, who seizes a living man. The vaulted pits, shaped like inverted funnels, which are found in some Etruscan cities, are identified by some as *mundi*.[3]   " As far as I can judge, from the accounts of those who have gone into a *mundus*," says Cato, " the construction [4] of these objects recalls the vault of heaven above us."   In Italy the blood of the victims was poured into the *mundus*, for the dead were greedy for blood, which infused a semblance of life into them ;   dances were performed at the mouth to rejoice the shades, a parasol being used to prevent the sun from penetrating into their dark domain ;   and bits of precious metal were piled up as an offering.[5]   So, in our own time, we have kept the custom of placing coins in the foundations of our buildings, an uncomprehended survival of the propitiatory offerings to the infernal spirits of the *mundus*.   These rites come, at least in part, from the East.   A Chaldaean inscription from Khorsabad, which describes the foundation of the palace of Sargon, mentions that at the base of the future edifice " the people cast their amulets." [6]

With all the gods thus conjured up and called to witness, with the Capitoline trias looking down from their acropolis on the dwellings and circuit entrusted to their keeping, with the ghosts of the dead pouring from the gaping *mundus*, with the internal plan traced according to the divine plan of the world, and with its territory separated from the surrounding country by the sharp line of the furrow, the city was properly founded.   It was a complete organism and a holy

---

[1] Macrob., following Varro, *Sat.*, i. 16, 18 ; Festus, 154, 157.
[2] Stackelberg tomb at Corneto.
[3] E.g., at Marzabotto in the Apennines, not far from Bologna.   Grenier, **LXXXI**, p. 102.
[4] *Ap.* Festus, 157.   [5] Tac., *Hist.*, iv. 53.   [6] Thulin, **CLVIII**, p. 9.

thing. The accomplishment of the rites gave it life and the
right to rule over men. The confusion and chances of old
times were gone ; a new age was commencing under the
auspices of a new civilization.

The date, at least approximate, of this great event is
supplied to us by the soil of the Forum itself. The synoecism
was marked, as we have seen, by the occupation of this once
marshy depression which lay between the principal hills,
Capitol, Palatine, and Quirinal. Hitherto it had served as a
cemetery for the villagers of the neighbouring heights. The
moment when the Forum ceased to be a necropolis was
evidently that of its inauguration as the centre of the city.

The primitive tombs discovered in the Forum, in front of
the Temple of Antoninus and Faustina, in the last years of
the XIXth century,[1] fall into two groups which are chrono-
logically quite distinct. The earlier of them contain ashes
enclosed in an ossuary of clumsy earthenware. The grave-
furniture consists of one or two small vases of local make
and a few fragments of bronze. The pottery is similar to
that of the Alban Hills and the earliest pit-graves of Tuscany,
and dates from the IXth and VIIIth centuries B.C. These
first tombs belong to the beginning of the occupation of the
Roman hills. The second group is characterized by bigger
graves, containing remains of buried bodies. The skeletons
are sometimes enclosed in a primitive coffin formed of the
two scooped-out halves of an oak-trunk. This mode of burial
is later than the other. It is dated by the presence of
imported Greek vases of the earlier types, Geometric and
Proto-Corinthian. The later tombs of the Forum are, therefore, posterior to the beginning of Greek colonization in Italy
and of commercial intercourse between Campania and
Etruria. They cannot be older than the VIIth century,
and, indeed, they belong rather to the second than to the
first half of that century.

When, therefore, traditional chronology places the foundation of Rome in the year 754, and exactly on the 21st April of
that year, it either antedates or postdates. It is certainly at
least a century too late if it refers to the establishment of the
village on the Palatine, and it is almost equally previous if
it refers to the synoecism of the Roman villages. If any date

[1] G. Pinza, **XIV**, xv (1905), col. 274 ff., "La Necropoli dell' Argileto."

in Roman history nearly corresponds to that event, it is that of 614, the year in which tradition places the arrival in Rome of the Etruscan Tarquin, the son of Demaratos of Corinth. But it is vain to ask the legends for exact information of this kind.

After all, the occupation of the Roman hills by small bodies of outlaws, herdsmen, or husbandmen, is only an episode of minor significance in Italian prehistory. The important fact, that which really marks the beginning of a new age, is the appearance on these hills of a city of the type which, with the general advance of civilization, was springing up on all the shores of the Mediterranean.

Religious rites, composed, among other ingredients, of ideas taken from the most ancient traditions of the East, consecrated its foundation. Foreign political thought—Etruscan expansion—brought the native ethnical forces together and organized them. Economic conditions—the development of the wealth of Italy by industry and commerce—gave the Tiber bridge an importance which would only increase. The citizens of the new city thus found themselves torn from the isolation of old times ; a wider horizon opened to their eyes ; they would learn to be aware of themselves and to take an ever more active part in the life of the peninsula and the movement of civilization all over it.

The synoecism of the villages was really the first blossoming of the Roman people and the first link in the religious, political, and intellectual tradition which would be continued from now to the end of ancient times. The day on which the Etruscan trias was installed on the Capitol, and the Forum was marked by the orientation of its arteries as the sacred centre of the town, and the first circuit was drawn on a methodical plan, and the reasoned, deliberate image of a city was consecrated for gods and men by solemn ceremonies, that day was truly the day of the birth of Rome ; it marks the origin of Roman development and of the Roman spirit.

CHAPTER II

ETRUSCAN ART AND CIVILIZATION IN ROME

I

IONIAN CIVILIZATION AND ETRUSCAN ART

THE VIth century before our era was the period of the full development of Ionian civilization. In Asia Minor and in the islands of the Aegean Sea, great cities, enriched by trade and industry, gave art, literature, and science an impulse which marks the beginning of the radiance of Greece.[1] In the West, the brilliance of Etruscan civilization was a reflection of the light which came from Ionia. Great industrial and commercial cities used their wealth to make life beautiful. Architecture, sculpture, painting, metal-engraving, jewellery, beautiful vases of clay and bronze, scents, wine, rich clothing, games, and music transformed the native rudeness of Italy. Ionian ships frequented the Etruscan ports, just as Etruscan mariners, as merchants or as pirates, scoured the seas of Ionia.[2] In Etruria imported articles were mingled with native manufactures, so that it is usually hard to tell one from the other. Moreover, Greek artists came regularly and settled among the Etruscans, working for them and among them.[3] Etruscan civilization at this time, though doubtless heavier, less refined, and less spirited than Ionian, seems to have been quite as wealthy, and perhaps even more luxuriant. Never, perhaps, was Italy so like Greece.

Rome was at this time a great city, founded by the Etruscans and governed, in any case, by Etruscan tyrants. If we can believe her historians, it was during this period, the Royal period, that her civil, military, and religious laws

[1] Jardé, **LXXXVII,** English pp. 189 ff. ; Ducati, **LXV,** pp. 138 ff.
[2] Mueller, **CXIV,** i, pp. 271 ff.
[3] Körte, art. *Etrusker,* **CXXVII,** p. 745 ; Pliny, *N.H.,* xxxv. 152.

were established; and at this time the preponderance of Rome in Latium began. In these traditions it is difficult, for want of documentary evidence, to say how much is true and how much is exaggeration due to pride in ancient origin. Let us be content here to note some of the traces which this ancient domination of the Etruscans left on Rome.

II

ETRUSCAN MONUMENTS IN ROME. THE CAPITOLINE TEMPLE AND THE WOLF OF THE CAPITOL

The civilization of the great cities of Etruria is revealed to us chiefly by the tombs scattered round their sites. At Rome there are absolutely no burials which could belong to the Royal period. Various cemeteries have been explored on the outer slopes of several Roman hills, on the east of the Esquiline, on the north-east of the Quirinal, on the south-west slope of the Caelian, and even in the Vallis Murcia, between the Palatine and the Aventine.[1] None of these fills in the gap which divides the humble, archaic pits which were made before history from the burials of the IVth and IIIrd centuries B.C. The successive enlargements of Rome no doubt caused the disappearance, in antiquity, of those of the tombs surrounding the city which took up most room, and these would be the tumuli and funerary chambers of the Etruscan type.

Of the monuments of civil or religious architecture which might go back to this period, most have of course disappeared. Those which have been preserved, which tradition attributed to the Kings, have been so much altered that they are now hard to recognize, and critics find in them excellent reasons for ascribing them to much more recent periods. It is, for example, very doubtful what the Tullianum originally was, that prison at the foot of the Capitol, used from the early Republic onwards and made into the Mamertine prison in the Middle Ages, which was said to have been built, as its name indicates, by King Servius Tullius.[2] The Cloaca Maxima, which carried off the stagnant water of the valley

---

[1] G. Pinza, **XIV**, xv, cols. 43-265.
[2] Thédenat, **CLVI**, pp. 107 ff.; Pinza, **III**, 1902, pp. 37-45.

of the Forum, must clearly go back to the first occupation of this site. It represents one of the drainage works which the ancient Latins made all over the country. But what we see of it to-day cannot be older than the beginning of the Empire.[1] Its turning vault was made by the engineers, not of Tarquin, but very probably of Agrippa, who restored most of the drains of ancient Rome.

There was, however, one monument which preserved the memory of Etruscan architecture down to the end of the

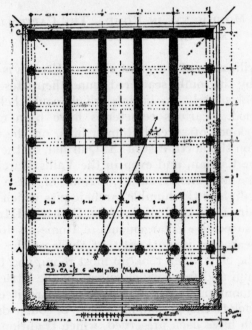

Fɪɢ. 1.—Plan of the Etruscan Temple on the Capitol.

classical period. This was the chief temple of the city, that of the Capitoline Trias.[2] It was rebuilt several times in the historical period, but always on the old plan, for the gods did not allow any transformation of the places to which they were accustomed.[3] After the fire of Sylla's time, the wood had been replaced by marble. Later, under Vespasian, the

[1] C. Huelsen, **XIII,** 1902, pp. 42-4 ; **XVII,** xiii (1904), pp. 28-9.
[2] Saglio, art. *Capitolium,* **LVI** ; Martha, **CIV,** 269 ff. Rodocanachi, **CXXXIX,** pp. xxvi ff.
[3] Homo, **LXXXV,** pp. 173 ff. ; cf. bibliography in Kiepert and Huelsen, *Formae urbis Romae,* s.v. *Capitolium.*

augurs did not authorize the Emperor to do more than raise the height. Moreover, the descriptions of it which we possess enable us to recognize it easily as an Etruscan monument.

Roman tradition agreed in ascribing its construction to Tarquin the Proud. "He brought craftsmen from all Etruria," says Livy.[1] The arrival of these crowds of Etruscan workmen was believed to be the origin of the name Vicus Tuscus, Etruria Street, which was kept by the quarter at the foot of the Capitol. The most detailed information on the work of Tarquin is supplied to us by Dionysius of Halicarnassus,[2] a contemporary of Augustus.

"The Temple was built on a high foundation measuring 8 plethra (774 ft.) round and about 200 ft. in length. The difference between the length and breadth was insignificant—less than 15 ft. The south front has three rows of columns, and there is a row of columns down each side. The interior is divided into three sanctuaries, parallel and adjoining ; in the middle is that of Jupiter, with those of Juno and Minerva on either side. All three are beneath the same ridge-piece and are covered by the same roof."

In this description we clearly see the essential features of the Etruscan temple as they are laid down in the theory of it which Vitruvius expounds,[3] and as they appear in the foundations of several temples excavated in Etruria.[4]

"The site destined for the Temple," says Vitruvius, "should have the proportions of six in length and five in breadth. The length should be divided into two, the rear part being reserved for the cellae and the front part being occupied by a colonnade. The breadth should be divided into ten ; three tenths, on each side, will be occupied by the subsidiary cellae, and four tenths by the central cella." [5]

Such, indeed, are the arrangements which we find at Florence, Marzabotto, Fiesole, Orvieto, Città Castellana (Falerii Veteres), and Città Lavinia.[6]

This plan seems to have prevailed at an early time in Tuscany and in Latium under Etruscan influence.

---

[1] i. 56.   [2] iv. 61.
[3] De Arch., iv. 7 ; cf. Martha, **CIV,** pp. 269 ff.
[4] Grenier, **LXXXI,** pp. 104 ff.
[5] De Arch., iv. 7.
[6] P. Ducati, "Contributo allo studio dell' arce etrusca di Marzabotto " in Atti e Mem. R. Deput. Storia Patria per le Romagne, xiii (1923), pp. 18 ff. of the reprint. The temple of Segni (Signia) has the three cellae, but is much longer than broad. Cf. Delbrueck, **LIX,** pl. iv.

The platform of earth on which the Etruscan temple stood was surrounded by a wall of stones, joined without mortar. Of stone, too, were the foundations, and, probably, the walls of the cellae. But the greater part of the construction was of wood. The columns and all the roofing and its supports were simply of wood, faced, it is true, with protective plaques of terra-cotta adorned with decorative motives and painted in bright colours.[1] Until about the middle of the VIth century, the Greek temples had been built in exactly the same

Fig. 2.—Elevation of an Etruscan temple.

way. The old sanctuary of Hera at Olympia was a wooden temple. Even in classical times provinces which remained undeveloped, like Aetolia,[2] retained this primitive mode of architecture. Like them, Etruria long remained faithful to the materials used by the earliest Ionian architects.[3]

[1] Durm, **LXVIII**, pp. 75 ff.
[2] E.g., the temple of Thermos, the sanctuary of the Aetolian League.
[3] On the terra-cotta decoration of early architecture in Asia Minor, Greece, and the islands, cf. Herbert-Koch, "Studien zu den campanischen Dachterra-kotten," in **XIII**, xxx (1915), pp. 1-115.

The Capitoline Temple was decorated with terra-cottas in this way. For the execution of these, Tarquin applied to Veii, which was at that time, according to Pliny, who probably has it from Varro, the most flourishing centre of this art. He called in an artist named Vulca, from whom he ordered the cultus-statue.[1] For the Jupiter of the Capitol was originally of terra-cotta. Like all terra-cotta statues, it was polychrome, and, in accordance with the convention of archaic Greek art, the flesh, particularly the face, was painted red.[2] In one hand he held the sceptre, and in the other a thunderbolt—*inque Jovis dextra fictile fulmen erat*.[3] On the ridge of the roof stood a terra-cotta quadriga, which was made at Veii, and was only delivered by the Veians, after the fall of Tarquin, with great difficulty.[4] There were other statues on the flanks of the pediment, not to mention the acroteria, the pediment itself, of which we know nothing, the antefixes, and all the facings of the roof-timbers and other works of art which may have been placed in the front vestibule. To judge from the many testimonies which we possess, the early Temple of the Capitol was adorned with quantities of plastic decoration.

All this tradition, like the rest of the traditions regarding the early centuries of Rome, must naturally be taken with caution. It has been attacked by Sig. Ettore Pais.[5] According to this critic, the arrangement of the Capitol and the construction of the temple only date from the IVth century. The defensive advantages of the hill were first revealed to the Romans by the invasion of the Gauls. The reference to the Veian artist *Vulca* is simply due to confusion with the fire-god *Vulcanus*, identified with the god Summanus who preceded Jupiter on the Capitol. And it is true that one cannot fail to be struck by the very great dimensions given by Dionysius for the Capitoline Temple—about 200 feet a side. The sides of the ancient temples of Etruria are generally between 60 and 100 feet. The columns along the sides of the temple also seem to be an architectural arrangement later than the VIth century. They are found at Città

[1] Pliny, *N.H.*, xxxv. 157.   Cf. Plut., *Publicola*, 13.
[2] Pliny, *N.H.*, xxxiii. 111.
[3] Ovid, *Fasti*, i. 202.
[4] Pliny, *N.H.*, xxviii. 16 ; Serv., *ad Aen.*, vii. 188 ; Plut., *Publicola*, 13.
[5] Pais, **CXXIV**, i, p. 523 ; iii, p. 337.

Castellana, in the Temple of Juno, which is of stone, and appears to be a reconstruction of the IVth century.[1] Moreover, this early temple of wood, if it was inaugurated in 509 and not destroyed until the fire of Sylla's time, managed to last very long—over four centuries—whereas the temples of stone or marble which succeeded it had to be rebuilt at much shorter intervals. One will readily grant Sig. Pais that the temple whose appearance was preserved in the later restorations cannot have been older than the IVth century.

But a mass of archaeological facts revealed by recent excavations confirm our information about the existence and the decoration of the VIth century temple. The first of these is the discovery, in the lowest strata of the Capitol, on the site of the temple, of fragments of terra-cotta which can only date from that period.[2] Thus, we have a large flat tile, with a band of meanders painted along one edge, and several fragments of a cornice and antefixes, likewise painted, of a type common in Graeco-Etruscan architecture at the end of the VIth century and the beginning of the Vth.[3] Above all, the discovery at Veii of a whole series of excellent statues or fragments of statues of terra-cotta supplies striking confirmation of the memory preserved by Pliny of the fame of the Veian coroplasts of Tarquin's day, and proves that the name Vulca, far from being the result of confusion with the fire-god, may quite well have been that of an artist, and a great artist, of Veii at the end of the VIth century.[4]

Excavations at Veii led to the discovery, in May, 1916, of a splendid archaic statue of Apollo, life-size and hardly lacking anything but the arms. (Plate II.) By its side was found the lower part of a statue of the same size, with the body of an animal, apparently a roe, lying on its back with its legs tied. The figure of Apollo and this fragment must have formed parts of a single group representing the dispute of Apollo and Heracles over the roe with the brazen feet. Two other deities were present at the scene—Hermes, whose head in the winged *pilos* has been found, and probably Artemis, of

---

[1] Observation of Ducati on pp. 22-3 of article quoted above, p. 21, n. 6.
[2] Gatti, **III**, xxiv (1896), pp. 187-9, pls. xii, xiii.
[3] Pinza, **XVI**, xv, col. 500, fig. 152.
[4] Giglioli, **XVIII**, 1919, pp. 13-37, pls. i-vii. Cf. Della Seta, **CXLIX**, pp. 205-6, figs. 215-17.

PLATE II

APOLLO FROM VEII
Terra-cotta, about 75 in. high. (Rome, Museum of Pope Julius)

[face p. 24

PLATE III

ANTEFIX AND FRAGMENT OF A STATUE FOUND AT SATRICUM (CONCA)
Terra-cotta. (Rome, Museum of Pope Julius)

[face p. 25

whom only insignificant fragments remain. The style and technique of these works date them, without any possibility of doubt, at the end of the VIth century or the beginning of the Vth.

The myth and the gods portrayed are Greek, but the technique is Etruscan. It looks rather later than that of the great sarcophagi of Cervetri, in which a less pure clay is used. These statues must have been made at Veii itself. "The artist who modelled them," the happy author of this fine discovery, Sig. Giglioli, says very justly,[1] " whether he was a Greek established in the West, or an Etruscan, or an Italian, who had been trained by the Greeks, has succeeded, while imitating the models which came pouring into Etruria from Ionia, in creating a truly individual work of art. The complexity of the figures, the knowledge shown in the modelling, the gracefulness of the forms, the perfect taste of the polychrome colouring, all the life which animates the execution of these bodies with their vigorous legs and powerful chests, the expression of the faces, marked with deep furrows about the eyes and mouth, everything makes these terra-cottas the masterpieces of archaic art in Etruria."

These fine statues from Veii recall other archaic fragments, no less admirable, discovered by Monsieur H. Graillot in 1896 in the ruins of the Etrusco-Latin temple at Conca, the ancient Satricum, on the borders of Latium and the Pontine Marshes.[2] (Plate III.) A female antefix with half-closed eyes and a pronounced smile has all the impenetrable subtlety of great art. A male head, bearded, with large conventional curls framing the brow and almond eyes wide open, presents the majesty imbued with gentleness and benevolence appropriate to a Jupiter. A head of a dying barbarian, found later, displays an interesting attempt to express suffering and the grimace of pain. Acroteria from Conca represent very living groups of satyrs and Maenads.[3] One of the early temples of Falerii has also yielded a fine acroterion representing fully-armed warriors fighting, antefixes of grotesque satyrs' heads with goat ears and deep wrinkles and of pleasant faces of

---

[1] **XVIII,** 1919, p. 29.
[2] H. Graillot, **X,** xvi (1896), pp. 131-64, pl. i, a-v. Cf. Della Seta, **CXLIX,** pp. 206-7, figs. 218-19.
[3] Della Seta, **CXLIX,** p. 175, fig. 176.

Maenads, and great quantities of fragments of decorative facing which protected the wooden roof-timbers.[1]

We have here, between Cervetri, Veii, Falerii, and the south of Latium, in other words all round Rome, at the end of the VIth century and the beginning of the Vth, the exuberant efflorescence of a plastic art of the very first order, which fully justifies Pliny's statement regarding the orders which Tarquin gave to Vulca and the artists of Veii. Roman tradition had, therefore, preserved, in connexion with the building of the Capitoline Temple, a true memory of the brilliance of Etruscan art in the archaic period. The cultus-statue of Jupiter, the quadriga on the roof-ridge, the acroteria, perhaps the decoration of the pediment, the ornamental facings, fragments of which have been found, the secondary statues of Hercules and Summanus which are also mentioned, were of the same kind as the terra-cottas from Veii and Conca. All this terra-cotta art had disappeared from the Capitol, at least since the time of Sylla. But it had been produced in such abundance that other specimens still kept the knowledge of it alive in the time of Pliny.

" Statues of this kind," he says, " are still found in many places, crowning the roofs of temples, in Rome and in the municipia. Their admirable modelling, their art, the solidity which they owe to their technique alone, make them more precious than gold—or at any rate purer." [2]

A well-known masterpiece of sculpture, one of the gems of the Capitoline Museum, conjures up at this day that living art of early Italy, vivified by Ionia. That is the bronze Wolf of the Capitol. (Plate I.) It indisputably represents a work of the end of the VIth century or the beginning of the Vth, contemporary, therefore, or nearly so, with the first building on the Capitol.

So far as memory goes back, the Wolf has been in Roman collections ; in the Middle Ages it was in the Lateran. We do not know when and where it was found. Formerly it was identified with a figure of the Wolf suckling Romulus and Remus which was dedicated on the Forum by the Ogulnius brothers in 296 B.C. The *putti* whom we see to-day sucking

---

[1] *Ibid.*, p. 208, figs. 230-1 ; pp. 172-3, fig. 175 ; p. 177, fig. 177. On this decoration, cf. E. Rizzo, **III**, 1910, pp. 281-322 ; 1911, pp. 54-67. All these fragments are in the museum of the Villa of Pope Julius in Rome. Cf. Della Seta, **CXLVIII**, pp. 120 ff.

[2] *N.H.*, xxxv. 158.

her dugs are modern ; they date from the Renaissance. The wolf alone is ancient, and the style has nothing in common with the time of the dedication of the Ogulnii. Petersen considers that it can be established that the Wolf which is now called " of the Capitol " really did stand on the Capitol from the beginning.[1] In that case it would be one of the original monuments of the first consecration of the sanctuary of the Roman city. Indeed, Cicero speaks several times of a Wolf suckling a gilt Romulus, which was struck by lightning in his own time, in 65 B.C., and had been torn from its base and thrown to the ground, where he saw it lying. Now, careful examination of the present bronze has revealed two longitudinal rents down the hind legs, edged with small balls of molten metal, which certainly look as if they could only be due to lightning. If so, the lightning only destroyed the *putto*, which was alone gilded, for the bronze of the wolf shows no sign of gilding ; the wolf itself suffered only a little.

No doubt there were many images of the Wolf in Rome. Yet it seems difficult to suppose, however frequent Roman thunderstorms may be, that many of them were thus struck by lightning.[2] It is also very unlikely that the Wolf which we possess was booty brought by the Romans from Greece or Etruria. The legend of the foster-mother wolf is, doubtless, not peculiar to Rome. In Ionia, Miletos was said to have been reared in this way. A stele from Bologna, in northern Etruria, represents a wild beast, a she-wolf or a lioness, suckling a child.[3] This myth really belongs to the folk-lore of all countries, since Mr Kipling has found it in India and developed it in the way we know. Yet it does not seem to have anywhere enjoyed the same popularity as in Rome. No decisive reason has yet been produced to prove that it did not originally belong to the Latin tribes or the Etruscans, but was borrowed by Italy from Greece. It is not enough to say that nothing excludes the hypothesis of a foreign origin for the legend or for the Roman statue ; that foreign origin should be established. Until proof of the contrary, it seems legitimate to believe that the Roman

[1] E. Petersen, " Lupa capitolina," in **IX,** 1908, pp. 440-56 ; 1909, pp. 29-47 ; Carcopino, **XXV,** 1924, iv, pp. 1-19 ; v, pp. 16-49.

[2] G. de Sanctis, **XXII,** xxxviii (1910), pp. 71-85.

[3] Ducati, " Le Pietre funerarie felsinee " in **XIV,** 1911, no. 195, col. 530, fig. 24 ; Grenier, **LXXXI,** p. 536, fig. 140.

Wolf is really autochthonous, and to regard the image of her which we possess as identified by the marks of lightning with that which stood in ancient times on the Capitol.

Need we be surprised, now that we know the objects from Veii, especially the fragment representing the body of the roe for which Apollo and Heracles contended, that a work of art like the Wolf should have been modelled in Italy, for Rome, about the end of the VIth century ? We find in the terra-cottas of Veii, of Falerii, and of Conca the same true and living realism associated with powerful conventionalization, the same care for detail, the same harmony of masses, and, above all, the same energy of expression and simplicity of line. The Etruscans had a reputation as bronze-workers, and could render in metal the same conceptions as they expressed so admirably in terra-cotta. Moreover, we find in Etruria another masterpiece of bronze, rather later than the Wolf—the Chimaera of Arezzo (Plate I), a composite monster of the kind the Ionians loved to invent, with a lion's head and body, a goat's head and neck rising from the middle of its back, and a snake's head at the end of its upturned tail.[1]

Let us, then, regard the Wolf of the Capitol as an Etruscan work of the time of Tarquin, made for Rome, like the cultus-statues and acroteria of the Capitoline temple, and an expressive souvenir of the great art which, in the VIth century B.C., was the art of Rome as well as of Etruria.

III

THE INTRODUCTION OF WRITING IN ROME

So we see that the Etruscans were the educators of the Romans. It was they who taught the Romans writing, and that as early as the VIIth century B.C.

The generally accepted theory, which is still set forth in most classical manuals, is that Rome received her alphabet, not from the Etruscans, but direct from the Greeks of Cumae.

---

[1] In the Florence Museum. Martha, **CIV,** p. 310, fig. 208.

The Etruscans are supposed to have transmitted their writing only to the Umbrians of central Italy and the Oscans of southern Italy, and not to the Latins.[1] This is the theory consecrated, since 1850, by the authority of Mommsen, though Mommsen himself afterwards suggested—without going into details, it is true—a less paradoxical solution.[2] If the Oscan neighbours of Cumae got their writing from the Etruscans, and the Latin neighbours of the Etruscans got theirs from Cumae, there must have been a curious kind of *chassé-croisé*. On the contrary, it now appears that the Latins obtained their alphabet from the Etruscans, like the Oscans and Umbrians, but not the same alphabet. The Latin alphabet is the early Etruscan alphabet, and that of the Oscans and Umbrians is a later Etruscan alphabet.

Writing was in common use in Etruria from the beginning of the VIIth century at the latest. A recent discovery supplies the proof; in a tomb containing a rich furniture of carved ivories of Oriental style, which may be dated approximately in the year 700, an ivory writing-tablet has been found, bearing a complete alphabet engraved with a pointed instrument on one side of the frame.[3] This alphabet, the earliest of all those known, in Italy or in Greece, is fundamentally the same as many others previously found in Etruria, incised on vases from Cervetri and Veii or painted on the wall of a tomb near Sienna.[4] The vases may be dated in the second half of the VIIth century, or perhaps the beginning of the VIth; the alphabet from Sienna is perhaps not earlier than the beginning of the Vth century. Between them they cover the whole archaic period of Etruscan civilization. One single alphabet, therefore, was in use in Etruria for at least two centuries. Whatever its origin may be, whether it comes from Cumae, as is commonly believed, or represents an earlier type than that of the Chalcidians of Cumae,[5] it is indisputably derived from a Greek model. The archaic Etruscan alphabet is nothing but a complete Greek alphabet of twenty-six letters.

---

[1] Sommer, **CL,** p. 25 ; Buck, **XLI,** p. 25 ; Kirchhoff, **LXXXIX,** pp. 129 ff.
[2] **V,** 1882, p. 95.
[3] Minto, **CXII,** pp. 236 ff.
[4] Alphabet of Cervetri : Lepsius, **VI,** 1836, pp. 106-206 ; Anziani, *Mélanges Cagnat,* 1912, pp. 17-30. Alphabet of Formello, near Veii : **V,** 1882, pp. 91 ff., Bréal, **X,** 1882, pp. 147-168. Alphabet of Colle, near Sienna : **LIa,** no. 176 *b*.
[5] Grenier, **X,** 1924, pp. 1-42.

This is the alphabet in which our earliest inscriptions are written, not only in Etruria, but also in Latium and Rome. These are not numerous ; but they are sufficient to enable us to criticize the writing. First, there is the celebrated fibula from Praeneste, which bears the inscription : *Manios me fhefhaked Numasioi* (*Manius me fecit Numerio*), which is placed, by the shape of the fibula, in the VIIth century, or in the VIth at the latest.[1] Then there is the inscription on the mutilated cippus found in 1899 under the black pavement of the Forum, in front of the Comitium.[2] As Sig. Pais very justly says, one cannot state with certainty that this inscription belongs to the VIth, the Vth, or even the IVth century. But the writing is quite clearly that of the archaic Etruscan

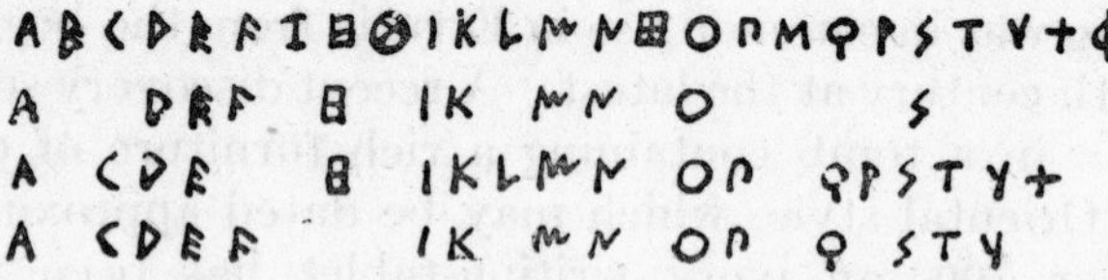

FIG. 3.—The archaic Etruscan and Latin alphabets.

Line 1. Archaic Etruscan alphabet.—2. Praeneste.—3. Forum.—4. Duenos.

alphabets. Connected with the same alphabets is the inscription incised with a point on the vase known as the Duenos vase, although this is clearly later, and can only belong to the IVth century.[3] The adjoining table (Fig. 3) shows these connexions.

About the end of the VIth century, or rather the beginning of the Vth, we find in Etruria a modification of the early Graeco-Etruscan alphabet. The voiced occlusives *b* and *d*, which, in Etruscan pronunciation, were not distinguished from the mute occlusives, disappear, and so does the vowel *o*. So the alphabets begin with the letters *a, c, e, v, z.* . . .[4] Some also drop the letter *c*, which does the same work as *k*. Two cippi from Chiusi, for example, give the series *a, e, v, z.* . . .[5] The vowel *o* never appears ; *u* was sufficient for the Etruscans.

---

[1] Helbig and Duemmler, **XIII**, ii (1887), pp. 37-43.
[2] **XVIII**, 1899, pp. 151-200 ; Comparetti, **L** ; cf. Thédenat, **CLVI**, pp. 80-2.
[3] Dressel, **VI**, 1880, pp. 158-95 ; Bréal, **X**, ii (1882), pp. 147-68 ; Pinza, **XIV**, xv, cols. 643-653.
[4] E.g., the Bomarzo vase, given as typical of the Etruscan alphabet by Bréal, **XI**, vii (1892), pp. 129-54 ; cf. Barnabei, **XVIII**, 1897, p. 509.
[5] **LIa**, nos. 1372-3, and Gamurrini, **VI**, 1871, pp. 155-66, pl. L.

On the other hand, a new sign appears in the alphabets and inscriptions—the sign 8 (=*f*), the origin of which is still a matter of discussion.[1] A reform of this kind, bringing writing into harmony with pronunciation, looks like the work of a thoughtful and intelligent will; it is a veritable spelling-reform. It is this alphabet, shorn of its voiced consonants and the vowel *o*, and augmented by 8 (=*f*), which is found in use among the Oscans and Umbrians, whether it was that these peoples did not learn to write until after Etruscan spelling was reformed, or that they blindly followed the example of the Etruscans, without taking the different character of their languages into account.

Rome, on the other hand, remained faithful to the old alphabet. Only those letters which did not correspond to any Latin sound, such as the aspirates ϕ (=*p* + *h*) and χ (=*k* + *h*), have disappeared. To express the sound *f*, indicated in the inscription on the Praeneste fibula by the group *digamma* + *h*, FH, the Latins were later content with the *digamma* alone, F. They never used the Etruscan 8. They only completed their reform of spelling at the end of the IVth century, in 312 B.C., when, on the authority of the Censor Appius Claudius Caecus, the third letter, C, was finally given its value as a mute guttural, and in the seventh place, instead of Z, which was not used, a new sign, G, was introduced, to indicate the voiced guttural. From the beginning of the Vth century, then, the evolution of Latin writing is independent of that of Etruscan writing.

So long as the reformed alphabet of the Vth century was believed to be the only Etruscan alphabet, it was natural to seek the origin of Roman writing elsewhere than in Etruria. Given the relationship of the archaic Etruscan alphabet with that of Cumae, it was legitimate to derive that of Rome direct from that of the Greeks of Cumae. But we now have in Etruria a complete alphabet containing all the letters which were used in Rome. It is surely more likely that the Romans learned writing from the Etruscans, their nearest neighbours, than from the Greeks of Cumae.

One detail removes all doubt on the matter. That is the transformation of the Greek *gamma* into the Latin C. If the Latin alphabet gives the third place to C and not to G, it

---

[1] See, lastly, Nogara, **IV,** 1920, p. 13, n. 1.

can only be the fault of the Etruscans. Etruscan pronunciation confused the voiced *g* and the mute *c ;* therefore it was in Etruria that the Greek γ was used for the sound intermediate between *g* and *c* which existed in the Etruscan language. The Romans, on the contrary, never confused voiced consonants with mute ones.[1] The proof of it is that they introduced into the alphabet the new sign G to indicate the voiced guttural. If the confusion, which did not exist in pronunciation, remained for a time in writing, it was because the writing was of Etruscan origin. For both sounds the Etruscan alphabet used the sign C. Thus we find, on an inscription from the Forum, the word RECEI=*regei*=*regi*. In this word the C has the value of γ. This letter appears in the same text in HONCE (=*hunc*) with the value of *c*. So, too, in the inscription of the Duenos vase we find, side by side, the words *cosmis* (=*comis*, *comes*) and *virco* (=*virgo*). It was in consequence of this old uncertainty that the Romans continued to write *Caius*, with the abbreviation *C.*, for the praenomen which they pronounced *Gaius* and the Greeks always wrote Γαίος. If Rome had taken her alphabet direct from the Greeks, the third letter C would always have kept the value *g*, and K would have been used for the mute guttural.

So the Romans must have been taught to write by the Etruscans, and that in the VIth century, at the latest, since the alphabet preserved by the Romans had disappeared from Etruscan use by the beginning of the Vth century. Rome learned her lessons under the tawse of the Tarquins.

IV

Etrusco-Roman Legendary Traditions

Through the darkness of a long age of forgetfulness, we see the Royal period of Rome, which was acquainted with writing and had its monuments of architecture, sculpture, and no doubt painting too, as a great period of civilization. It also seems to have had—still in common with the Etruscans

[1] Bréal, **XI**, vii (1892), p. 131.

—its legendary traditions, which were epic in character, if not in form.

In Greece, the VIth century is marked by the diffusion of imaginative literature. From its oral state, the Homeric epic was transposed into a written edition. It does not seem improbable that the Etruscans, who imitated all the arts of Hellas, also had their own epic legends. Whether they were written, and in what form, we do not know. But a memory of them, and a very definite memory, as we shall see, survived until the Imperial epoch. We find it also about the IVth century B.C. in Etruscan art. It no doubt had its share in the formation of the historical tradition of Rome. The

MACSTRNA   CAILE VIPINAS   LARθ   LARIS   PESNA   RASCE   VENθI AVLE   MARCE   CNEVB
                             VLθES   PAPAθNAS ARCMSNAS   VIPINAS CAMITLNAS TARXV
                                     VELZNAX   SVETIMAX   CAVLES   RVMAX
                                                                ...PLSAXS

FIG. 4.—Tarquin and Mastarna.   Painting from Vulci.

detailed but fabulous accounts which we possess of the period of the Kings probably came into history from Etruscan legends. Certainly there was a cycle about Tarquin and his companions.

A detailed examination of Etruscan representations of figures on mirrors, urns, funerary cippi, and the walls of tombs would perhaps make it possible to collect a certain number of elements of Etruscan historical legend. Let us be content here to mention, and to analyse from this point of view, a monument which is well-known—the paintings of a tomb at Vulci.

In 1857 the French consul and archaeologist Alexandre François discovered on the walls of a funerary chamber, in the neighbourhood of Vulci, a large composition, at the end of which was a person described in an inscription as *Cneve*

C

Tarchu Rumach, that is, *Cneius Tarquin of Rome.*[1] The painting itself, from its style, cannot be earlier than the first half of the IVth century. In representing an episode of the wars between Tarquin of Rome and certain Etruscan heroes, the artist was following an ancient tradition which had remained popular among his contemporaries. The names which he carefully wrote under each figure were intended to call up in the minds of spectators definite memories and a whole cycle of legends. A story, then known to everyone, was the foundation of this picture, just as the *Iliad* and *Odyssey* were the foundation of the innumerable works of art which they inspired.

The composition is arranged in a triptych. On the left, *Caile Vipinas* unbinds *Macstrna,* who must have been a prisoner of Tarquin. In the centre, the companions of Vipinas, named *Larth Ulthes, Rasce,* and *Aule Vipinas,* slay the companions of Tarquin, *Laris Papathnas Velznach, Pesna Arcmsnas Svetimach,* and *Venti Caules Plsachs.* Finally, on the right, one *Marce Camitlnas* is about to kill *Cneve Tarchu Rumach.* Each of the hapless guards of Tarquin bears, like Tarquin himself, a triple name, the last term in which is a race-name. But the race-names cannot be connected with definite cities. These figures remain unknown men for us.

This is not the case with the leaders, at least, of the opposing side. The two brothers Caile and Aule Vipinas are found on Etruscan urns, performing another exploit ; they surprise a mysterious individual named *Cacu.*[2] The memory of one of them, Caile, lived on in Roman historical tradition. Tacitus introduces him to us as the eponymous hero of the Caelian Hill in Rome.[3]

" This hill," he says, " was in old times called Querquetulanus, from the abundance of oaks upon it, and later Caelius, from Caeles Vibenna, the chief of an Etruscan tribe, who brought help, and was given that seat by Tarquin the Elder or some other of the Kings."

The grammarian Festus, in a very corrupt passage, seems to associate the two Vibenna brothers with the Vicus Tuscus in Rome, and even to mention in connexion with them

[1] Martha, **CIV,** p. 398, fig. 270 ; G. Koerte, **XII,** xii (1897), pp. 57-80, fig. p. 70.
[2] He was said to be a magician, sent by Marsyas to Tarchon, the king of the Tyrrhenians. He may have been the prototype of the fire-wizard Cacus whom Hercules slew on the Palatine, according to the Roman story.
[3] Tac., *Ann.,* iv. 65.

another person represented in the Vulci paintings, Macstrna.[1]

He, too, is known to us from the detailed account of him given by the most celebrated of students of things Etruscan, the Emperor Claudius, who, indeed, may very well be the source of the statements of Tacitus and Festus. In the famous speech which he made in favour of the admission of the Gallic nobles to the Senate, which is summarized by Tacitus and reproduced *in extenso* in an inscription from Lyons, the learned Emperor expressed himself thus :

"Servius Tullius, the truest comrade of Caelius Vibenna and the companion of all his adventures, being driven out of Etruria with all the remnants of the army of Caelius, came and occupied the Caelian Hill, to which he gave this name in memory of his chief. Then, having changed his own name (for in Etruscan he was called Mastarna), he reigned under the name of Servius, for the greater good of Rome."

The episode to which Claudius referred must have been a sequel to that depicted in the Vulci painting. Mastarna had been captured by Tarquin. The two Vibennae released their comrade and slew Tarquin. Then a series of adventures must have followed, in the course of which the Vibenna brothers perished in their turn. Mastarna collected the remnants of their army and settled in Rome, where he finally reigned in Tarquin's place. Here we have the material of part of an epic, in which the Etruscan rulers of Rome and Roman topography were mingled with the adventures of famous heroes of Etruria. In the time of the Emperor Claudius the exploits and misfortunes of the Vibenna brothers were still known, as well as the wonderful fortune of their faithful friend Mastarna. If the books devoted by Claudius to the past of Etruria had come down to us, they would no doubt have told us in what form these memories were transmitted. Certainly there is nothing improbable in the supposition of an Etrusco-Roman epic cycle.

---

[1] Fest., s.v. *Tuscus Vicus.* This is the text, according to Garrucci's restoration : *Volci*]entes fratres, Caeles et [*A*] Vibenn[*ae quos dicunt ad regem*]Tarquinium Romam se cum Max[*tarna contulisse eum incolue*]rint. Cf. G. de Sanctis, "Mastarna," in **IX,** ii (1902), pp. 96-104.

V

VARIOUS SURVIVALS OF THE ETRUSCAN PERIOD IN ROMAN CIVILIZATION

The fact of having thus taken part, during a long and brilliant period, in the life of Etruria left many traces in all the Roman civilization of later centuries. The first result of this early association with Etruria was that Rome was particularly accessible to Etruscan influences. Always, even when they found themselves the masters of a conquered Etruria, the Romans regarded their northern neighbours as possessing many secrets, which they never ceased to borrow from them. It is, therefore, almost impossible to distinguish what they retained from the time when they were themselves Etruscans from what they acquired later in the course of their history. In Rome, religion, art, even literary culture, and family and social life, all betray the lasting influence of her first teachers.

Capitoline Jupiter, in his Etruscan temple, always remained the chief god of the city. The priestly colleges, especially those of the soothsayers, augurs or haruspices, were always inspired by the Etruscan discipline. When some prodigy was beyond their competence, the Senate hastened to ask Etruria for its most highly qualified specialists. We shall find at every step, in the study of the rites and doctrines of Roman religion, this profound influence of Etruscan religion.

With reference to intellectual matters, Livy recalls that in old times it was the custom for young Romans of noble family to go to Etruria to finish their education, as later they went to Athens.[1] No doubt the Roman games were mainly Greek, but that was because the Etruscan games were so already.[2] In the pomp with which they were opened, which seems to have been the same in its essentials as that of the triumph, Hellenic elements were mingled with others which seem to have been peculiarly Etruscan.[3] Jupiter on his chariot, like the triumphant general, was dressed in Etruscan

[1] Livy, ix. 36. 3. Cf. Mueller, **CXIV**, p. 323.
[2] F. Weege, **XII**, xxxi (1916), pp. 137-8.
[3] Piganiol, **CXXXI**, pp. 15 ff.

fashion.[1] The heavy gold wreath, which adorned Jupiter's head, and was held by a slave over the head of the triumphant general, was Etruscan. The Lictors and their bundles of twelve rods round an axe were Etruscan.[2] The double axe seems to be the symbol of the great god of the pre-Hellenic peoples of the sea, many of whose beliefs survived among the Etruscans ; the twelve rods appear to correspond to the twelve cities of the Tyrrhenian confederation. Music in Rome was Etruscan.[3] The first actors, the *histriones*, came from Etruria. Roman funerals, which were so peculiar and so imposing, seem to have been imitated from Etruscan funerals. In Etruria, as in Rome, hired mourning-women chanted the dirge round the funeral bed. From Etruria the Romans learned the use of the mask, modelled on the dead man's face, which was afterwards preserved in the family.[4] The collection of these masks formed the ancestral portrait-gallery. For the funeral procession, the ancestral masks were taken from the wooden boxes in which they were kept, and were worn by men who impersonated the originals. These men strove to reproduce the physical peculiarities of the persons whom they represented, limping if the ancestor in question was lame. In this way past generations accompanied their descendant to his last dwelling, and it was before this assembly that the nearest kinsman spoke the funeral eulogy.

From the death-mask, from the care which the Etruscans took to preserve the likeness of the departed, the art of portraiture was derived. The Italian portrait, in Etruria from the VIth or even VIIth century, and later in Rome, showed a marked tendency to realism. It sought to represent the individual with his particular features, and was therein unlike the Greek portrait, which idealized the individual, and chiefly sought to bring out a general type in a particular image. This realism reigns supreme in all Etruscan funerary sculpture, from the first attempts [5] to the innumerable series of urns which show us the Etruscan as he was, fat or wrinkled, lying on the lid of his sarcophagus or of the casket which holds his ashes.

[1] Mueller, **CXIV**, ii, pp. 198 ff.
[2] The Tomba del Littore, at Vetulonia (Florence Museum).
[3] Mueller, **CXIV**, ii, pp. 209 ff.
[4] Minto, **CXII**, pp. 211, 276.
[5] Further most interesting information on this subject will be found in C. Albizzati, " Ritratti etruschi archaici," in **IV**, xiv (1920), pp. 3-22.

In architecture, just as the early Roman temple is Etruscan, so, too, the old Roman house, before the addition of the Greek *oecus*, reproduces an Etruscan plan. All the ancient authors agree in admitting the Etruscan origin of the atrium round which the dwelling-rooms are arranged. While hesitating to follow them in their etymology, and without being able to determine exactly the true character of the atrium, modern critics can only look for its model in Etruscan architecture.[1]

Perhaps even the constitution of the Roman family is indebted to Etruria for one of its characteristic elements. In Rome, the wife holds a place in the family infinitely more important than in Greece and amongst most peoples of the same stock as the Latins. Her moral position is in complete contradiction to the legal status assigned to her by the true Latin tradition. Legally, the wife does not count ; she has no rights. The celebrated sentence of Cato the Elder defines her position of perpetual minority : " Our ancestors wished that the wife should be in the husband's possession and power —*in manu et potestate virorum*." She cannot inherit ; kinship through women is of no account in the legal relations of one family with another. In all these features Roman law corresponds fairly exactly to Greek law.

Nevertheless, in spite of the law, we find in Rome that the wife is mistress, at least in the house. Whereas the Greek wife is relegated to the gynaeceum, the materfamilias is enthroned in the very centre of the house, in the principal room, opening wide on the atrium, from which she directs the whole of family life. The Latin inscriptions frequently show women to us as the counsellors and faithful companions of their husbands, whose dangers they share. In the Royal period, legend gives them a preponderant rôle in political life. Down to the end of the Republic, they never ceased to exercise considerable influence on their sons and husbands, and, through them, on the city. Manners greatly modified the rigour of law in their favour.

Is this situation to be explained by especial tenderness and refinement on the part of the early Romans ? It is surely more reasonable to see in it a survival of Etruscan family organization, which was matriarchal, in contrast to the

[1] Grenier, **LXXXI**, p. 120 and n. 1 (bibliography).

Latin patriarchal system.[1] In Etruria the mother is the centre of the family, and kinship lies in the distaff side. The Etruscan funerary inscriptions commonly mention the name of the mother, and often omit that of the father. The nobility of his maternal ancestors is as important to the Etruscan as that of his paternal line. The woman, in Etruria, really seems to be at least equal to the man. This is probably the reason why, in spite of the *deminutio capitis* laid upon her by the law, the Roman matron enjoys the importance and authority in the house which were given to her by Etruscan custom.

Moreover, the Roman marriage continued to reproduce, well into Imperial times, the rites and ceremonies of the Etruscan marriage. On the Roman sarcophagi, as on the Etruscan urns, the marriage scenes show us the bride veiled and surrounded not only by her girl companions, but by her kinsmen. The formula " *Ubi tu Gaius, ego Gaia* " certainly seems to allude to Etruscan equality and community rather than to the strict subordination of Latin law. In moral life as in that of the mind, in the family as in the plan of the house, part of the special character of Rome seems to come from Etruscan traditions, mingled in a more or less coherent fashion with the tradition of the Latins.

VI

The Population and Proper Names of Rome

The early population of Rome is presented by tradition as a mixture of Latins and Sabines, both belonging to the Italic family and speaking fairly closely related dialects. That of historical times appears, from the proper names in use throughout the classical period, to be composed of natives and a great number of families of Etruscan origin.

To establish a clear distinction between these two classes would be an almost impossible task, for even in Etruria properly Etruscan names are found together with many others which seem to be Italic. What is more, the same name, both in Etruria and in Rome, may contain purely

[1] Mueller, **CXIV,** i, pp. 373 ff.

native elements associated with elements which are foreign to the Italic languages and can be regarded as specifically Etruscan. For even in Etruria the Etruscans seem never to have been more than a racial minority, a ruling caste, open, moreover, to the natives, which imposed its methods of nomenclature on its neighbours, and at the same time allowed itself to be influenced and invaded by the names in use in the regions over which it extended its sway.

Proper names, both Etruscan and Italic, are formed on the same principle, namely by derivation, with the aid of one or more suffixes. So we divide them into root and suffixes. Now, many of the roots are found also in the proper names of Asia Minor; therefore they belong to the Etruscans, who in all probability came from that country. Similar instances are found among the suffixes.[1] But Italic suffixes may be attached to Etruscan roots, and vice versa. Nevertheless, the majority of Roman proper names seem to be, if not completely Etruscan, at least strongly contaminated with Etruscan.[2]

Let us first note, as examples, some roots of Roman names which, being found both in Etruria and in Asia Minor, or even in Asia Minor alone, may be qualified as Etruscan.

ASIA MINOR	ETRURIA	ROME
Τυλος	Tule	Tul-lius
Καδος	...	Catus
Ουαρος	...	Varus
Κεισος	Ceise	Caes-ius
Κασ-ιος	...	Cass-ius
Μαρ-ιος	Marie	Mar-ius
Αυλ-ια	...	Aul-ius
Ρουβ-εις	Rup-iias	Rubius
Τατ-εις	Tat-iial	Tatius
Etc.		

Of the suffixes, one which may at once be ascribed to the Etruscans is that of -ηνος, Latin -enna, which appears in the name of the Etruscan people: Τυρσ-ηνοί, Ras-enna.[3]

---

[1] G. Herbig, "Kleinasiatisch-etruskische Namengleichung," in *Sitzungsber. d. Münch. Akad.*, 1914, 2. Abhand., 39 pp. For place-names, cf. A. Kannengiesser, **IX**, xi (1910), pp. 26-47, and Kretschmer's reservations in *Glotta*, iv (1913), pp. 311-12.

[2] Schulze, **CXLVI**.

[3] De Saussure, quoted by Meillet, **I**, 1913-14, p. 122.

It is found in the names of persons, in Etruria and in Rome, in the forms -na, -ina, -ena, -enna : Caecina, Murena, Sisenna.[1] The Romans frequently develop it with the aid of the Italic suffix -ius : Herennius (formed on Herenna), Largennius (formed on Largenna). Certain families, like the Caecinae, kept in classical times the memory of their recent arrival from some Etruscan town. Such, too, was the case with Maecenas, Mecenas. The number and variety of true Roman derivatives in -nius, -inus, -enius, -ennius, -innus, -inius, -innius, formed on the top of this Etruscan suffix, are sufficient to show that this type of name was extremely ancient in Rome.

It is also generally agreed that the suffixes -a and -u are of Etruscan origin. Take, for example, the Etruscan name Papas-a,[2] which appears in another Etruscan inscription in the later form Paper-is,[3] to which the Latin name Papir-ius corresponds as exactly as can be. Proper names in -a are numerous in Rome : Cotta, Helva, Sulla, Volca (Etruscan Velχa). Still more numerous are those in which this suffix -a is developed by other suffixes. The Etruscan name Ap-as, for example, lies beneath such Roman names as App-e-ius, App-a-ienus, App-a-edius. So Latin names in -anius, -arus, -atius, -atinius, are seen to be secondary derivatives of a primary Etruscan formation in -a.[4] It is the same with the suffix -u.[5] An Etruscan root Tarχ, for example, produces a double series of names. With the suffix -ni the name Tarχ-ni Tarqu-inius, is formed. With the suffix -u we have Tarχ-u, Tarch-on, and its derivative Tarch-on-ius. In the same way an Etruscan name Velu underlies the Roman gens-name Velo-nius, and Capru is the origin of Capr-onius. Roman names in -onius, then, are generally based on an original Etruscan formation.

These Etruscan suffixes -a and -u served to form not only family names, but many cognomina which, from descriptive nicknames, developed into proper names : Agrippa, Galba, Pansa, Nasica, Seneca ;[6] Capito, Fronto, Naso, Strabo,

---

[1] Schulze, **CXLVI,** pp. 75, 81, 265.
[2] **LIa,** nos. 2951 ff.
[3] Schulze, **CXLVI,** p. 331 ; **LIa,** no. 834.
[4] **CXLVI,** pp. 388 ff.
[5] *Ibid.,* pp. 265 ff.
[6] Vendryes, **XI,** xxii (1921), pp. 97 ff.

Labeo, *Cato*.[1] The roots to which they are attached seem to
be in most cases of Italic origin ; *Agrippa* means " born feet-
foremost," *Galba* means " fat," and the other names mean
" big-headed," " big-browed," " big-nosed," etc. But in
some of these, at least, it is uncertain whether the root is
Latin or Etruscan. The cognomen *Labeo*, for example, may
come from *labea*, lip, or from the root which is found in the
names *Lab-ius*, *Lab-inus*, *Lab-enius*, *Lab-erius*, *Lab-onius*,
some of which appear to be of Etruscan formation. *Cato*,
too, may be derived from the adjective *catus*, wise, or from
the root which has given the names *Cat-ni* (Etruscan), *Catina*,
Catinius, *Catonius*, *Catunius*, *Catullus*, *Catedius*, *Catellius*,
Catillius, etc. Virgil's cognomen, *Maro*, certainly comes from
the Etruscan name *Masu* which has given the names *Masonius*
and *Maronius* in Rome.

In general, Roman nomenclature seems to be formed
indiscriminately of Latin and Etruscan roots, followed by
more or less developed series of suffixes. Among these
suffixes, the first, those immediately following the root,
-a, *-u*, *-l* (*Coc-l-es*, *Orb-il-ius*), *-r* (*Semp-ro-nius*, *Lab-er-ius*),
-s (*Fu-s-ius*, *Furius*, *Vol-u-s-ius*), and *-t* (*Pisi-d-ius*, *Tarc-
on-t-ius*), very often appear to be of Etruscan origin, since
they are found not only in Etruria, but also in Asia Minor.
But the termination *-ius* is Latin. Most Roman names,
therefore, either are entirely Etruscan, and Latinized only by
their ending, or bear the Etruscan stamp only in a part of
their suffixes. Therefore there were many Roman families
which took their names from an Etruscan or Etruscanized
ancestor. Moreover, the two languages, Latin and Etruscan,
seem, at the beginning and during a fairly long period, to
have mingled their methods of derivation in the formation of
proper names. The impression given by the study of names
certainly confirms that which seems to result from the consideration of the earliest Roman civilization as a whole ;
we see the effect of long and intimate mingling between the
two peoples and of the predominant position held by the
Etruscans.

So, on the Palatine or Forum, when the archaeologist
clears away the debris of Imperial times and goes deeper
into the ground, he finds the foundations of the Republican

[1] Schulze, **CXLVI**, pp. 314 ff.

period, themselves resting on mighty courses of obscure tufa blocks. Of these he can tell neither the exact date nor the purpose, but it is they which, lying buried and unknown to the Romans of historical times, have given the ground its shape and its stability. Thus, even if we study Roman civilization casually, we see, at the base of its development, the obscure but mighty foundations which, at the beginning of history, the Etruscan people laid down all over Italy. No doubt the details of the history of the Kings are still uncertain. But no one can question either the reality of this Etruscan period or its extreme importance.

CHAPTER III

ROME AND ITALY

I

THE NATIVE REACTION. LATINS AND SABINES

IN all times, and with especial intensity in the earlier periods, Italy must have presented the contrast, which strikes one at this day, between the brilliant civilization of the towns and the primitive simplicity of the country. The towns, in which men not only from all parts of Italy but from the whole world meet and live side by side, are on the highest level of culture. The countrysides, on the other hand, especially those which lie off the great ways of communication and are isolated by the nature of the land and the poverty of the inhabitants, even now live an extremely primitive life. If one goes even a short distance away from Rome or Naples, one finds oneself among a very backward population. Semi-barbarism lives next door to the most admirable artistic and intellectual development.

All these peasants and highlanders, whom modern civilization has hardly yet touched, constitute both a weakness and a valuable reserve of strength. These backward families take only the smallest part in the social and economic life of the country, but they bring up for the future a vigorous race, which is capable of developing, once educated, all the intelligence and resourcefulness of the townsman, in addition to an energy, a self-denial, a contempt of hardship, and a power of resistance, which the sons of the city, accustomed to an easier and softer life, have lost. To the artist, the Italian peasant is delightfully picturesque and primitive; to the statesman and economist he is a deplorable anachronism. To the historian he may, perhaps, afford an example by which to arrive at a conception, at least intelligible and probable, of the true character and the vicissitudes of early Roman civilization.

The history of Rome and early Italy is not only that of the Etruscan and Greek cities, but also that of the many native tribes of the plains, uplands, and mountains.

The Etruscans in central Italy and the Greek settlers in the south had, by creating cities, introduced into the peninsula the seeds of a new political and social life. In their cities, industries, arts, and ideas, which were the result of the long development of Asiatic and Mediterranean societies, bore fruit which had hardly any flavour of Italy. But all round them, in the vast tracts of the back-country, the native tribes carried on the traditions of primitive agricultural and pastoral life as they had been formed in the long centuries of prehistory. The country escaped the influence of the towns.

Unlike the Greeks, the Etruscans at least tried, it seems, to mingle with the surrounding natives. They assimilated some, admitting them into their cities. As their power advanced, from the VIIth century, and especially during the VIth, we see them sending out a whole series of swarms, from the coast towns to the interior of Italy. The confederation of Tyrrhenian cities seems to have conceived and attempted to realize the great project of an Italian empire, which should rule, by means of further confederations of cities, over the Po valley north of the Apennines and the plains of Campania south of Latium.[1] In order to have labour for its industries, customers for its trade, and food for its towns, Etruria became the teacher of the Italians. But its power, securely established on the coast, encountered, beyond the Tiber, the barrier of the mountains of Umbria. South of Umbria, the Sabines, and beyond them the various small peoples which separated them from the Samnites, remained independent on all the heights which gradually rose from the sea-board plain to the Apennines. Etruscan efforts at penetration and attacks must have caused a movement of the native peoples.[2] The kind of education which these brave and numerous hill-tribes gained in the course of defensive wars in the end made them a serious danger to the rich Tyrrhenian cities.

[1] Cf. Homo, **LXXXVI**, ch. iii.   [2] Cf. *ibid.*, ch. iii, § 4.

In Latium, Etruscan Rome succeeded in destroying Latin Alba. By the foundation of Tusculum Etruria ensured safety for the Roman Campagna and its roads against any return to the attack on the part of the hillmen. At the beginning of the Vth century, in 499 or 496, we find the Latins fighting for Tarquin against the Romans at Lake Regillus,[1] but a few years later, in 493, the Roman annals speak of the treaty of Spurius Cassius, which seals the alliance of the Latins and Rome and makes no mention of Tarquin or the Etruscans. These Latins are doubtless certain towns, Etruscanized like Rome itself, in the ruins of which foundations and other fragments of Etruscan architecture are found, the *clara oppida* of which Pliny speaks,[2] but they are principally the thirty *populi* or tribes united by the yearly common sacrifice to the Latin Jupiter of the Alban Mount.[3] In addition to the Alban Hills, Latium contains the Lepine Hills, which are still very wild to-day, and part of the plains below them. All through the Vth century and the first half of the IVth, down to 342, when Rome finally gained the upper hand over Tusculum, we find the Latins and Romans closely united. It even seems that the conduct of the Latin League was dominated by Latin interests, the policy of Tusculum, more than by that of Rome.[4] The Latins had assumed on the left bank of the Tiber the preponderance which had formerly been enjoyed by Etruria.

The defeat of Etruria in Rome and Latium seems to have been due to another native people, the Sabines, who, though they show many traces of Etruscan influence, had managed to safeguard their full independence. It was the Sabines who, about the end of the VIth century, or rather at the beginning of the Vth, took Rome from the Etruscans.[5]

Roman tradition places the Republican revolt against Tarquin in 509. It was in 504 that the annalists placed the arrival in Rome of the Sabine Atta Clausus, the ancestor of the family of the Claudii, with all his clients, 5000 of whom were capable of bearing arms.[6] There was, then, if we can believe this figure, a Sabine immigration of 20,000 or 25,000

[1] Livy, ii. 19 ; Dion. H., vi. 3.   [2] *N.H.*, iii. 69.
[3] Grenier, **LXXXI,** pp. 50-4.
[4] Piganiol, " Romains et Latins," in **X,** xxxviii (1920), pp. 285-316, espy. 297 ff.
[5] Cf. Homo, **LXXXVI,** bk. ii, ch. i.
[6] E. Albertini, " La Clientèle des Claudii," in **X,** xxiv (1904), pp. 247 ff.

souls. This was the nucleus of the Claudia tribe, whose lands lay towards the Sabina, north of the Anio.

Other Roman families, such as the Valerii, also claimed Sabine origin. Now, the Consular *Fasti* mention several Valerii during the first half of the Vth century. Claudii hold the consulship in 495 and 471. In 487 one Sicinius Sabinus appears. Lastly, in 460, tradition speaks of a Sabine chief, Appius Herdonius, who took the Capitol by a surprise. Down to Cato's time, Rome was often regarded as a Sabine city, and it was commonly admitted that the Romans were descended from the Sabines. We can fully associate ourselves with the hypothesis, suggested by Sig. Ettore Pais, of a Sabine conquest of Rome about the middle of the Vth century at the latest.[1]

The Latin alliance and the Sabine conquest mark, at the beginning of the Republican era, a reaction of old native traditions against the Mediterranean, urban civilization of the Etruscans. The Latins were peasants rather than townsmen. The Sabines were chiefly highlanders. When, later, the Romans conquered the Sabina, they found the population still scattered in small groups, in villages or even in isolated farms. So the men who took possession of the city of Rome were country-dwellers. The new families who henceforward enjoyed political predominance there remained settled on their estates. The patrician *gentes* were essentially rural. The land was their fortune. All their members were taken up with farm work. Chiefs and clients went to the city every ninth day, the *nundina*, for marketing and the despatch of public business. On the Forum, once consecrated by the Etruscans, peasants called their onions. The inscription carved on the mutilated cippus of the Forum seems to have said that beasts of burden, *jouxmenta* (=*jumenta*), might not be tethered near the alleged tomb of Romulus. Not far from that spot, the *Patres* met at the Comitium to prepare the motions which would presently, when the sales were over, be laid before the citizens who were thus brought together in the city for a few hours. Henceforward country prevailed over town, agriculture over trade, earth over mind. The Roman people became a people of peasants, governed by an aristocracy of land-owners.

[1] Pais, **XXIII,** ii (1909), pp. 358-79, and **CXXIII,** i, pp. 347-64.

Two centuries of rustic life, obscure and almost as uncertain as the age of the Kings, thus followed the first brilliant development of the Etruscan period. They consummated the union of the Roman people with the Latin land. They confirmed the nation, formed of different elements, in its qualities of tenacity and hardness. All this time, the Roman people was tilling the soil and fighting for its life, meanwhile developing the features which were its glory in the eyes of posterity, unwearying energy and grim patriotism. The ideal of the Roman, farmer and soldier, was to preserve the land of his fathers and to increase it by conquest. He was hard on himself and hard on others. With obstinate loyalty he clung to his old customs and turned aside from every novelty. The foreigner with his ways, the neighbour, was the enemy ; a single word, *hostis*, was used both for what was not Roman and for what was hateful. Roman simplicity and virtue were protected by utter narrowness of mind.

Classical tradition has done everything to popularize the ideal portrait of the old-time Roman, who devoted all his strength to the work of the fields and only left the plough to take up the sword. So we have Cincinnatus,[1] and Manius Curius, whom the Samnite ambassadors vainly tried to corrupt, who threw back their gold, preferring to remain poor and to rule over rich peoples.[2] So we have the sumptuary laws of the old Republic, jealously watching over the expenditure of individuals.[3] The historians in their retrospective enthusiasm love to contrast Roman austerity with " foreign " luxury. They glorify this spirit entirely absorbed in practical cares. According to them, abstract thought and the play of imagination and intelligence were utterly unknown to this

[1] Livy, iii. 25-9. The envoys of the Senate found him ploughing his land beyond the Tiber, and told him to put on his toga and hear the order of the Senate making him Dictator. Sixteen days later, having defeated the enemy, Cincinnatus went back to his ploughing.
[2] Flor., i. 13, 22. The Samnites found him in his simple hut, cooking turnips for his dinner.
[3] A marriage trousseau might contain only three purple-bordered robes. Gold wreaths in the Etruscan style were forbidden. Mourning-women might not be hired for funerals. Not more than ten flute-players must be used at the greatest internment. In 275 the Consular P. Cornelius Rufinus was struck off the Senate for being found in possession of silver plate weighing 10 lb. At the end of the first Punic War the Carthaginian ambassadors recognized the same dinner service on the tables of all the Roman Senators who entertained them. The old Roman is content with dishes of black earthenware, and only has a silver salt-cellar. And so on.

dour virtue. And this rudeness is supposed to have made the strength of Rome. It was because the Roman deliberately remained the most backward of the Italian peoples that he conquered all the rest.

That this picture, consecrated by tradition, has a foundation in fact, I would not deny. No doubt it exactly represents certain features of the Roman character, let us even say the dominant features of a part of the population of Rome, the most important part of that population, that, at least, which held the political power. But do not let us forget that, even in the hands of the Latins and the Sabines, Rome was still a city, and a great city. The natives took possession of the city founded by the Etruscans, but they did not destroy it. The old inhabitants remained. They had no land ; they could only live by their industry. The prosperity and importance of Etruscan Rome had been due, it seems, to the great amount of trade of which it was an entrepôt. Sabine Rome still had all the advantages of the position on the Tiber crossing, between central and southern Italy. Many of the inhabitants must have continued, though perhaps with greater difficulty than before, to act as middlemen between the Etruscan cities and the peoples of the centre and south of the peninsula. This activity was absolutely necessary, both for themselves and for the city. The poorish soil round Rome was incapable of feeding even a small urban community. Being obliged to import corn,[1] the city had to procure the wherewithal to pay for it by industry and trade. It had to work and produce in order to feed itself.

Moreover, by the side of the country aristocracy, surely we see in traditional history, directly after the Republican revolution, an essentially urban plebs appearing, whose work is considered indispensable to the life of the city. We know the parable of the Members and the Belly which was told to the plebs when it withdrew to the Sacred Mount. This plebs looked back with regret on Etruscan times. When Porsenna besieged Rome, the Republican leaders feared that it would open the gates to the enemy, and took all precautions against it.[2] It is in this population of craftsmen and traders, formed during the Etruscan period, that we shall look for the much-discussed origin of the Roman plebs. It was a typical urban

---

[1] Livy, ii. 34 ; iv. 25, 52 ; etc. [2] Livy, ii. 9.

population, preserving the spirit, the traditions, and the industries of Etruscan Rome. Its political victories, from the Vth to the IIIrd century B.C., witness to its continually increasing importance in national life. By the side of the rustic Latin and Sabine it represents the intelligence and the art of the Mediterranean.

Rome, moreover, could not live for two centuries in complete isolation from the rest of Italy. By its trade, by the thousand needs of daily life, it found itself in relations with Etruria and with Magnia Graecia and Sicily. It did not fail to be affected by their influence. Itself a great city, it was bound to vie with the other great cities which surrounded it or came within its ken. The general life of Italy, in which it necessarily took part, reviving the memories of the Etruscan age, must always have maintained an intellectual and artistic life, and a level of civilization in general far higher than that which one usually expects from the strict austerity of antique virtue.

It is on these elements, often neglected, of early Roman civilization that I would lay emphasis in this chapter.

II

ROME AND THE GREEKS OF ITALY

Having revolted against Tarquin and the Etruscans, Rome found, in the Vth century, natural allies in Italy. These were the Greeks, and more especially the Syracusans, who played the chief part in the war of Hellenism against Etruria.

The relations of Rome with the Greeks of Italy must have been conducted by land and by sea. The importance of the land road, which ran east of the Alban and Lepine Hills down the valleys of the Sacco and the Liris, is seen from the interminable wars of the Romans and Latins against the Aequi and Volsci who barred their way.[1] But large consignments of heavy material, corn, for example, certainly came to Rome by sea. Were they trans-shipped at the mouth of the

[1] A. Piganiol, **X**, xxxviii (1920), p. 298. Aequi and Volsci—in other words, Praeneste and Antium.

Tiber, so going by water all the way to Rome, or did sea trade for Rome not rather take the Etruscan port of Caere for a long time ? The first Roman settlement at Ostia, at the mouth of the Tiber, does not seem to be earlier than the IVth century.[1] Caere, moreover, though an Etruscan town and the refuge of the Tarquins, seems always to have been on excellent terms with Rome, no doubt to the material advantage of both parties. Its port may well have served the Romans regularly until Rome became a maritime power in the IIIrd century.[2]

What Rome wanted from Sicily was, first of all, corn. Livy mentions purchases of Sicilian corn in the years 486, 435, and 411 B.C.[3] From Sicily, too, Latium probably obtained its wine and oil at the beginning, and the Sicilians may have taught the Latins to cultivate the vine and olive. We seem to find a record of these civilizing influences in the erection in Rome, at the beginning of the Vth century, of a temple to the Sicilian goddess Ceres, associated, in the Etruscan way, with Liber (Bacchus) and Libera (probably Demeter). The architecture of this temple was Etruscan. But for its decoration two Greek artists were called in, Damophilos and Gorgasos, who established themselves in Rome.[4] The cult of Ceres seems to have been served until classical times by a priestess of Sicilian origin.[5] It was during this period, too, that Mercury, the Greek god of trade, and Apollo, the great pan-Hellenic deity of the Vth century, were introduced into Rome.[6]

The Romans were also dealing with Marseilles by the Vth century. From Marseilles Diana was said to have come ; a temple was built to her on the Aventine, and the cultus-statue reproduced the appearance of Artemis, the great protectress of the Phocaeans.[7] Somewhat later, in 396, when,

---

[1] Carcopino, **XLII**, pp. 6 ff.

[2] D. Anziani, **X**, xxxi (1911), 444 ff.

[3] ii. 33. According to another chronology, the two last dates were 427 and 403. Cf. Pais, **CXXII**, p. 309. One may, moreover, ask on what documents Livy's information is based.

[4] Pliny, *N.H.*, xxxv. 154. Cf. Merlin, **CIX**, pp. 140 ff.

[5] Pais, **CXXII**, pp. 250-2. We have no confirmation of the traditional date of 493-2. Nor, however, is there any proof that the worship of Ceres was, as Sig. Pais is inclined to think, only slightly earlier than that of the *Magna Mater* (204).

[6] One may add Castor and Pollux, the two horsemen whose worship was probably transmitted from Tarentum to Tusculum and Rome about the time of the battle of Lake Regillus. Cf. W. Helbig in *Hermes*, xxxix (1904), pp. 101-15.

[7] Diod., xiv. 93 ; Strabo, iv. 179-80. Cf. J. Bayet's remarks in **X**, xxxviii (1920), pp. 137-8.

after long struggles, the Romans had taken Veii, the golden crater which they offered to Delphic Apollo in gratitude for the counsels of his oracle was deposited in the Treasury of the Massaliots. When Rome was burned by the Gauls, Marseilles contributed to its reconstruction. Rome was at this time in such excellent relations with the Greeks of the West that the echoes of its capture by the Gauls which reached Greece Proper represented it as a Greek city which had fallen victim to Hyperborean barbarians.[1]

With the consignments of food-stuffs, not only did Hellenic deities come into Latium, but also ideas of every kind, moral, social, and political.

The Latin and Sabine aristocracy of peasants, being in possession of a great city like Rome, naturally came to look for rules of organization. Where should they find the models for a political system likely to satisfy the urban plebs, if not in the thriving, populous cities of Sicily and Magna Graecia ? For these cities the Vth century was a period not only of very great material prosperity, but also of extreme intellectual brilliance. In rhetoric, Sicily was ahead of Attica. Plato took refuge in Syracuse, and Herodotos settled at Thurii in Magna Graecia, an Athenian colony founded in 466 near the site of Sybaris, which had been destroyed by Croton at the end of the VIth century. Moreover, this part of Greek Italy, Bruttium, was the field of very remarkable social experiments.

This region was the scene, at the end of the VIth century and the beginning of the Vth, of the activities of Pythagoras, whose memory left such a deep impression on the imagination of all Italy, and of Rome in particular. On his return from his travels in the East, and as far as India, after an unsuccessful attempt to establish his school in Greece, Pythagoras came and taught at Tarentum. Then, having been summoned by the Crotoniates, he exercised an absolute moral dictatorship over their city. In 510, after the capture of Sybaris, he built near the ruins of that city the famous institution in which he collected his disciples in a kind of mystico-philosophic brotherhood. We cannot estimate the quality of his teaching. The precepts preserved under his name give us only a grossly superstitious picture of it. But

[1] Plut., *Camill.*, 22.

his mathematical discoveries and his cosmic theories rank him among the great thinkers of antiquity. He applied his intelligence to morals and politics as well as to metaphysics.[1] All over southern Italy we find many lasting traces of his influence. His name, at least, had reached Rome at an early date.

We know that, in spite of the obvious anachronism, Roman legend made Numa a disciple of Pythagoras. If it is true that tradition sums up under the name of Numa all the long process of social and religious organization which went on in Rome under the Sabine domination, the anachronism disappears. In that case, the legend represents a memory of the influence exercised on Rome by the moral ideas and legislative activity which had resulted, in southern Italy, from the teaching of the great philosopher.[2]

In 454, according to Roman tradition, the Laws of the Twelve Tables were drawn up.[3] It was said that these laws had been inspired by Greek models, the laws of Solon or others, and that the Decemvirs entrusted with their preparation had been sent to Athens and the Greek cities of Italy with instructions to find out the best laws everywhere. Did they really go to Athens ? To what extent was their work inspired by Hellenic antecedents ? We shall not discuss here a matter which so many have already discussed. Let us be content to observe that the mere idea of drawing up a code independent of religion and publishing laws was altogether Greek. The old native laws, the " Royal Laws," *Leges Regiae*, being part of the Law of Religion (*Jus Pontificium*), were kept secret by the priestly colleges down to the end of the IVth century. In the history of Roman law, the Twelve Tables represent a veritable revolution, the origin of which, it seems to me, can only have come from the Greek cities.

Of Roman political institutions, those which the plebs caused to be adopted also seem to be copied from Greek models.[4] The Tribuneship of the Plebs, instituted, according to tradition, in 471 or 466, recalls the office of the Demarchs

---

[1] Robin, **CXXXVIII**, pp. 57 ff.
[2] Zaleucos, who was a friend of Pythagoras, and was said, like him, to have been given Roman citizenship, made laws for Locri, and Charondas for the Chalcidian cities. At Thurii, rather later, Protagoras placed his constitution under the patronage of Charondas. Cf. Pais, **CXXII**, p. 331.
[3] De Sanctis, **CXLII**, ii, p. 42, 62 ; Pais, **CXXI**, i, pp. 446 ff. and **CXXII**, p. 332.
[4] Pais, **CXXII**, pp. 260 ff.

in Syracuse. The Plebeian Aediles correspond to the *Agora-nomoi* of various Greek cities. The *sacrosancta potestas* seems to be equivalent to the ἱερὰ καὶ ἄσυλος ἀρχή of the Greeks. Certainly the right of asylum attaching to some Greek sanctuaries in Rome, such as the Temple of Ceres, is a Greek institution. Greek, too, was the statue of Marsyas, the symbol of liberty, on the Roman Forum. Even the institution of the colonies, which began in the IVth century, was evidently inspired by Greek colonization. Greece, through her Italian offshoots, completed the organization of the Roman city.

So the special character of Rome never included an attitude of complete exclusiveness towards the more civilized regions of Italy, and, indeed, it would have been impossible. On the contrary, her originality lay in the variety of elements which she took from all the peoples of the peninsula. From the Vth century onwards, Rome seems to have deliberately gone to the Greeks for lessons. When, in the following century, she conquered Italy, she took possession not only of the land, but also of the civilizations which had developed there in the last four hundred years.

III

The Conquest of the Italian Civilizations

At the beginning of the IVth century the Gauls took Rome and burned it. This catastrophe seems to have been the cause of the sudden political rise of the Roman state. For it was not so much Rome as her enemy Etruria that suffered. Etruria was robbed by the barbarian invasions of the richest, perhaps, of its provinces—the plain of the Po. Above all, the proximity of the Gauls, and the perpetual menace of other inroads, turned the attention of the Etruscan Confederation northwards. The forces of Rome being liberated, the south of the peninsula was delivered into her hands.

In the middle of the IVth century, in 342, began the inexpiable war against the Samnites, the last consequences of which were the capture of Tarentum in 272 and the submission of the whole of southern Italy to Rome.

On the great plateaus of the central Apennines and in the upper valleys of the little rivers which flow from them to the Adriatic and Tyrrhenian Seas, there had lived, since prehistoric times, the Samnites, near kin of the Sabines. Life was rough in this mountain country. Snow on the crests for most of the year, a hard climate, a meagre soil, all made it difficult for a large sedentary population to settle there. The great resource, to this day, is stock-raising. From May to September, the herds of great light-coloured oxen and the tens of thousands of sheep and goats, accompanied by their herdsmen, fill the highland pastures with life.

From the top of their mountains, the Samnite herdsmen saw below them, on the east, the vast plain of Apulia with its ports, and, on the west, green Campania. These delectable plains were necessary to them. As soon as winter drove them from the hills, it was there that they must graze their beasts. Passing once more through the village in the valley, where their families lived, they made for the lowlands, where, moreover, people awaited them and their beasts, in order to buy wool, hides, and meat. This going to and fro between the plain and the mountains has always been the movement of life in southern Italy.[1]

This traffic between the two regions had not been established and was not continued without conflicts. The wealth of the countryside and cities of the lowlands was a constant temptation to the poor, hardy highlanders. It seems to have been from Samnium that the tribes to whom the Greeks gave the name of Oscans descended into Campania and peopled it. At the end of the VIth century, in the dawn of history, hillmen appear again as allies of the Etruscans in the valley of the Vulturnus. At the end of the next century the Samnites overwhelmed the whole plain and took possession both of Etruscan cities, like Nola and Capua, and of Greek cities, like Cumae and Naples, while the hillmen of Lucania occupied Paestum.[2] On the eastern side, towards Apulia, we do not know what relations may have been established between the

---

[1] A. Grenier, " La Transhumance des troupeaux an Italie et son rôle dans l'histoire romaine," **X**, xxv (1905), pp. 293-328.

[2] Nissen, **CXV**, ii, 2, pp. 681 ff., espy. pp. 700, 893.

tribes of the Apennines and the natives of the plain, Daunians, Iapygians, Peucetians, Messapians, and others.[1] In Calabria we find flourishing Greek cities, Brundisium and Tarentum, and in Apulia, on the coast and inland, large, wealthy, prosperous native towns. For all alike, the herdsmen of Samnium were a constant menace.

In Apulia, as in Campania, the civilization of the Greek colonies conquered the natives, Oscan or Iapygian. From the middle of the Vth century, these two regions were centres of

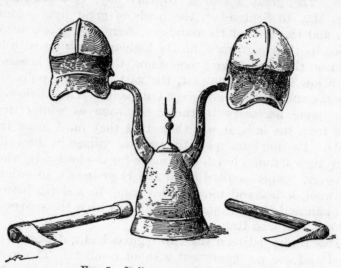

FIG. 5.—Italic arms. (Naples Museum.)

a brilliant development, of an artistic, if not of an intellectual, kind. In Apulia and Lucania workshops manufactured painted vases, which gradually drove out Attic wares.[2] A few tombs which have been methodically excavated, among numbers which have been neglected or destroyed, enable us to observe a diffusion in these provinces of manners, ideas, and industries comparable to those of Tarentum or Heracleia.[3] The same is true of Campania, where Greek influence was followed by that of the Etruscans, who commanded the district

[1] Nissen, **CXV**, ii, 2, pp. 835 ff.
[2] Dugas-Pottier, art. *Vasa*, **LVI**, pp. 651 ff.
[3] Pagenstecher, **CXX**, 1912, and " Grabgemälde aus Gnathia," in **XIII**, xxvii (1912), pp. 101-23 ; M. Jatta, " Tombe canosine del Museo di Bari," *ibid.*, xxix (1914), pp. 91-126 ; H. Nachod, " Gräber in Canosa," *ibid.*, pp. 260-98.

for at least a century, at the time when their power was at its height. Here, too, there was a native painted pottery which competed with Greek imports.[1] Here, too, certain tombs, at Cumae, Nola, Capua, and Paestum, afford specimens of funerary architecture and painting which follow the movement of Greek and Etruscan art at no very great distance.[2]

Even the Samnites of the mountains seem to have had in the IVth century a civilization copied from that of the plains. Their capital, Aufidenum, in the upper valley of the Sangro, on the Adriatic slope of the Apennines, was a citadel, no doubt of rude architecture, but built on the scientific principles of Greek fortification. The buildings appear to have been chiefly of wood, with stone stylobates ; but they contained columns, and seem to point to the existence of some sort of social life, copied from that of the lowland cities. The tombs, in any case, give a high idea of the wealth of these hillmen and of the volume of their trade with the Greek or Hellenized towns of the plains.[3] These vigorous tribes of an unkindly region formed a people which was raised by its dealings with Apulia and Campania to a level considerably above primitive barbarism.

Apparently, war broke out between the Latins and Samnites in consequence of an appeal of Capua and, at the same time, of the intrigues of Tarentum. Rome was the ally, at first, of the cities of Campania and Apulia. Her armies occupied these districts, and it was here that the struggle was waged. The three quarters of a century during which she fought in the wholly Hellenized south of the peninsula completed her education.

It was then, apparently, that the Romans began to be acquainted with riches, the luxury which they engender, and, consequently, the pleasure of art. Livy lays emphasis on the lustre of the Samnites' arms, with their gold and silver plating,[4] the whiteness of their tunics, their purple ribbons, their tall crests ; he enumerates the spoil in metal—copper, gold, and silver—which every triumph brought in. What we know of Oscan civilization fully confirms the picture which

[1] Dugas-Pottier, art. *Vasa*, in **LVI,** p. 651.
[2] F. Weege, " Oskische Grabmalerei," in **XII,** xxv (1909), pp. 99-141.
[3] L. Mariani, " Alfedena," in **XIV,** x (1901), espy. pp. 247 ff. ; cf. **XVIII,** 1901, pp. 442 ff. ; 1902, pp. 516 ff.
[4] ix. 40.

he draws of it.[1]   A painting on a tomb at Capua, for example,
shows us a Samnite horseman.   He wears a bronze helmet
with a large crest and a huge flowing mane, on either side of
which rises a stiff feather.   He has a white tunic, held at the

Fig. 6.—Samnite horseman.   Tomb-painting.   (Capua Museum.)

waist by a broad belt with metal fittings.   The horse's head
is protected by a plate of gilt metal and bears two tall feathers.
The leather harness is adorned with gilt disks.   The painted
vases of Campania sometimes show the same armament,[2]
in which Greek forms are overloaded with barbaric fancies.
These folk loved show.   They had themselves painted on the

[1] Weege, "Bewaffnung u. Tracht der Osker," **XII,** xxiv (1909), pp. 141-62.
Our figs. 5, 6, and 7 are from this publication.
[2] Dugas-Pottier, art. *Vasa,* in **LVI,** p. 650, figs. 73 ff.

walls of funerary chambers in their most gorgeous garb,
setting forth to war or returning from the fight laden with
trophies. These trophies consisted simply of the many-
coloured tunic of the enemy fixed on the shaft of a lance.[1]
One may see in this the origin of our cavalry pennons.

They were tough and skilful fighters, from whom the
Romans took many details of armament. In particular, the
Roman cavalry adopted the javelin, shield, and movements
of the cavalry of the Samnites of Campania.[2] For these
latter had been able to profit by the tactical lessons of the

Fig. 7.—Samnite gladiators. (Capua Museum.)

Greeks, and the Romans themselves must have already had
some scientific military education to be able to measure
swords with them. Prosperity and civilization had not
affected the fighting spirit of this people, which had continued
to have constant dealings, friendly and hostile, with its kinsmen of the mountains. The tomb-paintings bear witness to
it. They sometimes show ladies at their toilet or matrons
laden with heavy jewels ;[3] but still more often do they depict
combats in which opponents, already full of wounds, hurl
themselves at each other, shield forward and lance down, or
with javelin poised in the air.[4]

[1] Weege, **XII**, xxxiii (1909), p. 102, fig. 1, pl. x.
[2] *Ibid.*, p. 143 ; cf. Pais, **CXXII**, p. 323 ; cf. pp. 319-21.
[3] **XII**, 1909, pls. 7 and 11.   [4] *Ibid.*, p. 119, fig. 8 ; p. 133, fig. **13**, pl. xi.

In many cases, it is true, these combats appear to be simply games. In some, the presence of spectators and umpires leaves no doubt on the matter.[1] Moreover, we know that in Rome the name " Samnites " was used for a class of fully-armed gladiators, and that until Imperial times Capua was an important centre for gladiatorial schools. Did the Romans, then, acquire their taste for this kind of spectacle in Campania ? The first performance of the kind in Rome was said to have been given by M. and D. Brutus on the occasion of their father's death in 264 ; that is to say, shortly after Rome had established her power in Campania. But gladiatorial combats seem to have been an Etruscan no less than a Samnite institution. The generic name used in Rome for the gladiator, *lanista*, is of Etruscan origin. It is hard to decide to which of their neighbours the Romans were indebted for their love of these sanguinary games. At any rate, it was from Magna Graecia—from Thurii, where they had a garrison in 285—that they are said to have learned horse-racing.[2] But chariot-races must have been much more ancient among them, and must have been taken from the Etruscans.

The policy and wars which took their armies into Campania, into Apulia, and into Lucania brought the Romans into direct contact with brilliant native civilizations, the daughters of the Greek civilization of Italy. Far from evincing the least repugnance towards them, they imitated them eagerly.

Rome now became the capital of Graeco-Etruscan Italy. Mistress of the greater part of the peninsula, she benefited by all the work of civilization which had been developed for centuries by the various peoples which she had conquered one after another. With their spoils and part of their wealth, she gleaned at least some of the factors of prosperity which they had possessed—industries, trade, ports, ways of communication. She opened her doors to their men, and, more then ever, to their ideas and their arts.

The year 300 really marks the end of the exclusiveness of Rome. The city state was succeeded by a new political and social system, the association of many towns and large districts in a whole which was, no doubt, still ill-defined, but was subject to a central authority. This very character-

[1] **XII**, 1909, p. 133, fig. 13.   [2] Tac., *Ann.*, xiv. 21.

istic development in Italy closely followed the corresponding
transformation of Greece and the Hellenized countries of
Asia, where the empire of Alexander and the kingdoms of
his successors put an end to the independence of the cities
and constituted large, highly centralized states.

If we adhered to the Roman historical tradition, as Livy
gives it to us, for example, we should conceive of this conquest of Italy by the Romans as the victory of a rude people
over enemies who were infinitely stronger in appearance, but
were weakened by their wealth and the refinement of their
civilization. In fact, it would be a kind of first barbarian
invasion. Rome destroyed Italian Hellenism. In depriving
her neighbours of their independence, she dealt a mortal
blow to the arts and industries which they had created.
Proud of her rude simplicity, and contemptuous of the
luxury which had ruined her enemies, she remained immovably
faithful to her old traditions until the day when conquered
Greece seduced her severe virtue. So, too, according to this
view, the conquest of the Mediterranean world after that of
Italy was the triumph of a people which had kept all its
youthful strength and rustic energy over the more advanced
civilizations of the East. So the history of Rome shows
throughout the superiority of coarse simplicity to intellectual
development.

This picture, on which so many have enlarged, does not
seem to correspond to the facts. No doubt it cannot be
pretended that the Rome of the IVth century before our era
was like Capua or Tarentum. But there is no fact which
compels us to accept the picture of a still barbarous Rome,
brutally destroying on every side, without drawing any
advantage from it, all the ancient progress of Magna Graecia
and Etruria. If the Romans conquered all the other peoples
of Italy, it was because, in certain respects at least, they were
their equals in intelligence. Brute force may, no doubt,
sometimes overcome civilization, but that is when civilization
itself suffers from some internal vice which makes its weakness. From what we know of the early civilizations of Italy,
it does not appear that they were struck with any such mortal
sickness. It does not even seem that they died of the
Roman conquest.

No doubt, Rome was guilty of much looting and destruction in Italy. She grew rich on the spoils of the conquered. But both in Magna Graecia and in Etruria she went into many cities—Capua, Thurii, Canosa—as an ally and protectress rather than as an enemy. Even Tarentum, which was taken by force of arms, was not destroyed, and reappears as a flourishing city at the time of the Punic Wars. We cannot, therefore, believe that the set-back of the artistic industries in southern Italy, and of painted pottery in particular, can be dated from the appearance of the Roman armies.[1] The decline through which these industries went during the first part of the IIIrd century was due to more general causes, and chiefly to the new flight taken by Hellenism after Alexander's time, and to the changes in aesthetic taste which ensued from it.[2] Then Magna Graecia found itself behind the rest of the Hellenic world. We see it, under Roman dominion, making up this lost ground as early as the second half of the IIIrd century, with its vases of the type of Cales, near Capua.[3] Let us admit that Rome was likewise behind Magna Graecia. She none the less shared in the same civilization of Greek origin, which had been implanted in Italy with the establishment of the Greek colonies, and had spread fairly uniformly over the various regions of the peninsula, from Bruttium to Etruria and the valley of the Po. Even after the Sabine and Latin reaction Rome had not ceased to participate in the general life of Italy. First her relations with Sicily and Magna Graecia, and then her conquests in the south and centre, merely equalized, as it were, little by little, the general level of civilization enjoyed by herself and regions which were more precocious or more favoured by circumstances.

IV

ARTISTIC DEVELOPMENT IN ROME FROM THE FIFTH TO THE THIRD CENTURY

The Roman historians seem to have made it a point of honour to separate their city from the rest of Italy and to

---

[1] V. Macchioro, " Per la storia della ceramografia italiota : la cronologia," in **XIII,** xxvii (1912), pp. 21-36.
[2] C. Picard, " La Fin de la céramique peinte dans la Grande-Grèce," in **II,** xxxv (1911), pp. 203 ff.
[3] Pagenstecher, **CXIX.** Cf. Dugas-Pottier, art. *Vasa,* in **LVI,** pp. 655, 658, 665.

contrast her with the peoples which she conquered. I believe
that she should, on the contrary, be brought nearer to them.
I imagine a development in Rome parallel to that of the other
great cities of the peninsula. Let us try to find at least some
indications of it.

Even in the early Republic, the Romans showed themselves great builders, and they were not long in proving good
architects. Their piety filled the city with temples. In 484
they are said to have dedicated a temple to Castor on the
Forum.[1] In 433 they erected another to Apollo on the Campus
Martius.[2] Vestiges of these venerable buildings have recently
been found, and the study of them has permitted some very
interesting observations.[3]

In the basement of the Temple of Castor dating from the
time of Augustus parts of the foundations of the earlier
building have been found. They consist of large blocks of
blackish tufa, fairly roughly hewn, and arranged in exactly
the same way as the courses which form the basement of the
temple of Capitoline Jupiter, or the very ancient walls which
can still be seen on the Palatine. Of the Temple of Apollo
there has been found, near the Theatre of Marcellus and the
Portico of Octavia, a strong breast-wall which must have
supported the *podium*. The tufa blocks of which it is composed are very finely and carefully cut, and the courses show
in the middle a slight convexity of ·045,[4] an architectural
device invented in Greece in the Vth century, to correct the
natural error of vision. So considerable progress was made
in the fifty years which lay between the construction of the
Temple of Castor and that of the Temple of Apollo, and this
progress shows us that the architects who worked in Rome
were acquainted with the most ingenious devices of Greek
craftsmanship.

Other remains of early temples which have been found
beneath the soil of Rome and identified enable us to state
that until about the middle of the IIIrd century, that is,
just before the first Punic War, the Tuscan order prevailed in
Rome, as in the rest of Latium.[5] Only at the beginning of
the IInd century did the elongated Greek plan and the Greek
orders finally supplant the old Etruscan architectural tradition.

[1] Livy, ii. 42.   [2] *Ibid.*, iv. 25, 29.   [3] Delbrueck, **LIX**.
[4] *Ibid.*, pp. 8, 14.   [5] *Id.*, **LX,** pp. 24, 60.

These old Roman temples, like the Etruscan temples, are only wooden buildings faced with polychrome terra-cottas. But this plastic decoration follows the general movement of Greek art. Human figures are introduced, separate from the mere ornament, and become more numerous. In addition to the acroteria and friezes, we find true pediment-decoration appearing, containing the gods of Hellenic mythology.[1] The fragments found at small places in Latium like Antemnae,[2] Ardea,[3] and Lanuvium,[4] are in no way different from the much more abundant remains found at Falerii, for which the destruction of the city in 241 gives the latest possible date.[5] These terra-cotta reliefs and statues are exactly the same in Etruria, Umbria, Latium, and Campania.[6] They are the product of a true Italic art, and one is naturally led to suppose that there were wandering artists, who were called in by any city which had a temple to build or to decorate. Rome did not stand aloof from this artistic movement. A fine terra-cotta statue of a seated female deity, which was found near the Palatine and is now in the Conservatori Museum, comes from the pediment of some vanished Roman temple.[7] (Plate XI, 1.) The religious edifices which were built in Rome from the Vth to the IIIrd century before our era must have had the same decoration of human figures as those of the other cities of Italy.

These temples were adorned with paintings. The evidence of the ancient writers leaves no doubt on the matter. Greek artists, as we have seen, had been summoned to Rome to decorate the Temple of Ceres, and they had settled permanently in the city. Pliny, to whom we owe this information, shows us Fabius Pictor, a Roman of the aristocratic family of the Fabii, decorating the Temple of Salus in 304. He states, in this connexion, that painting, which was very ancient in Italy, had always been highly appreciated by the Romans. At Ardea and Lanuvium, he says, he admired the astonishing freshness of paintings which he judged to be older than Rome itself; among them, he recognized nude figures of Atalanta

---

[1] Della Seta, **CXLVIII**, pp. 132 ff.   [2] *Ibid.*, p. 211, pl. 49.
[3] Duruy, **LXIX**, i, p. 45, fig.   (From the Campana Collection in the Louvre.)
[4] Della Seta, **CXLIX**, p. 250, fig. 279.
[5] *Ibid.*, pp. 213-15, figs. 229-33 ; **CXLVIII**, pp. 120 ff., pls. 34-49.
[6] Koch, **XC**.
[7] Della Seta, **CXLIX**, p. 215, fig. 234.

PLATE IV

PAINTING FROM A ROMAN TOMB ON THE ESQUILINE
(Rome, Conservatori)

[face p. 64

and Helen, of excellent drawing.[1] In Rome, Quintilian
declares that he saw ancient paintings on which he deciphered
the names of *Alexanter, Cassanter, Hecoba,* and *Pulixena.*[2]
This is the spelling which we find on the IVth century mirrors
and caskets of Praeneste. It is due to Etruscan influence,
and shows that it was through Etruria that the stories of the
Trojan cycle reached Rome. So painting had made them
popular there at the same time as in the rest of Italy.

It was very probably also in some temple that the slave
in Plautus' *Captives*[3] had seen the picture of the torments
of Acheron. These infernal scenes were common motives
from the IVth century onwards in Etruscan tomb-paintings.[4]
Their appearance in Rome testifies to the diffusion of both
the ideas and the art of Etruria. Long before the beginnings
of literature, then, the Roman people had, to teach it Greek
legends and Etruscan ideas, the pictorial and plastic representations which are the books of the ignorant.

We even find among the Romans, at this time, the expression of an original artistic tendency, which was destined later,
in the sculpture of the end of the Republic and of the Imperial
epoch, to receive a majestic development—the representation
of historical facts.[5] I refer to a fragment of fresco found on
the Esquiline on the wall of an ancient funerary chamber.[6]
(Plate IV.) The paintings are arranged in three horizontal
bands. Below, there are a few fragments of a battle scene.
Immediately above it are two large figures conversing. One,
the Roman Q. Fabius, is clad in the toga, and is escorted by
four smaller figures in tunics ; the other, M. Fannius, wears
a heavy white cloak over his left shoulder and stretches his
right hand towards his interlocutor. We find this same
person, M. Fannius, again in the top band, this time wearing
a crested helmet of a definitely Samnite type. He advances
towards a very mutilated figure holding a lance, who must
be Fabius. The subject is no doubt the surrender of a
stronghold, the wall and battlements of which can be seen.
These paintings are simple pictures of events, not works of
art. This is just what makes them interesting. Works of
art were inspired by traditional motives—chiefly mythology

[1] *N.H.,* xxxv. 17. [2] *Inst. Orat.,* i. 4. 16.
[3] *Capt.,* 998 ff. [4] Weege, **CLXIX,** pp. 25 ff.
[5] Courbaud, **LII,** pp. 195 ff.
[6] **III,** xvii (1889), pp. 340-50, pls. xi, xii ; **XIII,** vi (1891), p 111 ; **LI,** vi, 29, 827.

—or by the subjects common in Magna Graecia and Etruria, triumphal processions or funeral scenes. Here, on the contrary, we see an awkward effort to render, without any artistic model, particular deeds, to the glory of a person who has accomplished them. It is not certain who this Q. Fabius was. His adversary Fannius is equally unknown ; he was no doubt a Samnite chief. So the painting is a document representing some episode in the Samnite wars of the end of the IVth century or the beginning of the IIIrd. It is an original Roman work, the first of those figure compositions inspired by history which were intended to relate to the people the exploits accomplished by its leaders.

Another class of works of art seems to have been especially abundant in Rome in early times—statues representing, not gods or mythical heroes, but real persons. We may ignore, as being impossible to confirm and probably tinged with fancy, to say the least of it, the references of ancient authors to statues of the Kings dedicated by themselves on the Capitol and to portraits of the founders and first defenders of the Republic, such as Brutus and Horatius Cocles, or of heroines like Lucretia and Cloelia. But it is hard to doubt that a statue which was supposed to represent the augur Attus Navius stood for a long time near the Curia, and we cannot reject the whole of tradition regarding the early monuments of Rome, since, at the very point where our texts mention the monumental tomb of Romulus or Faustulus, beneath the black pavement of the Forum, the basement has been found of a building which resembles a tomb, whatever its real purpose may have been.[1]

Honorary monuments continued to be built, if we can believe tradition, all through the Vth and IVth centuries. The Roman ambassadors murdered by the people of Fidenae in 438, Camillus who conquered Veii in 396, C. Maenius who vanquished the Latins, Tremulus who vanquished the Samnites, all had their statues. Evidence regarding works earlier than the burning by the Gauls (390) is evidently to be taken with caution. But the monuments of the time of the Samnite Wars survived until the Ist century. The alterations of Sylla caused the disappearance from the Comitium of the statues of Pythagoras and Alcibiades which

[1] Thédenat, **CLVI**, pp. 76 ff.

were set up during those wars on the order of Pythian Apollo.[1]
In spite of the uncertainty attaching to the examples quoted
for the early period, we may take it that the alleged severity
of Rome caused no break in the Etruscan tradition of raising
public portraits of citizens who had served the State well.[2]
What these honorary statues of early times were like, we can
imagine from a celebrated example, the fine statue of the
" Orator," which was found in the XVIth century near Lake
Trasimene and is preserved in the Florence Archaeological
Museum.[3] (Plate XI.) This work is rather later than the
period which we are discussing. It must date from the IIIrd
century, or at any rate from a time after the conquest of
Etruria, when Etruscan art and Roman art were no longer
distinct. It is a bronze statue of perfect workmanship,
representing one Aulus Metilius, who is otherwise unknown.
Draped in his toga, and lifting his arm to command silence,
the orator rises to his full height to dominate the crowd.
The wrinkles on the brow and a slight contraction of the mouth
seem to awake expectation of the thought which he is about
to express. The face is austere and grave, and the whole
figure is profoundly living. Such a work looks like the result
of a long tradition in the art of portraiture. It is a masterpiece, heralding the countless series of Roman honorary
statues.

By the side of religious architecture and decoration, therefore, the early Republic possessed a profane art. The play
of memory and imagination were not unknown to it. So
far from wishing to display an austere nakedness in contrast
to the abundance of monuments which adorned the Greek
and Etruscan cities, it rather seems, at all times, to have
tried to rival them.

Did it also possess artistic industries ? The IVth century
is marked all over Italy, from Tarentum to Clusium and
Volaterrae, by a new efflorescence of artistic handicrafts.
The Peloponnesian War and, above all, the disastrous enterprise of Athens against Syracuse had put an end to the
preponderance of Attic manufactures all over the Mediterranean. About the middle of the Vth century the workshops

[1] Pliny, *N.H.* xxxiv. 26 ; cf. Pais, **CXXI,** i, 594.
[2] When the Romans took Volsinii (Orvieto) in 265 B.C., they seized 2000 bronze statues there. Pliny, *N.H.,* xxxiv. 34 ; xxxvi. 135.
[3] Martha, **CIV,** p 375, fig. 261.

of Magna Graecia had begun to manufacture for the Italian market painted vases similar to those of Attica. By the beginning of the IVth century they commanded the market.[1] Not far from Rome, Falerii, a native town, but strongly subject to Etruscan influences, seems to have been a manufacturing centre of the first rank. Its products are superior, in make and even in art, to those of Etruria. The models of Tarentum and Magna Graecia seem to have had some influence on this peculiarly brilliant development of Faliscan pottery.[2]

Another native city, the neighbour and once the rival of Rome, Praeneste, had at the same time made a speciality of chasing on bronze. From Praeneste we have a great number of engraved mirrors and caskets. The manufacture of mirrors was originally a Greek industry, which was transplanted into Etruria at the beginning of the Vth century and from there had moved to Praeneste.[3] The caskets, on the other hand, at least in the form which they have at Praeneste in the IVth century, represent a true local industry.[4] They are boxes made entirely of metal, intended to hold ladies' jewels and toilet articles. The body, usually cylindrical, is covered with fine engraving done with the graver, the motives being those of the contemporary painted vases of southern Italy. It stands on three moulded feet, generally shaped like lion's paws, over which there are sometimes figure motives. The lid has for a handle a small group of two or three figures. (Fig. 8.)

The style of most of the caskets is feeble and fairly careless. Both mirrors and caskets are similar, in their industrial rather than artistic character and in the subjects which they represent, to the painted pottery of Falerii.

Now, the most beautiful of the Praeneste caskets—and the most beautiful are the oldest—the Ficorini casket, which has been in the museum of the Villa of Pope Julius since 1913, bears a signature which proves that it was made in Rome itself: *Dindia Macolnia fileai dedit. Novios Plautios med Romai fecid.* (Dindia Macolnia gave me to her daughter, Novios Plautios made me in Rome.)[5]

[1] Dugas-Pottier, art. *Vasa*, **LVI**, p. 651.
[2] C. Picard, **X**, xxx (1910), pp. 108 ff.
[3] Matthies, **CVII**.
[4] Schumacher, **CXLVII** ; Martha, **CIV**, pp. 535 ff.
[5] Behn, **XXIX** ; Martha, **CIV**, p. 535.

The casket comes from Praeneste itself; the name Dindia Macolnia is Praenestine. The artist's praenomen, on the other hand, is Campanian. The name Plautios is that of a great Roman family. Novios Plautios seems to have been some freedman of Campanian origin established in Rome.

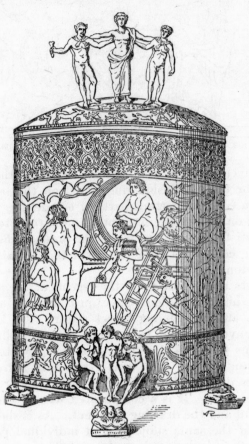

FIG. 8.—The Ficorini casket.

What was his share in the manufacture of the casket? For this included several operations, which were not necessarily all done in the same workshop or by the same craftsman. The feet and the group which forms the handle of the lid were cast separately; there are many very similar pieces; they were taken almost at random in the shop where the caskets were put together. The fitter took his bronze sheet,

FIGS. 9-10.—Engravings on a casket of Praeneste type.

ready engraved, and cut it, sometimes damaging the engraved subject ; for the suspension rings fixed on the body of the casket often cover important parts of the design.   Although it is incised on the lid, the inscription must refer to the chief, and only artistic, part of the work, the bronze chasing on the body of the casket.   Therefore it was the actual engraving which was done in Rome.

It depicts an episode from the legend of the Argonauts. Jason and his companions have just arrived among the Bebrycians, and are landing to get water.   The king of the country, Amycos, wishes to prevent them.   Pollux defeats him with his fists, and ties him to a tree.   Victory crowns the hero, and Castor and some Argonauts surround him, while others descend from the ship with kegs or lie on the deck or the shore.   It is a complicated scene ; the composition is skilful and the drawing excellent.   As is shown by the repetition of the same subject or of individual passages on other caskets, mirrors, and even painted vases of southern Italy,[1] it is inspired by a celebrated large painting, very likely a work of Polygnotos.   So the influence of Attic art of the middle of the Vth century was felt in Rome a century later, most certainly through the intermediacy of southern Italy.

It has long been suggested, on the strength of the inscription on the Ficorini casket, that the so-called Praeneste

[1] Behn, **XXIX,** pp. 61 ff.

COENALIA.—Kitchen scenes.

caskets and mirrors were really made in Rome.[1] The arguments against such a hypothesis seem fully justified. The
art of the Ficorini casket is much more delicate than that of
most of the Praeneste caskets and mirrors. It seems to
represent the art of a capital, as against that of provincial
workshops. Most of the caskets found at Praeneste are
certainly of local make, but the signature of Novios Plautios
shows that the principal centre of this art, or at least the
intermediary between southern Italy and the Aequian city,
which was politically subordinate to Rome from the middle
of the IVth century, must have been Rome.[2]

There are such analogies of style and subject between the
caskets of Praeneste and the painted vases of Falerii that if
Rome furnished patterns for the one she must equally have
influenced the other. The Ficorini casket shows her in
possession of an artistic tradition emanating direct from
Magna Graecia. The events which, during the second half
of the IVth century, linked the history of Rome so closely
with that of southern Italy make it comprehensible that
artists of Tarentum, Capua, or other places should have come
and settled in Rome, just as, a century before, Attic artists
had come and settled in Magna Graecia. In this way Rome
would have become the secondary centre from which this

[1] Gamurrini, **XIII,** ii (1887), pp. 228 ff.
[2] Ducati, **LXVI,** p. 469.

Italo-Greek art radiated in the various regions of central Italy over which her political dominion grew steadily stronger.

The Greek legends, which a century later were to inspire the beginnings of Roman literature, had, therefore, long been popularized in Latium by the crafts as well as the major arts, painting and sculpture. Nor was a vein of realism lacking. Another casket of the Praeneste type, but of unknown provenance, shows us preparations for a meal, a perfect illustration of the scenes which are so frequent in the comedies of Plautus and Terence. The legends accompanying the design might come from a piece of comic dialogue.[1] " *Confice piscim* " (clean the fish), we read near a very mutilated figure which seems to be employed in this task. Another appears to be cutting up a quarter of beef which hangs on hooks. Two other serving-men are face to face, one presenting a dish on which bits of meat are arranged, the other taking an empty dish back to him. " *Cofeci* " (I have prepared the meat), says one. " *Feri porod* " (cut some more), says the other. At a fire, a cook turns the meat which is cooking in a wide pan—" *Made mi recie* " (cook it right royally). Another picks out the pieces on a fork and puts them on a dish— " *Misce sane* " (turn it well), he says to his mate. Finally, another cook runs to the right with two spits on which gobbets of meat are speared—" *Asom fero* " (I am bringing the roast ; or, I am bringing this to roast). The whole is entitled *Coenalia*,[2] in a writing which is different from that of the other inscriptions, and seems older. The cist can only date from the end of the IVth century ; the form *recie* (= *regie*) places it before the spelling-reform of Appius Claudius. The drawing is rapid and rather careless, but easy, and is inspired by the details of common life. Similar scenes are found on the walls of Etruscan tombs from the end of the Vth century or the beginning of the IVth.[3] So the influences of the various parts of early Italy meet and mingle in Latium. Mythology and realism are found together. Pictorial and plastic art came long before the blossoming of literature, and gradually prepared men's minds to understand its subjects and to appreciate its tendencies.

[1] L. Duvau, " Ciste de Préneste," in **X,** x (1890), pp. 303-16, pl. 6.
[2] The *o* is a true Greek Ω.
[3] E.g. in the Golini tomb at Orvieto. Martha, **CIV,** fig. 266, p. 301 ; fig. 279, p. 413.

V

ROMAN MONEY

All these indications of a flourishing artistic and intellectual life in Rome, which probably existed in the Vth century and certainly in the IVth, belie the classical tradition of a long age of Roman simplicity. Amid the uncertainty resulting from this contradiction, we receive valuable light from an important body of evidence. The history of the earliest coinage of Rome bears witness both to long fidelity to old habits and to remarkable mental adaptability. While they obstinately kept their own habits among themselves, the Romans seem to have been well acquainted with the innovations effected by the other peoples of Italy, and to have set out to profit by them.

The standard of trade value among the peasants of Latium was cattle. *Pecunia*, wealth, is derived from the word *pecus*, which means a herd. Down to Varro's time, the Roman law-courts continued to assess the fines which they inflicted in oxen or sheep.[1] But from the beginning of the Republic official conversion-tables made it possible to reduce head of cattle to current coin.

Moreover, from the first Iron age, and perhaps before, copper seems to have been used as money both in central Europe and in Italy. Well into the historical period it remained the normal standard of value among the various Italic peoples, like gold in Asia and silver in Greece. In prehistoric times, unminted copper was used, in pieces which were weighed ; this was *aes rude*. *Aes rude* still appears in Latin finds by the side of minted coins of the end of the IIIrd or the beginning of the IInd century B.C.[2] Throughout the period of the civil law, that is, to the end of the Republic, the legal ceremony of sale continued to be performed *per aes et libram*, that is to say, with a piece of unminted metal and the scales.

All over central Italy, the bronze intended in early times to serve as money is found, often cast in lumps of different

---

[1] Varro, *R. R.*, ii. 1. 9.   [2] E.g., at Falerii, **V**, 1880, p. 111.

shapes and essentially variable weights,[1] or in spits, which were convenient for division. The spit, ὀβελός, represents an early money which was in use on the Mediterranean coasts, and notably in Etruria, until about the VIth century B.C.[2] At this time a practice was started, in northern and central Italy, of marking the rectangular bits of metal which were used as money with a rudimentary sign—a central ridge with oblique strokes at the side, like a dry branch or the bones of a fish, or else a star, or a half-moon.[3] This was *aes signatum*. Roman tradition is perhaps correct in ascribing to one of the Kings, Servius Tullius, the innovation of marking with a sign the lumps of bronze which were intended to replace the cattle in which the farmers used to pay.[4] But it anticipates when it speaks of relief figures of oxen and sheep in this period. The heavy rectangular coins marked with an ox belong to a much later time, the beginning of the IIIrd century. For they seem to belong to the same series as the pieces bearing a figure of an elephant, clearly an allusion to the victories over Pyrrhos.[5] Therefore Rome continued to cast these primitive coins even when much more perfect types had long been in use.

It was in the second half of the IVth century that the Romans began to strike a true coinage, the *aes grave*, of lentil shape, the value and weight of which were reckoned on a fixed scale of division, and were guaranteed by the impression of the State. These are the well-known coins with the head of Janus on the obverse and a ship's prow on the reverse. The unit is the *as*, corresponding to the copper pound of 272 grammes and divided into 12 *unciae*. Its multiples are the double *as*, *dupondius*, and the five-*as* piece, *quincussis ;* its submultiples are the *semis* ($\frac{1}{2}$), the *triens* ($\frac{1}{3}$), the *sextans* ($\frac{1}{6}$), and the *uncia* ($\frac{1}{12}$). These coins were issued concurrently with the rectangular pieces, enabling us to note, from the beginning of the IIIrd century, a progressive reduction of the weight of the unit until it was about 36 grammes, which limit seems to have been reached at the time of the Punic Wars. Henceforward the copper money was only a fiduciary money.

---

[1] Haeberlin, **LXXXII,** pp. 4 ff.   [2] Déchelette, **LVII,** ii, 2, p. 799.
[3] Haeberlin, **LXXXIII,** pp. 10 ff.   [4] Pliny, *N.H.*, xviii. 12.
[5] Haeberlin, **LXXXII,** pp. 141 ff., 146.

History places in the year 269, after the taking of Tarentum and just before the first Punic War, the beginning of Roman silver money. Does this mean that Rome had hitherto been content with her copper coinage ? We find in many parts of central Italy, and particularly in southern Italy, silver coins bearing the epigraph ROMANO, and later ROMA, which are contemporary with the beginning of the *aes grave*.[1] This is a coinage which the Romans caused to be struck at Capua for the requirements of their policy in southern Italy. It is based on the decimal system, not the duodecimal. The unit is the didrachm of 6·82 grammes, representing $\frac{1}{5000}$ of the Greek talent. Similar coins struck at the same time in Etruria show that the Graeco-Roman weights were henceforward regularly observed in the Etruscan issues. Furthermore, Rome herself took pains to find a common measure between her new money and the traditional silver standard of Etruria, the *scrupulum* of 1·137 grammes. The Campano-Roman didrachm is exactly 6 *scrupula*. So the Roman silver currency of the end of the IVth century was intended to circulate all over Italy.

When, in 269, Rome found herself richer than southern Italy and Etruria which she had conquered, she judged it wise to concentrate within her own walls the minting activity which for more than fifty years the Campanian workshops had been carrying on for her. A new reform of weights and measures brought not only her money, but all her weights and measures, into line with the Attic type then prevailing on all the coasts of the Mediterranean. She made the Attic drachma of 4·37 grm. into her *denarius ;* the *quinarius* or double sesterce was equal to the Greek triobol. But she kept the Etruscan standard of the *scrupulum*, which represented two and a half tenths of the *denarius*, and became the sesterce; *semis tertius* = $2\frac{1}{2}$. For an old tradition which she refused to abandon bound her to the Etruscan silver coinage. Before she was drawn into southern Italy and had the mints of Campania at her disposal, it was from Etruria that she had had to obtain the gold and silver money which she needed.

From the Vth century onwards, we find in Etruria a silver coinage with an archaic Gorgon's head, the unit of which seems to be a piece weighing 8·53 grm., corresponding in

---

[1] Babelon, **XXVIII,** i, pp. 10 ff.

value to the *quincussis* (5 *asses*) of Roman copper. In the IVth century, before it imitated Rome, Etruria struck a silver stater of 11·37 grm., corresponding to the *decussis* (10 *asses*) of copper. Still earlier, in the VIth century, gold and silver coins of Asia Minor made their way to Etruria, and have been found at Clusium and Volaterrae.[1] During the Etruscan period coins of the same origin cannot have failed to circulate in Rome. In the Vth and IVth centuries the issues of Etruscan silver must have been accepted in Rome, just as, later, Roman issues were valid in Etruria. Only the richest state coined money, and this money circulated among the neighbours who traded with it.

The late appearance of Roman money confirms, beyond dispute, the statement that the Romans long remained faithful to the oldest Italic traditions. For the patrician farmers who composed the Senate, cattle were the measure of wealth. Metal, either raw, or in the form of bars or lumps, marked with a sign or not, sufficed as the small change of exchanges in kind. Cattle were counted, metal was weighed. But in a city like Rome, forced by its situation and the necessities of life to engage in trade, national economy could not be confined to the barter of farm produce and a few minor purchases paid in copper. The coins of the cities of Magna Graecia and Sicily circulated in Rome at an early date. In Latin a coin is designated by the Greek word νόμος, *nummus;*[2] the Latin *uncia* corresponds to the Sicilian οὐγκία; *libra* probably comes from λίτρα.[3] This use of the same terms and the concordances between the Greek, Roman, and Etruscan monetary systems show that coins of various origins circulated all over the peninsula. But the Roman State long abstained from giving its official sanction, in the form of a coinage bearing its stamp, to the economic movement which was left to the activity of that part of the population which did not exercise political power.

It did not make up its mind to this measure until the second half of the IVth century, when its armies entered southern

---

[1] Mueller, **CXIV**, i, pp. 385 ff.

[2] Mueller, **CXIV**, i, p. 296. The change from *o* to *u* may perhaps be explained by transmission through Etruscan.

[3] Cf. W. Schulze, *Kuhn Zeitschr.*, xxxiii (1893), p. 225. The true origin of these words is unknown. See the hypothesis of Ernest Assmann, " Die babylonische Herkunft von *as, aes, raudus, uncia, libra*," in *Nomisma*, v (1910), pp. 1-9.

Italy. For Rome it struck its copper *asses ;* for the Latins, rectangular pieces exactly sized ; and for Magna Graecia, silver coins. Finally, only after the fall of Tarentum, it consented to give up the old copper standard and to establish the silver standard in Rome. But silver money had long been known there. Years of habit, unnoticeable but deeply rooted, had consecrated its units, the drachma which became the *denarius* and the Etruscan *scrupulum* which became the sesterce. Senatus Consulta were needed only to ratify the usage.

Let us not confuse Roman life with Roman politics. The politics of Rome were altogether those of an aristocracy of peasants and soldiers. This aristocracy might obstinately shut its eyes for centuries to the progress which was going on outside it, but all round it, in Italy and in Rome itself ; it could not prevent it. Within the city, it found itself obliged, every day, to compromise with the urban plebs which was so alien to its traditions. Outside, every enlargement of the Roman State was a blow at the exclusiveness of the conservative spirit, until the day when, having become capital of the greater part of Italy, Rome finally opened her doors to all the Italian civilizations.

VI

APPIUS CLAUDIUS CAECUS [1]

One man represents in his own person, by his manifold activity, the state of civilization attained by Rome towards the end of the IVth century. This is Appius Claudius Caecus, Censor in 312, Consul in 307 and 296, general, jurist, poet, grammarian, and, above all, great constructor of public works.[2] Appius was an aristocrat, a descendant of the great Sabine family of the Claudii, whose pride, obstinacy, and hardness were legendary. It was he who fought the last battles for the privileges of the patricians ;[3] he was especially indignant at the idea of seeing plebeians holding the priest-

---

[1] Cf. Lejay, " Appius Claudius Caecus," in **XX,** xliv (1920), pp. 92-141.
[2] Livy, ii. 56 ; Tac., *Ann.,* i. 4 ; Suet., *Tib.,* 1-3.
[3] Livy, x. 7 ; cf. ix. 34.

hoods. He had all the uncompromising patriotism of the old Roman. When, in 279, the Senate was allowing itself to be tempted by the peaceful proposals of Pyrrhos presented by Cineas, Appius Claudius, old as he was, and already the representative of a past age, came out of the retirement in which he had shut himself up and, by a speech which became famous, caused the rejection of the peace offered by a victorious enemy.[1]

Yet Mommsen has been able to present him as an innovator, a revolutionary demagogue, almost a forerunner of the Gracchi.[2] An innovator he certainly was. Although he tried to deny the plebeians admission to the Consulate and equality of religious rights, he helped them by opening the Senate even to the sons of freedmen who had the required income. He allowed citizens without landed property to enter the tribes, and gave movable fortune rights equal to those which had hitherto attached only to landed property.[3] Above all, he made his Quaestor Cn. Flavius divulge technicalities of legal procedure, the knowledge of which had hitherto been reserved to patricians. The difference between his political action and that of the Gracchi is that the Gracchi championed the unfortunates of the plebs, whereas he favoured the successful plebeians. He appreciated the new power which movable wealth placed in their hands, and, while wishing to confine the exercise of power to the patricians, he strove to incorporate the best of the plebeians in the old aristocratic State.

He was an imitator, says Mommsen, of Cleisthenes and Pericles. He took as his models, Sig. Pais thinks, Dionysius and Architas of Syracuse.[4] That a knowledge of Greek and, still more, of Sicilian politics had some influence on his ideas is highly probable. But the reforms which he carried out seem to be more simply the effect of a Roman intelligence endeavouring to give official consecration to progress already accomplished, and to make it serve the good of the State. Appius Claudius sought to adapt the patrician organization of the Republic to new social conditions and to the new extension of the power of Rome. He wished to legalize,

---

[1] Cic., *Sen.*, 6 ; *Brut.*, 16 ; Plut., *Pyrrh.*, 19.
[2] Mommsen, **CXII**, i, 287 ff.
[3] E. Albertini, " La Clientèle des Claudii," **X**, xxiv (1904), pp. 248 ff.
[4] **CXXII**, p. 294.

at least to a certain extent, the situation acquired by the plebs, whose traditions constituted a bond between the various regions of Italy and Rome, their new capital. Appius Claudius was an enlightened Roman patrician, not a demagogue.

He knew the law, and could make skilful use of words. This science and this art were not novelties in Rome. Livy contrasts Claudius with military bunglers in politics like Fabius and Decius, and suggests that he was more efficient on the Forum and in administration than as a general.[1] In addition, he was a moralist and poet. Should his versatility class him outside the Roman line ? He composed, in Saturnian verse, a collection of " sentences " which, according to Cicero, was admired by Panaetios.[2] Was it simply an imitation of the Pythagorean golden maxims which were popular in southern Italy ? Some have seen in it also the influence of the New Comedy, and of Philemon in particular.[3] Certainly the Romans of this time, who for thirty years had been fighting and living all over the south, from Campania to Apulia, were acquainted with this literature. But maxims like those which have come down to us under the name of Appius Claudius—" Every man is the artificer of his fortune," " Work is better for the Roman people than idleness," " When you see a friend, forget your own troubles "—might equally well be the summing up of the practical experience of the Latin peasant, which expresses itself to this day in countless proverbs, often racy and pointed.

Greek influence seems to have helped the Latin to bring out his own native originality. It may have been the knowledge of Greek which decided Appius Claudius to reintroduce the letter G into the Latin alphabet. But the character itself was new ; it took the place of a Greek letter, the Z, which was dropped as useless. It was purely in view of Latin pronunciation that s between two vowels was officially replaced by r—Furii instead of Fusii. Reforms like these point to a Censor who appreciated grammatical subtleties.

The most memorable work of Appius Claudius, that which is the best evidence of the development of Roman civilization

[1] x. 23.   [2] Tusc., iv. 2. 4.
[3] F. Marx, Zeitschr. f. oester. Gymn., 1897, pp. 217, 394.

in his time, was the construction of the first aqueduct and of the great road which has kept his name.

By hereditary tradition the Romans were experts in drainage works.[1] But the idea of bringing water to a city from a distant spring is somewhat different from that realized by the innumerable *cuniculi* of the Latin Campagna. It was, without any doubt, inspired by some example noticed in Apulia, which was rich in towns but poor in water. Syracuse, the real capital of all Italian Hellas, had an aqueduct,[2] the subterranean channels of which ended in the citadel. Like the aqueduct of Syracuse, the Aqua Appia ran chiefly underground. It caught the water of a spring situated not far from the Anio, about ten miles from Rome. The conduit only came above ground where it entered the city; here it was carried on arches from a point near the Porta Capena over the depression between the Caelian and the Aventine, a distance of about 60 *passus* (98 yeards). Forty years later, in 272, the Censor M. Curius Dentatus built a second aqueduct, which was likewise subterranean throughout its length except near the Esquiline, where there were arches for 330 yards. Only in the middle of the IInd century, in 144 B.C., did the Aqua Marcia have 7 miles of arches out of a total length of 57 miles. The first aqueducts, then, were works of tunnelling rather than of architecture. No doubt they had Greek models, but their construction was based on the oldest technical traditions of the Latin peasants.

One cannot fail to recognize the vastness of conception displayed in the construction of the Appian Way from Rome to Capua, over the Pontine Marshes.

Other roads already existed in ancient Italy. Communication between central and southern Italy had always been possible by the road which became the Via Latina, from Rome to Beneventum. The Via Salaria, which ran from the coast to the Sabina, also appears very old. The Etruscans, long before the IVth century, had built good roads.[3] The Greeks had laid many in southern Italy. In this art, again, old native traditions and foreign examples met.

According to tradition, the Romans learned the art of road-building from the Carthaginians in Sicily. But the

---

[1] Cf. p. 4 above. [2] Saglio, art. *Aqueduc*, **LVI**, p. 388.
[3] Martha, **CIV**, p. 253 ; Anziani, **X**, 1913, p. 231.

Carthaginians do not seem to have done more than introduce into Sicily the use of lime mortar, which spread to the Romans through Magna Graecia.[1] It is, indeed, in the use of mortar that the Appian Way differs from the old roads of Latium and Etruria. Excavations have made it possible to recognize in the substructions the four courses arranged in the order which continued to be orthodox until the end of the Roman age. At the bottom is the *statumen* of flat stones, intended to drain away the water; it is surmounted by a layer of coarse concrete (*rudus*) and by a second, thicker layer of fine concrete (*nucleus*); on the top is the *summum dorsum,* of gravel or paving-stones.[2] The Appian Way was only paved bit by bit, the sections near Rome at the beginning of the IIIrd century and the part near Tarracina not until the Empire.[3]

But the original construction of the road involved considerable works of engineering, which are still admired for their boldness and perfection—the portion built on the side of the Alban Hills near Aricia, and the embankment, from ten to thirteen feet high, which runs for seventeen miles across the Pontine Marshes. Under the Empire, Statius still described the old work of Appius Claudius as *Regina viarum*, the Queen of roads.[4]

If, on her first intimate contact with the Greeks of Italy, Rome attained this perfection in the construction of roads and aqueducts, if the coinage which she then issued, without any preliminary experiments and failures, at once circulated all over Italy, if the Roman casket of Novios Plautios stands out as a model in the midst of the whole Praenestine series, if Latin architecture succeeded in introducing into Campania, at Paestum itself, by the side of the most majestic examples of the Greek temple, the Etrusco-Latin temple with a podium,[5] it was because this sudden efflorescence was based on a long native tradition. The examples of Magna Graecia bore fruit in Rome because they found the soil prepared, and were not altogether novelties. First Etruria, and then relations with Greek Italy, established since the beginning of the Republic and maintained inconspicuously during the Latin period, had gradually educated the Romans. A character like Appius

[1] Nissen, **CXV**, ii, pp. 42, 50.
[2] M. Besnier, art. *Via*, **LVI**, pp. 785 ff.   [3] *Ibid.*, p. 783.
[4] *Silv.*, ii. 2. 12.   [5] Delbrueck, **LX**, p. 32.

F

Claudius, Niebuhr used to say, would not be surprising in Greece, but he appears out of place in Roman history. To me he seems, on the contrary, the perfect representative of the union of old experience with new tendencies.

We do the Romans wrong when we look for the whole of their special character in their grossness. Pig-headed peasants and narrow-minded soldiers would never have created a great people. We should not contrast the Rome of the early centuries with the rest of Italy, but rather try to distinguish in her the inheritance of the old Italian civilizations absorbed by her, whose substance she assimilated.

That she had also a character of her own, we shall not deny. At the beginning of the Vth century she had thrown off the Etruscan hegemony and associated herself closely with the rustic peoples of the Latin and Sabine hills. Then she had to fight hard for her life, by work and by war. Circumstances forced upon her childhood a sense of realities, rigid discipline, and long acquaintance with poverty. From these she may have derived, in later years, her timidity of imagination, her habit of moral observation, her care for practical things and logic. *Cui non risere parentes.* Whatever his merits, the Roman never has the charm of the Greek. His breadth of conception does not make up for his lack of imagination. His ideal never rises from the ground. He has learned to calculate too much ; his reasoning never loses sight of the action which will be its consequence. His art always has a utilitarian purpose, or else it betrays the effort of the scholar's application.

Yet the Roman mind lacks neither activity, nor versatility, nor delicacy. It adheres to traditions which have been tested by use, but it is none the less eager for new experiences and ideas. It borrows institutions, ideas, and arts from neighbours with discernment. It does not copy slavishly, but stamps its own character on what it adopts. Even in the early centuries which we have been considering, the Romans' capacity for assimilation appears as highly developed as their originality. Rome triumphed over the whole of Italy, not because her people had remained the most primitive of all, but because, having become about equal to the others in civilization, it was also better disciplined and more energetic.

THE OLD ROMAN RELIGION

LIKE Roman civilization in general, Roman religion presents a mixture of ancient traditions obstinately maintained and borrowed elements. " The most ancient religious institutions," said Cicero, " are the best, because they are the nearest to the gods." [1] And, indeed, in Cicero's time, and down to the end of the Empire, the calendar ascribed to Numa continued to govern the religious year of the Roman. He celebrated according to the ancient rites feasts the meaning of which was lost. He celebrated other feasts, too, and the new gods from Greece and the East had taken in the Roman Pantheon the place once held by primitive deities of whom little more than the name was known to scholars. Respect for ancient institutions had not been able to prevent religion from following the political, social, and intellectual evolution of Rome.

One might try to distinguish, in the early period, the original religious foundation from its successive transformations, and to note the contributions of the different peoples of Italy, Sabines, Etruscans, Campanians, with whom the Romans found themselves in contact. But, while we have a fair knowledge, thanks to a body of literary [2] and epigraphic [3] evidence, of the character of early Roman religion,[4] we lack precise information regarding most of the Italic cults. The first transformations and amalgamations seem to be previous to the oldest state of religion which the Romans have recorded.

[1] *Leg.*, 2.
[2] Most of the information scattered among the scholars, gloss-writers, and Fathers (especially St Augustine) comes from Varro and from learned men of the Augustan age like Verrius Flaccus.
[3] In particular, the official calendar, dating from the beginning of the Empire, fragments of which were found in the Forum in 1893. **LI,** i, 2, pp 205 ff. ; vi, nos. 32481-32502.
[4] Details will be found especially in Wissowa, **CLXXI,** and an extremely perspicacious and well-documented general account in Warde Fowler, **CLXVII.**

Moreover, these everlasting attempts at analysis, which necessarily contain much mere conjecture, end by making us lose sight of the facts which we have. Let us rather try to see what were the religious conceptions of the beginning of the historical period, and to ascertain their general characteristics. This religion has very few features in common with that of classical times. But, though beliefs were forgotten, they left their stamp on the imagination and character of the Roman. Roman gravity, for example, seems to be largely composed of respect for those gods which the primitive mind had imagined in numbers all around. Above all, from the point of view which concerns us, a general survey of the old religious system will complete and define the idea which we may obtain of Roman civilization in the early centuries of the Republic.

I

The Roman Conception of Divinity and the Principal Gods

We know the admirable picture which Fustel de Coulanges draws of the religious life of the Roman : [1]

" His house is for him what a church is for us ; there he finds his worship and his gods. His hearth is a god ; the walls, the doors, the threshold are gods ; the posts which mark off his field are also gods. The tomb is an altar, and his ancestors are divine beings. Each of his daily actions is a rite. . . . Birth, initiation, the assumption of the toga, marriage, and the anniversaries of all these events are the solemn acts of his worship. . . . He makes sacrifice every day in his house, every month in his curia, and several times a year in his *gens* or his tribe. In addition to all these gods, he owes worship to those of the city. In Rome there are more gods than citizens." Taking an example from the very period which we are now studying, Fustel de Coulanges shows us Camillus, who was Dictator five times and was victorious in ten battles, in the rôle of a priest as much as of a warrior.

" As a child, he had worn the *praetexta* garment which

---

[1] **LXXVIII,** pp. 254 ff.

indicated his caste and the *bulla* which warded off evil.   As
he grew up, he had taken part every day in the ceremonies
of worship ; he had spent his youth in instructing himself
in the rites of religion.   It is true that war broke out, and the
priest turned soldier. . . .   A day came when they thought
of him for the Dictatorship.   That day the magistrate in
charge, after meditating all through a fine night, consulted
the gods ; his thoughts were fixed on Camillus, whose name
he pronounced in a low voice, and his eyes were on the sky, in
which they sought for omens.   The gods sent none but good ;
Camillus was agreeable to them, and he was accordingly
appointed Dictator.   Now he was the leader of an army, and
he marched out of the city, not without first consulting the
auspices and sacrificing many victims.   He had many
officers under his orders, and nearly as many priests—a
pontifex, augurs, haruspices, *pullarii, victimarii*, a hearth-
bearer. . . ."

We may deny the existence of Camillus ; we none the less
see his likeness, more or less complete, more or less sincere,
according to the period, in every magistrate and even in every
citizen of Rome, down to the end of ancient times.

Even in the days of Camillus such a state of mind represented an extremely ancient inheritance.   It certainly was
that of prehistoric times ; it was far older than Rome.
Indeed, it corresponds as exactly as possible to the mentality
which modern ethnology has revealed to us in peoples which
have remained at a primitive stage of civilization.[1]

For primitive man, as for the prehistoric Latin, the distinction which is so deep in modern societies between the
sacred and the profane, between the spiritual and the material
world, does not exist.   On every side primitive man feels
himself surrounded by mysterious powers, intangible and
invisible.   He does not define them, he could not even tell
their number, but he knows well that on them depend, at
every moment, his lot and that of all that is dear to him,
his undertakings, his goods, his family, his city.   Everything
is god—rocks, earth, trees, springs, beasts, sky.   He himself
partakes of the divine ; every one of his actions, every one of
his words creates repercussions extending infinitely, of which

[1] Two books are essential for an understanding of this subject : Durkheim,
LXVII, and Lévy-Bruhl, **XCIX**.   See also **C.**

he cannot know. At certain moments of his life he has a special power, or, on the contrary, is peculiarly subject and vulnerable to these forces which are scattered all round. Some men, either by a natural gift or in virtue of an initiation or a mere act—even involuntary—are held to be in closer relation with the divine ; these know the means to influence the hidden powers. These means are formulas or rites, which act of themselves, driving away evil, attracting, strengthening, and multiplying good. The Roman, like primitive man, feels for these formulas and rites and the persons who know their secret a blind, unshakable confidence, a faith which no experience can weaken. The magician is a king. The king, or the magistrate who replaces him, is necessarily a magician.

For a period like this we cannot speak of gods, or Geniuses, or necessary connexions of will and action. Mind, matter, external form, substance, causality are categories which do not exist for primitive man. There is no distinction of things on the one hand and minds on the other, there are no mechanical actions, there are no laws of nature. There are forces in everything, and these forces obey no law but their caprice or the constraint imposed on them by superior forces. It is not even man that acts. The mason does not build the house, nor the general win the battle, nor the lance slay the adversary, but it is the force which is in the mason which determines the force which is in the house, it is that of the leader or the city which prevails over that of the enemy, and the lance is only the accidental sign of the combat of forces of which death is the result. This attitude of mind is older than logic, and long remained stronger than it. It only yielded little by little, in Rome as elsewhere. Neither in Rome, nor elsewhere, not even among ourselves at this day, has it even completely disappeared.

There are innumerable traces of it in early Roman religion, infinitely more developed, it seems to me, than in Greek religion, where they can only be found buried under a myth or at the origin of a rite. The heir of the long intellectual development of the prehistoric civilizations of the Mediterranean, Greece arrived, as early as the Ionian period and the Homeric poems, at the conception of personal gods who think, will, and act. The very foundation of Roman religion remained much more primitive. The autochthonous gods

(original or native)

are hardly gods ; they have neither form, nor personality, nor will. They were not defined, and seem only gradually to have been given names, from their function or the place where they were supposed to reside, or even, in many cases, from the formula or rite intended to influence them.[1] Lack of imagination, some will say. Not that, but an imagination which remained much longer than elsewhere in the primitive forms of human thought, and only emerged from them to find all round it a mythology already completely formed, which it adopted.

Political circumstances seem to have taught the Roman, at a very early date, perhaps in prehistoric times, to conceive of a higher god, stronger than all the others, who presides over the destinies of the group, and originally represents the force or genius of the people. But this social god never eliminated the others, and did not supersede them in their proper functions. The Roman Jupiter never found himself relegated to the firmament or the summit of some Olympus, where his competence would be cut down every day, until it finally became a kind of potential presidency over the working of the laws of nature. He was never anything but a god like the others, acting, like them, within a strictly defined sphere ; he was not a supreme god to whom the others were subordinate. Only Hellenism gave him omnipotence.

Though his conception of the divine had not yet broken loose from the case of primitive mentality, the Roman of the time of Camillus was no longer a primitive man. Through Etruria, and through Magna Graecia and Sicily, Mediterranean ideas had penetrated into his city, and had already partly imposed themselves on his mind. He had organized his political and social life. His religion already formed a whole which has an appearance of regular organization.

The family, first of all, is the centre of a number of cults which remained living long enough to be taken up by the official religion of the classical period. The domestic hearth is the family altar at which the father consecrates by traditional rites all acts which affect the life of his folk. It is at the fire of the hearth that he presents the new-born child,

---

[1] L. Deubner, " Zur Entwicklungsgeschichte der altrömischen Religion," in **XVII,** xxvii (1911), pp. 321-35. Anna Perenna, for example, the goddess of the New Year, seems to have been born of the wish-formula " *annare perennareque commode liceat.*"

holding it up in his arms and declaring it to be his. It is to this altar, of which she will be the ministrant, that the new wife is led, to share with her husband the sacred cake of *confarreatio*. Beside the hearth, the store-cupboard, the *penus*, has its kindly, generous gods, the Penates. The altars of Pompeii show them to us in the shape of light Geniuses, crowned with flowers, clad in short garments, dancing joyously amid their flying ribbons. The various parts of the house all have their divine function. Limentinus, the threshold, welcomes the people of the house and keeps away undesirables. Forculus is the protective power of the door ; Cardea, that of the hinges. Janus with the two faces, who is often explained as representing the door—*janua*—with two fronts, seems rather to be the god who watches to right and to left of him, the prime defender of the group which dwells in the house, village, or city. The monumental door was probably called after him, not he after the door.

So, too, every act of family life calls up a Genius. We know some of them from St Augustine, who quotes Varro. When a child is born, Cunina watches over his cradle, Rumina teaches him to take the breast, Educa and Potina make him eat and drink, Statulinus holds him upright, and Fabulinus makes him talk. The *Acts* of the Arval Brothers give us another example of this multiplication of deities. One day a fig-tree which had grown on the roof of Dea Dia had to be removed. To do this, Deferunda was invoked to take it away, Coinquenda to lop the branches, Commolenda to chop it up, and Adolenda to burn it. When sacrifice was made to Tellus and Ceres for the work of the fields, an ancient text [1] says that the flamen called upon Vervactor for the first plough-ing, Redarator for the second, Imporcitor for the harrowing, Insitor for the sowing, Oberator for the dunging, and Occator, Sarsitor, Subrincator, Messor, Convector, Conditor, and Promitor. Gods, Geniuses, we call them, wrongly ; they are much rather survivals from days before the gods and Geniuses, as we imagine them with the eyes of the Greeks and of classical times, from days when every thing, every being, every act was divine, when divinity was not distinguished from nature, when not man, but an undefined force, cut the tree, turned up the soil, and caused the harvest to grow.

[1] Fabius Pictor, *ap.* Serv., *ad Georg.*, i. 21.

THE OLD ROMAN RELIGION

It is gods of this kind, incompletely personified, named artificially and late, that we chiefly find in the calendar traditionally attributed to Numa, which must represent a first attempt to systematize the old religion, dating from the beginning of the Republic. Most of them are closely connected with agricultural life. Pales, a god or goddess whose festival is held on the 21st April, reigns over flocks and herds, and Faunus and Lupercus, who is apparently called after the rites of the Lupercalia intended to drive wolves away (15th February), have a similar rôle. The wealth of the harvest is entrusted to the goddess Ops conjointly with the barn-god Consus, who hides and preserves. The Opsiconsivia are held on the 25th August, about the time the harvest is taken in, and the Opalia on the 19th December, at the end of the farmer's year, about the same time as the Saturnalia (17th December). The agricultural feasts begin again on the 15th April with the sowing festivals, during which pregnant cows are sacrificed to Tellus to increase her fertility. The 19th April brings the Cerialia, in honour of Ceres, and the 25th April the Robigalia, to exercise Robigo or Robigus, the rust which spoils the corn.

From this swarm of *numina*—that is, wills, energies, or powers—some emerge who became genuine gods—Saturn, Janus, Jupiter, Mars, Quirinus, Neptune, and Vulcan.

Saturn seems to have been originally the god of the sowing (*sata*). He was said to be the most ancient of the gods of Italy. When the Aborigines entered Latium, they found him reigning peacefully over their Siculian predecessors. It was he who had united them in an ordered people ; he had taught them to feed on himself and, almost without toil, so posterity related, supplied all their needs in plenty. The youth of Saturn had been the Golden Age. So, in spring, and above all in winter, men made believe, for a few days, that the Golden Age had returned, in order to rejuvenate Saturn— these were the Saturnalia. No more masters, no more servants, no more slaves, no more work, no more private property ; joy alone must reign. Everybody put on the clothes of others as he pleased, and ate and drank his bellyful. The December Saturnalia have disappeared ; the French *Mardi Gras* keeps those of spring alive. Apparently a strong young man represented the god ; at the end of the feast, he or his effigy was sacrificed to the god to convey his strength and youth to him,[1] just as Mr Carnival is solemnly burned to-day. There seem to be an ancient god and Mediterranean memories in Saturn and the legend of his Golden Age.

Janus, whom we find reduced to the humble office of a watchful porter, must in early times have been a powerful god, the Genius of the sky and the predecessor of Jupiter, as Saturn was the Genius of the earth. The first month of the annual solar cycle bears his name ; his feast is held on the 9th January. His name Janus, Dianus, indicates in him the *numen* of which Diana is the female personification. In Latium, Diana seems to be the deity of vegetation, reborn every year, whose strength must never diminish. By the Lake of Nemi, she is the goddess of the forest, Diana Nemorensis. The ritual murder of her priest, when he has no longer sufficient strength to be victorious, is intended to ensure the perpetual fertility of the goddess, by replacing him by a stronger man.[2]

There are many Jupiters in Rome. He who reigns on the Capitol, between Juno and Minerva, is Etruscan. He does not appear in the calendar of Numa. He who is honoured on the Ides of every month and in the rites of the Vinalia (23rd April and 19th August) and of the Meditrinalia on the 11th October, when the new wine is drunk with the words

" *Vetus novum vinum bibo,*
Veteri novo morbo medeor "

(I drink wine, old and new, I am cured of ills, old and new),

this Jupiter, who also presides over the ceremonies of the Regifugium and the Poplifugium, the Flight of the King and the Flight of the People, seems to present some analogies to Janus. His flamen bears the title of Flamen Dialis. He is also probably not very different from Jupiter Latiaris or Latialis, a racial deity common to the Latin tribes, whose shrine stood on the top of Monte Cavo, in the middle of the Alban Hills. But Latin Jupiter has nothing in common, at the beginning, with Hellenic Zeus. He has no features, he is not the divine king whose frown shakes heaven and earth. He is manifold, and is divided into as many persons as functions—

[1] Frazer, **LXXV**, pp. 583-5.   [2] *Ibid.*

Jupiter Lucetius, Genius of the clear sky, Jupiter Elicius, Fulgur, Summanus, god of the stormy sky, of the thunderbolt, of the lightning. He is the meteorite which falls from the firmament, and probably, too, the old, mysterious stone axe which is regarded as an instrument come from heaven, Jupiter Lapis. He is the god by whom oaths are sworn, Dius Fidius. In the nuptial cake, he presides over the union of husband and wife, Jupiter Farreus. He is revered, as the epithet *Pater* regularly attached to his name shows, but there is no attempt to know him and to define him.

Mars became in classical times, beyond dispute, the war-god and the protector of Roman armies, but his original character is uncertain. He, too, would seem to be an agrarian god, the Genius of spring vegetation. If he was always a war-god, it would be hard to explain the name of Arvales borne by his priests, and the character of the feast of the Ambarvalia, the procession which went round the fields in spring to purify them and make them fertile. On the other hand, the Salii, who perform an armed dance and wear the costume of the Roman soldier of the IVth or Vth century, are also priests of Mars. The double feast of Mars, in spring and in October, certainly seems to correspond to a lustration of the army before its departure to war and a purification on its return. On the 14th March the Equirria are observed, a lustration of the horses ; on the 19th comes the lustration of the shields, and on the 23rd that of the trumpets, the Tubilustrium, and the dancing procession of the Salii. In the autumn these ceremonies are repeated as rites of return ; on the Ides of October (15th) a horse is sacrificed, and on the 19th, after the Armilustrium, the Salii put away their shields. The double character of the feasts of the god, Ambarvalia and Armilustrium, and of the god himself may be explained by the fact that spring, when the work of the fields is resumed, is also the season when armies go to war. The same spring god presides over the simultaneous undertakings of the peasant and the soldier.

What was Neptune originally, he who became a great god in consequence of his identification with Poseidon ? What was Volcanus before he became the Roman Hephaestos ? We do not know.[1] We know still less of other gods and

---

[1] Neptune was especially honoured at Veii and Volcanus at Ostia. On this god cf. Carcopino, **XLII**, pp. 87 ff.

goddesses, who were no doubt important, since they all had their flamen—Carmenta, whose feast was on the 11th and 15th January, Falacer, Furrina, Volturnus. A goddess named Caca seems to have in early times played on the Palatine the part of a fire-goddess which was later filled by Vesta on the Forum.

These are only some of the known gods, *dii certi*. By their side there are countless undetermined gods, *dii incerti*, who reveal themselves as circumstances arise. Such gods were discovered even in historical times. When money was first minted, a god Aescolanus appeared and presided over the operation. There was a special god for silver minting, Argentinus, but not for gold. A god hitherto unknown, Aius-Locutius, warned the Romans of the approach of the Gauls in 390. In 211, when Hannibal beat a retreat after caracoling with his Numidian troopers beneath the walls of Rome, his retirement was attributed to the formal order of Rediculus Tutanus. This was the last divine revelation in Rome.

There were gods available in infinite numbers, not only in Latium, but all over the world. The neighbours' gods were powerful too ; it was the business of the Roman to conciliate them. He felt no aversion to adopting them. By the side of his native gods, *dii Indigetes*, the pious Roman invoked, collectively, the foreign gods, many of whom, moreover, were established in Rome, *dii Novensiles* or *Novensides*, gods newly installed. The formula of devotion pronounced by Decius gives us an idea of the complexity of the early Pantheon : *Janus, Juppiter, Mars Pater, Quirinus, Bellona, Lares, divi Novensiles, divi Indigetes, divi quorum est potestas nostrorum hostiumque.*[1] These new gods were chiefly, according to Varro, of Sabine origin,[2] like Feronia, whose place of worship, on the territory of Capena, at the foot of Soracte, was frequented by the Sabine herdsmen, or Vacuna at Reate, who seems to have been a Vesta. Others were Greek—Mercury, Apollo, Castor and Pollux, Hercules. Many were the gods of conquered cities, taken in by Rome, such as Queen Juno of Veii, Juturna of Lavinium, Fortune of Praeneste. Then

[1] Livy, viii. 9.
[2] Varro, *L.L.*, v. 10. 74. Moreover, the pronunciation *Novensiles* for *Novensides* is Sabine.

there were all those who corresponded to new ideas or facts—the Tempestates, whose dignity can only have dated from the birth of a Roman navy, Salus, Spes, Honos, Virtus, Concordia, abstractions which did not seem at all out of place beside the older deities. Among the new gods, too, we must rank the *dii Consentes*, who went together, and formed the council of Jupiter, six gods and six goddesses of Graeco-Etruscan origin, whose gilded statues were to be seen on the Forum, at the foot of the Capitol ; later they were identified with the twelve great deities of the Hellenic Pantheon. Thus all ancient Italy was represented in Rome by its gods.

Among these deities there are great gods, whose office is important, and lesser ones, whose activity is confined to a particular place or to minor interests. But we do not see at the origin of the gods or of their classification any great cosmological hypothesis, any general conception of the order of the universe, any wide horizon. There are gods in the sky, no doubt ; Janus and Jupiter are celestial gods. But the contemplation of the heavens did not engross the Roman particularly. He lived on the earth, so he chiefly concerned himself about the gods of the earth ; he obtained his living from the fertility of the fields, so most of his gods watched over the fields. He was little troubled about the universe, or the mystery of life and nature. What interested him was his family, his house, his land, his beasts, his crops, and also his city and his people. For all these interests he never had enough familiar and useful gods. He made up for lack of quality by quantity.

Since the divine was conceived as a mysterious force spread all through nature, there was no reason why it should not reside in material objects or animals. There was a time when the Genius of the flint made the power of man. It was natural that the flint should be a god. Jupiter Lapis represents the memory of this. The baneful or helpful power of animals also had something divine in it, and so had that of the tree, the spring, or the river. Some traces of these fancies survived in cult and legend. The Lupercalia seem originally to have been a rite intended to act on the divine force of the wolf, to keep him away from the flocks and herds. There was a definite connexion between Mars and the wolf-god ; the wolf was sacred to him ; Romulus and Remus, sons of Mars, were reared by a she-wolf. The eagle was the attribute of the sky-god Jupiter; the birds by which the divinity manifests his will have also something divine in them. The woodpecker Picus seems to have been the national god in Picenum. But we do not find in early Italy clear traces of true totemism, in which the spirit of the animal is identified with that of the tribe, and the animal is regarded as the father of men, and communion between the social group and its divine ancestor is renewed periodically by special rites. The Roman mind was too careful of precision and practical utility to attach itself to such mysteries. The gods, animal and other, had a function ; they were made for service, or at least they had to be prevented from doing harm. There was no idea of mystic union between beast and man.

But there was a divine force present in man—the Genius. The Genius of the paterfamilias was at the same time that of the whole family ; it was he who ensured its well-being, prosperity, and also continuity. He was the same who had been the Genius of the old, departed heads of the family ; he was identified with that of their ancestors, and this character entitled him to new worship. It was necessary to make him favourable to the new generations, to give him his place in the life of the family and his share in the offerings on the hearth. Above all, he must not be angered by departure from the rules once established by his will. This permanence of the family Genius was one of the foundations of the Roman conservative spirit ; it made the *mos majorum* sacred for ever.

The materfamilias also had her Genius, her Juno, who was with her in all her acts. She had met her on the day of her marriage, beneath the veil from which she emerged to a new life, Juno Pronuba. Her Juno gave her happy fertility and made childbirth easy for her, Juno Lucina. Every woman had her Juno, every man his Genius, sharing in all the vicissitudes of their life.

After death, the spirit which was in man continued to live, but it was a diminished, faint life. It was believed to abide in the tomb, where the kindred brought it their offerings. Regarding the dead, only one idea seems quite definite and unchangeable in the whole of Roman tradition—the belief that they absolutely required the nourishment with which the living sustained them. There was always something

material about the Genius. When they were satisfied, the
dead were the favourable Manes. In old Latin the word
manus meant " good." They were identified with the
Geniuses of the family group who protected the family, often
represented, at Pompeii, in the form of serpents which come
to take their share of the offerings laid on the hearth. When
neglected by the living, they suffered and took vengeance,
becoming dreaded Larvae or Lemures.

From the cult of the dead Fustel de Coulanges believed
that the whole organization of the family and of the social
state of antiquity could be derived. This worship certainly
occupies a considerable place in family life. The Genius of
the ancestors, embodied in the paterfamilias, gives him his
authority over the whole *gens ;* he is to some extent confounded with the Genius of the *gens* itself and with that of
the hearth of the house, the centre of the *gens*. But these
conceptions, which are, moreover, rather confused, seem to
be the consequence rather than the origin of Roman family
organization. Even the worship of the dead seems to be a
continuation of that of the personal Genius of individuals,
which does not itself do more than reflect the general idea
of life and the world which dominates the whole of early
Roman religion.

The specially Roman conception of life beyond the grave
and the abode of the dead appears extremely vague. This
was a problem devoid of practical interest, a purely individual
concern, to which the Roman mind attached little importance.
The Roman did not venture into hell any more than into
heaven, preferring to remain on solid earth. But he did not
escape the influence of the ideas on the subject current among
neighbouring peoples. The primitive goddesses of death,
Mania, mother of the Manes, Acca Larentia, mother of the
Lares, are themselves perhaps of Etruscan origin.[1] Subterranean Orcus, where the dead are gathered together under
the dominion of a powerful god, Vedius or Dis Pater, who was
easily assimilated to Pluto later, seems to have been inspired
either by Etruria or by Magna Graecia. Orcus afterwards
became Virgil's underworld, in which Greek and Etruscan
fables are mingled with the moral and metaphysical ideas of
the Pythagoreans and Greek philosophers. The old Roman

[1] Mueller, **CXIV**, ii, pp. 101 ff.

religion does not seem to have troubled itself with systematizing these beliefs of diverse origin.

From primitive times onwards, we find, in the Roman tombs, rites of burning and of burial appearing alternately, but we cannot trace a corresponding development in ideas regarding the future life. The survival of the Genius underground in the tomb seems to fit the rite of burial. Mother Earth, the primitive consort of Saturn, she who brings forth all life, she to whom a pregnant cow is sacrificed on the 15th April to make the beasts fertile, is also imagined as she who receives into her vast bosom all that has lived. As goddess of the dead, Earth is closely associated with the Manes. " To the Manes and Mother Earth," Decius cries, " I dedicate the legions and auxiliaries of the enemy, with myself." [1] In the classical period, when the practice of burning prevailed, which released the soul from the body, bearing it, so to speak, on the wings of flame to the distant regions of an airy empyrean, men still continued to believe in the subterranean life of souls, to offer them nourishment, and to imagine them received and guarded by Mother Earth. This idea is clearly expressed in a funerary inscription : *Ereptam viro et matri, Mater me Terra recipit*—" Torn from my husband and mother, Mother Earth receives me." [2]

In all the conceptions regarding the next life we find more literature and philosophy than religious beliefs.

When, on coming into contact with the personal gods of Magna Graecia and Hellenized Etruria, in emulation of them and under the influence of the myths introduced at least by art, these native *numina* had taken on bodies and really become deities, the Roman Pantheon found itself overpopulated. Its superabundance fully justified Polybius' remark : " The Romans are more religious than the gods themselves." But these gods remained vague, without personality, without form, without legend, almost nameless, often sexless,[3] only distinguished by their functions, and most of them designated by a mere adjective indicating their rôle. Gods like these did not inspire their worshippers with any sentiment or emotion. The memory of them, at least that of local gods,

---

[1] Livy, viii. 9. [2] Warde Fowler, **CLXVII**, p. 122.
[3] We know the forms of address : *Sive mas sive femina es . . . seu quo alio nomine te appellari mavis.*

might live long among the country people, of whose religion, however, we know very little. But in the city, and above all among cultivated minds, these pale deities were bound to fade away before the living gods of Greece. The surprising thing about early Roman religion is that it left so many traces in classical times which can still be recognized. It was indebted for this to a work of systematization which, while preserving the old gods, completely altered, if not the form, at least the spirit of their worship.

II

CHARACTERISTICS OF ROMAN WORSHIP

The great originality of this religion with its very primitive conceptions lies in the essentially rational character of its organization.

If the presence of so many gods seems never to have disturbed the Roman, it is because he had adopted towards them, at an early date and once for all, the same attitude as towards men—that of law. *Jus divinum,* covering *fas* and *nefas,* what is allowed or forbidden by religion, was as strictly regulated as *jus civile,* and on the same principle—to every one his due.[1] Man owed god the accomplishment of certain rites ; god owed man the regular performance of the function with which he was charged. In his *Complete Farmer's Handbook,* Cato the Elder notes the ceremonies which the paterfamilias must accomplish, and the words with which he must accompany them. In prayers everything is specified by word and gesture as carefully as in the procedure of civil law. Every offering is accompanied by the statement " *Ut tibi jus est* "—" As is thy due." [2] Provided that this is done, the god, having his due, will render to the pious man—that is, to the man who has strictly fulfilled his duty to him—the protection to which that man has a right.

The duty of the Roman to his gods is not thought, for he need not know them ; still less is it feeling, for there is no question of loving them ; it is simply action, it consists in

---

[1] Warde Fowler, **CLXVII,** pp. 168 ff.   [2] Cato, *R. R.,* 139.

the rites of worship. But this worship is rational, it is addressed to the will of the god.

So far back as our evidence regarding Roman religion takes us, we find no survival, save in exceptional cases, in which, moreover, it is almost dead, of the primitive magical notion according to which the rite acts directly on the god, strengthening or weakening him, and possesses the virtue of compelling him, as it were automatically, to perform his function. The essential rite was sacrifice ; like other peoples, the Romans offered their gods nourishment. But their object in doing so was to win the good will of the god. Indeed, their sacrifices shed blood very sparingly. Pliny states that worship, as organized by Numa, included no offerings but the fruits of the earth and cakes.[1] This means that it was un- necessary to have recourse to the magical power of blood to vivify the gods. Instances of human sacrifice may be quoted from historical times ; but this rite was foreign to the Romans, as Livy carefully says when he mentions it.[2] Modern scholars may recognize traces, feeble enough, of human sacrifice in particular rites of certain Roman cere- monies,[3] but it is none the less true that the Romans of the Republican age had lost all memory of the notion that a god benefits by the life sacrificed to him. The Roman gods did not even insist upon the blood of animals, and readily accepted substitutes. " It is permitted," a scholiast of Virgil says definitely, " to substitute effigies for the real victims. If the necessary animals are hard to obtain, the gods accept their image in bread or wax." [4] Therefore the vital force of the animal cannot have been supposed to exert any binding influence on the god. The appearance of the offering was more important than its real nature. The god chiefly insisted on the shape. Sacrifice gave him a moral satisfaction.

Sacrifice was always accompanied by prayer. This was probably a rhythmical formula, generally accompanied by

---

[1] *N.H.,* xviii. 7 : *Numa instituit deos fruge colere et mole salsa supplicare.*
[2] xxii. 57. 6. In the excitement of the second Punic War, the Senate, after consulting the Sibylline Oracles, caused two Greeks and two Gauls to be buried alive in the Forum Boarium, *minime Romano sacro,* says Livy.
[3] For the ceremony of the Argei, in which puppets representing old men were thrown into the river, cf. H. Hubert, *Année sociologique,* iv. pp. 237 ff. For the Regifugium, see Frazer, **LXXV,** pp. 157, 301.
[4] Serv., *ad Aen.,* ii. 116.

music, a true *carmen*. The least alteration in the wording destroyed its efficacy, for the god took pleasure in the rhythm and the traditional words. But these words were not a mere charm, not, at least, in official religion ; they expressed a reasonable meaning, and they tell us clearly what man expected from his prayer. Prayer was not intended to constrain the gods forcibly ; it was addressed to their good will and begged for their peace, *pacem deorum*, that is, for their contentment and friendship.[1] To obtain their good will, it made promises to them. Above all, the worshipper accompanied his prayer with the strict performance of the rites and sacrifices which constituted his obligations, and he asked the god to fulfil his obligations likewise. The forms of prayer quoted by Cato fully agree with those of which the historians tell us, and may be taken as typical of Roman prayer.[2] First, the god addressed must be named, not because of the magical power of the name, but from scrupulous care for precision : [3] *Mars, te precor quaesoque*. It would be unnecessary to pray and beseech if the name was efficacious by itself. *Te precor quaesoque uti sies volens propitius, mihi, domo, familiaeque nostrae.* After indicating to whom it is addressed, the prayer states on whose behalf it is made ; thus the two parties are, as it were, brought face to face. Cato next mentions the rite accomplished : *quojus rei ergo, agrum, terram, fundumque meum suovetaurilia circumagi jussi.* Then the worshipper enumerates at length the services which he requests from the well-disposed heart of Mars. Finally he concludes : *Sic uti dixi, macte hisce suovetaurilibus lactentibus immolandis esto.* When the immolation has been done, he repeats his prayer to the god to accept the sacrifice and not to forget its object : *Mars pater, ejusdem rei ergo, macte his suovetaurilibus lactentibus esto.* Here we have the various phases, and often the very terms, of legal proceedings.[4]

The ceremonial of the religious festivals included sacrifices, prayers, and rites of very diverse origin and date. Some of them can only be explained as practices which were originally of a magical character. This seems to be true of lustration,

---

[1] Wissowa, **CLXXI**, p. 390, n. 3 ; Appel, **XXVII**, pp. 120 ff.
[2] Appel, **XXVII**.   [3] Cato, *Agr.*, 141.
[4] G. Appel, **XXVII**, pp. 145 ff. In many cases the form of prayer and the legal formula can be placed side by side.

which made a man able to act or rendered a thing capable of being influenced by the divinity. The procession of the sacrificial animals round the estate and that of the Arval Brothers across the fields seem to have been intended to gather up and neutralize the influences which might hinder the favourable action of the god. But at an early date lustration took on an idea of purification, which was expressed either by the use of lustral water, or by passage through fire, or by the use of smoke. Material purity was still sought rather than moral purity. Man must bring himself into a condition to please the gods. When, later, justice became the essential quality of the gods, the first condition for obtaining their good will was that a man should be just, and the object of lustration was to purge him of past ill deeds. The notion of mystical purity conceived by the " prelogical mentality " was transformed into an idea of rational justice and pity. The terms *justus* and *pius* took on a moral meaning.

It is perfectly legitimate, and even necessary, to look to a magical origin for the explanation of the details of most rites. But the understanding of them which we may thus obtain to-day entirely escaped the Romans, from the time when their religion was officially established. Every year they went through the traditional ceremonies, in order not to offend the gods by defrauding them of their due. They also added new ceremonies. Several of the names designating feasts in the calendar of Numa seem to be of recent formation, such as Armilustrium, Tubilustrium. The chariot races held in March and October do not appear very old. This kind of spectacle was only brought into Italy in the VIth century by the Greek colonies of Croton and Sybaris, and they reached Rome, through the Etruscans, about the beginning of the Vth century. When they arrived, they must have already lost all magical significance. At the end of the October races the slaying with javelins of the off horse of the winning chariot was a survival from an earlier stage of savagery, if it was not of foreign origin. The animal's head and tail were cut off, the people of the Subura and the Sacred Way fought for the head, and the tail was carried with speed to the altar of the Regia, while the Vestals gathered up the blood which dripped from it. This cruel rite was contrary to the very spirit which enjoyed the swift grace of the horse during the race. We do not know its meaning ; that is all that can be said of it.

But scenes of this kind are exceptional in Roman religion. At an early date we find official worship shorn of all primitive barbarism. It is not surrounded with the reek of blood ; there is no horror in it. All the feasts of gods were days of joy for the people ; they never degraded it. This religion was above all utilitarian. It celebrated the departure and return of flocks and of armies, calling down on both the same protection of the same god ; the processions winding over the countryside were intended to draw upon it the favourable eye of the divinity. In honour of Vesta, from the 7th to the 15th June, when the harvest was ripening, the Penus Vestae, the symbolic store-closet of the city's corn, was opened, thoroughly cleaned, and made ready to receive the new corn. At the end of August, the feasts of Ops and Consus were those of the harvest-home. It was a cold religion, without enthusiasm, grave and severely official, but essentially public, knowing none of the dark by-ways of mysticism, clear, honest, and fundamentally healthy. Not without reason did the poets of the classical period see beauty in these old country rites.

III

RELIGIOUS ORGANIZATION AND THE PRIESTLY COLLEGES

So the forms of worship, by their rational, legal, utilitarian character, were in strong contrast to the conception of the divine, which remained very primitive. The reason was that the gods had been conceived by the people, whereas worship was regulated by the magistrates of the city. Between the gods and the people the College of Pontifices was set up, to govern their relations. It was this college which established their relations on the basis of law.

The Pontifices, who first numbered three, then five, then nine, under the presidency of the Pontifex Maximus, the inheritor of the royal power in religious matters, had authority to settle everything connected with the relations of men with the gods. Yet they were not a priestly caste cut off from the rest of the people. They were not priests, properly speaking, or at least they were only priests for a time, like every citizen when he was called by his position to fulfil his sacerdotal duties. They were much rather a kind of magistrates, religious magistrates. They were recruited by co-optation from the élite of the Roman educated classes. They were at the same time Senators, jurists, and generals. The College of Pontifices, which was exclusively patrician until about 300, then opened its doors to plebeians, and even to foreigners, like the Latin Tiberius Coruncanius, who left a name as an altogether remarkable man.[1] It acted as an administrative committee, commanding both the priests and the people.

The Pontifices had directly under their orders the flamens—the major flamens, who were annual priests of the three great gods, Jupiter, Mars, and Quirinus (Janus), and the twelve minor flamens. The Vestals were subordinate to them. They managed all the other religious colleges, those of specialists like the augurs and the *Decemviri Sacris Faciundis*, and the various brotherhoods, Salii, Arvals, Sodales Titii, etc. In a word, they controlled the whole religious life of the city.

Their special mission was organization and the making of rules. Being depositaries of tradition, they had to adapt it to circumstances. Thus, it was the College which fixed the calendar every year, and intercalated the days required to make the civil computation fit the course of the sun, so that the spring festivals should fall in the spring months and so on. Consequently, it was for the College to say what gods should be honoured, and on what days. The so-called calendar of Numa is its work. It was the Pontifices who had to decide on the admission of foreign gods, on the site, plan, and dedication of temples, and on the rites to be observed. They intervened in all new or disputed cases. All prodigies were reported to them, and they were asked for the methods of expiation. They represented a permanent authority, whose charge it was to lay down and to administer the whole of *jus divinum*. To them religion owed its formal and rational character.

There was another important priestly college in Rome—that of the augurs. The augurs were specialists, whose business it was, under the authority of the Pontifices, to observe the signs of the divine will and to interpret them.

[1] Cic., *Brut.*, 14. 55.

For, though they dwelt among men, the Roman gods were less familiar than the Greek. Only very exceptionally did they let themselves be seen; they did not speak; they had no oracles; to give their warnings, they were content with omens, usually of a childish kind, the meaning of which was left to the augurs to discuss. In addition, there was a whole organized system for consulting the gods; the augurs presided over it, not on their own account, but in the name of the magistrate whose assistants they were.

Here again we find a system of rules intended to rationalize a body of primitive practices.

The signs interpreted by the augurs were divided into five classes: [1] those which came from the sky, namely lightning, those which the birds gave by their flight, those which they gave by their song, those which came from four-footed animals, and in particular from the examination of the entrails of victims, and, lastly, miscellaneous portents, the *dirae*. The meaning of lightning was supposed to depend on the quarter of the sky where it appeared. Lightning by day was a warning from Jupiter; lightning by night came from Summanus or from Vedius, the god of the dead; the shape of the flash made its signification quite certain. Thunderclaps in a clear sky were considered especially serious.

In the matter of birds, the most usual form of divination consisted in observing their flight. Here, again, attention was paid to the region of the sky, which might be favourable or unfavourable, no less than to the number of the birds and their species. According to tradition, Romulus used to rise at daybreak to take the auspices at the awakening of nature. Some time before the Punic Wars, the Romans found a convenient substitute for this old practice in the sacred fowls. The magistrate had them brought to him when he woke up, and in the propitious silence conducted the following dialogue with the augur in charge of them. " Tell me, is there silence ? " " It seems so." " Tell me, do they eat ? " " They eat." [2] We know the story told of the first Punic War. The fowls taken on the general's ship refused to eat. " Let them drink, then ! " said the general, and ordered them to be thrown overboard. He engaged battle and was defeated.

We have already mentioned the general theory which

[1] Mueller, **CXIV,** ii, pp. 114 ff.   [2] Cic., *Div.*, ii. 34. 71-2.

underlay the examination of the entrails of victims, and of the liver in particular.[1]   The word *haruspicium* used for this process of divination is, at least in its first half, Etruscan. The purely Latin term is *extispicium*.   The science itself seems to be of Etruscan origin.   It is based on exact knowledge of the anatomical topography of the liver, supplemented, no doubt, by that of the entrails, and on the distinction of the parts supposed to depend on each of the gods.   Modern palmistry indulges in similar speculations on the forms and lines of the hand.   The authority of the Pontifices conferred the official sanction of the State on this mode of divination.

From the Vth century onwards we also find in Rome many traces of divination of the Greek type.   Whereas the Roman sought to know the present will of the gods, the Greek preferred to question them about the future.   The Greek gods, and Apollo in particular, knew what was destined ; their prescience was far beyond the intelligence of the blind gods of Italy.   At Praeneste a goddess, perhaps of Greek origin, or at least deeply influenced by Greece, Fortune, the eldest daughter of Jupiter, Fortuna Primigenia,[2] gave oracles in the manner of Delphic Pythia, in the form of obscure sentences which had to be interpreted.   But the *Sortes Praenestinae* were too near at hand, and seem to have enjoyed little credit in Rome, for in 242 the Senate forbade one of its members to consult them.[3]   This was not the case with the Sibylline Oracles of Cumae.

In one of the volcanic caves which surrounded Cumae, the Greeks must have found or established an oracle, served by a priestess called the Sibyl.   How she gave her oracles, Virgil tells us at the beginning of the sixth book of the *Aeneid*.[4] How a collection of these oracles can have been of any interest to Rome does not seem to have occurred to the ancients. Their tradition simply related that the Sibyl herself made Tarquin buy them.[5]   In any case, they must have been brought into Rome before the capture of Cumae by the Samnites in 423, or perhaps at that very moment.   We seem to have here an obscure episode in the diffusion of Hellenic influences in Latium.   The Sibylline Oracles were deposited

---

[1] Cf. p. 13 above.
[2] Wissowa, **CLXXI,** pp. 259 ff.
[3] Val. Max., i. 3. 2.
[4] vi. 41 ff.
[5] Dion. H., iv. 62 ; Pliny, *N.H.*, xiii. 88.   Cf. Wissowa, **CLXXII,** pp. 536 ff.

in the Temple of Capitoline Jupiter, where they were destroyed, with the temple itself, in 83 B.C. Special officials, at first two, and later ten, *Duoviri* and *Decemviri Sacris Faciundis*, who were under the authority of the Pontifices, had been created to guard these oracles and consult them. Resort was only had to them in exceptional circumstances, or in the presence of portents the interpretation of which was beyond the competence of the augurs. More than anything else, the Sibylline Oracles contributed to the introduction of Greek rites into Roman religion—*supplicationes, lectisternia,* meals offered to the statues of the gods—thus gradually transforming into idolatry the less picturesque but more ideal religion of early Rome.

IV

RELIGION AND THE BEGINNINGS OF LITERATURE

This religion, hospitable though it was to foreign gods and rites, was none the less deeply marked with the original stamp of the old Roman spirit. The instinct for order and the desire to preserve records soon made it familiar with writing. The Pontifices seem to have made extensive use of this art. Since it was their business to indicate the various acts and formulas which ought to satisfy the gods, they took note of portents and the action taken on them. A list of cases of this kind formed the *Indigitamenta*, which must have been compiled in the IVth century, or in the IIIrd at the latest.[1] The general rules enacted on every subject, morality, law, religion, were collected, about the same time as the *Indigitamenta*, in the *Libri* or *Commentarii Pontificum*, which were veritable religious archives of the Roman State.[2] This was not all. Being entrusted with the care of the calendar, the Pontifices found themselves obliged to keep an exact record of past years, of their total number and the intercalations which they had required. Originally, it was said, they had marked them by a nail hammered into a board. Then they noted the names of the Consuls, and even added a brief summary of the most important events of the year. These records were written on planks, which were first kept secret,

---

[1] Warde Fowler, **CLXVII**, p. 285.   [2] *Ibid.*

but were later exhibited at the house of the Pontifex Maximus on the Forum. It was the collection of these tables which was published in 123 B.C. by Mucius Scaevola, the Pontifex Maximus, under the title *Annales Maximi*.[1] It is a precious document, which constitutes the chief and only authentic source of our knowledge of Roman history. From the registers of the Pontifices, too, come the *Fasti*, the Consular *Fasti*, giving a list of the Consuls, and the Triumphal *Fasti*, which Augustus, in his reverence for old tradition, caused to be exhibited, as they used to be, on the walls of the Regia, where they were engraved by the side of the calendar.[2] It was these Pontifical *Annals* which drove Roman historians, Livy and Tacitus alike, to adopt the form, so strange to us, of annals in which the events are arranged in years. No doubt there will still be much discussion about the authenticity of these documents, at least for the years previous to the burning of the city by the Gauls in 390. The fact that they were edited by the Pontifices explains the character of the information which we possess about the early days of Rome. We know the names of the magistrates, the laws passed, the wars and the treaties, the temples dedicated, and, especially, the portents to which even Livy gives such a large place. But we need not look to them for general surveys or for reflections such as we find in Thucydides or Polybius.

So the Pontifices, who laid down the first rules of Roman law in their *Commentaries*, were also the first historians of Rome. Their college represented both the directing intelligence and the conscience of the people. The site of the Regia, on the Forum, the place where it met and exercised its activity, was venerable above all others.

In religion, too, we must look for the origin of the earliest Latin poetry. The feasts of the gods gave it its first impulse in combining, round the altar of sacrifice, the rhythmic words of prayer, music, and sometimes the exaltation of the dance.

We know the importance enjoyed in Rome by the guild of the *Tubicines*, in virtue of the part they necessarily played in every ceremony of public worship. When they were absent all worship stopped. The acts of sacrifice and the words of prayer were accompanied by the flute. So every invocation

[1] Cichorius, in Pauly and Wissowa, **CXXVII**, s.v. *Annales Maximi*. See also Kornemann, **IX**, xi (1911), pp. 245 ff.

[2] Pais, **CXXV**.

of the gods was a rhythmical text. Though we cannot define it, in consequence of our ignorance of ancient music, we find this rhythm in all the rituals which have come down to us, in the Eugubian tables of Umbria and in the incomprehensible Etruscan text inscribed on the wrappings of the Agram mummy.[1] The Roman musicians were the pupils of those of Etruria,[2] who were themselves, it seems, the heirs of the Ionian or Graeco-Oriental tradition. When classical authors refer to the old Etrusco-Roman music they commonly speak of the " Lydian modes." So in music, at least, Etruscan art guided the first mode in which Roman sentiments were expressed.

The same music enlivened the dance. It was perhaps from Etruria, from her neighbour Veii, that Rome took the armed dance of the Salii.[3] Wearing helmets and carrying spears and the *ancilia*, the sacred shields believed to have fallen from heaven, the two groups, of twelve Salii each, performed their evolutions under the direction of the *vates* who directed the words and the *praesul* who conducted the music and dancing.[4] Thanks to Varro, we possess some fragments of their hymn. Its words were unintelligible to the Romans themselves, and modern commentators have not cleared up all its obscurities. But they agree generally in seeing in it at least a rough suggestion of the Latin verse, the Saturnian, containing two series of three feet, each marked by a stress.[5]

The Arval Brothers also danced, in honour of the peaceful Mars and of Dea Dia, to a three-time rhythm. The happy discovery, in the precinct near Rome where they met, of the *Acts* of the brotherhood, engraved in the Imperial epoch, has given us their hymn.[6] It is a kind of litany, each verse of which was repeated thrice.

> *Enos Lases iuvate*
> *Neve lue rue Marmar | sins incurrere in pleoris*
> *Satur fu fere Mars | limen sali sta berber*
> *Semunis alternei | advocapit cunctos.*
> *Enos Marmor iuvato.*
> *Triumpe. Triumpe. Triumpe. | Triumpe. Triumpe.*[7]

[1] Thulin, **CLIX.**   [2] Mueller, **CXIV,** ii, pp. 200 ff.
[3] *Ibid.*, pp. 294 ff.   [4] *Ibid.*, pp. 218-19 ; Livy, i. 20. 4.
[5] Schanz, **CXLIII,** i, 1, pp. 14 ff.   [6] **LI,** 28 ; vi, 2104.
[7] It is interpreted as follows : *Nos Lares juvate. Neve luem, ruem* (plague and ruin) *sinas incurrere in plures. Satur esto fere Mars, limen sali, siste verber* (check thy whip (?) ; Lindsay). *Semones alternatim advocabit cunctos* (all the Geniuses). *Nos Marmor juvato. Triumphe.*

The directions of the ritual say that the priests tuck up their robes, take the books, and dance in three-time, singing the litany.[1]

Prayer, therefore, represents an early form of poetry. When, for the celebration of the Secular Games, Augustus caused Horace to compose the hymn to be sung by alternate choirs of girls and lads, he was only reviving a tradition the origin of which may have been older than Rome itself.

We should note the presence in Rome, from primitive times, of the *vates*, skilled in composing the rhythmical words of the sacred hymns, the *praesul*, who conducted the dances, and the *tubicen*, who accompanied dances and words. In practice the three professions must have been merged. They came within the guild of the *Tubicines*, the artist auxiliaries of religion.

But did these artists devote their talent exclusively to religion ? Were they not sometimes, like the bards who assisted the druids, tempted by other themes than prayers ?

We cannot here enter into the question, so much debated since Niebuhr first raised it, of the existence of Roman epic lays. The theory of Niebuhr, who sees traces of an epic at the bottom of the legendary history of the first centuries of Rome, is based on a literary impression which is hard to deny. Most of the episodes in that history, the dramatic legend of the Tarquins, Horatius Cocles, Cloelia, Coriolanus, the Three Hundred and Six Fabii, Torquatus, have an undeniable poetic colour.[2] Nor is there any serious reason for rejecting the ancient evidence to the effect that it was the custom of the old Romans, at the end of a banquet, to sing the glory of their ancestors in lays accompanied by the flute.[3] But we cannot prove the connexion of these lays with the Roman legendary tradition, the origin of which remains obscure.[4] In Etruria, the paintings on the Vulci tomb, in which Tarquin and Mastarna appear, certainly seem to prove the existence

---

[1] **LI**, vi, 2104, a : *Ibi sacerdotes, succincti, acceptis libellis, carmen descindentes tripodaverunt.*

[2] See also De Sanctis, **CXLII**, ii, pp. 502 ff.

[3] Cic., *Tusc.*, i. 2. 3 ; iv. 2. 3 (quoting Cato) ; Val. Max., ii. 1. 10 ; Festus (quoting Varro), p. 77 (M.) ; Hor., *Odes*, iv. 15. 29. Cf. Pais, **CXXI**, i, p. 9, n. 1.

[4] The formation of the tradition is generally explained by an efflorescence of myths, mostly of religious origin. Sig. Pais carries this theory to extremes. The hypothesis of the myth has supplanted that of the popular epic. Despite the ingenuity and learning which they display, these interpretations very often appear arbitrary.

of a romantic cycle with which the heroes of early Roman history were connected.[1] Latin epic lays may have found models in them. It is now admitted that you cannot have a poem without a poet. In Etruria, the poets would have been the professional musicians and players, *ludiones* and *histriones ;* in Rome, they would have been the *tubicines*, musicians who were indebted for their technical education to Etruria, and, though of humble condition, were not necessarily lacking in liveliness of wit or imagination. If this was so, these auxiliaries of religion certainly deserved the right of feasting on the Capitol at Jupiter's expense, and of filling the city with their foolery on the day of their annual festival.[2]

The drama, in any case, had some roots which penetrated through the surface layer of the " games " of Greek type to the deeper soil of the old native festivals. The Roman Games, according to tradition, were instituted by Tarquin. In the VIth century, probably, and certainly at the beginning of the Vth, the Etruscans held games, of which they have left us pictures in their tomb-paintings.[3] These were athletic sports, chariot-races, and contests of various kinds, which may well have been borrowed from Greece. Whether they dated from the Royal period or not, the Roman Games were held in honour of Capitoline Jupiter ; they always kept the clear mark of their Etruscan origin. They opened with a procession of all the participants, which was an almost exact reproduction of the procession of the triumphant general going up to the Capitol. Behind the competitors, and before the statues of the gods or the chariot which bore the triumphant general, himself dressed as Jupiter, marched the bands of Lydian dancers, *ludiones* or *histriones*, and the flute-players or cithara-players.[4] The part played by these choruses in the old games seems to have been confined to miming dances accompanied by music, but without words. So, in Greece, the choruses of satyrs represented by their evolutions and mimicry the fables of the satyric drama. The first appearance of these actors in Rome was said to have been in 366,

---

[1] See above, pp. 32 ff.
[2] We know the anecdote related by Livy, ix. 30. Dissatisfied at losing these rights, the *Tubicines* withdrew in a body to Tibur. The Tiburtines made them drunk and brought them back to Rome, where their privileges were eagerly restored to them.
[3] F. Weege, **XII,** xxxi (1916), pp. 105 ff. ; **CLXIX.**
[4] Mueller, **CXIV,** ii, pp. 196 ff. ; Piganiol, **CXXXI,** pp. 15 ff.

when they were brought from Etruria to procure the aid of the gods against an epidemic.   The Roman Games, according to Mommsen, were no earlier.[1]

In the long description which he gives of the beginnings of the Roman theatre, Livy[2] goes on to speak of the jokes, in doggerel verse, which the young men bandied about, trying to fit their gestures to their words.   These were the Fescennine Songs, an old native custom, perhaps, as Horace says, or else a recent adoption from Etruria.[3]   " Fescennine licence," in any case, seems to have been definitely satirical.   It reminds one of the vein of parody which flourished in the IVth century in Sicily and the whole of Magna Graecia.

Then there appeared, Livy continues, professional actors, who were given the Etruscan name of *histriones*.   No longer content with their improvised cross-talk in rude, artless verse, similar to the Fescennine Songs, they came to represent " Satires," accompanied by music, the words being sung and keeping time with the flute.   These were genuine theatrical performances, copied, no doubt, from the Phlyac farces and the Rhintonica of southern Italy.[4]   Moreover, they were the immediate predecessors of the plays of the classical type of Livius Andronicus.

But the young Romans, leaving this too clever art to the *histriones*, kept up their old buffoonery mingled with verses. These were what were later called *exodia*, a type which seems to have been confused with the *Atellanae*, which were of Campanian origin, as their name shows.[5]   " The young men," says Livy, "kept this type of play to themselves, and did not allow it to be desecrated by the *histriones*.   That is why the actors of *Atellanae* are not excluded from the tribes, and do their military service, as not being mere play-actors." [6]

So, by the side of skilled performances, the rhythmical evolutions of the *ludiones* and the Satires of the *histriones*, we find a popular vein which reflects the same tendencies and gradually introduces dialogue into the dramatic " games." And this tradition, which was born of religious festivals, was

---

[1] Mommsen, **CXIII**, ii, p. 53.
[2] vii. 2.   Cf. Piganiol, **CXXXI**, pp. 109 ff.
[3] The town of Fescennium, which was supposed to have furnished the model of these songs, was in Etruria, near the present Viterbo.
[4] Croiset, **LIV**, v, pp. 172 ff.
[5] Atella, a small city in Campania, between Capua and Naples.
[6] vii. 2.

maintained until the Imperial epoch, by the side of the classical drama. The *Atellana* remained popular; we still find it in our own time, rejuvenated by Italian verve, in the *Commedia dell' Arte*. Punchinello, Harlequin, Pierrot, Columbine are descended in a straight line from Maccus, the hump-backed gowk with the great parrot nose and the big ears, Bucco, the braggart, Pappus, the old dodderer, Dorsenus, and other burlesque types of ancient Italy. Puns, parodies, and facetious topical allusions cheered the old Romans on the festivals of their primitive gods. The play of the mind, however simple it may have been, had a part in their religion.

CONCLUSION OF PART I

ROME, ITALY, AND GREECE

IN religion we recognize the same features as in the whole of early Roman civilization. Its foundation appears extremely primitive. The very conception of divinity and the organization of worship round the hearth and fields of the family seem to be earlier than the foundation of cities, and, without any doubt, come from the herdsmen and ploughmen who were descended from the old prehistoric tribes. Of these primordial elements, some seem to have belonged rather to the Indo-European invaders of the Italic peninsula, and the others, such as Saturn and Mother Earth, for example, to the Mediterranean autochthons, Siculians or others.[1] But this primitive substratum was covered by the sediment brought by all the successive vicissitudes of the earliest history of Rome. As in the section of a piece of ground, we see, in the solidified mass of Roman religion, a thick stratum of Etruscan influences, hardly distinct from the primitive strata, and, immediately over it, increasingly numerous traces of the relations of Rome with the Greeks of southern Italy and Sicily. The Hellenic tinge becomes more pronounced as the power of Rome advances towards the Hellenized regions of Italy ; the Greek gods and representations of them grow more numerous, Etruscan and Greek legends are mingled with those of Latium, and Graeco-Etruscan rites, dances, perhaps some rudiments of poetry, and games, assume a larger and larger place in worship. Roman religion is not only Roman ; it is Italian, and for that reason, from a very early period, it is permeated with Mediterranean, and especially Greek, influences.

Its characteristic feature, perhaps taken from Etruria, is its strong administrative organization under the authority of

[1] This distinction is drawn with great discernment by Piganiol, **CXXX**, pp. 93-139.

the colleges of specialists, and of the Pontifices in particular. From the heterogeneous mixture of religious traditions, the Pontifices seem to have set themselves to develop the rational element into a coherent system, giving it the cautious, strict form of legal relations between man and god. Thanks to them, Roman religion became an essentially formal and official cult. As far as we can go back we find it as a State religion.

Yet beneath this cold outward covering there was a pulsing popular life, of which we know little, but see glimpses in the family and rustic worships, the countless local cults, and certain manifestations like the Fescennine plays or the *Atellanae*, as well as in many rites of magical character and meaning incorporated in the official religion.

What was the Roman people, then, during the long period which we have just surveyed ? What was its spirit, and what did it owe to Greece ?

The Roman people and its civilization were a mixture of prehistoric elements, European and Mediterranean, blended by a discipline, which was Etruscan, that is, was permeated with Hellenic elements, before it became properly Roman. At the time when history begins, we find in Rome a city plebs and a country population, two peoples, so to speak, the second of which is further divided into a patriarchal aristocracy and a crowd of humble peasants. The necessities of the struggle for existence imposed cohesion on this aggregate. But the spirit of the two parties seems to have been profoundly different. The sons of the soil, whether patricians or simple peasants, brought the stability of their rustic traditions and their conservative obstinacy. The children of the town, more versatile, more enterprising, and less backward, established ties between the city of Rome, the great Etruscan or Etruscanized cities all round, and the more distant cities of Hellenized Italy. By them the ideas and the arts which the sea bore to the shores of Italy were diffused along the great land roads into the interior of Latium and came into the city itself.

Then the conquest of Italy introduced still other elements into the Roman people. In it, the man of Samnium, Campania, Apulia, or Bruttium met the Faliscan, the Etruscan, and the Umbrian, and Greek gods encountered those of the

H

conquered Italian cities and the local divinities of country shrines. In all this crowd the Senatorial aristocracy alone represented an element of permanence ; it maintained its own authority, and thereby imposed law and unity all round it. But the unity was only superficial, and the law, which dealt with the smallest details, with the alphabet no less than with religion, was obliged, in order to preserve its force, to adapt itself and to sanction, one after another, the innovations which were introduced by outside agencies.

The Roman people did not exist all at once—it formed little by little, and with it its spirit, which at first had little character of its own, like that of a child, was in a perpetual state of transformation. When, about the end of the IIIrd century and the beginning of the IInd, we see it, in the light of more definite history, arrived at adolescence, and its poetry allows us to perceive its thoughts, we shall find it Italian rather than Roman, and already, before any direct contact with Greece, steeped in Greek legends, Greek ideas, and Greek feelings.

PART II

ROME AS A MEDITERRANEAN CAPITAL

In his attempt to give a general picture of Roman history, Florus [1] compares its successive stages to those of the life of a man. He brings the childhood and adolescence of the city down to the Consulship of Appius Claudius, at the beginning of the IIIrd century before our era. Then comes her lusty youth, lasting to the death of Caesar. Rome, he observes, had taken nearly five hundred years to conquer Italy ; less than two centuries were to make her mistress of Africa, Europe, Asia, and, in short, the whole civilized world.

Let us adopt the plan drawn by Florus. For this period of exuberant, ambitious youth does indeed produce a decisive change in Roman civilization. The intellectual horizon of the Romans henceforward goes beyond Italy and embraces, little by little, the whole of the Mediterranean world. The great struggle of Rome against Carthage puts her in possession first of Sicily (first Punic War, 264-241) and then of the whole western Mediterranean (second Punic War, 218-201). She goes on, almost without interruption, to bring down and then conquer Macedonia (200-168), Greece (146), Asia Minor (132), Syria (65), and, lastly, Egypt (31). The ambition of individuals, raised to the pitch of frenzy by greed for booty, creates the upheaval of the Civil Wars, in which the old state of society and all the old ideals go under. Even the population changes. Endless troops of prisoners of war from every land, brought in as slaves and later freed, take the place of citizens, decimated by the wars, and small country land-owners, ruined by economic changes. Into Rome goods and traders from beyond the seas come pouring, with pedagogues, philosophers, hostages, ambassadors, artists, and craftsmen, Greek or Hellenized, who exercise great influence around them.

[1] At the beginning of the IInd century of our era.

115

Not without reason has the whole of antiquity been regarded as the development of one same civilization, the centre of which moved from Athens to Rome, and then from Rome to Constantinople.   From now onwards Rome is the depository of it.

The essential fact of this period is the development of a Roman literature.   In general, this literature is inspired by that of Greece, and it has the appearance of a scholarly, artificial creation.   Nevertheless, it is, at the very beginning, an imaginative literature, poetic in form, and it commences, just like an original literature, with the epic and popular spectacles.   Moreover, its earliest works are previous to any direct contact with Greece.   The Roman armies attacked Philip of Macedon in 200.   The writings of Livius Andronicus go back to 240.   Naevius, rather later than he, disappears about 200.   Ennius was born in 239, Plautus in 254, and Cato in 234 ; they therefore belong to a generation which received all its education from a still wholly Italian Rome. Livius Andronicus was a Greek from Tarentum, Naevius a Campanian, Ennius a Bruttian, Plautus an Umbrian.   So the flowering of Roman literature cannot be regarded as a sudden revolution, resulting from the conquest of the Greek countries, but rather as the last effect of Rome's assimilation of the Hellenized regions of Italy.

It was in Sicily, above all, during the first Punic War, that the Romans became acquainted with Greek literary forms.   Greece was first revealed to them through schools and books.   This explains why the earliest Latin literature tells us so little of its own time.   It is not inspired by contemporary writings of the Hellenistic world, but by models of the classical age.   Its masters are Homer and the tragedians. Comedy alone is an exception.   For comedy, in Sicily and the whole of southern Italy, was an exceptionally living and popular form.   No doubt the source of Roman poetry is Greek, but it springs from Italian soil.

Far from feeling intimidated by the perfection of such models as these, and withdrawing into themselves before the austere nobility of the classical ideal, the Romans were able to appreciate it, and adopted it with enthusiasm.   They had, indeed, been preparing themselves to understand it through the dim centuries of slow initiation during which they had been in contact with their neighbours of Italy. They came to Greece as pupils who were docile but already formed, capable of profiting by the education offered to them, and capable also of selecting from it. They borrowed much, but they did not completely forget their previous development, and they sought, as a rule, to adapt their imitations to their own traditions, their needs, and their aspirations. Beneath Greek forms many Italian features can be seen. While we must recognize the former, it is chiefly the latter that I shall try to bring out.

Chapter I

THE EARLIEST POETS

I

LIVIUS ANDRONICUS AND NAEVIUS

ANDRONICOS formed part of the spoil taken from Tarentum in 272, and he fell to the portion of the family of the Livii, who liberated him later; hence his name of Livius Andronicus.[1] As far as we can tell from the little we know of him, he is a very inconspicuous individual; his personality is colourless, and his writing is without fire. Brought up with his master's children, he was later employed to teach Greek and Latin to the sons of the friends and clients of the house. He was the schoolmaster, not only of his direct pupils, but of the Roman people.[2]

It was no doubt for his pupils that he thought of translating the *Odyssey*, the great school-book of Greek children. Of this work we have about forty lines, quoted in scraps by grammarians. In them we see Livius labouring, like a conscientious dominie, to render each Homeric hexameter word for word in a heavily stressed Saturnian. It is a line-for-line construe, such as a lower-form schoolboy makes to-day.

Ἄνδρα μοὶ ἔννεπε Μοῦσα πολύτροπον,
Virum mihi Camena insece versutum.

Livius translates quite literally, except images and flights of expression which were beyond the resources of Latin.[3]

---

[1] For the personality of the Livius who was the master of Andronicus, see Schanz, **CXLII**, i, p. 56.

[2] For details of fact and a critical study of his works, we may refer, in general, to De la Ville de Mirmont, **CLXIV**, and Plessis, **CXXXIII**.

[3] Grenier, **LXXX**, p. 153 and n. 1; Turiello, " L'Influenza ellenica sull' origine della poesia latina," in **XXII**, xx (1892), pp. 77-9.

Creation is not for him, either because he is incapable of it, or because he does not venture to indulge in it in consideration of his pupils.

Nevertheless, through the favour of his aristocratic protectors and pupils, he enjoyed some esteem in Rome, both as an official interpreter of Greek poetry and as a national poet. After the first Punic War the Senate wished to give the Roman Games the same character as those held in Greek countries. Andronicus was commissioned, for the occasion, to translate a Greek tragedy and comedy. His success was no doubt considerable, for he was not content with this first essay. Of his tragic works we have a few titles and about forty lines.[1] The style shows all the dull, stiff accuracy of the Latin *Odyssey*.

But through these prosaic translations the Romans saw the Greek heroes, greater than ordinary men, yet profoundly human, passionate, reasoning, heroic, daring, or resigned. Their tragic adventures brought them into conflict with the invincible forces of fate. They afforded signal examples of the vicissitudes of life. The story charmed the imagination ; the poverty of the form was not perceived.

Out of consideration for the translator of these beautiful legends, the Senate granted musicians, authors, and actors, the fellow-artists of Livius, a place for meeting and worship in the Temple of Minerva on the Aventine. In 207, during the second Punic War, the poet was instructed to compose the hymn to be sung by a choir of twenty-seven young women to thank the gods for the victory of the Metaurus.[2] With Livius Andronicus, and through him, Greek poetry obtained freedom of the city of Rome.

After the conscientious industry of Livius came the fire and enthusiasm of Naevius. He was an Italian from Campania, who fought in the first Punic War and was an ardent champion of the plebs in its political struggles against the aristocracy, which imprisoned him and finally banished him.

Naevius was an epic poet, and he was a creator, in that he blended Greek lessons with Italic traditions. Livius Andronicus had translated the *Odyssey ;* Naevius set out to write

[1] *Aegisthus, Ajax Mastigophorus, Equus Trojanus, Andromeda, Hermione* (Ribbeck, *Tragic. Rom. Fragm.*). An excellent selection of these fragments of early Latin poets will be found in Ernout, **LXX.**
[2] Livy, xxvii. 37. 7.

an *Iliad*, but a Latin *Iliad*. He took the idea and the epic
form from Homer, but the war in which he had just fought
seemed to him as great a subject as the struggle of the Greeks
against Troy. So he sang the Punic War. Moreover, since
Greek legend seemed to be the source of all epics, he was at
pains to attach his poem to the Trojan cycle. He gave
history an atmosphere of myth. He was the first, to our
knowledge, who referred to the Trojan origin of Rome and,
in connexion with the Punic War, to the unhappy loves of
Dido and Aeneas.[1] No one can deny that his poetical relation
of the combats in which he took part was perhaps connected
with some tradition of Latin or Campanian epic lays, celebrating in words the feats which were shown to the people on the
day of the triumph in paintings, and were recorded in paintings in tombs like that on the Esquiline. It was not in
Homer, in any case, that Naevius found the source of the
exploits and loves of Aeneas. He was inspired, according to
Sig. Pais,[2] either by the poetry which must have flourished in
his time at Tarentum or Syracuse, or even by the histories of
Italy composed in Sicily from the IVth century onwards, in
which ingenious writers strove to attach to prehistoric Greek
tradition the origins of the city whose power was gradually
extending over Italy. However this may have been, what
matters to us is the originality of this deliberate combination
of history and fable.

The form of Naevius's poetry is also new. He still uses
the Saturnian metre. But he does not hesitate to introduce
expressions exactly copied from those of Greek poetical
language. With him the artistic enrichment of the Roman
language begins. Finding in Homer the phrase ἄναξ ἑκάεργος
Ἀπόλλων,[3] Livius was content to translate : *filius Latonas*.
Naevius tries to reproduce both the image and the majestic
sound of the words :

> *Deinde pollens sagittis, inclutus Arquitenens,*
> *Sanctus Jove prognatus, Putius Apollo.*[4]

He had a sense of poetic style, as being different from

---

[1] The *Punic War* seems to have begun with an account of the fall of Troy :
Noctu Trioad exibant capitibus opertis . . . (fr. 5). It was doubtless to Dido that
Aeneas related his adventures : *Blande et docte percontat Aeneas quo pacto Trojam
urbem liquisset* (fr. 24).
[2] Pais, **CXXI**, i, pp. 40 ff.   [3] *Od.*, viii. 323.   [4] *Pun. War*, p. 32.

prose, particularly in the use of special terms. In Greece the poet used archaic terms, generally taken from Homer, or dialect words ;[1] or else he invented compounds, giving a whole image in a single word, which were repeated from one work to another. For Naevius, and after him for Roman poets in general, the words which gave poetry its special sound and colour were either terms not used in common speech, or combinations of words generally imitated from the Greek, or compound words.[2]   The two lines quoted above give examples of these various methods. Thus Naevius created for Latin the artistic language, that of the gods and heroes, who did not speak as men did for the practical purposes of their daily life.[3]

For the Games, the great artistic manifestation of the time, Naevius wrote tragedies and many comedies. Most of his tragedies were copied from Greek plays, or were at least inspired by Greek legend.[4]   But he was an innovator in drama as in epic. He dramatized the childhood of Romulus and Remus. For the triumph of Marcellus in 222, he staged one of the achievements of the campaign, the capture of Clastidium, thus bringing into the theatre the spectacle of the victories of the general, animated by the tragic spirit and poetic dialogue. The actors in these historical dramas wore the real costume of Roman leaders, the purple-bordered toga, *praetexta*, from which came the name of *fabulae praetextatae*. If Naevius's bold inventiveness had found the same support among the people and the aristocracy as the plain translations of Livius, a native Roman tragedy might have come into being and developed.

Of his comedies, some bore Greek names and others true Latin names. In the former he seems to have made use of the process of " contamination " with which Terence was afterwards reproached ;[5] that is to say, he combined the argument and episodes of several Greek models in a single play. Some fragments which appear to come from his

---

[1] Meillet, **CVIII,** Pt. ii, ch. ii (1st ed., p. 136).
[2] Grenier, **LXXX,** p. 156.
[3] *Ampullae* and *sesquipedalia verba* are, for Horace (*A.P.*, 95-8), the privilege of tragedy. Grenier, **LXXX,** p. 119. For the meaning of *ampullae*, see E. Pottier, **XXI,** 1900, pp. 225-32.
[4] We know of his *Trojan Horse, Hector, Hesione, Danae, Iphigenia, Lycurgus.*
[5] Ter., *Andr.*, Prol., 18 : *Qui cum hunc accusant, Naevium, Plautum, Ennium accusant.*

comedies on Latin themes suggest that in them he gave free rein to the boisterous raillery of the old Fescennine songs and to jokes of the kind with which the plebs and soldiery sometimes accompanied the triumphal progress of the victorious general. " At the feast of Liber, at least," he said, " let us speak freely." [1] A fragment, preserved by Aulus Gellius, makes satirical allusion to some youthful adventure of Scipio Africanus :—

" He, who had done so many glorious things, whose deeds still live, who alone stands out among the nations, even he was once carried off by his father from his girl, with nothing on but his cloak." [2]

No doubt all these original efforts of Naevius drew their sap from the old traditions of the Latin or Campanian *vates*. We can recognize in him the native vein of epic and comedy, amplified and raised to the dignity of literature by the artistic form of the Greek poetical styles.

II

ENNIUS

The great poet of this early period was Ennius, who was both learned and inspired. He, too, was an Italian from the south, born at Rudiae in Calabria, who became, however, thoroughly Roman. He belongs to the generation which followed that of Naevius, and his talent well shows the rapid progress made by Rome between the first and second Punic Wars. His literary work, contemporary with that of Plautus, embraces all forms—epic, tragedy, comedy, and also satire, a medley of raillery, moral and philosophical ideas, polemics, and didactic exposition of knowledge of the most varied kind. It really forms a transition between the age of beginnings and the classical development. Ennius is still closely related to Livius and Naevius, while, through Lucilius, the form which

---

[1] *Libera lingua loquemur ludis Liberalibus* (fr. 113).
[2] Aul. Gel., v. 7. 8. 5 :

> *Etiam qui res magnas manu saepe gessit gloriose*
> *Cujus facta viva nunc vigent, qui apud gentes solus praestat,*
> *Eum suus pater cum pallio uno ab amica abduxit.*

he introduces is developed by Horace, and there are many close resemblances between his *Annals* and the epic of Virgil.[1]

Like Naevius, Ennius wished to be the author of a Roman *Iliad*. But it was not only one episode in Roman history, but the whole of it, from the beginning to his own day, that he set out to present in epic form. He took his title of *Annals* from the historical work of the Roman Pontifices. Between the Pontifices and the poet, the first Roman historians, his contemporaries Fabius Pictor and Cincius Alimentus, certainly acted as intermediaries. But these latter wrote in Greek, and, therefore, spoke only to an educated few. It was the people itself that Ennius wished to reach by his poetry ; his name and his words should be familiar in the mouths of the mass.

The second Punic War, in which he fought, seemed to him the apogee and culmination of the destiny of Rome. It must have formed the central episode of the poem, since we find it commencing in the VIIIth Book and the XVIIIth Book concluded the *Annals* in 174. After the legends of the foundation of the city, which Ennius had already related, and the memories of the early centuries, the poem must have presented a long procession, in attitudes copied from those of the Homeric heroes, of the leaders who during those forty decisive years had guided the destinies of Rome.

This epic, while artificial and learned, as, indeed, is every work of art, was of such living, present interest that it could be understood and enjoyed as those of Ariosto and Tasso have long been, and still are, in Italy. Ennius and Naevius were not merely students, living on Greek books ; they were men of action, who sought to render in artistic form the impressions and feelings which they had experienced and their contemporaries had shared. The *Punic War* and the *Annals* were true Roman epics, and not mere translations of the *Iliad*.

Yet, among the Romans who read his works, Ennius was held to be more steeped in Greek influences than Naevius. This judgment must have referred chiefly to his language and style, which, though they showed the use of the same methods, certainly appear more scholarly than those of his predecessor.

His metre, first of all, is not the old Saturnian, but the hexameter, copied from the Greek epic verse. His images,

[1] Norden, **CXVII.**

his combinations of words, and his tricks of style, such as apostrophes and comparisons, are modelled on Homer. Yet there is no mere translation, but rather adaptation and transposition. The poet does not let imitation of his master change his own character, which is sometimes rough and forceful, with a strong tendency to emphasis, and sometimes charmingly sweet and graceful.[1] Poetic flights alternate with strokes of realism which are rather heavy, with prosaic and clumsy passages, but as a rule the expression has the fulness of meaning and the sonorous phrasing which show the great poet. In France the poet who reminds one of Ennius is Ronsard. Here we see the same troubled, inquiring genius, the impetuous passion, the love of greatness and beauty, the combination of the inexperienced zeal of archaism with the grace, sometimes rather finical, borrowed from some model admired for its artistic dexterity.

The tragedies formed a fairly considerable part of Ennius's work ; the ancients have preserved the titles of about twenty.[2] Two of them represented Roman subjects, the *Rape of the Sabines* and the *Fall of Ambracia*. Most of the others belonged to the Trojan cycle, become Roman by adoption. Almost all, it has been observed, seem inspired by Euripides. Ennius reproduces not only the pathos of his model, but his argumentative habit and his philosophical, moral, and religious discussions. He argues against fate, he tries to analyse the character of men and even of gods ; his drama is one of passion and of ideas. Here is quite an Epicurean profession of faith, worthy of Lucretius, from the tragedy of *Telamon :*

Ego deum genus esse semper dixi et dicam caelitum,
Sed eos non curare opinor quid agat humanum genus ;
Nam si curent, bene bonis sit, male malis, quod non est.

"That there is a race of gods in heaven, I have always said, and will say ; but I do not think that they care what the race of men may do. For if they cared it would go well with the good and ill with the bad ; and it is not so."

---

[1] See, e.g., the description of spring, imitated from Aesch., *Eum.*, 885, 903 ff., in fr. 151 ff. : *Caelum nitescere, arbores frondescere, | Vites laetificare, pampinis pubescere*, etc. In *Ann.*, fr. 457, Jupiter, talking with Venus, smiles : *Juppiter hic risit, tempestatesque serenae | Riserunt omnes risu Jovis omnipotentis.* Fr. 352 : *Et simul erubuit ceu lacte et purpura mixta.*

[2] *Achilles, Ajax, Alexander, Andromache, Eumenides, Hectoris Lutra, Hecuba, Phoenix, Telamon, Thyestes,* etc.

It is the great argument of the existence of evil as against divine perfection.

He is chiefly concerned with morality, like his model Euripides. A fragment of uncertain origin gives a beautiful image, both familiar and striking, of the fellowship of men :

> *Homo qui erranti comiter monstrat viam*
> *Quasi lumen de suo lumine accendat facit :*
> *Nihilominus ipsi lucet, cum illi accenderit.*

" A man who kindly shows a wanderer the way does as if he gave him a light from his lamp. His own light burns no less when he has kindled the others."

But his morality is based on a very Roman idea ; law is above everything else, even virtue.

> *Melius est virtute jus, nam saepe virtutem mali*
> *Nanciscuntur, jus atque aequom se a malis spernit procul.*

" Law is better than virtue. For bad men often happen upon virtue, but law and right withholds itself from the bad."

One great thought, much more philosophical than religious, and more dramatic than philosophical, that of inexorable fate, dominates all his plays, as it dominated the Athenian drama. The lot of men does not depend on the caprice of the countless ancient gods, supposed to be present everywhere. Gods, like men, are subject to Fate. Whatever they do, neither gods nor men can escape from the supreme, blind law, fixed from all eternity. Its power takes hold of individuals, and, whether they will or no, makes them play the part to which they are destined. The hapless Cassandra is the living embodiment of this fatal law. Possessed by her gift of prophecy, she wails in vain over the trouble into which she casts her family and her city.

" Dear mother, far the best of all women, I am sent for mysterious prophecies. Apollo, against my will, by a power outside myself, compels me to declare what is fated. I blush before my maiden companions, I am ashamed before my good father. Mother, I pity you and I loathe myself."

And the prophecy preserved in another fragment is expressed in words which must have profoundly stirred the souls of a generation which had grown up amid the anxieties of the war against Hannibal. The downfall willed by fate is preparing for the City ; it is at hand, and nothing can stave it off.[1]

From the theatre and by the theatre Ennius was led to philosophy. But the philosophy which he knows does not seem to be that of the great schools of Hellenistic Greece, or at most he catches an echo of it through Sicily. One of his satires was called *Epicharmus*, after the Sicilian poet, who was not afraid of making fun of the gods as well as of men, and, moreover, filled his works with philosophical maxims and discussions. It seems to have recounted a dream of Epicharmus, in which the poet thought that he was dead, went down to Hades, and conversed, among others, with Pythagoras himself. A fragment gives the tone of the poem and of the teaching expounded in it ; it was a form of naturalism, interpreting the old religious myths by naturalistic ideas. Jupiter is simply the universe in a perpetual state of change, the air which becomes wind, and cloud, and rain, the element which nourishes all life.

Istic est is Juppiter, quem dico, quem Graeci vocant
Aerem, qui ventus est et nubes, imber postea
Atque ex imbre frigus, ventus post fit, aer denuo.
Haec propter Jupiter sunt ista quae dico tibi
Quando mortales atque urbes beluasque omnes juvant.[2]

Later, no doubt, Ennius carried his criticism even further. For there had just appeared, in Hellenistic Greece, a new theory, at once romantic and rationalistic, according to which the gods were merely old heroes deified by the imagination of men. Ennius appropriated it, and translated or imitated the *Sacred History* of Euhemeros. He had long been troubled by the mystery of the gods. Here, it seems, was the solution which attracted him. On a distant island, Euhemeros related, there stood a temple of Jupiter, bearing

---

[1] *Jamque mari magno classis cita*
Texitur, exitium examen rapit ;
Advenit, fera velivolantibus
Navibus complebit manus litora.

[2] In the next generation, in Pacuvius, likewise a philosophic poet, even Jupiter has disappeared ; there are only sky and ether.

Id quod nostri Caelum memorant, Grai perhibent aethera.
Quidquid est hoc, omnia animat, format, alit, auget, creat,
Sepelit recipitque in sese omnia, omniumque idem est pater,
Indidemque eadem aeque oriuntur de integro atque eodem occidunt.

on one of its columns a long inscription recording the whole early history of the world. Cronos and Jupiter and all the other gods were only ancient kings. It was a fanciful echo of the great discussions which at that time raged between the Greek Epicureans, Stoics, and Sceptics, and was well calculated to attract the turbulent imagination of the poet of the *Annals*.[1]

The result of this succession of live achievements effected, since the beginning of the IIIrd century, by her first poets, was a number of permanent gains for Rome—first, a poetic language equally suited to tragedy and epic, then specimens of these two forms, and, lastly, comedy and satire, not to mention the beginnings of a philosophic thought based entirely on reason. In all these directions Ennius appears as the chief, leading the Romans to the conquest of the things of the mind with ardour equal to that which carried their armies from Sicily to Carthage, to Macedonia, to Asia, and to Greece.

III

PLAUTUS

Of the three first poets and of their successors, the tragic poets Pacuvius and Accius, we possess only fragments. Of Plautus, Varro's care has preserved twenty complete comedies out of twenty-one which he recognized as authentic.[2] All are imitated from Greek models. Plautus himself boasts of it : *Fabula tota Graeca est*, he announces ; it is a kind of recommendation with the public. Greece was regarded as an ideal land of intelligence, beauty, and joy, and all the more

[1] One need mention only, as a proof of the poet's versatility, in addition to the epigrams and the elegy on the death of Scipio, the *Heduphagetica*, an adaptation of a Greek gastronomical treatise, which must doubtless be regarded as a mere exercise in verbal virtuosity.

[2] According to Aulus Gellius (iii. 3. 10), about 130 comedies were attributed to Plautus. Aelius Stilo recognized 25 of these as authentic ; others said 40. There were 21 in Varro's *Corpus*, but we have only fragments of the twenty-first, the *Vidularia*. The others are : *Amphitruo, Asinaria, Aulularia, Captivi, Curculio, Casina, Cistellaria, Epidicus, Bacchides, Mostellaria, Menaechmi, Miles Gloriosus, Mercator, Pseudolus, Poenulus, Persa, Rudens, Stichus, Trinummus, Truculentus.* The most convenient edition, pending the appearance of that which Monsieur L. Havet is preparing for the *Collection Budé*, is Lindsay's, CI. The *Asinaria* is only a pastiche by Plautus (Havet, *C.R. Ac. Inscr.*, 2nd May 1924, pp. 158-9).

because it was still only known indirectly, and from afar, through its literature. The first play of Plautus in alphabetical order, *Amphitryon*, bears a marked Sicilian stamp. It is one of the *hilarotragoediae* which were so popular at Syracuse and Tarentum.

"Why do you scowl?" Mercury asks in the prologue. "Is it because I have just announced a tragedy? Well, I am a god; I'll be off and put that right. If that is your pleasure, I shall make the tragedy into a comedy, without touching the words. Will you have it, or won't you?"

Fig. 11.—*Amphitryon*. Jupiter and Mercury beneath Alcmena's window. Vase-painting from southern Italy.

Rhinton himself, the creator of this form, had written an *Amphitryon*. For the other plays, we can point to models, often on Plautus's own authority, in Menander, Diphilos, and Philemon, the most celebrated authors of the Greek New Comedy. To what extent Plautus follows the footsteps of Naevius, we cannot say. In any case, it is quite a Greek form which he nationalizes in Rome.

But Plautus was neither a learned man nor a theorist; he had no powerful patron whose protection might enable him to become the apostle of a literary ideal. His patron was the crowd; his only principle was to please; his only object,

I

success. Although we cannot say exactly what changes he made in his models, we can be certain that he adapted them to the taste of the Roman public. His work truly constitutes a historical document on the Roman spirit about the end of the IIIrd and the beginning of the IInd century before our era. This is its especial interest for us here.[1]

Plautus was a plebeian. Born at Sarsina in Umbria before 250, he kept himself alive until he was over forty by various trades, all equally humble, first as an entertainments contractor and then as a merchant, in which capacity he was so unsuccessful that he had to take on a job as baker's man. It was to escape from the grinding-mill, he says, that he became a comic author. He knew life and its difficulties; he must have moved in very different circles, travelling, perhaps, when he was in trade, and in any case rubbing shoulders with all conditions of men from the days when he supplied material and personnel for the theatre to those when he produced his own plays. His rich young men and pimps, slaves and slave-dealers, inn-keepers and usurers were drawn from personal acquaintance. The most astonishing thing in Plautus is his literary accomplishment, the purity and flexibility of his diction, which were recognized by the ancients,[2] the art, often very skilful, of his composition and poetry. It may be replied that he combined natural genius with stage experience. But if the stage itself could form such a writer, he must have had a strong literary bent already; if such a writer could come out of the crowd, the crowd itself cannot have been without culture.

What is there truly original and characteristic in the comedy of Plautus?

Not the subjects. We may allow that they are Greek. We shall be forgiven for thinking them drearily commonplace and wholly devoid of interest. Read the comedies of Plautus, shut the book, and try to describe the exact plot of any one. All are confused in the memory; such-and-such a scene or episode might equally well come in the *Stichus* or the *Mercator* or the *Truculentus*. Almost without exception, you will find a lover, served by an artful, comic slave; the lover has

---

[1] For Plautus and Roman comedy in general, see Michaut, **CX**.
[2] Quintilian (x. 1. 99) quotes the remark of Aelius Stilo: "If the Muses wished to speak Latin, they would speak the language of Plautus."

trouble with his father, or the pimp, or a bombastic soldier, or some puppet or other; the slave swindles them out of money, which serves to redeem the heroine from slavery. She has remained pure through all dangers. The play ends happily with a wedding, generally accompanied by a recognition. Stories of sea-voyages, shipwrecks, and pirates, unexpected home-comings, mystifications, mistaken identities, slaves' rascalities, and quarrels furnish the most common episodes. The plot is clearly only an accessory. Save in exceptional cases, such as the *Aulularia*, it is of little account;

MILES   PARASITVS

Fig. 12.—*Miles Gloriosus.*   Painting from Pompeii.

it is only a conventional scenario, a commonplace peg on which to hang the various incidents. Plautus obviously does not attach any importance to it. Without taking the trouble to invent, he accepts the themes and tricks of Greek comedy as they are. In order to enjoy a play, it is almost unnecessary to make an effort to follow the story, which is often fairly confused.

The characters themselves are conventional. They did not yet wear the mask in Plautus's time, but nothing can have been easier, when his plays were revived, than to give it to them. For they are reproductions of models which wore the mask; they have no individuality; they are merely "parts." We find the old man, sometimes indulgent and

good, but more often severe and avaricious.   The two types
are sometimes opposed, as in the *Aulularia*, where the worthy
Megadorus has a foil in the testy and virulent Euclio.   Every
play has its *senex*.   Then we have the youth or youths, all
in love, but some virtuous and tender and the others licentious,
violent, and jealous.   Sometimes they have with them their
pedagogue ;   it is for them that the slave intrigues, a devoted,
scurrilous, cunning fellow, who raises a laugh at the expense
of the miserly father, the yokel, or the braggart soldier.   Add
the parasite and the *leno*.   In every play we find the same
characters under different names.   The female characters
are fewer but even more insignificant.   We know, moreover,
that they were played by men ;   they might have been played
by marionettes.   Men and women alike come from the Greek
theatre.   The New Comedy, though it charms by its liveliness
and good humour, its unexpected repartees and its wise
reflections, is in no way a comedy of character.   We find
morality in it, but no psychology.   Do not let us look for
more in Latin comedy.

What remains, then, in Plautus's comedy, which made its
success ?   Its comic power alone, comedy of situation and
comedy of words.

The comedy of situation is not, as a rule, of a very lofty
order.   It is produced by easy and rather crude methods, the
commonest of which are antics, blows, drunkenness, brag,
and trickeries of all kinds.   Certain vase-paintings from
southern Italy give us an idea of this drama, in which grimacing characters indulge in exaggerated but expressive and droll
contortions.[1]   It was there, even more than in the New
Comedy, that Plautus must have found his " business."
He makes use of it with such high spirits and prodigality,
surprises are repeated and varied so frequently, comic scenes
are carried on, sometimes rather too long, with such ease,
good humour, and fancy, that the most critical cannot refrain
from laughing.   These comedies have a " go," rather childish,
but simple and healthy, which carries one away.   The author
is enjoying himself, we feel ;   even the actors must have
enjoyed themselves ;   and we, at this day, merely reading
the plays, provided we do not trouble too much about analysis,
find ourselves infected by the general gaiety.

[1] Bieber, **XXXI,** pp. 138 ff., pls. 75 ff.

Plautus's special virtue, which remains inimitable, is his use of language. His phrases are simple, short, made to be understood immediately, taken from ordinary conversation, but dazzlingly rich in words. The poet calls upon all the resources of expression in Latin—trade-terms, popular expressions, learned words. With perfect ease, he gaily borrows from the vocabulary of the priest, the magistrate, the peasant, the soldier, the slave, the whore, and the gossip, from the talk of the market-place and from the diction of serious poetry.

He is not content to use words; he plays with them. This is one of his favourite resources. Wealth of words and of plays on words were considered in antiquity the special mark of his style.

Plays on the sound and meaning of words, puns, nonsense, and comic formations make his dialogue an uninterrupted fire of wit—not very refined wit, perhaps, but the rather coarse salt of the Latin salt-pans with which Cicero liked to season his speeches when he wanted to charm his hearers.

This verbal wealth does not lie only in the fancy with which Plautus makes use of the resources of Latin; it also comes from his creative imagination. The poet invents not only plays on words and combinations of words, but also, without any doubt, a great number of new words, which he forms on roots or words already in use, in such a way that they can be understood at once, yet their novelty strikes the audience and makes it laugh. For us, to-day, it is very difficult to distinguish these neologisms, at least in the case of simple or derived words. For the methods of derivation are common to the language; there is nothing which clearly reveals the personality of the writer who first used it for one word or another. The comedies of Plautus are the earliest literary text in Latin which we can read continuously; it is impossible for us to estimate how much they enriched the speech of Rome.

It is not so with his compound words. Serious poetry, that of Naevius and Ennius, obtained fine effects from this method of composing words. Terms of this kind, the *sesquipedalia verba* of Horace, are one of the characteristic features of the epic and tragic style. Plautus transfers them into comedy, using them with the most comic effect. The old man in the *Captivi* is told that one of his slaves is the son of a

very rich and well-known personage named Thensaurochry-
sonicochrysides. " Doubtless it was because of his wealth
that they gave him that beautiful name," says the simple
old man. The soldier in the *Pseudolus* is called Polymachaero-
plagides, and the one in the *Miles* is Pyrgopolinices. This is
probably only an imitation of the comic writers of Sicily, if
not of Greece. But Plautus also transposes the process into
Latin. Here is a whole passage of abuse thus formed of a
mixture of Greek and Latin, addressed to a *leno* :—[1]

> *Vaniloquidorus, virginesvendonides,*
> *Nugiepiloquides, argentumextenebronides,*
> *Tedigniloquides, nugides, palponides,*
> *Quodsemelarripides, nunquameripides.* Em tibi.

Plautus plays on proper names :—

> *Credo hercle nomen mutabit mihi*
> *Facietque extemplo* Crucisalum *ex* Chrysalo.[2]

He also plays on common nouns. With him fists become
" tooth-crackers," and teeth " nut-crackers."

> *Ne tibi, hercle, hau longe est os ab infortunio*
> *Ita dentifrangibula haec meis manibus gestiunt.*

The parasite :—

> *Quom ejus verba interpretor, mihi cautio est*
> *Ne nucifrangibula excussit ex malis meis.*[3]

All kinds of comic insults are thus formed by composition.[4]
Sometimes, too, the expressions of tragedy and the epic are
parodied in this way.

> *Salsipotenti et Multipotenti Jovi' fratri et Nerei, Neptuno.*[5]

These comic compound formations clearly bear the stamp
of Plautus. For to combine two previously independent terms
so as to create a new word is to do something of your own.
The imagination and will of the writer have a share in this
creation. The unexpected, intimate alliance of two words
provokes surprise ; the amusing image is as it were packed

[1] *Persa*, 702-5.   [2] *Bacchides*, 362.   [3] *Ibid.*, 595 ff.
[4] E.g., *Trinummus*, 1021 ; *Pseudolus*, 357-70, etc.   [5] *Trinum.*, 820.

in the unity of the compound. Such formations are an integrant part of a literary work.

It is a quality of the great poet that he creates his own language. Naevius and Ennius created the language of serious poetry, Plautus that of comedy. This makes his true originality his chief claim to the high place which he has always held in Latin literature.

The actual form of his comedy is Greek ; the plot, the characters, the moral ideas, the sentiments are Greek. We should not attach great importance to occasional allusions to Roman institutions or customs ; in his free and easy way, the poet mingles Greek and Roman things in the fairyland of the theatre. With him all these elements are simply accessories. For him the main thing is to make people laugh. He and his public are indifferent to the logic of the plot ; so long as the incidents are amusing, it does not much matter how they are introduced. Psychological analysis and sentimental subtleties do not interest the Roman public ; they do not go to the theatre to see themselves, and still less to see man in general. So Plautus simplifies, suppressing or exaggerating into caricature the indications of this kind which he finds in his Greek models. On the other hand, he pours out, in a profusion unknown to the New Comedy, all the comic devices, and above all the humour of words, which he raises to its highest pitch. Such is his mastery in this that he is able to treat any subject—tragi-comedy like *Amphitryon*, free, licentious comedy like the *Casina*, or serious, sentimental comedy like the *Captives*. The subject is of little importance ; the form in which he clothes it is the essential, and it is by this that Plautus is sure to please.

He boasts of producing purely Greek plays, because Greece is the fashion ; she has just been given her liberty by Rome ; one is glad to know her, and sometimes pretends to understand her. But we must not take this too seriously. Plautus's comedy is certainly more Sicilian than Greek, or rather it is Italian, for the influence of Sicily must for a long time have been spreading, through southern Italy, all over the peninsula, and penetrating into Rome. The fancy of Plautus certainly preserves much of the unrestraint of the old national farces, Fescennine songs, *Atellanae*, and satires. As in the *Atellana*, his characters are simply conventional outlines. As in the Fescennine song, jokes and foolery are more important than logical plot. If we knew the *Atellanae* of the Imperial epoch, we should doubtless find in them the characteristic features of the comedy of Plautus. But what we probably should not find is the rich, full language of the old poet and the boisterousness which, in its archaism, inevitably calls up, to a Frenchman, the memory of Rabelais.

The Latin poet has not the depth of thought, nor the satirical audacity, nor the sense of observation of Rabelais. The substantific marrow is lacking in him. But outwardly the two writers are alike. Both are great artists in words. They excel in transforming the speech of the people into literary material, concocting words so as to bring out all their meaning, striking them together so as to produce the spark of laughter. In spite of Greek influence, Plautus comes from the old comic genius of Italy, just as, in spite of the Renaissance, Rabelais embodies the popular high spirits of Gaul. Both are fed by the sap of their soil.

The comedy of Plautus has all the appearance of a holiday show of a naturally gay people, still too young and exuberant for the refinements of psychological analysis, and delighted by antics and scurrility. But we must be careful not to exaggerate this aspect. Plautus's audience seems to have been able to listen to simple ideas of practical morality and even to certain delicate sentiments, expressed in humorous form. The comedy of the *Captives* is a proof of it.

"This play," Plautus warns them, "is not made like the others. You will hear none of those bawdy lines which one dares not remember ; you will not even see a *leno,* nor a cursed whore, nor a bragging soldier."

The theme is the noble, tender friendship and mutual devotion of two young men who are full of the highest sentiments. The bustle and noisy foolery of the slaves are followed by speeches impregnated with feeling and moral maxims. Here we are much nearer the Greek New Comedy than the *Atellana.* We must not forget that the performance of a comedy included a great deal of music. The dialogue was interspersed with *cantica,* lyrical, or, more particularly, pathetic pieces, accompanied by the flute. These were veritable flights of poetry, and they were the true literary part of a comedy, addressed to the intelligence and the

aesthetic sense.   In Plautus the development of the farcical
side does not exclude art ; boisterous abundance of words is
often allied with clear and graceful expression of ideas and
delicately witty dialogue skilfully conducted ; the play of
bodies and words alternates with that of thought.

When we try to picture the crowd which, after a tragedy
by Ennius, applauded the comedies of Plautus, we should
forget the pictures consecrated by tradition.   The Roman
people of the end of the IIIrd century and the beginning of
the IInd was neither the King-People, heavily conscious of
its majesty and imbued with a slightly stupid gravity, nor
yet a demoralized, vile plebs which cared only for the violent
and bloody entertainments of the amphitheatre.   It was the
Italian people ; in it the Latin or Sabine peasant mingled
with the Umbrian, the Etruscan, the Campanian, the Apulian,
and the Messapian, and even the Greek from Sicily.   Slaves
from all parts of the Mediterranean world had not yet come
pouring into the city, there to be freed and to raise offspring.
The crowd was composed of small free artisans, many of
whom might be artistic craftsmen, traders of too small means
to be classed among the Knights, but with an intellectual
horizon which went far beyond the city and the Latin countryside, and small farmers who had fought all over Italy, in
Sicily, in Spain, and even in Africa.   It was a population of
free origin and of Italian stock, living by its labour, which
filled the city.   Plautus came from its ranks, and had lived
all his life among it ; he wrote for it ; and for it he combined
the traditions of the Italian comic show with the literary
lessons of Greek comedy.

Like the comedy, the epic and tragedy were made for this
people.   In form they are Greek ; they mingle the fables of
the Greeks of old time and those invented by the Sicilians
with local legends and the story of the contemporary exploits
of the armies and leaders of Rome.   Burning Roman patriotism inspires every effort of Naevius and Ennius.   The Italian
soul lives in their work no less than in that of Plautus.   The
Greek bough picked in Sicily was grafted on to the native
trunk.   The fruit kept the flavour—rather rough, perhaps,
but native—of the soil of Italy.

CHAPTER II

THE NEW SPIRIT AND THE OLD IDEAL. SCIPIO AFRICANUS AND CATO THE CENSOR

THE importance of the first Roman literary attempts lies in the fact that they are not merely an intellectual exercise, but truly express a new conception of the world and of social life. This was the reason for their success. The poets did no more than express in Latin and spread among the mass of the people the ideas with which the more intelligent and daring among the newer generations were already completely imbued. They gave these ideas a wider and more lasting influence. Literature was at once the expression and one of the chief causes of the transformation of ideas.

Greek epic and tragedy, and, after them, the earliest Roman poetry, are the glorification of the hero. Loved or persecuted by the gods, the hero stands half-way between mankind and them. Prometheus defies Jupiter; the ingenuity of Ulysses finally prevails over the hatred of Juno. Above the mass of men, in a fairy world, not bound by the narrow rules of reality, the hero gives a free rein to all human faculties—intelligence, activity, passion. Heroic poetry is the exaltation of human personality; it reveals to the imagination the radiant path of glory.

The example of the heroes inspires well-born souls with noble emulation. Through it, man conceives the sentiment of his own importance and his power. He acquires confidence in himself. Henceforth he will see life as a kind of theatre, in which the superior man must compel the admiration of the mass by his audacity, his breadth of action, the unexpectedness or majesty of his attitude. The greatness of the interests at stake will only excite his daring. He dreams of unprecedented exploits; whether he succeed or fall, heroic renown will be his portion. Ambition becomes a virtue.

138

The individual rises above collective interests ; he no longer acts for his country alone, but for himself as well.

Clearly a conception of this kind is at variance with the old Roman tradition. The old ideal takes no account of personality. Strictly subordinated to the family and the *gens*, the individual only counts in the group to which he belongs ; he does not act or think by himself, but in accordance with the principles or interests of his group. The highest virtue is nameless sacrifice to the laws of the city. Literature lifts the Roman out of the mass. By awaking personal thought, it teaches him to see in himself the man in the citizen. It sets up imagination against material interests, play against strict duty, the hero against the paterfamilias. It creates and develops the personality. The Romans made no mistake ; they rightly gave intellectual culture the name of " the humanities."

I

SCIPIO AFRICANUS

We find the perfect type of the Roman of the new age embodied in Scipio Africanus. The art of Livy may, perhaps, have contributed to an over-emphasis of his heroic features. But our information about the facts of this period is based on evidence which is certain enough for us to be able to accept it as being on the whole true.

We know the scene which marks the beginning of his career. Scipio sprang up, as it were, from the assembled people, radiant with confidence in himself and adorned with all the gifts which the gods bestow on mortals whom they cherish.[1] It was in the darkest days of 212, four years after Cannae. Messengers of misfortune came to the Senate one after the other. Syracuse had just gone over to Hannibal, Tarentum was taken, Italy, hitherto faithful, was revolting, Capua had opened its gates to the enemy. In Spain, Scipio's father and uncle, who had succeeded for years in barring the way to the reinforcements which Carthage tried to send round into Italy, had both been defeated and killed. No one

[1] Livy, xxvi. 18.

dared to sue for the heavy honour of taking their place. The Comitia had been convoked, the people were waiting for the candidates to present themselves, all eyes were turned on the magistrates, who looked at one another. Suddenly P. Cornelius, a young man of about twenty-four, stood up and said that he asked to be chosen to replace his father and uncle. One shout of general approval was an augury of a successful command ; the citizens unanimously entrusted him with the mission in Spain. His eloquence and wisdom quickly disposed of the doubts of the cautious and the uneasy vacillations of the crowd.

All the acts of his life were equally spectacular. On every occasion Scipio did the reassuring thing and spoke the effective word. He knew no obstacles. Laws prescribing the age of candidates, superstitious fears, strict traditions of administration, were no more difficulty to him than adverse circumstances. He was the hero whose personality prevails over things and men.

The almost miraculous character of every one of Scipio's actions impressed the enemy as much as his fellow countrymen. In Spain, his first act was to take by surprise, " by the help of Neptune," the citadel of New Carthage, Hasdrubal's treasury and arsenal.[1] The generosity he showed after his victory at once made him popular with the native chieftains. A rumour went about that there had come to the Romans a young chief " like a god." [2] Certainly he is like some Dioscuros, who guides mariners through the dangers of the sea, whose dazzling apparition on the field of battle decides the day. Moreover, he himself was well aware of this reputation, and was pleased to allow popular imagination to draw a halo of divinity about him. Livy notes that he had genuine talents and also great skill in making the most of them, which he cultivated from his youth up.[3]

" Many of his proposals to the multitude, he said, were inspired by dreams or by some divine power. . . . From the day he assumed the man's toga, he never took any public or private action before he had gone to the Capitol, entered the Sanctuary, and sat there, alone and in secret, for some time. This habit, which he observed all his life, caused some to believe that he was

[1] Livy, xxvi. 45. New Carthage was taken by use of the phenomenon of the tide, which was a prodigy to the Romans. *Neptunum jubebat ducem itineris sequi*, says Livy.
[2] Livy, xxvi. 50.   [3] xxvi. 19.

of divine origin, and revived in Scipio's case the story, which was told of Alexander the Great long before, and was equally absurd, that he was begotten by a huge snake, which was often seen in his mother's bedroom, but slipped out of sight whenever anyone went in. Scipio himself never attacked this legend, and indeed was clever enough to increase its credit by never denying it, nor confirming it."

This searching for attitudes, these conversations with Capitoline Jupiter, and, above all, these legends showing imitation of Alexander, the typical hero, whose example haunted the imagination of all ambitious men from the princes of Macedonia, Syria, and Egypt to Caesar, all this takes one a long way from the simplicity of the Roman leaders of other days.

For Scipio, as later for Caesar, his admirers, at least in non-Roman countries, dreamed of the title of king. He was still Roman enough to spurn the word, but the idea corresponded too well to the image which he conceived of himself and of his position in the city for him absolutely to refuse the homage paid to a king.[1] " For me," he said to the Spaniards, " the title of Imperator, which my soldiers give me, is the highest. . . . If that of king seems greater to you, you may believe, without speaking it, that there is a king's soul in me." A king's soul, for Scipio, was evidently that of an Alexander or an Achilles. His ideal was no longer in old Rome, but in that transfigured humanity which Greece had created.

Moreover, his attitude displeased and disturbed the old Romans. By his nobility of mien no less than by his graciousness and lively intelligence he had been able to charm the Numidian chieftains Syphax and Masinissa, and even his enemy Hasdrubal.[2] But Cato, his Quaestor, sourly complained of his display and arrogance, accusing him of corrupting the ancient discipline. In the Senate old Fabius Cunctator opposed with all his might the young general's proposal to cross into Africa and to terminate the long war of exhaustion by one daring blow, which might be as disastrous as the expedition of Regulus.[3] Instead of Africa, Sicily was assigned to him as his province. It made no difference to him. In Sicily, he prepared his expedition against Africa, landed before Carthage, and so compelled Hannibal to leave Italy. Between the two heroes, victory fell in favour of the Roman.

There is a story that afterwards, at the court of Antiochos,

[1] Livy, xxvii. 19.   [2] Livy, xxviii. 18. 35.   [3] Livy, xxviii. 40 ff.

Scipio met his former adversary, and talked familiarly with him of the virtue and order of excellence of the great captains.[1] The first of all, in Hannibal's opinion, was Alexander, whose phalanx had dispersed innumerable hosts. Next to him came Pyrrhos, a master in the art of choosing and fortifying a position. " And third ? " asked Scipio. " Myself," Hannibal replied. " Where would you have placed yourself if you had defeated me at Zama ? " " Then I should have placed myself before Alexander and before Pyrrhos and before all the others." The anecdote is obviously apocryphal. It is interesting because it shows how the anecdote-writers insisted on presenting Scipio as comparing himself to the Greek heroes. The other pictures of Scipio's life, such as we find in Livy, probably owe as much to the *Annals* of Ennius as to historical truth. In that case they are a literary work which enables us to judge of the trend of men's imagination at the time. But there is nothing to prove that Scipio's conduct was not very often inspired by an imagination keenly susceptible to romantic and literary influences. We must not, even for these early times, underestimate the part played by literary influences in the life and actions of men. At bottom, is it not imagination which determines their career and animates most of their exploits and crimes ?

It was through his too enthusiastic adoption of Greek literature as a rule of life that Scipio in the end found himself in opposition to the majority of his fellow-citizens. The charge of peculation brought against his brother and himself on their return from the expedition in Asia, in 190, was clearly only a pretext.[2] Scipio scorned to defend himself, and in a last display of bravado led the whole people in his train to the Capitol to thank Jupiter for the victory over Carthage of which this day was the anniversary. Nevertheless, he was found guilty ; the authorities did not dare to arrest him, but he ended his life in semi-exile at Liternum, refusing his ashes to his " thankless city."

A hundred years earlier, before the days of Livius, Naevius, and Ennius, Scipio would have been a Roman like the rest, a brave soldier and an energetic magistrate, anxious only to carry out the decisions of the Senate and the people for the greater good of the Republic. Poetry would not have

---

[1] Livy, xxxv. Epit.   [2] Livy, xxxviii. 50 ff., espy. 55. 56.

exalted his personality above the people and the laws.   He would have defeated Hannibal just the same, but without the epic air with which his imagination invested the last years of the war, in Spain and in Africa.   At the end he would have enjoyed the attention of the Senate and the respect of the people, and on his sarcophagus, laid by those of his ancestors in the family tomb, the traditional formula would have been engraved : " Aedile, Censor, Consul, he was among you."

Let us acknowledge, with the strictly orthodox Romans, that the new spirit embodied in Scipio was overthrowing the moral and social traditions of the Republic.   It was this spirit which gave birth, in after years, to men like Sylla and Caesar.   But, on the other hand, the patriarchal tradition of the small Roman city could not live in a great state.   The very victories of Rome passed the death sentence of the *mos majorum.*   The roads of all Italy, and even of the sea, were opening before the Romans.   How could they maintain the family, collected on its estate under the authority of the father ?   Subordination to a hard rule of work and economy and the sacrifice of each to the interests of the group—such were the foundations of the old morality.   The qualities demanded of the citizen by the new position of Rome were the opposite.   A leader needed the initiative and boldness which come from self-confidence and the habit of independence. The size of the task to be accomplished required a wider view of men and things.   Scipio's reply to the accusations of Cato was just : " I owe the Senate an account of results alone ; I do not need such an exact Quaestor."   Even the sentiment of honour had to change ; it must no longer be confined to sacrifice and obedience, but must be shown chiefly in action and creation.   As the city grew, it restored liberty to the individual ; the latter must find his laws in himself.   The old traditions no longer gave them to him. Greek thought might furnish them, and did furnish them to those who could understand it.   Its only fault was that it was too lofty for many.   It was not from excess but from lack of literature that the Roman people was to suffer.   More philosophical wisdom and less material appetite would have spared it the Civil Wars.

II

Cato the Censor

The infatuation of part of the aristocracy and of the city masses for Greece and its literature did not escape strenuous opposition. Attachment to the habits of old times was one of the forms of Roman pride ; excessive devotion to tradition, or rather to a part of tradition, surely represents one of the doctrines of nationalism everywhere. Opposition to the new spirit was incorporated in one man, a man, moreover, who represented a whole class of the Latin population, of which he possessed, in high degree, both the virtues and the defects. This man was Cato. The class which he represented was that of the small country land-owners, hard-working, bent on gain, soldiers of wonderful endurance, coolness, and energy, born fighters, on the public square no less than on the battle-field, with trenchant, incisive minds, sober, too, and shrewd, and passionately attached to their lands, their hearths, and all the memories which the hearth represented for them.

More than any others, these peasants had contributed to the triumph of Rome, a triumph of which they were becoming the victims. Hitherto the harvests of their farms had always held a preponderant place in the economic life of the Republic. But now the fertility of southern Italy and, above all, sea trade threatened their interests. Their great enemies were Sicily, which already supplied Rome with corn and obliged them to fall back on the cultivation of olives and vines, Africa, which might supply oil, Greece, which was to supply wine, and, more than anything, the spirit of adventure and novelty which developed movable wealth and decreased the value of their ancestral estate, preparing for its absorption by the great property. They were the class which was sacrificed and discontented. It was in their name, animated by their spirit and all their bitterness, that Cato set out to fight the new spirit.

Even the outward appearance of Cato and his character made a strong impression on antiquity. The portrait which Plutarch has preserved is legendary, but it is very probable that the main lines are correct. Cato was at once a Latin and a Sabine, having been born at Tusculum, in 234, and brought up on his father's little farm in the Sabina. Constant work, says Plutarch, plain living, and military service, on which he went when still young, gave him a strong and healthy constitution. An ancient epigram gives us his portrait : " With his red hair, great teeth, and grey glittering eyes, even when Porcius is dead Persephone will not have him in Hades."

Πυρρὸν, πανδακέτην, γλαυκόμματον, οὐδὲ θανόντα
Πόρκιον εἰς Ἀΐδην Περσεφόνη δέχεται.[1]

He was and always affected to be a plain, coarse man.

" Ever since he was young, his body was all scarred with honourable wounds got in the war against Hannibal. . . . In a fight, he stood immovable at his post, dealt frightful blows, and showed the enemy a formidable face, while he uttered threats in a terrifying tone of voice, being persuaded, and teaching others, that this play-acting often has more effect on an enemy than the sword you present at him. . . . Later, when he became a leader, he was still a soldier. On the march, he always went on foot, carrying his own arms, followed only by a slave with his provisions. Simple and easily pleased in all his personal requirements, in everything else he was severe and inexorable. He was like Socrates," Plutarch concludes, " of whom Plato said that he was outwardly homely, satyr-like, and outrageous, but was inwardly full of reason and gravity."[2]

But other qualities than his courage and integrity earned him promotion to office. What drew attention to him was the warmth and skill of his eloquence. In the morning he would go from his farm to the neighbouring towns and defend the clients who appealed to him ; then, returning to his fields, he used to work with his slaves for the rest of the day. This activity was quite in accordance with the old Latin tradition. A Roman patrician, his neighbour in the country, named Valerius Flaccus, is said to have advised him to settle in Rome and to take to public affairs. His forensic speeches soon earned him admirers and friends, and, aided by the credit of Valerius, he was able to set foot on the path of honours.[3]

That Cato was a remarkable orator cannot be doubted. The fragments of his speeches which we possess hardly allow us to judge of his eloquence, but Cicero's eulogy of it deserves

[1] Plut., Cato, 1.   [2] Ibid., 10.   [3] Ibid., 4.

K

credence.[1] " Who was ever able to praise more nobly, to condemn with more trenchant energy ? How delicate is his thought, with what ingenious simplicity he sets forth facts and arguments ! " The special feature of his mind seems to have been a kind of satirical humour, expressed in witty sayings, coined like proverbs. Plutarch quotes several examples, probably authentic, which are quite the aphorisms of a bantering peasant, with a quick eye for the ridiculous.[2] Many of them seem to be simply rustic proverbs neatly adapted to the occasion. One day, the Roman people was clamouring insistently and inopportunely for a distribution of corn. Cato, who wanted to dissuade them, began his speech thus : " Citizens, it is hard to talk to a belly which has no ears." Another time, condemning the amount the Romans spent on their tables, he said : " It is not easy to save a city where a fish is worth more than an ox." Being abused by a fool, he retorted : " It is not a fair fight. You like hearing folly and talking it ; I dislike hearing it and am not used to talking it."

No doubt this is not wit of a very subtle order. In many respects it is like what we find in Plautus.[3] Indeed, Cato's speeches are animated by the same caustic native vigour, and, moreover, they are addressed to the same public as comedy. The object is to raise, not a smile, but a hearty laugh, rejoicing the hearers or confounding the opponent. " To raise a laugh," said Cato, " is the business of a good orator." [4]

In his youth Cato had chosen his moral and political ideal. He had found it in the memory of his neighbour in the country, Manius Curius, who had enjoyed three triumphs and remained celebrated for his rustic simplicity. Some time later, in the army or in Rome, he had had the opportunity to set before him as his model Fabius Maximus Cunctator. It was not only on account of his personal temperament, but also in the name of the tradition represented by these great Romans, that he declared war on all fomenters of novelty.

---

[1] *Brutus*, 17. 65.   [2] *Cato*, 11 ff.
[3] The tricks of the two are often the same—alliteration, contrast of sounds, words, and images, and lively repartee. Compare Cato's invective against women, in the thoroughly Catonian speech placed in his mouth by Livy (xxxii. 2), with those of Plautus in the *Menaechmi* (110-17).
[4] Quintil., *Inst. Or.*, vi. 3. 105 ; Jordan, **LXXXVIII**, p. 83.

We have already mentioned his hostility to Scipio Africanus and his attacks on him.[1] Nothing disarmed his tenacious hatred. Twenty years after his first accusations, we still find him as the leader of the campaign which condemned the conqueror of Carthage to exile. Plutarch quotes a ferocious utterance made by him on this occasion, which well shows the bitterness of his coldly violent nature.[2]

"A young man who had obtained the condemnation of an enemy of his father, lately dead, was crossing the Forum some days after the sentence of Scipio. 'That is the funeral sacrifice one should offer to the shades of a father,' said Cato, embracing him. 'Not the blood of lambs and kids should be shed for them, but the tears of their condemned enemies.'"

Cato deliberately refused to understand the changes which the new political situation of Rome imposed on Roman civilization. This was the cause of his efforts, predestined to failure, against Greek luxury and culture. He had made up a character for himself, just as Scipio had done, and he had to maintain its austere reputation. So he was often led to overdo his part, and himself to yield to the vanity which exasperated him in others. Plutarch seriously discusses these exaggerations.[3]

"Having found a Babylonian carpet among the goods left him by a friend, he at once sold it. Of the many country houses he owned, not one was white-washed. When his horse and his slave grew old, they had to be sold. . . . Cato seemed to glory in his lack of feeling; he boasted that he had left in Spain the charger which he had ridden during his Consulship, in order that the Republic should not have to pay for its transport by sea."

"Magnanimity or meanness?" Plutarch wonders. "Vanity," we may reply.

The vanity of the Censor, who thinks himself alone impeccable, has not escaped his biographer.[4]

"He did not allow that a good citizen should receive praise which could not be turned to the public good. Yet he, of all men, praised himself the most; so much so, that when citizens committed errors of conduct he said, 'We must excuse them; they are not Catos.' . . . On the base of the statue which was raised to him in the Temple of Salus he did not have his military exploits or his triumph engraved, but the following inscription: 'In honour of Cato for having, in his Censorship, by salutary ordinances and wise institutions, raised the Roman Republic, which the decay of morals had set on the brink of ruin.'"

[1] Cf. Plut., *Cato*, 5.
[3] *Ibid.*, 6.
[2] *Ibid.*, 22.
[4] *Ibid.*, 28.

However obstinate Cato may have been in his fidelity to the past and his hatred of all novelty, he was not himself ignorant of the Greek literature which he would have excluded from the Republic. He was of too curious a mind, and also too greedy for all useful acquirements, to have failed to be initiated into it in his young days. While Plutarch shows him, according to the traditional story, learning Greek in his old age, he does not hesitate to mention several incidents which definitely contradict this legend.[1]

" When Fabius Maximus recovered Tarentum in 209 B.C., Cato, who was quite young, was serving under him. He was billeted on Nearchos, a Pythagorean philosopher, whom he wished to hear discoursing on philosophy. Nearchos professed the same doctrine as Plato ; he taught that pleasure was the greatest bait for evil, and that the body is the chief plague of the soul. . . . These discourses made Cato love temperance and frugality even more than before."

So there was some Greek influence even at the beginning of Cato's asceticism.

Nor do the lessons of Greek rhetoric seem to have been unconnected with his skill in oratory.

" He benefited somewhat," says Plutarch, " from the study of Thucydides, but much more from that of Demosthenes. . . . At least, his writings are enriched with many maxims and historical allusions taken from the works of the Greeks, and many of his moral sayings are translated from them word for word." [2]

In 191 Cato took part in the expedition to Greece and Asia against Antiochos, and stayed a fairly long time in Athens.

" People say," Plutarch relates,[3] " that a speech which he made in Greek to the Athenian people has been preserved. . . . It is not true ; he spoke to the Athenians through an interpreter, not because he did not know Greek very well, but because he was attached to the customs of his fathers, and scoffed at those who could admire no one but the Greeks."

When, moreover, we study the language of the only surviving work of Cato, *De Agricultura*, we are struck by the number of Greek words which have made their way into the treatise.[4] As a champion of the old Latin tradition, Cato claimed to be summarizing his own experience as a *bonus agricola bonusque colonus*. As a matter of fact, the very idea of writing a τέχνη of agriculture was suggested to him by a

[1] Plut., *Cato*, 4.
[2] *Ibid.*, 3.
[3] *Ibid.*, 18.
[4] Grenier, **LXXX**, p. 80 and n. 2.

Greek model, the Greek translation of an agricultural treatise by the Carthaginian Hanno.

The true note is given us by Cato himself.[1] He knows the Greeks and their literature, but he makes a profession of despising them. He does not dare to forbid absolutely the reading of their works, but he allows only a superficial notion of them. After having, very reluctantly, half-opened the door, he hopes to close it by solemnly cursing all this culture.

> " I shall speak, in the proper place, of those damned Greeks ; I shall say what I saw in Athens, and how it may be good to glance at their literature, but not to go into it deeply. I shall prove how detestable and worthless is their race. Believe me, Marcus, my son, this is an oracular saying: if ever that race comes to pass its literature to us, all is lost."

It was not the cultivation of the intelligence that Cato proscribed, but only what the Greeks of his day had made of it. His attitude at the time of the embassy of Carneades to Rome allows us to see this difference. Here is Plutarch's account : [2]

> " The two philosophers, Carneades, of the Academy, and Diogenes, a Stoic, had hardly arrived when all the young Romans with a taste for letters, having gone to see them, were ravished with admiration for them, and could not have enough of listening to them. Carneades' charm, the force of his eloquence, his reputation, which did not surpass his talent, his advantage in having for an audience the most distinguished and cultured of the Romans, made a great noise in Rome. It was like a violent wind sounding all about the city. Everyone said how a wonderfully learned Greek had come, who charmed and attracted all spirits, and inspired the young men with such a love of knowledge that, forswearing pleasure and all other pursuits, they were seized with enthusiasm for philosophy All the Romans were enchanted with him, and were delighted to see their children applying themselves to the study of Greek literature and eagerly seeking out these excellent men. But Cato was distressed to see this love of letters making its way into Rome ; *he feared that the young Romans, diverting all their emulation and all their enthusiasm to this pursuit, would come to set the glory of speaking well above that of doing well and distinguishing themselves in arms.* . . . He thought that it was necessary, on some specious pretext, to send all these philosophers away from Rome. He went to the Senate and blamed it for leaving these ambassadors so long without an answer. It should take note of their business as soon as possible and come to a decision about it, that the philosophers might go back to their schools and teach the children of the Greeks, and the young Romans might obey only the magistrates and the laws, as they used to do."

[1] Quoted by Pliny, *N.H.*, xxix. 7. 14. Jordan, **LXXXVIII**, p. 77.
[2] *Cato*, 34-5.

In this, Plutarch observes, he was not acting out of personal enmity to Carneades, as some have believed, but out of conscientious objection to philosophy and affected contempt, in which he gloried, of the Muses and Greek teaching.

The elder Cato was animated by a political notion, or rather sense, which was not altogether misguided. All this philosophy, that of Zeno no less than that of the Academy or Epicurus, this predominant and almost exclusive interest in the things of the mind and of art, certainly did represent the mentality of conquered men, resigned to political impotence and inaction. They were, in the true sense of the word, a diversion, no doubt a very estimable diversion, but one which disposed, if not the mind, at least the energy, to indolent acceptance of things as they were. By concentrating the moral forces on the inner life, they diverted them from the effort required to master things and men. For this practical Latin, who never thought without a view to action, and had come out of the bitter struggle, maintained all through his youth for the existence of his country, with an understanding of the urgent necessity of fighting and conquering yet again, Socrates was a babbler and Isocrates a useless person.[1] He scoffed, not without reason, at the disciples who grew old round their master, as if they only meant to exercise their art in the next world. Philosophy, like eloquence, was for him only a means, a means for action, and not an end.

Just as, after absolutely forbidding his son to deal with Greek physicians, he had himself written a medical work, in which he collected the old Latin prescriptions, so, too, he wished to give his fellow-countrymen a literature in which there was no danger, practical literature like the treatise *On Agriculture*, and a history. So little was he the enemy of letters in themselves, that he was one of the protectors of Ennius, whom he took with him to Sardinia in 195. He must have appreciated the poet's genius, and, above all, his burning patriotism. He certainly would have liked and encouraged a purely Roman literature, inspired only by national traditions.

History, for him, was essentially a practical lesson. He wished, we are told, to help his son by transmitting to him the fruit of experience and the traditions of his ancestors.

---

[1] Plut., *Cato*, 36.

History should be as useful to the citizen and statesman as the *De Re Rustica* was to the farmer.   So he wrote the seven books *De Originibus*.

As a historian, Cato had an immediate predecessor in Fabius Pictor, who, about 200 B.C., had written in Latin, in prose.   But Fabius belonged to the Gens Fabia, and his work must have been, before all, a manifestation of that aristocratic pride which Cato pursued everywhere with obstinate hatred.   Even Ennius, in his *Annals*, had had to indulge the genealogical fancies of his protectors.   In reaction, Cato, we are told, made a point of mentioning no proper name, or rather, he only mentioned one, that of one of Pyrrhos's elephants.   Individuals did not exist for him ; he only saw the " Consul " or the " magistrate."   As the title of the work shows, he concerned himself chiefly with the origins of the cities of Italy, dealing with each, it seems, as it came within the orbit of Rome.   He got his information either from the Greek historiographers, especially the Sicilian authors of the Κτίσεις 'Ιταλίας (*Foundations of Italy*), or from poets like Ennius.   Some of the fragments which have come down to us refer to the legend of Aeneas and the Trojan origin. " Plenty of industry and carefulness," was the opinion of Cornelius Nepos, " but no ideas." [1]

The atmosphere in which the Roman people lived at the time of Ennius and Plautus was too much permeated with intellectuality for Cato to be able to dream of altogether proscribing the things of the mind.   He would have liked a purely national literature, which should preserve everything which their ancestors had acquired.   It was Cato who, in the *Origins*, spoke of the poems which, many centuries before his time, used to be sung at banquets by each feaster, in honour of great men.[2]   But the state in which he saw Greece did not seem to him at all an ideal for his own country.   That is why, in his brutal way, he repudiated Greece, itself and its

---

[1] *Cato*, iii. 2. 4.   As far as we can reconstruct the work, it was as follows (Jordan, p. 4) : i. History of the Kings.—ii, iii. Origin of the cities of Italy.—iv. First Punic War.—v. Second Punic War.—vi, vii. Events subsequent to the Praetorship of Servius Galba (161 B.C.).   In the later books Cato was careful to insert some of the speeches he had made, no doubt rewriting them.   Cicero speaks of at least 150 speeches which he had traced and read, but does not say that they were in the *Origins* (*Brutus*, 17. 65).

[2] Cic., *Brut.*, 19. 75.

literature, and stormed against the infatuation of his contemporaries.

Cato lived long enough to see the defeat of all the ideas which he had so stubbornly defended. The new spirit finally prevailed over the old ideal. He himself admitted it in one of his last forensic speeches. " It is hard," he said, " to have to give an account of your life to men of another age than that in which you have lived." [1] Moreover, since he made it a kind of point of honour not to be among the vanquished, we find him himself yielding more and more to the new manners. He had defended Italian agriculture as the only stable base on which the fortune of individuals and of the State could rest ; he condemned trade on a large scale as too risky and traffic in money as shameful.[2] He saw at least the beginning of the ruin of the small Italian property, and he himself, in his old age, came to neglect his fields in order to buy ponds, in which he bred fish, and hot springs, and to organize fullers' workshops. He even practised—through intermediaries, it is true—the most decried of all forms of usury, the marine loan. He went so far as to trade in slaves, buying young boys whom he resold after training them. And he exhorted his son to attempt all these forms of business.[3]

The same must have been the case with his literary tastes. Although he declared that the finest way to grow old was to deal with public affairs to the end, the invasion of office by the younger generation finally gave him leisure. Study, which he had once regarded as matter unworthy to occupy a man's whole activity, must now have seemed to him a worthy ornament of ease. Now, at that time there was no other object of study than Greek literature. He must have devoted himself to it with an ardour which age did not extinguish. This, no doubt, was the origin of the legend of Cato setting himself at the end of his life to learn Greek. In reality, the austere champion of the old Latin spirit had long taken advantage of the achievements of Greek learning.[4]

His concessions to Greece, or rather to Mediterranean life in the form which it had been given by the world born of the

---

[1] Plut., *Cato*, 22.   [2] *R.R.*, 1.   [3] Plut., *Cato*, 33.

[4] In addition to the facts mentioned previously, we know that Cato accepted the chronological system of Eratosthenes in his *Origins*. As general in Greece, in the campaign against Antiochos, he repeated at Thermopylae the manœuvre of the Persians, *remembering the detour they had taken to enter into Greece that way* (Plut., *Cato*, 19).

conquests of Alexander, did not prevent Cato from standing, at the beginning of the IInd century, for the perfect type of the old-time Roman, keen-witted but obstinate, grimly pugnacious, and fundamentally utilitarian. He had all the characteristic qualities, comic gift, sense of justice, and indomitable but wary energy. He also had the defects, brutality, pettiness, pride. Take them all in all, we prefer Scipio, dying in exile, to Cato, trafficking in young slaves and finally marrying his clerk's daughter.[1]

Yet all his ideas have not died with him ; one, at least, is sometimes to be found at this day, namely, that refined culture of the intellect tends to corrupt the purity of morals. But we shall be compelled by illustrious examples to observe that the introduction of Greek thought in Rome did not cause a degeneration but rather an elevation of character.[2] Most of the vices which from now onwards spread in Rome had nothing Greek about them—gluttony, and unbounded greed for honours, power, and money. The illiterate Marius was not morally superior to the dilettante Sylla. If the faults of the Romans did not originally spring from rustic grossness, it is fairer to look for their origin in Asia,[3] as Livy does, rather than in Greece. Really, they were the vices of upstarts, and had nothing to do with literature and philosophy. They were solely the result of a too rapid increase of wealth. Rome was intoxicated with suddenly finding the world and all its gold in her hands. She had plundered in the general chaos, and her ill-gotten gains turned against her. This wealth was not even distributed among the whole of the conquering people. It remained the privilege of a limited class, the Senatorial aristocracy and the Knights, who, after ruining the small Italian land-owners, destroyed themselves by the Civil Wars. We have here a whole series of economic and social phenomena of a material kind, quite unconnected with the intellectual and moral evolution of the Roman spirit. Not Greek thought, but the gold of the looted world, destroyed the ancient virtues and finally the power of Rome.

[1] Plut., *Cato*, 37.   [2] *Infra*, chap. iv : Aemilius Paullus, Scipio Aemilianus.
[3] Livy, xxxix. 6 : " *It was the army of Asia which brought into Rome the beginnings of foreign luxury*," in 190, " beds adorned with bronze, precious carpets, veils and tissues of silk, etc. It was then that singing-girls, harp-players, and tumblers were introduced into banquets, and the meals themselves were prepared with more care and expense ; then the cook, who in old times was the lowest slave in price and in occupation, came into esteem, and what had been a menial service was regarded as an art."

CHAPTER III

CHANGES IN RELIGIOUS SPIRIT

WE may more readily grant that philosophic criticism was calculated to injure the old religious beliefs. But even here we must not exaggerate, for many Romans had advanced beyond primitive conceptions without waiting for Greek thought, making the sacred fowls drink, for example, when they would not eat.[1] On the other hand, we find cultivated men like Aemilius Paullus who continue to be the most scrupulous and convinced augurs. Even more than the philosophies of to-day, those of antiquity left many enigmas to be met by the answers which religion already provided. Reasoning might even serve to justify ancient religious practices. We find Cicero defending divination.

If Greece undermined the credit of the thirty thousand Italian gods found by Varro, who will blame her ? Zeus, especially the wiser Zeus of the philosophers, was infinitely superior to Janus and his crew. Even if he had become an idle and indifferent Zeus, there was no loss either to speculative thought or to morals, about which he had originally troubled himself little enough. In reality, it was not these new speculations which killed the old beliefs ; they died of themselves, because they no longer corresponded to the intellectual and social condition of the people. Having nothing to put in their place, the Romans adopted, rather at random, either philosophical notions or myths and worships from abroad. We may for the moment leave aside Greek philosophic thought, which hardly reached any but the intellectual élite. The very mingled stream which flowed about the public ways came from less lofty and less pure sources.

In it we perceive, first of all, as in the beginnings of literature, Italian influences, which are far more numerous

[1] Val. Max., i. 5. 3-4 ; Cic., *Div.*, i. 16. 29 ; Livy, *Epit.*, 19.

and stronger, and also older, than those which might come from Greece.

I

RELIGIOUS UNREST IN ROME DURING THE SECOND PUNIC WAR

The conquest of Italy attracted to Rome a mob originating from the various regions of the peninsula. Samnites, Etruscans, Umbrians, Campanians came in as prisoners, or as free craftsmen, or as refugees without goods or home, seeking an asylum and a fortune in the new capital. The effect of the second Punic War was to swell this last class beyond all bounds. As soon as Hannibal was removed, the Senate ordered these unfortunates to return to their districts, but probably its decrees were never more than partially carried out. These provincials mingled with the Roman plebs, and there was a constant and prolonged exchange of ideas between them. The effect was first seen in a recrudescence of superstition.

" As the war dragged on," Livy relates,[1] "and successes and failures altered the situation less than the spirits of men, such a religious feeling, and that chiefly from abroad, invaded the city that it seemed that either the gods or the men had suddenly been changed. Not only in secret and within walls were the Roman rites abandoned, but in public, even on the Forum and the Capitol, there was a crowd of women, whose sacrifices and prayers were not after the manner of their ancestors. Sacrificing priests and sooth-sayers obtained a hold on people's minds. Their following was swelled by the swarms of peasants driven into the city by need and fear from fields which were untilled because of the long war and unsafe ; and they made an easy profit from the ignorance of others, plying their trade as if it was author-ized. . . . The Senate entrusted the Praetor of the City with the task of rescuing the people from this superstition. He read the Senatus Consultum in the Assembly, and issued an edict that anyone possessing books of prophecies or prayers or written directions for sacrificing should hand in all such books and writings to himself before the 1st April, and that no one should make sacrifice by a new or foreign rite in any public or sacred place."

The authority of the Senate might put down the more conspicuous of these manifestations, but it had to consider the religious unrest raging in the masses. The credit of the

[1] xxv. 1.

old gods was exhausted ; they had not been powerful enough to protect Italy, their own land, against the foreigner ; the virtue appeared to have gone out of the traditional rites. No doubt, too, the old religion, which was so abstract and so exclusively formal, no longer satisfied the popular feeling and imagination. The inactivity forced upon the people by war, their anxiety in the presence of danger, the mingling of peoples, the echoes of poetry and scraps of philosophy which might even reach the masses, developed among them new preoccupations, like a ferment. Whence does man come, of what essence is he made, what is his destiny ? These questions, natural to a waking intelligence, must have been asked by the Roman people, and the religion of the Pontifices did not answer.

But the refugees from Campania and southern Italy and the Greeks of Sicily spoke of strange gods who suffered like men, and died like men, and like all nature, but to rise again. They were said to have revealed to certain sages the mysteries by which men might ensure their happiness after death and understand the secret of rebirth. The names of Iacchos and Zagreus who reigned in the Thracian mountains, of Demeter and Core adored at Eleusis, were mingled with those of Orpheus and Pythagoras. Those initiated into these mysteries carefully kept to themselves the secret, which only roused curiosity. They were seen meeting to celebrate rites of which the profane could know nothing definite ; they spoke of ineffable purifications and a divine intoxication which exalted the spirit and the senses ; there was something about descent into hell, and death, and resurrection. These people dressed only in white, and abstained from eating everything that had lived, even some plants being forbidden them ; they were the pure, and even after death they allowed none but the pure into their cemeteries. Being imbued with a wisdom greater than human, they seemed to be beyond the assaults of evil. And the women in particular flocked eagerly to them, to have a share in the secret.

This intensification of religious feeling in the people was met by redoubled activity in the administration of the Pontifices. The official heads of religion strove to give satisfaction to the new unrest by the regular methods. At every portent announced to them they consulted the Sibylline

Books.[1] These Greek oracles suggested to them the most varied expiations.   Clearly, the Pontifices called upon all the resources of their experience and imagination.

First, we find them having recourse to old Italic rites. In 217, after the first set-backs of the second Punic War, they caused the Senate to decree a " Sacred Spring." [2] Of the new-born creatures, only the animals were slain ; for the children, it was decided to wait till they reached man's age, when they must leave the city and seek a home elsewhere.

In the next year, after Cannae, the disaster was attributed to the infidelity of two Vestals.[3] The unhappy women were put to death.   The Sibylline Books were again consulted, and Q. Fabius Pictor, the future historian, was sent to Delphi to consult the Oracle.   Meanwhile, the Sibylline Books had suggested an abominable rite ; a Gaulish man and woman and a Greek man and woman were buried alive in the Forum Boarium.   As a rule, in each of the following years, the oracles were content to prescribe the accomplishment of certain ceremonies " by Greek rites," or the adoption of Greek gods, to whom temples were dedicated even within the *pomoerium*.   This was the time of the official adoption into Roman religion of most of the Hellenic deities, who had no doubt long been known, but had still been treated as foreigners.   In 215, for example, a three days' *lectisternium* was held.[4] The statues of the twelve great Greek gods were set, in the Hellenic manner, on six couches ; they were supposed to be offered a banquet, while the people passed in procession before them, bringing their supplications.   So the great games in honour of Apollo were organized, in 212, in the Greek manner, to act as a kind of derivation for the malady of religious innovation from which the spirit of the people was suffering.

" Among the prophetical books which were seized," Livy [5] relates, " the verses of a certain Marcius fell into the hands of the Praetor.   Of the two prophecies of Marcius, the authority of one, which was made public after the event which it correctly foretold, inspired faith in the other, the time for which had not yet come.   In the former, the defeat of Cannae was predicted. . . .   The second was more obscure : ' Romans, if you would drive out the enemy and the plague which comes from far countries, dedicate games to Apollo.   When the people has contributed publicly, let each give

[1] Livy, xxi. 62.   [2] Livy, xxii. 10.
[3] Livy, xxii. 57.   [4] Livy, xxii. 10.   [5] xxv. 12.

privately. Let the Decemvirs sacrifice by the Greek rite. If you do these things rightly, you will rejoice always, and it will be better with you ; for that god will destroy your enemies who browse peacefully in your fields.' ''

They took a whole day, Livy goes on, trying to understand this prediction. Next day, the Decemvirs were instructed by Senatus Consultum to refer to the Sibylline Books. On their report, the Senate decreed the exact accomplishment of the orders of the prophecy. The Decemvirs had, therefore, to sacrifice by the Greek rites ; they had to offer an ox and two white kids to Apollo and a heifer to Latona ; the horns of all these victims were to be gilded. At the opening of the Games, in the Circus Maximus, the Praetor caused it to be announced that while they lasted everyone should bring his offerings to Apollo. The people went to the Games crowned with flowers ; the matrons, with their hair unbound, made supplications ; all the doors of the houses were opened and meals were taken outside ; and the day was celebrated with ceremonies of all kinds. Greek rites and old magical practices like the opening of the doors were combined to give Roman worship an entirely new aspect.

II

Oriental Cults. The Great Mother of the Gods of Pessinus

All these new devotions, whether of Italic or Greek origin, did not succeed in removing the danger. Seven years later, in 205, the enemy were still browsing in the fields of Italy. There were more and more portents.[1] Rome was more than ever ridden by superstitious fears. When the Sibylline Books were again consulted, the following oracle was found : " When a foreign enemy brings war into the land of Italy, he can be driven out and vanquished if the Idaean Mother is brought from Pessinus to Rome." It was no longer to the Greek gods that the Romans appealed, but to those of Asia.

The Great Mother of Pessinus was the old chthonian deity

[1] Livy, xxvi. 19 ; xxvii. 28 ; xxviii. 11.

adored since prehistoric times in Crete and Asia Minor.[1]
Rhea, Cubebe, Cybele were her names. The mother of all
the gods and the principle of all life—divine, human, animal,
and even vegetable—she reigned on the high wooded plateaus,
over the beasts, over the springs and ponds, in caves under
the earth, and in tombs. Her earliest images were cut in
the rock, her human form hardly emerging from the stone.
She was associated with a young light-god, Attis, her lover.
She was a jealous goddess, demanding single loyalty from her
worshippers. He who resisted her went mad. In a frenzy
of mystic passion, Attis emasculated himself at the foot of a
pine-tree, and died of the wound. The Goddess Mother of
Ida was the national goddess of Phrygia ; the city of Pessinus
was her principal sanctuary and her special domain.

" On the Anatolian plateau," Monsieur F. Cumont writes,[2]
" the climate is extreme. The winter is hard, long, and icy ;
the spring rains bring a sudden efflorescence of vegetation,
soon burned up by the heat of summer. The abrupt contrasts
of nature, alternately bountiful and barren, radiant and
gloomy, inspire excesses of joy and sadness unknown in more
temperate regions. The Phrygians wept in despair over the
long agony and death of vegetation, and then, when the green
reappeared in March, they abandoned themselves to all the
exaltation of tumultuous joy. The violence of these opposite
feelings was expressed in savage rites. After the days of
mourning, in which the death of Attis was bewailed, an outburst of rejoicing celebrated his resurrection, that is, the
rebirth of nature. Amid yells and the din of tambourines
and cymbals, with the flutes skirling over all, there were wild
flights over the mountain, dishevelled dancings round the
altars, flagellations and mutilations. The blood of men
mingled with that of the victims. The priests, the ' Galli '
who had sacrificed their manhood to the goddess, formed a
sacred order, which had the gift of prophecy. Their orgiastic
rites produced the ecstasy which purifies the present life
and ensures a blessed existence after death." This was the
cult which, to drive out Hannibal, the Senate brought into
Rome.

The Great Goddess of Ida landed in Italy at the beginning
of April, 204, in the form of a black stone. She was received

---

[1] Graillot, **LXXIX** ; Cumont, **LV**, pp. 57 ff.   [2] **LV**, p. 62.

by the man whom the Senate had judged the most holy of all the Romans, P. Scipio Nasica, the cousin of the future Africanus, and by a matron of the old aristocratic family of the Claudii at the head of all the Roman ladies. Until she should have her own sanctuary, she was installed in the Temple of Victory on the Palatine, with all her clergy of castrated Galli in their long, gorgeous robes, prophets, beggars, bearers of sacred images of all kinds, and players of tambourines and screaming instruments. Like the games of the Greek type, the Ludi Megalenses were founded, to commemorate yearly the introduction of this exotic cult into the city.[1]

This religion of mysticism and exaltation was so contrary to the principles of Roman religion that the Pontifices soon imposed strict barriers on its manifestations. Citizens were forbidden to take part in it, and, of course, to enter its priesthood. It seems, too, that the sound sense of the people was not long in conceiving the most profound contempt, if not for the goddess, at any rate for her ministers—tambourine-bangers, not worth a nut-shell, as Plautus calls them.[2] When the danger was over, the goddess of Ida found herself relegated to her sanctuary. But the fact remains that, to give satisfaction to the religious emotion which had come over the masses, the Senate had introduced into Rome one of the grossest of all the orgiastic cults which raged in the East.

III

THE AFFAIR OF THE BACCHANALIA AND THE PONTIFICAL REACTION

At the price of all these concessions to the new spirit, the Pontifices had managed to safeguard their authority over religion. The innovations which they admitted took their place in official worship. The rest remained superstition. The great gods of Olympus, established in Rome, had relegated the innumerable *numina* of primitive times to the shade. In many cases they were assimilated to some ancient deity, to whom they gave their personality. The Italic Saturn, for example, was certainly blended with Cronos, and

---

[1] Graillot, **LXXIX**, pp. 25 ff., espy. 78. [2] *Truculentus*, 610.

Venus, apparently an ancient garden-goddess, had become Aphrodite. Sacrifices and rites in the Greek manner were superimposed on the native rites, and must often have superseded them.[1] Under the influence of poetry, in particular, Roman religion henceforward appeared as a younger sister of Greek religion. But it was as strictly regulated as before, and was still as hostile to sentimental exaltation.

In the people, however, the religious ferment of which the second Punic War had sown the seeds continued to develop its effects. In particular, we find a trace of it in the story, which Livy relates at length, of the scandal caused by the mysteries of Bacchus. The severity with which it was put down shows the energy with which the Pontifices exerted their authority when it was a matter of safeguarding the principles of the national religion.

The incident occurred in 186 B.C., fifteen years after Zama. Livy seems to regard the worship of Bacchus as having been introduced into Rome quite recently.[2] " A low-born Greek," he says, " came first to Etruria. . . . The corruption of this evil spread from Etruria to Rome as by contagion." In reality, the Bacchic mysteries seem to have spread, as early as the Vth century at least, all over southern Italy, where they were more or less confused with Orphism. They must have penetrated to Etruria at the same time, if it is true that we should recognize male and female Bacchants in a number of Etruscan tomb-paintings. Under whatever name he was known, Dionysos, Iacchos, Zagreus, Bacchus, and whatever his origin may have been, this god was, like Attis, a god of nature, dying and reborn.[3] His worship had once inspired Euripides to one of the most poetic and disturbing of his tragedies, the *Bacchae*. It united in the enthusiasm of life the sense of nature and the sense of the infinite. It was a hymn to beauty and joy, and a challenge to death. It is all to the honour of the Romans that they did not remain insensible to the disturbing, fanciful charm of the young Dionysos conducting his *thiasos* amid dancing Maenads and boisterous satyrs. The success and the spread of the mysteries simply shows that the old religious tradition was no longer sufficient

---

[1] C. Jullian, " La Religion romaine deux siècles avant notre ère," **Xa,** pp. 311-42 ; Warde Fowler, **CLXVII,** pp. 314 ff. ; Wissowa, **CLXXI,** pp. 60 ff.
[2] xxxix. 8-9.   [3] Loisy, **CII,** pp. 25 ff.

L

for the Roman spirit. The passionate thought which was awaking drew it, in spite of its prudence, to the exaltations of mysticism.

The severity with which Livy treats the followers of Bacchus is only an echo of the Pontifical tradition by which all Roman history-writing is inspired. The accusations which he repeats are only the commonplace, cruel calumnies which every new religion has provoked among those who do not know it.[1] Drunkenness and licence, it was said, were the means by which this cult attracted adherents; wantonness, perjury, and murder were its most usual effects. Nevertheless, so great was its success that over seven thousand persons, men and women, were implicated in the prosecution, which was still going on five years later.[2] The only conclusion to be drawn from these indications is that the Roman people had taken kindly to a teaching which had for centuries been so widespread in the rest of Italy and the Mediterranean world. The religious intoxication of orgiastic worship was not necessarily corruption. One should not confuse the symbol with the real thing, the rite with the act which it simulates.

The cult was put down with astonishing ferocity. The Consul Posthumius, entrusted with the inquiry, made an alarming report to the Senate,[3] and obtained a decree of prohibition of which Livy gives a summary and the full text was found in Bruttium in the XVIIth century, engraved on a bronze tablet.[4] It is clear that the whole cult was forbidden, and not merely secret meetings for its celebration. The prohibition was extended to the whole of Italy, to every citizen, to every person enjoying Latin rights, and to all allies; in other words, to all over whom the Senate had authority.

"There was a panic in Rome and all over Italy. . . . Numbers were arrested. Some of the initiates, both men and women, killed themselves. Those who pleaded guilty were executed, and the rest were kept in prison. Those slain were more than those imprisoned. The women were handed over to their relations or to those under whose authority they were, for private punishment.[5]

"'Nothing,' the Consul Posthumius declared, 'is of more deceptive appearance than a bad religion. How often our fathers gave the magistrates the task of forbidding foreign rites and all forms of sacrifice other than the

[1] Reinach, **CXXXVII**, iii, pp. 266 ff. [2] Livy, xl. 19.
[3] Livy, xxxix. 14. [4] **LI**, i, no. 196. [5] Livy, xxxix. 17-18.

Roman way ! For they wisely held that nothing is more destructive to religion than sacrifice by foreign ceremonies.' " [1]

The Senatus Consultum regarding the Bacchanalia was a very definite measure of reaction, religious as well as political.

Yet another episode, dating from the same period, may be compared to the attention paid by the Pontifices during the Punic War, in 212, to the prophecies of Marcius.   It was said that in 181 there were discovered, at the foot of the Janiculum, two stone coffins bearing Greek and Latin inscriptions to the effect that one contained the body of Numa Pompilius, son of Pompo, King of the Romans, and the other the books of Numa.[2]   The sarcophagus of Numa was empty ; the other contained seven books in Latin treating of Pontifical law and seven others in Greek on moral philosophy.   It was a vulgar fraud, says Livy, based on the tradition which made Numa a pupil of Pythagoras.   It was evidently an attempt to introduce, under the cloak of Numa, ideas or rites emanating from the Pythagorean sects.   The Praetor did not hesitate ; he declared that the books must be neither read nor kept, and the Senate had them burned by the executioner on the Forum.   They did not want any more Sibylline books.

The Senate, through the Pontifices, wished to keep control of religious matters.   It could conceive of no other religion than the official cults.   These cults might be broadened, but by the Senate.   They could admit any gods, as circumstances required, but on certain conditions.   The first was that they should receive only public worship.   Like other ceremonies, those of religion must have their regulations, laid down by a college, and responsible officials to preside over them.   Religion did not admit of secret worship or personal feeling.   Mysticism, being fundamentally individual, eluded the control of the authorities by its very nature and by the secrecy in which it was wrapped up.   This was the reason of the invincible distrust which it inspired.

In spite of the Senate, new ideas crept into religion, and chiefly through literature.   Tragedy certainly contributed to the introduction of the Greek gods.   Comedy, more popular, must have had still more influence, but in another domain ; it established a connexion, hitherto non-existent, between the gods and morality.   The prologue of Plautus's *Rudens*

[1] Livy, xxxix. 16.   [2] Livy, xl. 29.

appears characteristic in this respect. Jupiter becomes the judge and protector of virtue.

" He concerns himself with the actions of men, their habits, the faithfulness with which they do their duty, the use each makes of his wealth. *Day by day, messengers faithfully bring him the names of those who seek evil*, of the wicked men who try to win a law-suit by a false oath, who obtain from the judge that to which they have no right. And Jupiter rejudges the case ; on the guilty he inflicts a punishment greater than their gain. *Of honest folk, on the other hand, he keeps a separate list.*"

And here, in the same prologue, is a still greater novelty, overthrowing the old religious conceptions :

" Doubtless the wicked think to conciliate Jupiter by gifts, by sacrifices. Well, they waste their time and their money. For no prayer from the lips of a perjurer is accepted by Jupiter. When the dutiful man supplicates the gods, he has better success than the guilty man in obtaining their favour."

This seems to be, in terms of the common religion, the distinction which the mystic religions make between the pure and the profane. But here it is a question of moral purity and virtue.[1]

Such ideas no doubt come from the Greek comedy which Plautus used as a model. Among the very various elements which were mingled in the Roman religion of the IInd century before our era, those introduced by literature were not the least potent for the future.

[1] In the metrical inscription from Serapeion A at Delos, M. Roussel notes two lines which indicate that Serapis and Isis especially protect good people (33-4) : " Gods of salvation, you watch unceasingly over the good who have only pure thoughts in their mind." So, too, in Euripides, the Dioscuri declare that on the sea they only help the good (*Electra*, 1350 ff.). Roussel, **CXLI**, pp. 77, 293.

THE CIRCLE OF SCIPIO AEMILIANUS. TERENCE AND LUCILIUS

WHEN, at the beginning of the IInd century before our era, the Romans landed in Greece, their state of mind was rather like that of the young men who later, at the end of the Republic and the beginning of the Empire, set out, when they had finished their studies, to see at last for themselves the places of which they had been told so much. So their feelings towards Greece show, at any rate at first, the warmth of youthful enthusiasm. This age, which was that of Ennius and Plautus, was for the Romans a period of burning phil-Hellenism, which we have every reason to believe sincere. The proclamation of the independence of Greece in 196 is an evidence of it.[1]

But the Greece whose acquaintance the Romans made was no longer the Greece of the poets, nor even of the orators. The political relations which had begun in such an idyllic way soon degenerated into displays of brutality like the ravaging of Epeiros by Aemilius Paullus in 168 [2] and the sack of Corinth by Mummius in 146. In Athens, in her decline, serious poetry was silent ; eloquence had sunk to rhetoric ; philosophy drowned all other voices with the din of argument. Some, like Cato, saw in all this nothing but ridiculous hair-splitting. Others, less narrow-minded, were keenly struck by the intellectual profit which they might draw from it. Leaving metaphysics alone, they applied themselves to the theories which treated of the practical conduct of life. Morals had always had a strong attraction for the Roman mind. The lessons of the philosophers bore

---

[1] For the history of the relations between Rome and Greece before the conquest, see Holleaux, **LXXXIV**. For the conquest itself, see Colin, **XLVI**.
[2] Plut., *Aem. Paul.*, 32.

their fruit. The idealism of the previous period was succeeded in Rome by psychological observation and moral discussion.

Moreover, the severest of the Romans were not insensible to the charm of the intellectual culture and arts of Greece. Aemilius Paullus (227-158), after his victory at Pydna (168), took advantage of his command, Plutarch tells us, to visit the Greek lands and their cities and sanctuaries.[1] Of all the treasures which fell into his hands on the defeat of Perseus, he would keep nothing for himself but the king's library. Of the Athenians he demanded two things—their best artists, to paint the pictures which should present the incidents of his campaign on the day of his triumph, and their best philosophers, to complete the education of his children.

For his sons, Plutarch adds, he cherished an extremely tender affection.[2] At first he had taught them himself, following the old national tradition, as Cato had taught his son. " But he took even greater care that they should be formed by Greek education. He always kept with them, not only grammarians, sophists, and rhetoricians, but painters, and even men to manage their horses and hounds and to instruct them in hunting."

Such was the upbringing of the son of Aemilius Paullus, Scipio Aemilianus (185-129), who was adopted into the family of his uncle Scipio Africanus. This education, which made him one of the most cultured men of his time, had not prevented him from conceiving in his youth a strong attachment for Cato.[3] His friend Laelius, a son of the most faithful comrade of the first Africanus, was not less versed than he in Greek letters, and was even said to be of more brilliant intellect. While Scipio chiefly admired Xenophon, Laelius preferred the more subtle philosophy of the Greeks of his own time. In 155 he assiduously attended the discourses of the Stoic Diogenes. Somewhat later, he attached himself to Panaetios, likewise a Stoic, but of the broader kind, taking what was good from the greatest minds of all schools, especially Plato and Aristotle. It was in his intimate converse with Scipio and Laelius that Panaetios created the tradition of Roman philosophy, as we find it expounded by Cicero, entirely eclectical, standing half-way between the fundamental

---

[1] Plut., *Aem. Paul.*, 30.   [2] *Ibid.*, 7.   [3] Cic., *Rep.*, ii. 1. 1.

scepticism of the New Academy and the absolute doctrines of the Porch.

History, too, in the person of Polybius, found a welcome in the circle of Scipio Aemilianus. Twenty or twenty-five years older than the two young Romans, Polybius long stood to them as a kind of fatherly tutor.[1] In the years following 190 he had taken part, by the side of Philopoemen, in the last efforts of the Greeks to safeguard the liberty which the Romans had granted them. In 169 he was Hipparch of the Achaean League. It was in this capacity that the Romans claimed him as a hostage after the victory of Aemilius Paullus over Perseus. The loan of books led to long talks with the son of the Roman general. While the other hostages were interned in Italian municipia, Polybius was allowed to reside in Rome. In 150 he obtained permission to return to Greece. But Rome was henceforward a second country for him. He wrote its history. He often came back there. We find him at Scipio's side at the taking of Carthage in 146 ; and he even seems to have accompanied him to Numantia in 133.[2] " There was, so to speak," M. Croiset observes, " a pre-established harmony between the vigorous mind of Polybius and this new world. Amid all the intellectual gatherings of frivolous, chattering people, he was serious, practical, capable of action and reflection ; there was a touch of the Roman in him." Perhaps Polybius gained as much from Scipio and Rome as he gave them.

In this house of Scipio, where all the Roman aristocracy met, the two best poets of the day, Terence and Lucilius, were received on familiar terms. For this society they wrote ; at least it directed the tendency of their thought.

I

TERENCE (C. 192-159)

Terence was only a freedman, once a slave of the Senator Terentius Lucanus. The surname of Afer which he bore evidently referred to his origin, whether he was bought in

---

[1] Croiset, LIV, v, pp. 262 ff.
[2] Polybius outlived Scipio Aemilianus, who died in 129 at the age of fifty-six. He himself only died in 125, aged over eighty, of a fall from his horse.

Africa or was the son of one of the prisoners who must have come into Rome on the fall of Carthage in 204.[1] His literary activity commenced with the *Andrian* and the *Eunuch* in 166, a year or two after Scipio's return to Rome with Polybius. His career was short. He was of a delicate constitution, and died about 159 on a voyage to Greece. He had written six comedies, which we possess.[2]

He was accused of not being the author—or, at least, the sole author—of his works. A commentator has preserved this epigram :—

"The plays which are called yours, Terence, whose are they? Surely someone who gave laws to the peoples, someone crowned with honours, wrote those plays!"[3]

Some said Scipio, others suspected rather Laelius. Suetonius tells a story to the effect that Laelius, having asked his wife not to interrupt him because he felt in a mood for writing, then read her a passage which he said he had just composed, which appears in the *Heautontimorumenos*. Terence himself twice refers, in his prologues, to these accusations.[4] He does not formally deny them. It was difficult for him to make too definite a public denial of allegations which, true or false, were flattering to his protectors. "You call it an accusation," he replies. "I think it praise. I am proud of pleasing these men whom you all love." But the dispute is quite unimportant. We may take it that when Terence was writing these comedies they must have been discussed in the circle of Scipio ; an idea, a line, a retort might be contributed by Scipio or Laelius or one of their friends. In any case, the general tone was in accordance with their taste. The spirit of this circle of distinguished young men is expressed by the plays of Terence.

In his plays there is no mistaking the preponderant influence of the moral tendency which, from Greek philosophy, had spread to all the literature of this period. The comedies of Terence are, above all, studies of sentiments and characters. They belong to the psychological theatre. That is why they

---

[1] For details see Plessis, **CXXXIII,** pp. 71-96.
[2] *Andrian, Eunuch, Heautontimorumenos, Adelphi, Hecyra, Phormio.*
[3] *Tuae, Terenti, quae vocantur fabulae,* | *Cujae sunt ?   Non has jura qui populis dabat* | *Summo ille honore affectus fecit fabulas ?*
[4] *Heautontimorumenos, Adelphi.*

were so much appreciated throughout the classical age in France, and generally preferred to those of Plautus, which are much more living and infinitely more comic.

Yet Terence imitates exactly the same models as Plautus. He contaminates them, of course ; that is, he transfers episodes or characters from one play to another.[1] Plautus, on the contrary, boasted of translating exactly : *Plautus vortit barbare.* As a fact, both treat their models with equal freedom, each according to his temperament ; Plautus takes chiefly the fun and the amusing situations, Terence the sentiment and the psychological subtleties. All these different elements were to be found in the Greek New Comedy ; each of the Latin poets develops and strengthens that side which he thinks his public will like. Plautus brings into comedy even the traditional conventions of the *Atellana* and the very old native farce ; Terence adds the subtleties of a delicate, introspective spirit which analyses its own reactions to circumstances. His work truly marks the beginning in Rome of the moral literature, born of the " Know thyself " of Socrates, which studies man and life.

The recent discovery in Egypt by Monsieur G. Lefebvre of a papyrus containing considerable fragments of Menander enables us to form a clearer idea than we had before of the New Comedy by which Latin comedy was inspired, and of the liberties which the imitators took with it. The least incomplete of the four comedies discovered was one of the most celebrated which Menander wrote, the *Arbitrants.*[2] The subject is exactly that of the *Hecyra* of Terence. But a very close comparison cannot be drawn between the two plays, because the *Hecyra* is copied, not directly from Menander's comedy, but from an imitation of Menander by a second-rate author, Apollodoros of Carystos. The characters are not the same, and no scene corresponds exactly ; the analogy does not go beyond the general idea.

In the *Arbitrants*, the wedded life of a young couple, Charisios and Pamphile, tenderly attached to one another, has been destroyed by the premature birth of a child, the result of the violence done to the young woman by an un-

---

[1] For contamination, see L. Havet, **XX**, 1923.
[2] Translated into French by M. Croiset, **VII**, Oct. and Dec. 1907, and into English by F. G. Allinson (Loeb Class Libr.). Cf. Legrand, **XXI**, xx (1907), pp. 233-325 ; xxi (1908), pp. 1-33.

known man before her marriage. The child has been exposed. Charisios in his rage has taken a dancing-girl, with whom he tries to forget his grief. The child has been picked up by peasants. The chance award of Smicrines, the father-in-law, whom they happen to meet, puts into their hands a sign of identity which the mother has given to the unfortunate baby, a ring taken by her from the man who violated her. This ring comes into the possession of Charisios's dancing-girl. After various complications, Charisios recognizes the ring, and therefore the child, as his own. Husband and wife are reconciled, and the dancing-girl and her fellow-slave obtain the freedom they desire.

In the fragments which we possess, the interest is concentrated on the entrance on the scene of the peasant family and the pleading of the charcoal-burner against the herdsman in order to obtain the objects found with the child. As the title shows, this was the central point of the plot ; the chief scene was a kind of parody of the lawsuits in which the clever speakers of Athens displayed the ingenuity of their dialectic. There is a mixture of feeling, of a trifling kind, and impudence in the character of the little dancing-girl, Habrotonon, who is surprised at the conduct of Charisios, who has bought her but cannot be induced to love her. Her dream is to obtain her freedom through love, and, to this end, she devises simple ruses with the slave Onesimos. The comic element is supplied by the untimely outbursts of rage of the father-in-law Smicrines, who, without in the least understanding what is going on, fusses round the young couple in order to save the dowry. In spite of the lacunae, we can see what must have made the charm and the success of Menander—the variety and the fancy of the action, which carries the spectator with it and presents to him, in a series of entertaining pictures, a comic rendering of family life.

The argument of the *Hecyra* is more confused and much less skilfully set forth, either because the author followed by Terence was less dexterous than Menander, or because the process of contamination has overloaded and hampered the development of the plot. We again find the young couple, who have quarrelled in their own despite, but in even more improbable circumstances than in the Greek comedy. Pamphilus, who has long had an affair with the courtesan Bacchis, has allowed himself to be married to Philumena. But since his marriage he has gradually tired of his mistress, and then he has gone on a journey. He returns head-over-ears in love with his young wife. Like Pamphile in the Greek play, Philumena was violated by an unknown man some time before her marriage. Finding herself with child, she has, during the absence of her husband, taken refuge with her mother. Her father-in-law puts her flight down to the influence of his wife, whom he upbraids furiously. Pamphilus arrives just in time to surprise the secret of his wife's delivery. In despair, he renounces the married happiness which he was expecting and demands a divorce. The two fathers are unanimous in ascribing this decision to the young man's continued attachment for the courtesan Bacchis. As in the play of the younger Dumas, the father implores his son's mistress to retire. He easily obtains this renunciation, and sends her to reassure Philumena. On Bacchis's finger the young woman recognizes her ring, which had been taken from her by the unknown man who violated her. Bacchis had been given it by Pamphilus. All is explained, and the young pair are reconciled. " Applaud."

The play takes its name from the scene in which Philumena's father-in-law storms at her unhappy, innocent mother-in-law, whom he blames for the quarrel of the young people.

"Yes, you are all alike! Your one object is to see your sons married, and married to the girls you choose. You get them married ; and your one object is to see them drive their wives from the house !"

The scene is fairly entertaining, though commonplace. It is a device for amusing the audience. The mother-in-law is brought in, as it were, as a comic interlude. The real subject, which Terence takes an interest in treating, is the character of Pamphilus.

It is true that the hero only appears in the third act. But from the very first line, according to a classical practice, we hear of nothing but him and his sentiments. His mistress, his slave, his father, his mother, and his wife's father and mother talk about him all the time. When, after this abundant introduction, he comes on in person, he proceeds to confide his sentiments to his slave.

" Do not try to console me. Is there anyone, anywhere in the world, so unhappy as I ? Before I married, my heart was given to another. I need not remind you—everybody knows how I have suffered. Yet I did not dare to refuse the woman whom my father threw into my arms. This trouble is hardly past, and my heart, breaking loose from the bonds in which it was tied, is beginning to turn towards my wife, when a new trouble arises to divide us. This time I have to find either my mother or my wife guilty—one of them, certainly. In either case, what is before me but still more suffering ? As for my mother, I must overlook her sins—filial duty orders it. But my wife—what do I not owe to her ? In the past she has shown such patience towards me ; she has never spoken a word of all my insults . . . .," etc.

He is in this frame of mind when he surprises his wife at the moment of giving birth to a child. Again he analyses his emotion in a long monologue. Then we have the young man's devices to conceal the fact from his slave, to whom he has already said only too much, and his struggles against the self-sacrifice of his parents, who, for the peace of the young household, wish to retire into the country, and against his father-in-law, who wants to make him acknowledge the child. The whole play is simply an exhibition of the difficulties in which a weak young man, full of the most excellent sentiments, finds himself, between a mistress, a wife, a bastard, a tactless father-in-law, an indiscreet slave, and too well-meaning parents. The only true subject of the different episodes is the psychology of Pamphilus.

Dramatic literature comprises, in substance, two distinct elements. One appeals to the eyes and the imagination ; it is the spectacle of a world or a time which takes the spectator out of his everyday thoughts, and the animation of characters who act, grow excited, laugh, suffer, worry, and plot through episodes which are more violent or more comic or on a larger scale than the circumstances of common life. The other element, which interests rather the reflective capacity, brings the spectator back to himself and reality ; it asks him to recognize his own acts, thoughts, and feelings in the characters which are presented to him. It is chiefly the former element which Plautus develops. In Terence, on the other hand, it is only an accessory, affording an opportunity and means of bringing into play sentiments the analysis of which constitutes the main interest of the comedy.

Terence, Scipio, Laelius, and their friends were young men. They were less than twenty-five years old. Polybius, who was forty, and had taken part in the public life of his country twenty years before, was like a patriarch among them. What especially interested this circle was the character of the young man as a type, his sentiments, his passions, his education, his attitude towards paternal authority, the effect of a father's severity or indulgence on his character. These were the problems which they discussed. In Greek comedy they looked for examples and lessons. Greek philosophy, too, dealt abundantly with characters and passions, analysing, arguing, and drawing moral conclusions from its observations. Terence and his friends made these things the object of their reflections. If in Terence's plays the characters of the young men appear more living than the rest, it is because they are animated by the personal experience of the author and his friends. In these plays we may seek, not their portraits, but only an echo of their interests and ideas.

One problem seems to have been especially discussed, both in the circle of Scipio, and, no doubt, in the Rome of his day. It was, what attitude a father should adopt towards his son. In the *Heautontimorumenos*, Menedemus has been strict, as an old Roman of Cato's school would have been; he bitterly repents of it, and henceforward shows himself disposed to extreme indulgence. His neighbour Chremes steps in and recalls him to a sense of proportion, wisely counselling moderation. The theme is resumed and treated more fully and clearly in the *Adelphi*. Demea is a curmudgeon, and he makes his son a hypocrite. Micio forgives his adopted son everything, and the spoilt child abuses his indulgence. Micio is an egoist at bottom, and in the end it is he who is fooled. Evidently they believed in the happy mean at Scipio's.[1] But Terence does not maintain a thesis— he analyses and describes. Between the old severity and excessive modern laxity he adopts a tone, tempered with eclecticism, which must have been that of men like Panaetios.

It would be idle to look in his plays for a picture of specifically Roman manners. Neither the young men nor the other characters are Romans. Are they even the Greeks of the day? It would be rash to say so. We see no stroke of

[1] Moreover, this was the attitude adopted by Scipio in politics towards the end of his life, between the demagogic Gracchi and the reactionary obstinacy of the aristocracy.

realism in them. They are the young man or the father of all times and all countries. Guided by a philosophy which only cares for the " general," the author's observation leads to an analysis which disengages from all its particular characters a kind of abstraction stamped with universal truth. What we find in Terence, is, as in French classical literature, the ideal man, or rather characters, studied independently of all circumstances of time and place.

We must add that these persons are almost all fundamentally virtuous, or at least imbued with the most virtuous intentions. Even the rascalities of the slaves are inspired solely by absolute devotion to their young masters, and the courtesans reputed to be the most dangerous yield enthusiastically to the general tendency to generosity. The tone is often rather mawkishly sentimental. The shadows are lightly painted in this picture of life. The plays of Terence breathe a pleasant idealism. Was this Terence's natural disposition, or did Scipio and his friends, happy and favoured by fortune, wish in their youthful wisdom to see only the tender, affecting side of life ?

One cannot be surprised that these comedies, whatever their merit—and just because of their merit—enjoyed only a middling success with the general Roman public. The author, in his prologues, ascribes his failure to unlucky circumstances—the competition of a rope-walker, the announcement of a famous boxer or of gladiatorial combats. We can well understand that the public which applauded Plautus or his imitators was bored listening to Terence. The dialogue is all in fine shades of meaning, and lacks force and effectiveness. Subtleties of delicate psychology should be read, when they will delight an educated observer of the human heart. The crude tricks, destitute of all verisimilitude, of which Terence accuses his rivals, were much more likely to please the audience.[1]

The work of the friend of Laelius and Scipio was too devoid of artifice, too pure and cold in matter, to amuse the people. Abstract thought and the cultured exercise of the

---

[1] *Phormio*, Prologue : " The ill-natured old poet goes off repeating that everything that Terence has yet given to the theatre is as poor in invention as in style. It is true ; you find nothing in him like the scene in which a bright young fellow, subject to hallucinations, thinks he sees a deer fleeing, with the pack after her, and the poor thing weeps, and prays for succour."

intellect necessarily remained the appanage of a select few. In the poets of the preceding generation, the patriotism of the epic, the dramatic nature of the tragic legends, all that sprang from the imagination or from feeling, were naturally within the grasp of all. The Homeric and classical Greece of Naevius and Ennius was destined to greater popularity than the Greece of the Porch and of Polybius. From now we find in the formation of the Roman intellect the closed, aristocratic character which excludes the masses. The humanities become the privilege of a small circle of initiates. Literature moves away from the people.

Terence would not understand or allow this divorce. What pleased Scipio must please the people. He would be a pure artist, and yet he asked the crowd for its applause. " Encourage by your attention and kind silence," he never ceases to repeat, " those who truly cultivate the art of the Muses." The Muses whom he worshipped were not divinities of the market-place and the show-booth. They were the learned goddesses of a thoughtful, cultivated society, altogether cut off, by constant intercourse with Greek literature, from the crowd on the theatre benches. The Muses of Terence had no charm but for an élite.

II

Lucilius (185-103)

About ten years younger than Terence, Lucilius must have succeeded him in the intimacy of Scipio and Laelius.[1] Horace refers to an anecdote of him romping with Scipio and chasing him round the table, beating him with a napkin, until the cabbage should be cooked.[2] He is said to have served under Scipio at the siege of Numantia in 134-3. He was an Italian from Suessa Aurunca in Campania, on the border of Latium. Being a Knight, and of independent means, he wrote for his personal satisfaction, doubtless driven by some demon. Moreover, he did not begin to publish until very late, about 131, only a few years before the death of Scipio. His satires

---

[1] Cf Plessis, **CXXXIII**, pp. 97-119.
[2] *Sat.*, ii. 1. 71 ff.

are the work of the old age of that circle, as the comedies of Terence marked its noble adolescence.

The satire, according to the well-known and much-discussed remark of Quintilian, was a purely Roman form.[1] Without doubt it was Latin ; no model for it is found in Greek literature. In Rome, on the other hand, Lucilius encountered the example of Ennius and Pacuvius, who themselves perhaps carried on some tradition of parodying, critical fantasy of native origin. After him, Varro, in his *Saturae Menippeae*, mingled prose and verse, and also, no doubt, all kinds of subjects. Horace, who often invokes the precedent of Lucilius, while he does not hesitate to criticize him, gives the literary satire its final form. Juvenal makes it more bitter and introduces, in accordance with the taste of his time, declamation, while Petronius in his *Satyricon* makes it a comic review of the follies of the age. With him the satire, which probably originated in the dramatic form, leads to the new form of the novel.

But, if the form is Latin, we cannot speak with such confidence about the substance. Satire comprises, at least in Lucilius and Horace, two distinct elements—reviling and moralizing. Reviling is of all times and all countries. It does not seem that ancient Latium was at all free of it. But it flourished in Greece as a literary form in the iambic and in the Old Comedy, which did not fear to call by their names the well-known personages whom it turned to ridicule. Horace himself recalls the fact.[2] As for moralizing, Greek philosophy in all its schools gave plenty of examples. The master used to converse every day on various subjects with his pupils, as Lucilius does with his readers. Sometimes he must have been tempted to pour derision on the opposing system or even on the person of some philosopher of the sect next door. One of these philosophers, Timon of Phlius, about the end of the IVth century, had left a scoffing poem in which he passed in derisive review all the systems except that of his master, the Sceptic Pyrrhon. But we do not find that anyone ever thought of illustrating his lessons of morality by an amusing picture of the follies or vices of his day.

[1] G. Boissier, " Satura tota nostra est," in **I**, 1895 ; **XX**, 1893, p. 98. An able discussion of this subject will be found in the introduction to the Abbé Lejay's learned edition of the *Satires* of Horace, **XCV**.
[2] *Sat.*, i. 4. 1 ff.

The New Academy, for which no truth was certain, must have been particularly disposed to mock at the dogmatism of the Stoics and the faith of the Epicureans. Now, Lucilius was in particularly close relations in Rome with one of the chiefs of this school, Cleitomachos, who dedicated a treatise to him. But what was this treatise? What sort of mind had Cleitomachos? Was it from the Greek philosophers that Lucilius got his taste for moral dissertation, presented in amusing form and enlivened with personal attacks intended to make the reader laugh? Was he not content with simply imitating Ennius and Pacuvius? Presumably Quintilian was in a position to judge, since he could read Ennius and Lucilius and know the philosophers of their day by more than vague anecdotes. It would be presumptuous for us to contradict him. We have seen that in the house of Scipio, as in that of his father Aemilius Paullus, Latin tradition and Greek culture were held in equal honour. We may spare ourselves the trouble, which would be useless in any case, of trying to separate what Lucilius found indissolubly united.

As far as we can judge from what we are told and from the fragments which have survived, the thirty books of *Satires* of Lucilius were not without some kinship with the comedy of Terence. Satire is more abstract than comedy in that it discourses, but it discourses chiefly of morals; it describes the absurdities which comedy shows at work. It embellishes the development of the theme with humorous portraits, anecdotes, and sometimes even little dialogues intended to provoke laughter. Therein it is more precise and more realistic than comedy. It shows us, for example, not avarice or the miser, but So-and-so, mentioned by his name, who was a miser. It represents the application to life, the experimental test, one might say, of the moral philosophy and psychology which, in Terence, animated comedy.

This realistic precision, these portraits, these pictures of the life of the day, are what may have appeared original and peculiarly Roman in the satire. They must have caused the success of Lucilius's work; for us, they would have been its chief interest. What an abundant mine of information we should have found in these chronicles, in which, in his old age, the poet recorded his life's experience, his reflections, and his observations on his contemporaries! The style was

M

loose and the art mediocre, Horace says. But the whole must have been living, and would furnish a precious document on the time which Cicero regarded as the Golden Age of the Republic, and on the society which was still loyal to the old maxims, but already steeped in Greek thought. Of all the Latin poets, Lucilius is perhaps the one whose loss we should most bitterly regret.

CHAPTER V

FROM THE GRACCHI TO LUCRETIUS.
ACTION AND THOUGHT

I

STOICISM AND THE SOCIAL REVOLUTION

WHILE Lucilius, dwelling aloof in the domain of philosophy, wrote his satires in peace, the life of Scipio Aemilianus, which had begun under such favourable auspices, and had for long been so happy, ended in tragedy. One morning of the year 129 he was found dead on his bed, very probably murdered. For Rome was in the midst of a social revolution ; the Gracchi had commenced a war to the death against the aristocracy. Men like Scipio, fundamentally honest but lacking boldness and anxious above all to maintain the happy mean, incurred the anger of both parties alike. It was no longer a time for Xenophon's noble ideal and the amiable eclecticism of Panaetios.

A century of essentially aristocratic government had established the political sway of Rome over the Mediterranean world. The capital was the richer by all the spoils of the conquered, but the social fabric of early Rome was destroyed for ever. The true city plebs no longer existed, being supplanted on the streets and even on the Forum by the sons of Daos, now become citizens. The small rural property was gone, ruined by foreign competition ; it was gradually absorbed by the *latifundia* of the Senatorial aristocracy. But the Senate itself had its problem in a new class, enriched by trade on a large scale and daily growing stronger, namely, the Knights, who aspired to take or at least to share its political power. No less than the Senators, these financiers realized what a fine thing it was, in Cicero's words, to rule the world.[1] In this chaos of new men and new interests, what remained of the old Rome ? A few ideas and feelings which drew their strength and, as it were, their nourishment from Greek philosophical speculation.

For between the old Latin spirit and the intellectual culture of Greece there was no such incompatibility as Cato had supposed. The poems of Homer and Athenian literature of the Vth century expressed the spirit of a brave and enterprising people. The new literature, that of a Greece which had lost its liberty, took up at least some of the most noble traditions of a great past. Scientific curiosity and interest in moral questions could be reconciled with the practical activity dear to the old Roman. Indeed, certain forms of the most recent Greek thought presented a singular affinity to the absolute character, the rigidity, and the rather rude energy of ancient Latium. Such, in particular, were the Stoic doctrines.

The development of Stoicism in Athens and the rest of Greece in the IIIrd century before our era represented, as it would do later in Imperial Rome, a protest of generous souls against the present degradation. The simple, uncompromising vigour of an extreme doctrine seemed a kind of compensation for the inertia imposed by political circumstances. Zeno found the supreme good in effort towards moral beauty. He preached that in life men should use reason in order to attain temperance, courage, and justice. Such a morality did no more than, as it were, codify the principles of the old Roman ideal.

To the mere practice of virtue Stoicism added something still more noble, a rational foundation and an ideal end. The development of its theory further brought in new and generous principles. Reason being the common portion of men, all, whatever their birth, are equal, and, since virtue is the only merit, it confers on all good men, whatever their condition, the same high dignity. Against barriers of caste and distinctions of social rank, the Stoic sets up universal justice. He was able to teach the Romans respect for the conquered and charity to the unfortunate.

Moreover, the Stoics did not confine their speculations to metaphysics and morality. They also considered politics,

[1] *Quam praeclarum esset externis gentibus imperare.*

and we know that they did not hesitate on occasion to take active part in them, endeavouring to cause their ideal of equality and absolute right to prevail. The democratic ardour of the Gracchi was equally indebted to the old Latin traditions and to the teaching of the Stoics.

For the Gracchi were not new men. They belonged to the élite of the Roman aristocracy. Their father, Sempronius, was a friend and stout supporter of the elder Cato ; their mother Cornelia was the daughter of Scipio Africanus. They found in their family the same traditions as Scipio Aemilianus, and they were in a position to receive the lessons of Greece with the same profit as the older man. They did not meet another Panaetios, but a Stoic, the philosopher Blossius, who remained loyally attached to the elder brother, Tiberius, aided him in his work, and after his death was implicated in the prosecution of his supporters.

When Tiberius Gracchus addresses the people, not fearing to bring before them their grievances and sufferings, in his desire to arouse their passions, we hear in his words an echo both of the old Tribunes of the Plebs and of the teaching of the Porch. The fragment which Plutarch has preserved for us at all events reveals a powerful orator.

" The wild beasts have their lairs, and those who die for the defence of Italy have nothing but the air they breathe. Without a roof to cover them, they wander about with their wives and children. The generals are fooling you when they exhort you to fight for your temples, for your gods, for the tombs of your fathers. Of so many Romans, is there one who has his household altar and his family tomb? You only fight and die to feed the opulence and luxury of others. They call you the lords of the world, and you have not a sod of earth of your own."

The examples of Greek history had a share in the attempt of the Gracchi no less than the lessons of philosophy. Tiberius, inspired by Blossius, seems to have hoped at first to bring about in Rome a movement of generous idealism such as had been effected in Sparta, about a century earlier, by the king Agis with the assistance of the philosopher Sphaeros. Agis had tried to regenerate his city by putting an end to the monstrous inequality of wealth.[1] The revolution had sunk into bloodshed and anarchy, but had begun admirably. All the young people, with the women in the front rank, had

[1] *Tib. and C. Gracchus,* 10

enthusiastically given up their possessions on the altar of their country. Perhaps Tiberius expected equal disinterestedness from his fellow-countrymen.[1]

Caius, on his side, took his inspiration direct from Pericles. "His power," says Monsieur G. Bloch, "was personal monarchy based on opinion, born of the suffrage and depending on it, a Periclean monarchy."[2] The memory of the great Athenian seems always to have guided his thoughts. "The corn law, for example, by which doles to the multitude were made by the State instead of by the nobles, whose influence over votes was thus abolished, seems to have been inspired by the system of pay ($\mu\iota\sigma\theta o\iota$) by which Pericles tried to combat the influence of the wealthy Cimon. The great building works ordered by the State were for the proletariat a kind of complement to this law. And, just as in Athens, the constitution in Rome was, if not violated, at least strained by the prestige of eloquence and genius and by the concentration in the same hands of all the springs of government."[3]

The principle of the revolution attempted by the Gracchi was generous, and its success would perhaps have saved the Republic. Its failure was the fault, not of the Gracchi nor of their Greek masters or models, but of the Roman aristocracy, whose selfishness was incapable of understanding their ideas, and of the people itself, which was already too much debased, too much accustomed to idleness and the distractions of the town, to make, and above all to maintain, the effort required for its regeneration. After the death of Caius Gracchus,[4] thought of material and immediate interest alone dominated the whole of Roman policy. In 111 the war against Jugurtha began. In 91 the Social War broke out in Italy, and, immediately after, the war against Mithridates in Asia. Then came the strife of Marius and Sylla, the one as destitute of any ideal as the other ; and civil wars and proscriptions would continue for half a century, until the Principate of Augustus.

---

[1] Plut., *Agis and Cleomenes*, 6 ff.
[2] **XXXIV**, pp. 202 ff. [3] *Ibid.*
[4] Tiberius had fallen in 132 ; his younger brother, Caius, twelve years later, in 121.

II

LUCRETIUS

It was during this period of disturbances and exasperated passions that the great writers of the Republican epoch were born—Cicero in 106, Caesar in 100, Lucretius about 98, Sallust in 86, and Catullus in 84.

Of the personality and life of Lucretius we know nothing, or almost nothing. A gloss of Donatus, a commentator of Virgil, based on the authority of Suetonius, gives us the approximate dates of his birth (98) and death (54). We may add, for what it is worth, the extremely doubtful story, which comes from St Jerome, that Lucretius was driven mad by a love-potion, wrote his poem in his lucid intervals, and committed suicide at the age of forty-four. His work, which he completed but did not make perfect, was published, not very carefully, by Cicero, directly after the death of the poet.[1]

Though Lucretius never speaks of himself, he shows through his work. The wisdom which he sings, the calming doctrine of Epicurus, is not the fruit of indifference and a happy propensity to enjoy the pleasures of life without troubling. For him it is an object of passion. To know and to understand seem to be for him the consolation of an ardent nature which has not been able to act or has scorned to do so.

"Thirst for gold," said Sallust,[2] "and thirst for power were the source of all evils. Greed destroyed good faith, honesty, and all the other virtues. In their stead, it taught pride, cruelty, contempt of the gods, and unbounded venality. Ambition made most men assume a mask; one thought was hidden in the depths of the heart, another was on the lips; hate and friendship were not feelings, but policies; honesty lay in the face but not in the heart." "Unrestrained cupidity invaded everything, profaned everything, ravaged everything; it respected nothing, held nothing sacred, and in the end cast itself into the abyss."[3]

Lucretius, too, had seen his contemporaries " shedding the blood of citizens to swell their possessions; the greedy

[1] For all details, see Plessis, **CXXXIII**, pp. 120 ff. Martha's fine work, **CIII**, is still the best general study of the poem of Lucretius. A good critical analysis of his doctrine will be found at the beginning of Giussani's edition.
[2] *Cat.*, 10. [3] *Jug.*, 41.

doubling their wealth by heaping murder on murder ; the cruel rejoicing at the sad death of a brother ; and men hating and fearing the tables of their nearest kin." [1] He has seen the play of envy and treason with his own eyes.[2] He had seen Sisyphus in the ambitious man,[3]

"Who strives to obtain from the people the rods and the dread axes, and always falls back, defeated and saddened. For to seek power, which is an empty thing, and is never given, and ever to labour sore in that pursuit, is nought but struggling to push up the mountain a stone which rolls back from the very top and bounds away to the flat lands of the plain."

Perhaps he had himself once attempted this labour. In any case, he had repudiated it as vain. Yet it is not selfish indifference which inspires the beginning of his second book ; the end of the passage makes that clear.

"Pleasant it is, when the winds make turmoil on the mighty sea, to watch the hard toil of others from the land ; not that the distress of any man gives delight, but because it is sweet to see the ills which you yourself escape. . . . But nothing is sweeter than to dwell in the serene, well-fortified sanctuaries built by the teaching of the wise, whence you may look down on others. . . . Unhappy minds of men! Blind hearts! In what darkness of life, in what dangers, does our little time go by !"

Lucretius was a Roman, deeply grieved by the ills of his country, and anxious to cure them. He himself had found peace in the wisdom of Epicurus. That was why he spent his nights at work, in order to teach his fellow-citizens the remedy which would save them.

"Deign, Goddess," he says in his opening prayer to the mother of the line of Aeneas, "deign, Venus, to give my words eternal beauty. And meanwhile cause the brutal works of war, on all lands and seas, to rest in slumber. Thou alone hast power to delight mortals with tranquil peace ; for the brutal works of war are ruled by Mars, mighty in arms, Mars, who often lays himself on thy bosom, vanquished by the eternal wound of love." [4]

Art and beauty must lend their charm to wisdom, to lead men back from their errors and to assuage their ills.

History has preserved for us the memory of ambitious men and their followers, of their struggles and their crimes. It has left in oblivion all who, like the poet, remained in the shade, either because they were powerless or because they were reasonable and virtuous, all who were merely the victims of the evils of the time, and suffered from them

---

[1] *De Nat. Rer.*, iii. 70-4.   [2] iii. 75. 85.
[3] iii. 995. I quote Lucretius from Ernout's edition, **LXXI.**   [4] i. 1-44.

materially and morally. Yet these were far the greater number, in Rome itself as well as in Italy and the provinces. What did they think ? How did they seek to understand their time and themselves ? How did they react, at least in their conscience and their spirit, to the frantic struggles of which the whole world was the theatre ? They are the true representatives of the civilization of the epoch. And their influence must have been considerable ; otherwise we could not explain the sudden retirement, at the height of their success, of men like Sylla and Lucullus, or the seclusion in which a wise man like Atticus lived all his life. This was evidently the feeling of many Romans, it must have inspired Lucretius himself, and it was expressed by Sallust when, being reduced to compulsory inactivity, he declared : " Magistracies and military commands, in a word, all public office and all political action, seem to me, at this moment, utterly undesirable." [1]

Lucretius stands as the mouthpiece of these disillusioned ones. But in the retreat fortified by the teaching of the wise he displays all the passion of those who struggle in the plain. With the wisdom learnt from Epicurus he combines all the tenacious persistence of the old Roman character. He has his share of the frantic ardour of his age ; he directs it, not at ambition, but at truth. His philosophy is entirely Greek, but the tone in which he preaches it is certainly not.

It matters little whether the truth accepted with such fervour was that of Epicurus or of the Porch. The essential thing, it seems to me, in the poem of Lucretius, is his passionate adhesion to a wholly intellectual ideal. It is the same stern absoluteness of convictions which we seem to find in the sombre austerity of Cato of Utica, and perhaps even in the crime of Brutus and Cassius. For these Romans, as Cicero says, scoffing at Cato, philosophical ideas are not merely a matter for discussion ; they really become rules of life, principles of action.

One consequence of this complete adhesion of the soul to a philosophic doctrine is that the development of principles is directed by a logic without restriction and without reticence. Reason pursues its course imperturbably, and no considera-tion foreign to the doctrine itself can turn it aside. Lucretius

[1] *Jug.*, 3.

has made himself, as it were, an entirely new soul, the heart of a neophyte; he has made a clean sweep of all traditional opinions. He invokes a purely scientific and exclusively rational doctrine to govern all the beliefs of man and his whole life.

The first cause of all human vices, and especially of those which make the unhappiness of the age, is ignorance. Man does not know nature; therefore he does not understand himself, nor the conditions and limits of his existence. The poem shall furnish an explanation of the whole of nature. Intelligence will deliver man from his errors and his vain cares; it will save him useless endeavours and crimes. Morality is the aim of all knowledge.

This point of view is common to all the philosophic systems of the time. But Lucretius brings in the purely materialistic principle of Epicureanism. The universe is only matter; matter is uniformly composed of atoms—atoms of different kinds, being more or less subtle, but all obeying the same laws. They fall uniformly through infinite space; the angle of their descent leads to the coincidences which form different bodies. Nothing is ever created from nothing; all bodies owe their birth to specific germs. The laws which govern them are absolute and without exception. Nothing reverts to nothing. If in the whole course of past time there have been elements of a nature to remake our universe incessantly, it is because these elements are endowed with an immortal nature. These are the dogmas set forth in the first book. All the rest of the teaching proceeds from it as a consequence.

The properties of atoms and the mechanism of their various combinations suffice to account for the whole universe, our world, " with the mountain-roaming race of beasts, and the stock of men, the silent shoals of scaly ones, and all kinds of winged things," [1] and of the other worlds, also, which in infinite number gravitate in space. To explain their existence there is no need for the intervention of the gods or of a Providence.

Once these truths are known, " Nature will be seen free, released from her proud lords, doing her own work, spontaneously and without constraint." [2] The gods exist, no

[1] ii. 1080.   [2] ii. 1090.

doubt, but they can only be matter, like the rest of the universe. " In tranquil peace, they pass an untroubled life, a cloudless existence." [1] Their influence on the world is *nil*. Who, indeed, could govern the whole of this immensity, who could hold with a firm enough hand the strong reins capable of controlling the infinite ? Who could make all the heavens turn in harmony, heat all fertile lands with the fires of the ether, be everywhere always, ever ready to make darkness with clouds, to shake the clear spaces of the sky with thunder, to send forth the lightning, sometimes to destroy his own temple, and, withdrawing into the wilderness, to expend his fury in casting the bolts which often pass over the guilty and, by an undeserved chastisement, take the life of the innocent ?

The nature of the soul is in no way different from that of the rest of the universe. The soul is matter, like the rest, the product of a combination of atoms, which are only more subtle than those which form the body ; it is only a part of the body, it is born like the body, and it dies like it and with it. Why, then, fear death ? [2] It is nothing to us ; it does not touch us anywhere. We exist, death is not ; death comes, we no longer exist. Just as, in the past, before we were, we felt no pain, so we have nothing to fear or hope from a future in which we shall not be. And the third book ends in the deduction of the consequences of this annihilation. Lamentations are senseless, the cares of funerals are vain ! What does it matter to you whether your body is broken in the jaw of a wild beast, or burned on the pyre, or smothered in honey, or frozen on the icy stone of the tomb, or in the end overwhelmed and crushed by the weight of the earth which covers it ? As for the punishments of Hades, they are only legends or symbols. Death is the common law, and fear of it is only an effect of ignorance. Life, moreover, is nothing compared with eternity ; he who died but yesterday and he who died many months and years ago will both be non-existent equally long.

Man's psychological life, his illusions, his sensations, are explained as a function of the material nature of himself and of the world. This is the theme of the whole fourth book, which ends with an analysis of love. Wisdom is the avoidance

[1] ii. 1095. [2] iii. 830.

of passion, which is only error and slavery. And here all the austere prudence of the old Roman comes to reinforce the philosopher's aversion for the sentiment which troubles the peace of the soul.

"Those who yield to love dissipate their strength, and perish under their labour. Their life is passed at the beck of another. Meanwhile their fortune falls away and is spent in Babylonian hangings, their duties are neglected, and their reputation grows feeble and totters. . . . The wealth honestly earned by their fathers goes in hair-ribbons, bonnets, women's dresses, and fabrics of Alindos and Ceos. . . . There are banquets, games, oft-filled cups, perfumes, wreaths, garlands—all in vain! From the very fountain of pleasures there rises a bitterness, which takes the lover right in his throat."

A discourse like this could not but have delighted Cato the Censor, confirming him, as Plutarch says, in his love of temperance.

After man, Lucretius undertakes to explain the phenomena of nature. He gives us physics, and also history, or at least prehistory, considered as a natural phenomenon and set forth in a purely rational fashion, the accuracy of which, on the whole and in its main lines, agrees with the observations of modern experimental science. He also gives us the history of the origin of language. Speech, according to Lucretius, was invented little by little, by instinct and by necessity, and not by some individual of genius who gave each thing its name. The creation of the various crafts and of civilization, the origins of music, of science, of writing, of poetry, everything is explained by a slow, natural progress, without marvels or miracles.

"Navigation, agriculture, fortification, laws, arms, roads, clothes, and other such gains, and also all the delightful things of life, poems, pictures, cunning polished statues, all were taught to man by habit and the experience of the indefatigable mind, little by little, as he advanced at a foot's pace. So, little by little, time revealed each thing, and reason brought it forth into the light of day." [2]

The last book seems to be a kind of appendix, in which various passages were collected with a view to insertion in the body of the poem. It treats chiefly of meteorological phenomena, volcanoes, water and its habits, and disease. The work closes with a tragic picture of the plague of Athens,

---

[1] iv. 1121 ff.   [2] v. 1448 ff.

a gloomy ending to a poem without joy, but full of beauty and grandeur.

To-day the interest of the work no longer lies in the greater or less accuracy of the results which Lucretius declares established. In substance, his science is only that of Democritus, which Epicurus took over as it was. We cannot say that Lucretius treats any particular point with greater precision. The physical part of his poem seems childish, but the metaphysical problems are to this day the subject of our uncertain inquiries, and those which refer to men, to birth and death, have hardly been given a more definite answer. The originality of the work and its novelty in Rome lie in the boldness and vigour of the pure rationalism which, by force of reasoning alone, claimed to find the explanation of everything.

This is a stage in human knowledge which appears, in Lucretius, marked in a particularly clear fashion. The Latin poet has reached it by following the road already traced by his Greek master. His is dazzled by the brilliance of the summit. From there, he discovers the universe ; he proclaims, as news for Rome, the conception which he brings back with him, and sets it up against the old, incoherent mirages, already partly dissipated by the winds come from Greece.

Man's curiosity before nature was first satisfied by myths. Myth, born of the imagination—of feeling, if we prefer the word—is the reply, ready-made, to the great metaphysical problems which must not remain unknown to us, yet evade solution. The myth of Rome was the notion of countless little gods operating everywhere. There is no longer any question of it in Lucretius ; it was worn out. It is Greek myth, half poetic and half philosophic, which henceforward symbolizes the old error. Against it, Lucretius simply repeats the diatribes of Epicurus, but this criticism, Greek in origin, certainly strikes the conceptions current in Rome in his day. Lucretius does not attack one god or another, but the mythical, religious conception of the universe. He opposes it with the rational conception.

" As children tremble, and fear everything in the blind dark," he says on several occasions,[1] " so we in the daylight sometimes are afraid of things

[1] ii. 55 ; iii. 85 ; vi. 39.

which are no more to be feared than those which the children dread in the dark and imagine to be coming to them. This terror of the soul and this darkness must be dispelled, not by the rays of the sun and the shining shafts of the day, but by the sight of nature and reason."

The official Roman religion was really independent of this mythology. Its formal character, and the methodical spirit of the Pontifices which had presided at its constitution, had excluded from it sentimental effusions and the terrors of the soul. But it ascribed " marvellous deeds and cruel rages " to the gods ; [1] it made much of portents and strove elaborately to expiate them. Moreover, it lent itself to the contamination of foreign rites, Greek or even Oriental. After the Great Mother of the Gods of Pessinus came the Cappadocian Ma, a lewd and bloody goddess, whom Sylla and his soldiers had introduced into Rome.[2] All these cults, those of ancient Rome and those of Greece and the East, no doubt had ceased to have much influence on men's minds. There was a general tendency to incredulity during the last century of the Republic.[3] But this incredulity, so far from shutting out superstition, only made room for it. Mystery religions won more and more followers. From Delos and Puteoli, the great ports where the East mingled with Italy, Serapis and Isis, with their priests and their devotees, invaded the new capital of the Mediterranean world. Marius took with him on all his campaigns his Syrian prophetess Martha. Sylla, who was hardly deterred by respect of the gods when it was a matter of looting their sanctuaries,[4] none the less wore on his person a small statuette of Apollo which he invoked and kissed at critical moments. " Does the sight of your fierce legions marching over the plain, calling up the image of war, drive the superstitions from your soul in panic-stricken rout, and the fear of death, and leave your breast clear and released from care ? " [5]

Religions of every origin and every character and various superstitions all proceed from the same error, all are equally to be condemned and equally baneful. " Unhappy human race, what groaning you prepared for yourselves," by inventing the gods, " what pains for us, what tears for our posterity ! " [6]

---

[1] v. 1195. [2] Wissowa, **CLXXI**, pp. 348, 349 ; Cumont, **LV**, pp. 66 ff.
[3] Boissier, **XXXVII**, i, pp. 54-62. [4] Plut., *Sulla*, 29.
[5] ii. 40-5. [6] v. 1191 ff.

The gods exist, without doubt; it is not a question of deserting their temples, but simply of entering them with a tranquil heart.

"The gods are not cruel masters bent on hurting you. . . . Cease outraging them by ascribing to them unworthy purposes. It is your own error which prevents you from receiving in tranquillity and peace of soul the ideal images of beauty which emanate from their august persons." [1]

True piety is the knowledge and understanding of nature, of which the gods are only a part.

"It is no piety to be often seen veiled, turning towards a stone and approaching every altar, nor to lie prostrate on the ground, stretching out your hands before the shrines of the gods, nor to flood their altars with the blood of beasts, nor to make prayer after prayer; it is rather to be able to view all things with an untroubled mind." [2]

So we need not be surprised at the beautiful, pious invocation to Venus, the delight of gods and men, with which the poem opens, or at a picture like that of the triumph of Cybele, the mother of the gods, the mother of the wild creatures, and the creatress of mankind.[3] Understanding of the gods brings to man the joy of their perfect beauty. Only the error of primitive and irrational conceptions causes trouble and crime.

The nobility of this philosophy was that it proposed an ideal for a world which no longer had one. The *mos majorum*, the ancestral tradition taught and maintained by the family, was forgotten. The city, grown greater and wider, no longer constituted the citizen's reason for existence. To minds which now embraced the whole world, the old myths and the old rites, the cold ceremonies of the official religion, no longer gave satisfaction. Faith wavered between nothingness and the aberrations of mysticism. With many, no doubt, morality continued to be a habit and a kind of pious memory, but it was only an entirely individual rule, without foundation or authority. In this chaos, so painful to him, to which he rightly ascribes the evils of his country, Lucretius perceives the new truth which shall restore order. Intelligence is revealed to him as the sovereign mistress of proportion and wisdom. The triumph of reason—that is the great hope which animates and inspires his enthusiasm.

The peace of the wise man, the amiable indifference to

[1] vi. 63 ff.   [2] v. 1198 ff.   [3] ii. 598 ff.

practical things of the man who knows, the joy in living which understands nature and its beauty, such is the ideal which he would reveal. But the task is hard, for truth is obscure and error holds fast. No doubt the poet promises to sweeten the rim of the cup with yellow honey.[1] But his imperious enthusiasm overrides his promises. Against ignorance, his phrases are as definite as the old formulas of law. But in his work there is a flower of passion which gives his philosophy, the daughter of the old Greek speculation and of cold reason, the warmth of enthusiasm and the rather rude vigour of primitive poetry.

The serene sanctuaries of knowledge are for Lucretius like fortresses, which he takes by storm. The wisdom is that of Epicurus, but the tone is rather that of Stoicism, or, more simply, of a Roman with an antique soul, who has found in reason the weapon which he believes invincible against the shames and vices of his age.

[1] i. 936 ff.

CHAPTER VI

SCIENCE AND LEARNING

I

PHILOSOPHY AND SCIENCE

So, from the end of the IInd century before our era, and, still more, throughout the Ist century, Greek thought, in the form in which it flourished in the contemporary Hellenistic world, triumphed in Rome. Italy as a whole had become a province of Mediterranean civilization, and its capital tried to vie, even in the intellectual domain, with the other great cities of the Mediterranean.

The main current of this mental activity, aiming at knowledge, was represented by philosophy. For philosophy embraced all the physical and natural sciences. The second book of the poem of Lucretius, for example, gives us a whole treatise on physics. Science had not yet detached itself from metaphysics. It had not yet established a method of its own, and it still consisted in a mere series of logical developments based on nothing but superficial observations. Its aim, therefore, was confined to more or less fanciful explanations of phenomena, and every school had its own explanations.

Two orders of knowledge, however, were made the subject of special branches of teaching, independent of philosophical speculation, in the Hellenistic age—the abstract science of mathematics with its applications to astronomy, and the essentially practical science of medicine. Their progress in Rome at the end of the Republican period shows us at least the low-water mark of scientific development.

II

ASTRONOMY AND THE ROMAN CALENDAR

It was through astronomy and the measurement of time that mathematics won admittance into Rome. The Romans wanted first of all to learn the almanac.

The story goes that in 263 they set up on the Forum the first sundial, having carried it off from Catana.[1] Catana being situated four degrees south of Rome, the dial was inaccurate on the Forum. The Romans are said to have taken nearly a century to find out how to make the correction. But in 168, during the campaign of Aemilius Paullus in Macedonia, it is said that his Tribune C. Sulpicius Gallus was able to predict that there would be an eclipse of the moon on the night before an intended battle, and so to forestall the panic which would not have failed to fall on the army.[2] The same man is said to have calculated the distance of the moon from the earth, and to have left astronomical writings—most probably translated from the Greek—which were admired by his compatriots as works of profound genius.[3]

For all that, the calendar, under the control of the Pontifical College, continued to be regulated by pure empiricism, and often complicated by arbitrary interference for political motives. The chief difficulty arose from the lack of concordance between the months, which were governed by the course of the moon, and the year, governed by that of the sun. Twelve lunar months of $29\frac{1}{2}$ days give 354 days. The solar year contains 365 days. There was a difference of 10 or 11 days. The Romans had adopted the plan of fixing the year at 355 days and intercalating, every second year, between February and March, a month which sometimes had 22 days and sometimes 23.[4] So the complete cycle of four years contained two short years and two increased years. The average year came out at 366 days, so that you were a month

---

[1] Pliny, N.H., vii. 213.
[2] Such is Livy's account (xliv. 37). It seems rather that he merely explained the cause of the eclipse to the soldiers, and thus dispelled their alarm. Cf. Plut., Aem. Paul., 18; Polyb., fr. 29. 6. 8-10; Cic., Rep., i. 15; Senect., 14.
[3] Cic., Off., i. 6; Rep., i. 14. 16; Pliny, N.H., ii. 12. 9; 21. 19.
[4] See Sig. E. Mancini's study on the pre-Caesarian Roman calendar recently discovered at Anzio, Calendario e Fasti consolari e censorii, Lincei Press, Rome, 1921.

ahead every thirty years. That, no doubt, was why Manius
Acilius Glabrio, who defeated Antiochos in 191, on his return
from his expedition to Greece and Asia authorized the
Pontifices to make intercalations or not to make them, as
they saw fit. But the Pontifices only used this right to shorten
or prolong magistracies, or to damage or favour the farmers
of the public taxes. This confusion lasted until the intervention of Caesar.[1]

In the year 46, Caesar, as Pontifex Maximus and Dictator,
entrusted the Greek mathematician Sosigenes with the task
of re-establishing concordance between the civil year and the
solar year, and laying down the rules which the Pontifices
should observe in the future in order to maintain this concordance.[2] At that time they were two long months behind.
So two intercalary months of 67 days altogether were inserted
between November and December, although the year had
already been given an extra month of 23 days before March.
So this year 46 B.C. contained 445 days. In order to prevent
the return of the error, Sosigenes suggested that every year
ten days should be added to the lunar year of 355 days, and
Caesar decided to distribute these extra days among the
lunar months of 29 days, three of them receiving two more
days, and four others getting one. Between the lunar year,
thus rectified, and the solar year there was still a difference of
a quarter of a day. Every four years, therefore, yet another
day had to be added to the end of February, in the place
formerly occupied by the intercalary months.

The authority of Caesar carried through the reform of
Sosigenes. But the Pontifices themselves did not understand
it. The proof of it is that they made a mistake over the
intercalation of the supplementary day. The wording of
the decree ran : *quarto quoque anno*. They interpreted this
as " at the beginning of each fourth year," i.e., every three
years. This gave rise to an error which was only corrected
by Augustus in 8 A.D. Caesar's reform also established in
Rome a stellar calendar, fixing the rising and setting of the
stars on every day of the calendar, according to observations
made at Alexandria, which were not completely accurate in
Rome.[3]

[1] Censorinus, 20.   [2] Suet., *Caes.*, 40 ; Censorinus, 20.
[3] Cf. E. Ruelle, **LVI**, s.v. *Calendarium*, pp. 833 ff.

This reform was based, not on empiricism, but on an astronomical science which had exactly calculated the sidereal solar year. It was the work of Alexandria. But its science was not perfect. For the ancients could not appreciate the difference between the sidereal year and the tropical year, which is shorter on account of the precession of the equinoxes, that is, the annual retrogradation of the equinoctial points along the ecliptic. They had reckoned the solar year at 365 days, 6 hours, whereas it is really 365 days, 5 hours, 48 minutes, 49 seconds, so that there was an annual difference of 11 minutes, which in 129 years produced one day in advance. Thus, in 1582 the spring equinox fell on the 11th March. The Gregorian reform, by suppressing ten days, brought it back to the 21st March in the next year, and obviated a return of the discordance by slightly altering the bissextile intercalations.[1] The Orthodox peoples, who have kept the Roman calendar of Julius Caesar, are thirteen days ahead of us in consequence of the accumulation of the annual difference of 11 minutes.

There were mathematicians in Rome, but they were Greeks, or their direct pupils. We do not find any Roman school causing this science to make any progress or even developing it in a manner worthy of remark. Yet there were a good number of Romans who studied mathematics and could make practical use of them. Let us, for example, open the *De Architectura* of Vitruvius, an unpretending work by a modest technical writer. We shall find many instances of the use of geometry ;[2] we shall also find, at the beginning, in the form of a prologue, a programme of all the various forms of knowledge needed by an architect, among which mathematics hold an important place.[3] The architect must not only be a man of letters and able to draw, but he must *know his geometry, not be ignorant of optics, and have a good knowledge of arithmetic . . . and have at least some notion of astronomy.* The reasons by which Vitruvius justifies his demands are rather childlike.[4]

"The architect should be versed in letters in order to draft good memoranda of what he proposes to do. . . . Geometry is of great help to him, particularly in teaching him to use the rule and compass properly, to

[1] The last year of a century is only made a leap-year if it is divisible by 400. 1800 and 1900 were not leap-years, but 2000 will be one.
[2] Cf. Choisy, **XLV**, i, pp. 341 ff.   [3] i. 1. 4.   [4] *Ibid.*

take the alignments of buildings, and to get everything straight with the square and level. . . . Arithmetic is useful for assessing the cost of the work he undertakes and for reckoning lengths and proportions, which is sometimes done better by calculation than by geometry. . . . A knowledge of that part of philosophy which treats of natural things, what the Greeks call physiology, will enable him to solve a number of various questions, as is indispensable in many cases, especially when he has to lay a water-conduit. . . . Moreover, the architect would never be able to understand, without a scientific training, the treatises of Ctesibios, Archimedes, and other such writers. . . . Lastly, astronomy will be useful for setting up sundials, and telling the cardinal points, the equinoxes, the solstices, and the course of the stars." [1]

The architect, Vitruvius says more definitely, should have a knowledge of all these sciences, but it is neither possible nor even necessary that he should know them thoroughly.[2] This is quite the Roman point of view, which Cato had already expressed with reference to Greek thought in general : it is good, because it is profitable, to have a notion of it, but it is useless to immerse yourself in it. Leave it to the Greeks to specialize and invent ; let us confine ourselves to reaping the fruits of their discoveries. In every art, Vitruvius concludes, there is the general theory, which anyone may learn, and the practice, reserved to the specialist.[3]

The Greeks worked πρὸς φιλομάθειαν, for love of science. The Romans also loved science, but for themselves, not for its own sake ; they chiefly prized the profit which they might obtain from it. So they were never true scientists.

III

MEDICINE

So, too, there were doctors in Rome, mostly Greeks, but also Romans ; but there was no Roman medical science.

Greek medicine and surgery had made great progress. In the Alexandrian age they almost reached the level at which they stood in Europe about the middle of the last century, when they were still experimental arts.[4] The finds of surgical instruments at Pompeii and Latin literary evidence show that they had been completely adopted by Italy and Rome.

[1] i. 1. 7 ff.
[3] i. 1. 15 ff.
[2] i. 1. 13.
[4] Lecène, XCIV.

Pliny tells the story of the Peloponnesian doctor Archagathos, who came and established himself in Rome during the second Punic War, in 219.[1]   His surgical operations caused such a sensation that he was given the citizenship, and the State allotted a residence to him, in his own hospital.   But later " his mania for cutting and burning got him a name as a torturer," and probably contributed to that unpopularity of doctors and physic of which we hear an echo in the invectives of the elder Cato: " The Greeks have sworn among themselves to exterminate all the barbarians with their medicine, and have the impudence to take pay for doing so. . . . I bid you have nothing at all to do with doctors." [2] The *De Agricultura* contains some of the prescriptions of native medicine, mixed up with magical formulas.[3]   Cabbage is a panacea.[4]

" In the form of a poultice it cures all infected or gangrenous wounds. . . . If the trouble is internal, eat cabbage in vinegar ; this will drive away the trouble ; it will cure the belly, cure the head, cure the eyes.   But you must take it in the morning on an empty stomach.   This is the way to treat the bile, the spleen, the heart, the liver, the lungs. . . .   For rheumatism there is nothing like a raw cabbage, chopped and sprinkled with coriander," etc.

In spite of the advance of ideas, the Romans seem to have long kept some of Cato's prejudice against medicine and doctors.   The healing art was chiefly practised by freedmen or men of fairly low condition.   It was not so much, Pliny explains, medicine itself and the art of healing that were condemned, but the practice of a doctor's profession ; *non rem antiqui damnabant sed artem.*   The Romans would not allow that the care tending to preserve health should become a paid profession.   The practice of this profession, as indeed of most professions, seemed incompatible with Roman dignity. So those Romans who took to it went over like renegades into the Greek camp.   A doctor only inspired confidence if he spoke Greek ; the Roman patient, Pliny suggests, preferred not to understand too much when it was a matter of his health.

To raise the status of the doctor in Rome and to attract pupils and masters of the Greek schools, Caesar granted citizenship to all doctors practising or teaching their art in

[1] *N.H.*, xxix. 1. 6. 12.
[3] 127.
[2] *Ibid.*, xxix. 1. 14.
[4] 157.

Rome.[1] Under Augustus we hear of a celebrated physician, Antonius Musa. In 23 B.C. Augustus nearly died of a liver complaint.[2] Antonius Musa saved him by cold baths, and this cure won him the greatest reputation among the Roman aristocracy. Some years later, it is true, the same treatment killed, or at least did not save, Marcellus, the Emperor's beloved nephew, who had just married his daughter Julia. We know what an important, and often criminal, rôle doctors played later, under Claudius, at the Imperial court. Messalina had her own doctor, Vectius ; Agrippina made use of Claudius's doctor, C. Stertinius Xenophon, in having the Emperor poisoned. Vespasian gave doctors the same privileges as grammarians, rhetors, and philosophers.[3] At the beginning of the IIIrd century Alexander Severus organized official instruction in medicine, which we find, in the time of Constantine, not only in Rome but in the provinces.[4]

Valuable information regarding the state of the science at the end of the Republic or the beginning of the Empire has been preserved for us in a Latin medical work, the *De Medicina* of Celsus.[5]

The personality of the author and the dates of his life escape us. He was certainly a Roman ; it is not absolutely certain that he was a physician. His treatise on medicine is only part of an encyclopaedia, both literary and scientific, both theoretical and practical, the title of which was *Artes*. The Arts included Agriculture, Medicine, Warfare, Rhetoric, Philosophy, and Jurisprudence.[6] The original thing about the collection was the inclusion of a treatise on medicine, and this is the only part which has been preserved.

The medical science summarized by Celsus, for the use not of practitioners, but of the cultivated Roman reader, was that of the Alexandrian school of the time of the later Ptolemies. There opinion was divided between two doctrines —the empirical, according to which medicine consisted entirely of practice and experience, and the dogmatic, which maintained the principle that without an understanding of the causes of an illness, both the remote and the more im-

[1] Suet., *Caes.*, 42.   [2] Suet., *Aug.*, 81.   [3] Suet., *Vesp.*, 18.
[4] Reinach, **LVI**, s.v. *Medicus*, pp. 1674 ff.
[5] Text and French translation in Collection Nisard, 1846 ; Védrènes, **CLXIII** ; latest edition, Marx, **CVI**.
[6] Cf. Schanz, **CXLIII**, ii, 2 (2nd ed.), pp. 326 ff.

mediate causes, and without a knowledge of the natural
action of remedies, the art of the practising physician remained
blind and powerless.[1] The empirics chiefly sought to act,
the dogmatics to understand. In Alexandria the supporters
of rational medicine commonly practised the dissection of
corpses. What was more, in order to ascertain the working
of the organs, Alexandrian doctors had gone as far as
vivisection.

"Herophilos and Erasistratos," Celsus relates, "cut open living criminals
whom the king gave over to them from the prisons, in order to see in their
living state things which nature kept hidden. They claimed that there was
no cruelty in giving pain to a few criminals in order to find the means to
preserve innocent generations for centuries." [2]

The empirics, on their side, protested against the abuse of
philosophical reasoning, the abstractions and the hypotheses
of the rationalists, and accumulated exact observations. The
art of healing, they remarked, varies with the individual
and even with the climate ; it will be different in Egypt, in
Rome, and in Gaul. The discovery of the cause of a malady
is not that of its cure ; only constant experience teaches the
course of treatment to be followed ; all your conjectures on
the origin of the disease are of no practical use, for the important thing to know is, not what produces the disease,
but what cures it.

It was reasoning versus experience. The Alexandrians
did not think of combining the two methods and building a
rational science on experience. Their Roman interpreter is
content to seek a happy mean between the two, which will
make it unnecessary to take one side.

"I think," he says, "that medicine should be rational, but it should take
its data from evident causes only ; the investigation of occult causes may
exercise the physician's mind, but should be excluded from the practice of
his art. . . . It is useless and cruel to cut open living bodies, but it is
necessary for those who study this science to dissect dead bodies, for they
must learn the seat and arrangement of the organs. . . . The empirics are
right to devote themselves chiefly to looking for the remedy, but memory
and practice are insufficient, and reasoning must come in constantly ;" and
so on.

This is exactly the attitude which Vitruvius adopts, at
the beginning of his work on architecture, between the
champions of practice and those of theory.

[1] Cels., *De Med.*, 1.   [2] *Ibid.*

" Practice comes from long application of the usual processes. . . . Theory demonstrates and explains the execution of a work by means of the intelligence and reasoning. . . . The architect who has no theory and considers only practice has never succeeded in obtaining an authority proportionate to his efforts. . . . He who refuses to stand on any basis but theory pursues a shadow without reality. . . . But he who combines them is fully armed, and succeeds beyond his hopes." [1]

The quarrel, we see, sprang up in Greece over every one of the " arts." The Romans are not the people from whom to ask for a solution.

Quintilian called Celsus a mediocre spirit.[2] The rhetoric-teacher was perhaps thinking chiefly of the more literary parts of the *Artes*. It is certain that the *De Medicina* added nothing to the medical knowledge of the time. But it is a thoroughly sensible work. We may quote one example.

" The man with a good constitution, who enjoys health and can do what he likes, need not tie himself down to any regimen and can do without a doctor. . . . But delicate people, among whom I include a great proportion of town-dwellers and almost all men of letters, have to take more care of themselves." [3]

If Celsus was a doctor, he was probably a sound practitioner, but no scientist. His treatise shows very creditable medical knowledge, not science.

IV

HISTORICAL AND PHILOLOGICAL SCIENCE

The departments of knowledge which deal not with man but with men, their actions, their past, and their works, were organized, in Greek countries, separately from philosophy. Herodotos was independent of Socrates. But in the IInd century B.C. the spirit of the great schools of philosophy had an influence on history. Nor did the philologists at Pergamon and Alexandria who studied and commented on ancient writings escape the ideas generally propagated by philosophy. Into historical and philological study as a whole,

---

[1] *De Arch.*, i. 1 ff. [2] *Inst. Or.*, xii. 11. 24.
[3] *De Med.*, i. 1-2. And there is the picture of the surgeon. " The surgeon should be young, or fairly young. His hand must be strong, quick, and steady, his left must be as skilful as his right, his eye should be clear and keen, he must have confidence."

philosophy had introduced two essential elements—first, care for truth, and therefore criticism, and secondly, the notion of law.   Thereby it had transformed their character.

Care for the truth, it seems, is not a primitive feature of history.   Peoples in their childhood, like individuals, are less interested in facts than in legends.   Imagination and feeling are mingled with the account of the facts so intimately that they utterly distort it.   The Romans had at first been delighted with the Greek fables, which they unscrupulously wedded with their native myths.   The poets, Naevius and Ennius, and the first historians, Cato and Fabius Pictor, had in this way composed a heroic, imaginary tradition for their country.   For their generation the distinction between true and untrue was really meaningless.   People invented stories or repeated foreign inventions ;   they had not yet thought of observing and criticizing.

The Romans were taught to seek the truth by Polybius. The pages, inspired by philosophic thought, which serve as a preface to his history, are quite in the nature of a lesson to his readers.   The historian should forget his patriotism and national pride.

"Truth is to history what eyes are to animals.   Take out the eyes of an animal, and it becomes useless ; take the truth from history and it is no longer good for anything.   Whether one writes of friends or foes, for both alike one should consider only justice. . . .   In a word, the historian, without respect for the authors of deeds, must form his judgment on the deeds themselves." [1]

But it is not enough, when treating of human actions, to be able to discern the truth ;   one must also understand it— that is, perceive the connexion of cause and effect.   But to bring into history the logical connexions which constitute, as it were, the woof on which to weave the facts, one must consider events in their complexity and as a whole.[2]   Only thus will the historian succeed in discerning the plan of Fortune, that is, the actual concatenation of reality.   "*I shall gather together for the reader,*" says Polybius, "*in a single picture, all the means which Fortune has used for the execution of her design.   This is the chief motive which has led me to write.*" [3]

The plan of Fortune is, no doubt, only an arbitrary

[1] Polyb., i. 24. 4-8.   [2] *Ibid.*, i. 1. 4. 4-15.   [3] *Ibid.*, i. 4. 2.

hypothesis.   Nevertheless, the search for this plan represents, in history, the introduction of a logical connexion, something like the pursuit of remote causes by the doctors of the rational school, or the theory of architecture which Vitruvius contrasts with mere practice.   Henceforward it was the historian's business not merely to narrate, nor even to know, but to try to understand.[1]

This lesson was perhaps not understood by all Roman historians, but it was not lost.   Polybius's conception dominates all Roman histories down to and including Bossuet's *Discours sur l'histoire universelle*.   Fortune predestined Rome to the empire of the world.   " Since Fortune has caused all the affairs of the world to incline to one side only, and seems to have set herself but one aim . . . it seemed to me that I should not leave to oblivion the most beautiful and the most useful of her works." [2]   Livy does just the same—he prepares for and explains the triumph of Rome.   His philosophy of history is that of Polybius.

The *Histories* of Polybius were continued by a professional philosopher, Poseidonios of Apameia (133-49), who likewise came to Rome and there exercised great influence on all who were interested in the things of the mind.   Nourished on all the learning of the schools of Asia Minor, Poseidonios brought into history a conscientiousness in the matter of evidence which did not stop at facts, but aimed, above all, at ascertaining their causes.   A great traveller, like Polybius, he visited, like him, the countries in which the events which he was to relate occurred, but he also took pains to collect native traditions ; he observed, he encouraged men to talk, and he took notes.   The few surviving fragments of his work perhaps preserve the most valuable of all the information which we possess about pre-Roman Gaul.[3]   Being a student of physics as well as a moralist, he tried to discover the relations between the manners of men and nature.   He was very probably the author of the theory, which has had such

[1] From what point of view should facts be interpreted and judged ?   Historians are always faced with this problem.   Every effort, even unsuccessful, to solve it is creditable.   There is some foundation for M. Radet's severity on Polybius : " This typical retired army captain is richer in pretensions than in talent " (**XXI**, 1907, p. 6).   But it seems rather excessive.   The mere conception of " pragmatic history " and conscientious execution deserve esteem.
[2] Polyb., i. 4. 1.
[3] Cf. A. Grenier, " La Découverte du Rhin," in **X**, xxxviii (1920), pp. 16 ff.

a long and brilliant career, of the influence of climate, as it is set forth at the beginning of the sixth book of Vitruvius.[1] We find him going to Gades, both to study the phenomenon of the flow and ebb of the Ocean, and to try to get some news of the expedition of a Greek, Eudoxos of Cyzicos, who started from there, some twenty years before, in search of the route to the Indies.[2] Poseidonios was truly a master, and was regarded as such by the Romans who knew him personally or steeped themselves in his writings.

Caesar, in his *Commentaries*, does not hesitate to take much information from him and probably most of the descriptive digressions which here and there interrupt the record of military doings. He also seems to be the inspiration of at least some of the moral discourses which give such a special character to the historical works of Sallust. For example, the curious dissertation at the beginning of the *Catiline*, which gives a picture of the profound change which took place at this time in Roman manners,[3] is very like a passage which, according to Diodorus, comes from Poseidonios.[4] Both Caesar and Sallust learned from Poseidonios to observe countries and men, to note natural phenomena and manners.[5] He himself must have brought to this observation a purely scientific spirit, and have looked for the remote and immediate causes of facts. His Roman pupils were too much involved in active life or too full of passionate ambition to follow him on this path. They stopped half-way, at military and political history.

The true disciple of the Alexandrian scholars was M. Terentius Varro (116-26). He is a curious figure, this Roman Knight, born at Reate in the Sabina, a farmer, full of devices to make the most of his patrimony, soldier and sailor, Pompey's lieutenant in Cilicia during the war against the pirates and in Spain during the Civil War, a satirical poet like Lucilius, full of spirit and humour, critic, grammarian, archaeologist, historian, and organizer and director of the public libraries of Rome under Caesar and Octavian.[6] He

---

[1] vi. 1. 3 ff.   [2] Strabo, i. 100.   [3] Sall., v. 9-13.   [4] Diod., xxxvii. 3.
[5] On the small value of Caesar's ethnological information, cf. Grenier, op. cit., pp. 22 ff. Sallust, in his *Jugurtha*, probably used Poseidonios's geographical information on northern Africa, as Caesar used his information on Gaul.
[6] Boissier, **XXXV.**

might have known Marius and Sylla, and he only died after Actium, when Octavian was organizing his Principate. He represents a connecting link between the old Republic and the Empire.

From the old traditions, to which he was still very close, he gathered a quantity of facts, feelings, and beliefs. The pupil of the philosophers—Antiochos of Ascalon, whose course he followed in Athens—and of learned men like Aelius Stilo, the first of the Roman philologists, he treated these traditions as a matter for knowledge. In him, learned reflection was exercised on the Roman past in order to codify it. The form of his studies was Greek, the matter was Roman.

His love of literature and the teaching of Aelius Stilo first led him to philology. The critics of the Museum at Alexandria had made the *Canon* of the ancient Greek poets and orators ; Varro attached himself to ancient Latin poetry, and studied the comedies attributed to Plautus, over a hundred in all, out of which he recognized twenty-one as authentic. He applied himself to the beginnings of the Latin drama, and made a list of dramatic performances in Rome. He collected all that could be known of the poets of the century before his own. Altogether, he was the learned critic of ancient literature.[1]

From the works in the language he went on to its history and to that of Latin writing. So he came to history and even to prehistory. His treatise *De Gente Populi Romani* was an attempt to bring the origins of the Roman people into the scheme drawn by Greek prehistoric speculation and to give a scientific appearance to legend. Legend took him on to archaeology. His *Antiquitates Rerum Humanarum* and *Divinarum* were a collection in 41 books of all that could be known in his day regarding early Roman civilization, men, times, places, things, and gods. St Augustine's many borrowings from the *Divine Antiquities* show how abundant and how valuable was the information thus preserved.[2]

He also wrote for a wider public ; the diffusion of knowledge was the object of his *Imagines*, a collection of 700 portraits of famous men, each accompanied by a verse eulogy. This species of book-selling enterprise was suggested

---

[1] For the catalogue of Varro's works, see Schanz, **CXLIII**, 3rd ed., i, 2, pp. 423 ff.
[2] *Civ. Dei*, vi. 3 ff.

to him by Cicero's friend Atticus, who was his collaborator and publisher.

Varro was better qualified than anyone to compose the *Encyclopaedia*, regarding which we have a few scant allusions. It seems to have been the classical manual of the seven liberal arts—Grammar, Dialectic, Rhetoric, Geometry, Arithmetic, Astronomy, and Music. It probably also included treatises on medicine and architecture, not to mention a treatise on law of which we only know the title, *De Jure Civili*.[1] Varro's encyclopaedia must have become a model, often imitated and brought up to date. The *Artes* and *De Medicina* of Celsus and the *De Architectura* of Vitruvius were probably only improvements by specialists of parts of the old work of the great polymath.

Ritschl credits Varro with 74 different works, making a total of 620 books. However fertile and easy a writer he may have been, such an output is beyond human power, and, moreover, war and business must have robbed science of many of Varro's hours. We have no information about his method of work. It is not perhaps improbable that he made use of a sort of workshop of more or less Latinized Greeks or Latin scholars of second rank, working under his direction. In that case Varro " did " science rather as his friend Atticus did publishing, unless tradition has attached his name to much of the general scientific output of his time.

Of all this work we have only a part of the *De Lingua Latina* and the three books *Rerum Rusticarum*.

The *De Lingua Latina* was in 25 books. Books V to X alone have come down to us, and that with many lacunae. However, the synopses at the beginning of each book enable us to reconstruct the plan. The treatise was in three main divisions—etymology, declension, and syntax. What survives contains the end of the first part and the beginning of the second. A few valuable pieces of information are to be found mixed up with much rubbish.

At the beginning of the part about inflexion is an exposition of the great grammatical dispute of the day over *analogy* and *anomaly*. The anomalists were the empirics of grammar, and maintained that one should abide by the facts. In the presence of the great number of exceptions which they could

---

[1] Schanz, op. cit., pp. 438-9.

not explain, they declared that it was impossible, in the matter of language, to formulate general rules, and that everything in it was purely accidental. The analogists, on the other hand, saw in analogy the great law of grammatical formation, a logical law superior to all exceptions in fact. They were the rationalists. It was a version in the domain of language of the great philosophical dispute between the champions of pure and simple observation of the real and the logicians, who, starting from an abstract idea, chiefly sought, in experience, the effects of the general causes which they supposed.

Between the two parties Varro is content to adopt the Roman solution, which is no doubt superficial, but at that time was the common-sense solution, that of the happy mean. According to him, analogy and anomaly both exist side by side in language. It is wrong to try to bring everything under a rule, and it is wrong to see nothing but exceptions. Obviously he could not be expected to invent the laws of phonetics and the history of language.

If we would judge Varro's science by what remains of this treatise—and it certainly seems that we have a right to do so—that science was only a hasty compilation, presented in a literary form worse than mediocre.

Very different is the treatise on *Agriculture*. The style is vivid, and not without wit and charm; we can see the writer's personality. It is quite what one would expect from the canny, intelligent Roman of the old school, pleasant and companionable, but just a little pedantic. " My eightieth year," he says, " warns me that I must pack up and prepare to leave this life "; so he will put together his experience as a good Roman farmer. He draws a precise and highly instructive picture of the rural economy, and even the general economy, of the Italy of his day. The work is in the form of a dialogue, like most of Cicero's treatises, but the divisions and subdivisions and the plentiful reminiscences of reading betray the scholar beneath the farmer, and reveal the influence of the scientific teaching of the Greek schools in an emulator of the elder Cato.

Varro was not an isolated phenomenon in Rome. From his master Aelius Stilo onwards, a large school of learned men there pursued the same philological and archaeological studies as himself. Their reputation and influence were so great that Caesar himself in his youth thought that it would be good for his glory to write a treatise on *Analogy*. The Roman mind was not unresponsive to any of the branches of knowledge of Greece.

Latin learning was Greek in origin, methods, and ideas. But its object was the Latin past.

When the scholars of Pergamon or Alexandria study the past of Greece, they do so in an absolutely dispassionate spirit, with no other object than to ascertain and set forth the truth methodically. For this past is, as it were, foreign to them; in their eyes it represents the past of humanity itself, in its highest and most generally human form. Moreover, they readily include the whole of the world as far as they know it. Even the barbarians interest men like Polybius, and, still more, Poseidonios. The curiosity of Eratosthenes extends to the whole earth.

The spirit of the Roman scholars is quite different. Their learned zeal is animated by especial piety towards Rome. National pride inspires the inventories which they make of the antiquities of their country. To them these are riches which must not be lost. In Varro we seem to find a feeling not unlike that which lay beneath the poetic efforts of Naevius and Ennius. The old poets had the patriotic object of endowing Rome with a literature equal to that of Greece. So, too, Varro hopes to form for his country in a short time a treasure-house of knowledge equal to that which successive generations of learned men had patiently amassed for Greece. He wishes to show that the national antiquities of Rome are no less rich in intellectual elements and no less interesting than the Homeric past or the classical age of Greece.

No doubt Varro and his fellow-students do not expect any practical result from their researches. It would be wrong to ascribe to them any intention of restoring the Roman past to honour and resuscitating it. In raising it from oblivion, they only mean to do the work of scientists. But they do not study it purely as scientists. In them, patriotic feeling mingles with the scientific spirit. The affection with which they speak of the events, the beliefs, and the traditions of old days animates their studies with a kind of ideal life. The erudition which taught the Romans to see their own past clearly also awoke in them a veritable national consciousness, the policy of which would soon be a great active force.

It is in the studies of Varro that we must look for the origin of the poetic vein of national archaeology which appears in Tibullus, takes a larger and larger place in Propertius, and triumphs in Virgil. From the domain of the imagination, the tradition resuscitated by Varro's science passed into practice with the attempts of Augustus at moral reformation. So, without intending it, but in consequence of the special tendencies which it brought into science, Roman erudition, like everything else, led in the end to action. The Roman spirit excelled in seizing upon everything that was useful and in turning to profit even those forms of knowledge which were most unutilitarian in principle.

CHAPTER VII

ORATORY. CICERO AND LITERARY PROSE

I

ELOQUENCE AND RHETORIC

BEFORE they knew Greece, the Romans had no notion of either philosophy or science. It was, therefore, natural that in philosophy and science they should take all their lessons from the Greeks. But they had long practised the art of oratory. Skill in words was indispensable in a republic to anyone who aspired to dominate the masses. Political eloquence must have come into being among them at the same time as politics. Still more, the development of law and the custom of the client calling upon his patron for support in the courts made it a duty for the aristocrat to be able to defend a case. The desire to shine and the ambition of forcing oneself upon the attention of the citizens found the most usual and most certain means in public speaking. " In such a great and ancient republic," Cicero says, " in which the most brilliant rewards await eloquence, all have desired to exercise the gift of words." [1] So in the *Brutus*, when he undertakes to relate the history of Roman eloquence, he does not hesitate to trace its origin to L. Brutus who drove out the Tarquins, and he manages to cite a fair number of orators previous to Cato. We might therefore have expected Roman oratory to continue this old tradition, or at least to keep some original features and an independent character in the face of Greek eloquence.

Nothing of the kind is the case ; it is Greek rhetoric that we find triumphant in Rome in Cicero's time.

All the eloquence previous to the period of rhetoric

[1] *De Or.*, i. 4. 13.

appears of little account to Cicero. Even his eulogies of Cato condemn it. He praises Cato's natural gift; no one would have surpassed the eloquence of the old Censor, if he had been able to add to this gift the science possessed by later orators.

"Add rhythm and let his periods be more harmoniously constructed, make his words connect better and, as it were, fit into one another, and you will put no one above Cato."[1] "Servius Galba," a contemporary of Laelius and Scipio Aemilianus, "was without dispute the greatest orator of his time; *he was the first Roman to make use of the methods which are the privilege of the orator, digressions, amplifications, emotional passages, commonplaces.*"[2]

In Rome, as in Greece, true eloquence, in Cicero's opinion, only appears with the art of oratory.

This art, which is analysed at length in the *De Oratore* and the *Orator*, is that of the Greek rhetors. The orator undergoes an extremely delicate and complicated education, beginning, so to speak, when he leaves his cradle, and continuing to subject himself to it when he has left the period of his formation behind. It is an essentially practical art, distinguishing styles of eloquence and kinds of case, and cataloguing the type of argument best suited to each and the turns of phrase, arrangements of words, and effects most calculated to beguile the hearer. These devices should be such as to give strength to the weakest case and to make the strongest case appear weak. The rhetor is a master of arguments and words; his sole aim is success.

Brought into being in Sicily and Greece by the sophists, this purely empirical craft of eloquence was further developed in the schools of the Hellenistic world. In the kingdoms which issued from the inheritance of Alexander eloquence held an infinitely smaller place than in Rome. It was reduced to the very artificial form of the show speech or the narrow scope of the legal pleading. Driven from the public place, it took refuge in the porticoes of the school, where the teachers were left in peace to devote all the efforts of their subtlety to elaborating theories and methods. Each form of thought, each turn of phrase was studied for its own sake, and classified under a name of its own. Balances, oppositions, figures, strokes, everything was analysed and regulated. The very

[1] *Brut.*, 17. 68.   [2] *Brut.*, 21. 82.

form of words, their rhythmical value, their arrangement in the period, were made the subject of learned calculations and recipes. The masters of rhetoric laid down rules of prose rhythm, which were no doubt less strict than those of verse, but were not far removed from those of the lyric poem and the dramatic *canticum*.[1] They applied chiefly to the beginning and end of a phrase, but even within the period, according to the swing of the speech and the exact shade of thought or feeling, careful attention was paid to the quantity of syllables, the succession, alternation, or accumulation of longs and shorts. The speech became a sort of musical declamation, a monody governed by the most minute laws.

It was the pride of this learned and delicate art that it was based on experience alone, and was the fruit of long series of observations. It refused to recognize any reality but the word, which was stronger than facts, stronger than truth, the mistress of verisimilitude. For its devotees, the word was truly the principle of all things. The rhetors were the empirics of eloquence.

They gave eloquence its form and, let us acknowledge it, raised it from the state of spontaneous improvisation to the dignity of a literary composition.

Their teaching at first surprised the Romans, and for a long time met with energetic resistance from them. We remember the sally of Cato, who, deriding the long preparation which they demanded, asked whether it was with a view to making speeches in Hades that the pupils of the rhetors thus spent their whole life in studying. In 161 rhetors were lumped with philosophers in a Senatus Consultum expelling them. In 91 the orator Crassus, in the course of his Censorship, deported them again. Crassus is one of the speakers in the *De Oratore*. Cicero makes him explain the reasons for his edict.[2]

"The Greek rhetors of our time," Crassus says, "lack solid foundation, so that those of our young men who go to them only become spoilt and forget what they knew. Yet their knowledge is far more extensive than that of their Latin rivals. . . . I saw that these new masters could teach nothing but presumption. . . . That was all they did—they held a school for impudence, *ludus impudentiae.*"

Rhetorical cleverness seemed a danger to the morality and

[1] *Or.*, 168 ff.   [2] *De Or.*, iii. 24.

seriousness of eloquence. Crassus was right. The unrestrained development of rhetoric produced declamation.

While Cicero eagerly gathers the fruit of the teaching of
the rhetors and profits by it in his speeches, he takes care not
to place himself entirely on their side. Eloquence, like the
other arts, has its dogmatists as well as its empirics, and, true
to the Roman way, Cicero endeavours to hold the balance
equal between the two schools. " To limit the requirements
of an orator to a knowledge of the principles taught by the
rhetors," he says, " is to confine him within very narrow
bounds ; it is to reduce a vast career to a very small field." [1]
But what he contrasts with the rhetors is not Roman practice,
the breadth and passion of great political debates going
beyond the petty cleverness of the schoolroom, but another
theory, also of Greek origin.

In Greece the opponents, first of the sophists and then of
the rhetors, were the philosophers. Against Gorgias and
Protagoras, the artists in words, Socrates and Plato championed the rights of ideas. Aristotle, above all, showed the
superficiality of an art which claimed to tell men how to talk
without troubling about teaching them how to think. He
stood for truth against verisimilitude, and propounded the
theory of proof as the basis of eloquence. From the search
for methods and the collection of practical recipes he raised
rhetoric to the dignity of a true logical science. Perfect form
must be only the expression of coherent and fundamentally
true thought.

After Aristotle, the Hellenistic age separated eloquence
and philosophy still further. The rhetors regained their
liberty, while the philosophers, specializing their inquiries, in
general made the art of expression subordinate to the correct
definition of facts and ideas. Epicurus disdained eloquence
and its ornaments, and the Stoics made it the humble hand-
maid of dialectic. Only the New Academy strove to maintain
contact between the two arts and made philosophy and science
supports for rhetoric. It is the doctrine of the New Academy
that we find abundantly expounded, especially in the *De
Oratore*.

The superficiality and narrowness of the art of the rhetors
should, in Cicero's opinion, be corrected by the wide culture

[1] *De Or.*, iii. 19.

of the orator. Rhetoric will supply the form, philosophy and the whole cycle of human knowledge will furnish the foundation. The dialectic of the orator is simply a development of logic. Morality, that is the science of characters, sentiments, and passions, will give to eloquence the means to play on the various motive powers which actuate humanity. History and law will be for the advocate and the politician like an armoury of examples and arguments. Physics, the science of nature, and even metaphysics, to which all the problems of life come in the end, should complete the education of the orator. In short, the orator, in addition to rhetoric, should possess all the sciences.

But, as the speakers in the *De Oratore* remark, that is too vast a circle to embrace. Lost among all these various speculations, each one of which is sufficient to absorb the intellectual activity of a lifetime, the orator will have no time to apply himself to the special matter of his art. Useless, or nearly useless indulgence in general culture will be detrimental to his training in his special craft. Is eloquence merely the flower and crown of all knowledge, or is it a special art with its own rules and methods ? Surely it is chiefly developed by practice, and it is to the exercises proper to this art that the orator should above all apply himself.

Cicero's own opinion, as it emerges through the discussions of the dialogue, reflects the same eclecticism as we find in all Roman expositions of Greek intellectual controversies. Wisdom lies in the happy mean. We must not expect of the orator a profound knowledge of all the subjects which may give support to eloquence ; we must require from him only an adequate notion. Without being a philosopher, he must have the clear thought of philosophy. He need only be capable of taking from the various special sciences, as required, the wherewithal to feed and amplify the subject which he is discussing. A good orator (like the *honnête homme* in France) can be content with not being utterly ignorant of any branch of human knowledge. But in his education rhetoric, which gives him the special technique of his art, holds far the highest place.

So Roman oratory was entirely a Greek art. Among the speakers in the *De Oratore*, even those who raise their voice most energetically against the pretensions and practice of the rhetors, Crassus and Antonius appear well acquainted with the most subtle theories of rhetoric. No doubt they add their own experience, but their education, which has made them capable of presenting themselves at the law-court and on the Forum, has simply been that of the rhetors. The doctrines of the schools, developed in the intellectual centres of the Hellenistic world, came to Rome and were put to the test of life.

II

THE SCHOOLS OF RHETORIC

The only divergences between the Roman orators were due to the differences of doctrine of the Greek theorists.

For the various schools of rhetoric had not all the same ideal. Those of Athens adhered to a particularly sober and rather dry art. Thanks to the undying admiration of the perfection of the ancient models, the art of words kept a tendency to archaism. Lysias and Thucydides were the most admired masters. Men strove to reproduce the simplicity of the former and the restrained vigour and conciseness of the latter. The Attic school were the masters of the severe taste.

The schools of Asia, on the contrary, and that of Pergamon in particular, introduced into Greek eloquence the colour, the fluent rhythm, and the ornaments which were ever dear to the East. More imagination than logic in invention, immoderate use of figures, effective phrases, and contrasts, vocal tricks of delivery which turned speaking into a kind of chant, and exuberant gesture—these were the characteristics of the Asiatic style.

Between Attica and Asia, Rhodes tried to find the happy mean. Her rhetors equally condemned the rather dry severity of the former and the overloaded richness of the latter. The most celebrated master of the Rhodian school was Molon, a clever advocate, an excellent writer, and a teacher as remarkable for his criticism as for his lessons, if we are to believe Cicero.[1] It was to him that the Latin orator went to complete his rhetorical education.

[1] *Brut.*, 91. 316.

These are the three shades of Hellenistic art which we find in Rome in the Ist century before our era. We see them put into practice, embodied in celebrated orators, or rather expressed by three successive generations of orators. Public favour was transferred from one of these schools of eloquence to another, and the success of one after the other really represents the evolution of Roman taste between 100 and 50 B.C. We have simply to follow Cicero, a very sure critic of the art of his contemporaries.

The Asiatic style was the first to win popularity, and triumphed especially in the person of Hortensius, who was born in 115 and made his first appearance on the Forum in 96.[1] He displayed, Cicero tells us, impetuous talent and inexhaustible fertility, admirable natural qualities reinforced by constant practice. He abounded in brilliant expressions, lively figures, and trivial thoughts ; his voice was musical and sonorous, his gestures were very finished. He did not appeal to the taste of staid folk. " I have often seen Philippus laughing at him, and even growing angry and fuming, but the young men used to marvel at him, and the crowd was stirred." [2] In the general mediocrity of his time, Hortensius had no difficulty in coming to the front. Soon rising to honours and glory, he thought that he could despise his rivals, and enjoy his success without troubling about those who came after him. He ceased to work, and idleness " took the colour out of him as time does from an old painting. Everything in him degenerated, especially the easy, swift elocution which seemed to flow from a spring." [3] When his high position and dignified age required a more serious tone, he still remained the same orator as before. Only his zeal had grown cold ; he still had the abundance of ingenious thoughts with which his speeches were packed, but he could no longer clothe them in the adornment of a dazzling style. Asiatic brilliance was suited to youth ; it lacked the seriousness which gives authority.

Cicero, about fifteen years younger than Hortensius, saw him in his glory. " I used to follow in his very footsteps," he says.[4] Indeed, the two orators were closely associated

---

[1] *Brut.*, 64. 228 ff.
[3] *Brut.*, 93. 320.
[2] *Brut.*, 95. 326.
[4] *Brut.*, 90. 307.

throughout their careers. Cicero began by imitating the style of Hortensius.

"I made a whole speech, without lowering or varying my tone, with all the force of my voice and my whole body. . . . At that time I was very thin and weak in the body, with a long, lean neck; a physique like that runs a great risk, they say, if it is subjected to hard work and the chest is tried too much."[1]

He was exhorted to abandon the Forum. He only resolved to adopt a less violent and reckless manner, and left for Asia. After six months in Athens, he went to Rhodes.

"Molon did what he could to curb my redundance and the overflowing verbosity of my youthful unrestraint. . . . At the end of two years I came back a different man; my delivery was less violent and my style had, as it were, cooled down."[2]

It was then that he thought he saw the falling-off and defects of Hortensius. To the style of the older orator he opposed a soberer, more serious ideal, pretending to more moderation in taste and more depth in ideas. The style of Cicero was the Rhodian style.

His reign was uncontested nearly twenty-five years. About 56 a new generation appeared on the Forum, highly talented and very severe on its predecessors. Its most brilliant representative on the Forum was Calvus, whom we shall meet again among the poets of the circle of Catullus. These young men, in the name of the Attic ideal, made exactly the same criticisms of Cicero as he had once made of Hortensius, accusing him of excessive, artificial abundance and too much ornament of doubtful taste.

These attacks on his supremacy seem to have affected the great orator considerably. Calvus died young in 46. The *Brutus* and the *Orator*, both written in this same year, give us a very definite echo of the dispute.

In the *Brutus* one is surprised to see the Attic school and Lysias and Hypereides suddenly evoked apropos of Cato the Elder.

Why do our young men not admire and follow Cato? "It is sheer ignorance, that they should delight in the antique taste and simplicity of the Greeks, which they call Atticism, and not recognize the same qualities in Cato. Everyone wants to be a Hypereides and a Lysias. Very creditable. But why not want to be a Cato? They say that they love the Attic style of

---

[1] *Brut.*, 91. 313.   [2] *Brut.*, 315-16.

speaking. That, too, is very wise. Would to heaven they would imitate its life-blood, and not the dry bones only ! . . . Really they would do well not to be so utterly ignorant of Cato." [1]

The irony is somewhat heavy, and the note is not altogether agreeable. The discussion seems to be intended more seriously in the *Orator*.[2] Cicero is clearly in difficulties, and gets out of them by playing on the sense of the epithet " Attic."

"They say that the man who speaks in a careless, unpolished manner, provided it is precise and free from unnecessary ornament, alone speaks in the 'Attic' way. . . . But in that case Pericles himself was not an Attic orator, for if he had spoken in such a simple fashion Aristophanes would never have said that he 'thundered and lightened and set all Greece in a broil.' . . . Thus, either ornament, force, and abundance belong to the Attic style, or neither Aeschines nor Demosthenes is Attic."

We must not be misled by Cicero's apology *pro arte sua*. The difference is more serious and the principle of it is more interesting than Cicero wants to seem to admit. The Neo-Atticists were as expert in rhetoric as Cicero himself. They did not for a moment pretend to natural eloquence or main-tenance of the old Roman tradition. Their models, like his, were in Greece and came from the schools. But for their school the height of art was to appear artless. Knowledge of the subject—that was the true principle of eloquence. No doubt their oratory was aided by practice and experience, but was without any of the factitious devices intended to amplify and adorn a speech. For the Atticists, art was not something added to the idea ; it was one with it, emanated from it directly, was its soul. They wished to build an edifice which owed its beauty only to the quality of the materials and the arrangement of masses and lines ; they rejected extraneous ornament.

Cicero, on the other hand, cannot conceive of beauty without ornament, of art without artifice.

There is justice in the assertion that perfect knowledge of the subject is the principle of eloquence ; "it is still truer to say that no one can be eloquent on a subject of which he is ignorant, nor yet on a subject which he knows perfectly, if he is ignorant how to compose and polish his discourse." [3]

For Cicero, then, the orator's craft consists first in the

[1] *Brut.*, 17. 67 ; cf. 82-5. 283 ff.   [2] *Or.*, 9. 28-33.
[3] *De Or.*, i. 14. 63.

composition of a speech, *faciunda oratio*, and then in its adornment, *poliunda oratio*. The Neo-Atticists placed it entirely in the former operation. Too many beauties of indifferent quality—this was the reproach which Cicero had levelled at Hortensius, and Calvus now levelled it at him.

When one reads Cicero's speeches one cannot help agreeing with the new, severe school. The tricks of rhetoric are too abundant and too apparent. The arguments and their disposition, the ordering of phrases and words, and the tone of the speech, sprightly or indignant, display in Ciceronian eloquence an almost mechanical application of the principles of the school, as they are set forth in the theoretical treatises, the *De Oratore* and the *Orator*. Not only is everything calculated and deliberate, as is proper in art, but too often technique takes the place of inspiration and is something added on to the idea, which it distorts or overloads. The rhetor spoils the orator.

This scientific, overdone technique became second nature with Cicero, and the law of his mind. Certainly it made his task easy on many occasions, enabling him to speak almost impromptu on any subject, suggesting enlargements on the theme, and furnishing him with a reply or the means of rebutting his opponent's argument. This is his " stock-in-trade." He employs it with a virtuosity which must often have won him the applause of the public and even the favour of the judges, but does injustice to the sincerity of a magnificently oratorical temperament and lessens the literary value of his eloquence.

To rhetoric we must attribute all the apparatus of preparations and digressions in Cicero's speeches which often distract attention or weigh down the discourse. Rhetoric, too, is responsible for the superabundance of arguments, not all of them good, and, within the arguments, the superabundance of words which is wearying, at least to the reader. Each demonstration is too complete, each period too perfect. From rhetoric, above all, comes the abuse of small tricks and commonplaces. We expect the sincere expression of some profound feeling or some great idea, and we find only empty dialectic or pinchbeck emotion. G. Boissier notes, in the fourth Catilinarian Oration, a particularly striking example.[1]

---

[1] Boissier, **XXXVI**, p. 48.

" This was the matter which Cicero had to discuss, one of the most serious which could be placed before a deliberative assembly : how far may one deviate from legal methods in order to save the country ?   He did not even touch upon it. It is painful to see how he retreats before it, how he evades it, to develop petty arguments and to lose himself in vulgar emotion."

In all this eloquence, Boissier concludes, there is too much artifice and technical dexterity.   A concise, simple argument would be more suitable to the discussion of business.   Great philosophical tirades would be better replaced by a clear, sensible exposition of the orator's political principles and the general ideas which govern his conduct.   Calvus and the Neo-Atticists were absolutely right in their judgment.

III

LITERARY PROSE

The teaching of the rhetors was not strictly confined to eloquence ; it covered the expression of all ideas and every literary form—history, philosophy, didactic treatise, and even letter-writing.   If the whole of human knowledge should, as Cicero says, form the foundation of eloquence, eloquence, or at least rhetoric, on its side lent its form to the whole of intellectual activity.   The Greek schools and, after them, the Romans conceived of no literary work outside it.

History in particular, according to the ancient conception, is strictly subordinate to rhetoric.   When Cicero inveighs against his Neo-Attic adversaries, he distinguishes with much justice between the style suited to the exposition of facts and that required by the law-court or the Forum.   The rhetors had not failed to make this observation.   None the less, history is for him an oratorical form, *opus est maxime oratorium*.   So little does he distinguish it from the speech, the object of which is to please and to prove, so far, indeed, does he carry professional distortion, that he even concedes to the rhetor the right to lie a little in history, in order to embellish his narrative and to bring out his argument.[1]   Here

---

[1] *Brut.*, 11. 42.   True, it is Atticus who is speaking, and jestingly.   He draws attention to a piece of historical fancy in which Cicero departed from his own previous account of the death of Coriolanus.

rhetoric is at variance with the much more serious teaching of the philosophers.

The Roman historians of the end of the Republic, Caesar and Sallust, no doubt underwent the influence of the philosophical history of Polybius, and still more of Poseidonios. They took, chiefly from Poseidonios, information which might be useful to them. But on the whole they seem to be pupils of the rhetors much more than of the philosophers. History for them is really only a kind of forensic speech, in which the narrative is the principal element ; the technical methods and ornaments are essentially the same as in any other oratorical work. The political passion by which they are animated and the great part played by eloquence in Roman public life clearly contribute to this conception. But its origin none the less lies in the teachings of Greek rhetoric.

The intellectual formation of Caesar had been the same as that of Cicero and of all Roman politicians. He had intended to be an orator. It was by other means than eloquence that he sought political power ; but in his youth he had studied at Rhodes and attended the courses of Molon.[1] It is as a speech in his own defence, with a military report as basis, that we must regard his *Commentaries*. The style is that of narrative ; the sentences are short, the facts are the essential thing. This is all artistic effect. Caesar's limpidity of phrase is often more apparent than real. When we go into details and try to determine the reality behind them, we see how closely allied this simplicity is to that simplification which omits really essential things as merely accessory, in order to bring out only those features which are useful to the case. Caesar's acts and decisions appear in a fair light ; we do not so well understand the manoeuvres of the enemy, who is treated almost like the adverse party in the exposition of a case. Even his contemporaries noted all the artificiality of these alleged notes on operations.[2] It must be ascribed to rhetoric.

Rhetoric shows even more clearly in Sallust. Sallust chose his model in Greece, in the person of Thucydides. Now, for the Attic rhetors, Thucydides was the master whose

[1] Suet., *Caes.*, 4. For his eloquence, *ibid.*, 56. The eulogies of him which Cicero makes Atticus utter in the *Brutus* seem to have a tinge of flattery (*Brut.*, 72. 252-3).
[2] Asinius Pollio, *ap.* Suet., *Caes.*, 57.

methods they analysed, whose style they set up as an example to imitate. Sallust tries to reproduce his packed, vigorous conciseness. In contrast to the regular period of Cicero, he strives for effects produced by dissymmetry. The ends of his sentences do not obey metrical rules. He aims at an art of rather rude, archaic appearance. This, too, is a literary affectation. Sallust belongs to the young school of the Neo-Atticists, who, far from eschewing rhetoric, only endeavoured to bring it to a nicer perfection.

Sallust's form may recall the style of Thucydides, but the spirit of the *Catiline*, the *Jugurtha*, and the few surviving fragments of the *Histories* is very far removed from the lofty impartiality of the Greek historian. It was to serve his party, and, above all, to damage his opponents, that Sallust wrote history. The Forum was closed to him, so he sought elsewhere a platform where his voice would awake more lasting echoes. He moralizes in his prefaces, and pleads and vituperates all through his story, striving for a new effect in the contrast between the austerity and outward coldness of the style and the burning passion of the idea.

Neither Caesar nor Sallust is " Ciceronian," for they do not belong to exactly the same literary school as Cicero. They have not the same ideal, but they have the same art, which is, in a general way, that of Greek rhetoric. The orator and the two historians may equally justly be called pupils of the rhetors, for they have the same education, which is not distinguished from literary education in itself.

Of all the Greek " disciplines," oratory obtained the most complete success in Rome. Whereas in philosophy and science the Romans remained disciples, or were content to be compilers, in rhetoric they attained complete mastery. They had been prepared for it, no doubt, by the special importance of eloquence in Roman life. But in ceasing to be a mere practice, and becoming an art, Roman eloquence, and with it Roman literary prose, renounced all truly national character. The difference between Demosthenes and Cicero is not that one is Greek and the other Roman. It is no doubt due to the difference of their individual temperaments, but it should be explained, above all, by the development which rhetoric underwent, between the IVth and Ist centuries B.C., in the schools of the Hellenistic world.

CHAPTER VIII

POETRY. CATULLUS

WHETHER we consider political and social activity, in the Gracchi, pure speculation, in Lucretius, the applied sciences, or eloquence, in Cicero, we find the Roman spirit entirely subject to Greek forms. It is the same with poetry.

The form of poetry means not only the kinds, but the metres. Moreover, kinds and metres go together, and we know how important they were in ancient poetry. The kinds most cultivated in the Hellenistic age were, in addition to the epigram and the light occasional poems the flower of which is preserved in the *Anthology*, picturesque, erudite little poems such as Callimachos composed, and the sentimental and often erotic elegiac. These are what we find in Rome in Catullus. The metres, too, are all Greek. One of the chief merits of this poetry, in the eyes of contemporaries, was just the skill with which the types of verse created by Anacreon, Archilochos, and Sappho were adapted to Latin. No doubt other Romans before Catullus had imitated the same models. His originality lies in his delicate mastery of the form, as perfect as that of the Alexandrian poets.

Many of his expressions, combinations of words, and images also seem to have been inspired by the Greek. Herein Catullus follows what had been the tradition of Latin poetry from its beginnings. The similarities of this sort which his commentators manage to find would certainly be far more numerous still if the greater part of Alexandrian poetry had not disappeared. His imitation is often deliberate, and often, most certainly, unconscious. Formed by the reading of Greek works, by the legends, and also by the sight of works of art, sculptures, reliefs, and, above all, paintings, the Roman imagination can hardly be distinguished from that of the contemporary Greeks. The poets' minds are full of reminiscences which they have only to express in Latin. They know it, and do not conceal it from themselves.

> . . . *Veterum dulci scriptorum carmine Musae|Oblectant.*[1]

The old poets whose sweetness charms Catullus are, of course, the Greeks. In his time poetry could no more be imagined without Greek poetic training than literary prose without rhetoric.

Moreover, Catullus is not an isolated case. He belongs to the group of young men who, in the name of Atticism, set up a more sober, severe ideal against the abundance of Cicero. This new school established itself between the years 60 and 50. Its leader was Valerius Cato, the " Latin Siren," who, more than any man, excelled in reading the poets and could train them. The most vigorous and forcible spirit, who might have had a very great influence on his time if he had not died at the age of thirty-five, the victim of his passion for work, was Licinius Calvus, a son of the annalist Licinius Macer, " the eloquent wee man," *disertum salaputium*, as Catullus calls him. He was the man whose new style and success on the Forum alarmed Cicero. No less than for his eloquence, Calvus had a great name for his poetical works, epigrams, epithalamia, elegiacs, and a poem on the wanderings of Io, in which he was very probably inspired by Callimachos. After Calvus, one of the most celebrated of these young poet friends of Catullus was Helvius Cinna, the author of a *Smyrna*, much lauded by his contemporaries. The subject of this poem was the incestuous love of Smyrna for her father, of which Adonis was the result. Ovid sang the same theme later.[2] Of all this delicate efflorescence, chance has saved for us only the work of Catullus.

These young men, born between the years 90 and 80, and arriving at manhood about the time when the rivalry of Pompey and Caesar became definite, some of whom would live to see Actium and the establishment of the Empire, were not purely literary men, entirely given up to their art. Calvus, a man of action and an orator, but without political ambition—he never canvassed for office—was an exception among them. Most of the others, and Catullus in particular, set out to enjoy life ; they disdained action, but were very fond of society. Catullus is a poet of the world. The

---

[1] Cat., lxviii. 7.   [2] *Met.*, x. 298 ff.

epigrams and trifles which form the greater part of his work
are occasional poems. Many of them are perhaps inspired
by Greek models, for their technique and art are Greek ;
but they owe their existence to the small events of Roman
social life and above all to incidents in the sentimental life of
the poet. Let us leave their form on one side and seek what
makes their soul. Beneath the tricks of ingenuity we find
sincere emotion. A passion in which there is nothing
Alexandrian, which is sometimes brutal and often generous,
throbs in the skilfully chiselled verse. The warmth of a still
rather raw youth gives life to the mannerism of an artificial
poetry and transforms it into beauty. It places the Roman
stamp on it.

Catullus was born at Verona in a family in comfortable
circumstances, and came to Rome before he was twenty,
probably to finish his education and to make a political
career for himself. Social relations at this time were a useful
lever to ambition, and in society women were beginning to
play an important rôle. The Hellenistic age was the triumph
of woman ; the example of Alexandria, where the queens
ruled the kings, had influenced the whole Mediterranean
world. In Rome it was the same as elsewhere. Caesar had
been able to use his successes with women to good purpose,
and had done just the same as many others. Plutarch
relates how Lucullus went about it to obtain the government
of Cilicia. At the time the Tribune Cethegus was all-powerful
in the city ; now, Lucullus had a short time before conducted
a campaign against him, and was in his bad books.

"There was at that time in Rome a woman named Precia, one of those
who had become famous through their beauty and the charm of their wit ;
but at bottom she hardly behaved better than a professional courtesan. . . .
When Cethegus became infatuated with her, all power was in the hands of
this woman ; no public business was done but by Cethegus, and nothing was
obtained from Cethegus except through Precia. Lucullus, to win her over,
spared neither flatteries nor gifts ; he courted her with an assiduity which
flattered her pride and ambition. From then onwards Cethegus was loud
in praise of Lucullus, and got Cilicia for him."[1]

Catullus was not Lucullus. We do not know if it was
ambition which first guided him to the house of Lesbia. In
any case, he soon forgot every sentiment but love. Lesbia

---

[1] *Lucullus*, 9.

P

seems to have been none other than Clodia Metella, the sister of Clodius Pulcher (Cicero's enemy, who slew Milo), and the wife of Q. Caecilius Metellus, Consul in 60. She was of exactly the same class as Precia. Married in 63, she was a widow in 59; she was accused of having poisoned her husband; she was also accused of incest with her brother. In 56 Cicero had to defend against her one of her former lovers, whom she charged with having tried to poison her. This was Caelius, the former pupil, the friend, and afterwards the correspondent of Cicero. The *Pro Caelio* draws a cruel picture of Clodia which would well justify the last invectives of Catullus against Lesbia.

Directly after his arrival in Rome, about 62, and for about four years, the love of Lesbia seems to have been Catullus's chief motive in life. The death of her husband appears to have marked the end of his happiness. In 57 he had definitely broken with her, and left for Bithynia in the train of Memmius, the man to whom Lucretius dedicated his poem, a poor creature, to judge by what Catullus confides to us about him. It is about this time, from 58 to 54, that we must place the two longer poems which form the centre of the work of Catullus, the two *Epithalamia* (lxi and lxii), the *Attis* (lxiii), the *Epithalamium of Thetis and Peleus* (lxiv), the poem on *Berenice's Hair* (lxvi), an imitation of Callimachos, and, lastly, the wonderful elegy (lxviii) in which he expresses both the grief caused by the death of his brother and the profound melancholy of his unhappy love. He died aged a little over thirty, before the year 50 B.C.

In the brilliant, frivolous circle surrounding Lesbia, Catullus at first abandons himself to the happiness of his love. His wit and playful grace must have earned him triumphs which he is proud to lay at the feet of his mistress. There is certainly some affectation in two famous poems on Lesbia's sparrow, but the youthful freshness of the *Kisses* is not spoiled either by the Epicurean echo which underlies the first poem or by the mythological erudition which mingles with the motive of the second. At the same time Catullus chaffs his friends or fires off an epigram, sometimes of a coarseness which shows that the refinement of this society was of rather recent acquisition and very superficial, against somebody unpleasant or perhaps too pleasant. He is gay

and heedless.[1] He can on occasion sketch with clear strokes
and simple but charming colour a scene of common life [2]
or even a larger subject, in which feeling and picturesqueness
are combined. His light, graceful art recalls lightly-tinted
pictures framed in garlands and ribbons.

His love, drawn with a stroke, with an exactness beneath
which one guesses the turmoil of passion, is revealed in its
almost naïve sincerity. This is not a fancy of the imagination,
nor even intellectual love. Catullus loves with a burning
heart ; he loves with nobility. He faces his first mortifica-
tions with rather blustering courage.[3] But treason has
wounded his love " as the flower, at the end of the field, is
struck by the passing plough." [4] To paint the emotion which
he feels, he is doubtless inspired by Sappho, but that is
because the Greek poems seem to him to express his own
experience perfectly. His imitation is not a mere literary
exercise.

" He is like a god, he is above the gods, if that can be, who can sit near
you and see and hear you laughing sweetly ; from me, poor fool, it robs all
sense. For when I see you, Lesbia, everything goes . . . my tongue is
frozen, a thin flame flows through my limbs, my ears are full of drumming,
and my eyes are wrapped in night." [5] " I loved you then, not as any man
loves his mistress, but as a father loves his children. Now I know you ; and,
though I burn with a stronger flame, yet you are far less precious and of less
account. ' How can that be ? ' you say. Because such injury makes a man
love with more desire and less affection." [6] " From now, I could not feel
affection for you if you became perfect, nor cease to desire you whatever you
did." [7]

And in a few lines we have the story, commonplace, no
doubt, but deeply felt, of new oaths and new quarrels,[8] of
the man's efforts to break free,[9] of his fury against new
lovers, and, finally, passionate insults. The veil of preciosity
which concealed his happy love is rent, literary and philosophical memories, even mythology, all is forgotten. " I
hate and I desire. ' How can I do that ? ' you may ask.
I do not know, but I feel it and I am tortured." [10]

The romance of Catullus and Lesbia is one of the very few
documents of ancient sentimentality. It has been claimed
that antiquity, and Roman antiquity in particular, never
knew the whole range of sentiments which make a sort of

[1] xiii, xxvi, xxvii. [2] xviii, xix, xx. [3] viii. [4] xi. [5] li.
[6] lxxi. [7] lxxv. [8] lxx, lxxxiii, xci. [9] lxxvi. [10] lxxxv.

aura round love. It is true that the subtle and infinitely variable shades of passion which in France form one of the essential elements of lyric poetry, drama, and the novel have a very small place in Latin literature. Roman society generally made an absolute distinction between conjugal love, the quiet tenderness of which was full of gravity, and the sensuality of irregular attachments. For the materfamilias, the Roman felt a trustful affection, the seriousness and depth of which are expressed in many an epitaph of the end of the Republican period or the beginning of the Empire. Amorous love, on the other hand, was an act of passion. Between the two feelings there was the difference which Catullus expresses by the contrast of the terms *amare* and *bene velle*. It is the latter which is described and explained in No. lxxii. " I loved you as a father loves his children and those whom they wed." For his mistress, Catullus feels not only the sensual passion of an illicit amour, but all the tenderness of honest wedlock. " My Lesbia, the one Lesbia, Lesbia whom Catullus loved more than himself and all his own. . . ." Disillusionment has killed tenderness, but has not deadened passion. Passion still inflames the curses and insults which he hurls at her in her faithlessness.

This love, at once passionate and tender, seems in Catullus to be thoroughly sincere. It is pure of any alloy of convention, of passing fashion, of literary influence. Is it Greek ? Is it Roman ? Is it ancient or modern ? It is idle to ask ; it is simply love, felt by a soul at once violent and delicate, and expressed by a mind sufficiently master of its art to render it in all its vividness without suppressing or falsifying its shades.

Love, joy, anger, indignation, the whole range of fleeting sentiments and impressions is raised by Catullus to a literary form. He establishes the lyricism which develops and expands in poems of ampler scope. That is the great novelty in his work.

The strong sentimental vibration set up in the artistic soul of Catullus by unhappy passion seems to have given his talent its impulse. It released it from the mere game of scholarly imitation. His other poems, those which are not about Lesbia and are inspired by Greek models, owe to it a sensitiveness, never dead, which gives life to fictions, and feels emotion over myths and images, tinging them with a faint melancholy. It is like a wound, never quite healed, which aches at the least excitement and imbues the whole of life with a mournful pathos.

This is the kind of moral atmosphere which envelops the various pictures drawn by Catullus. It gives, as it were, a soul to his scholarly virtuosity. The short *Attis*,[1] for example, has no connexion with Catullus's own feelings or with love at all. Is it a mere imitation or development of some Greek model, or was it suggested to the poet by some scene observed during his travels in Bithynia ? It does not greatly matter. The most noticeable thing in it is the effect of exotic colour. The whirl of Phrygian orgies is given with swift, sure strokes.

"Come, Gallae, let us go to the high groves of Cybele, come, all you wandering herds of the Lady of Dindyma ! . . . Cast off slow delay ! Come, all of you ! Follow to the Phrygian house of Cybebe, to the Phrygian groves of the Goddess, where the voice of the cymbal sounds, where the timbrels clash, where the Phrygian piper wails on his curved reed, where the ivy-crowned Maenads wildly toss their heads, where they hold their sacred orgies with shrill screamings. . ."

But soon the melancholy plaint recurs, in which real feelings are mingled with fiction, and the poet's soul fills his art with touching sincerity.

"O my country, who made me ! O my country, who bore me ! Alas, I left you, as a runaway slave leaves his master. . . . Shall I no more see country, goods, friends, parents ? No more the Forum, the ring, the race-course, the gymnasium ? Oh sorrow, sorrow ! My heart must grieve, and grieve again ! . . . . I was a young lad, I was a boy, I was the flower of the gymnasium, I was the glory of the prize of olive. Mine were the crowded doors, mine the seething threshold, mine the flowery garlands. . . . Shall I now be a minister of the gods, a servant of Cybele ? "

The lions which the Goddess sends to bring back her faithless priest are surely a symbol of the invincible force which brings the lover back to the object of his passion.

"Great Goddess, Goddess Cybebe, Lady Goddess of Dindyma, far from my house be all thy frenzy ! Drive others in delirium, drive others in madness ! "

So, too, in the *Epithalamium of Thetis and Peleus*,[2] the plaints of deserted Ariadne are the centre and main motive of the poem.[3] We must surely see an outburst of sincere lyricism in the portrayal of the love which courses through the maiden and burns her very marrow.[4]

[1] lxiii.   [2] lxiv.   [3] 132-201.   [4] 86 ff.

"Ah, thou who dost lash up fury with pitiless heart, divine boy, thou who givest men care and joy together, and thou, Goddess of Golgi and leafy Idalium, what a storm have you raised in the burning heart of the maiden, who sighs for the fair-haired stranger!"[1]

Alexandria has been accused of the "elaborately concocted eroticism of its literary output."[2] Certainly there is no lack of eroticism in the Alexandrians of Rome. But in Catullus, at least, the only poet of the young school whom we know, these trivial images are animated by a breath of sincerity, generous and full of power. The refinement and wit, the too subtle art of his masters, become in this Roman a severe professional conscientiousness, which strives not only for colour but for simple, definite line.

In Catullus, poetical form reaches its perfection in Rome. It is full of condensed meaning. A few words, all carefully chosen, charged with meaning and artistically set in the verse, give images in masterly style. This art is that of the contemporary Greek poetry which continued the tradition of Callimachos. Yet there is something harder in it, something, too, which is more vigorous and purer. But there is no lack of grace. In Catullus we find plenty of very beautiful passages of delicate feeling and extremely fresh colour, which brilliantly express, in an idealized form, the sincere impressions of a mind sensitive to the beauty of things, passages which reveal both the style of the day and the talent of a true artist. We shall only quote one, the alternate strophes of the young men and maidens in the *Epithalamium*.[3]

"A flower which grows in the shelter of a fenced garden, unknown to beasts, untouched by the plough, caressed by the winds, strengthened by the soil, fostered by the dew . . . many boys, many maids desire it. But when it is nipped with a little nail, no boy, no maid desires it. So a maiden, while yet untouched, is dear to all her companions. . . .

"The lonely vine which grows in a bare field never lifts itself up, never bears a sweet grape . . . but its highest branch sinks to its root ; and no husbandman, no herdsman tends it. But if it is wedded to the elm, many husbandmen, many herdsmen tend it. So a maiden, while yet untouched, grows old untended, but when she wins a fitting marriage at the right time, she is the dearer to her husband and the less burdensome to her kin."

While Lucretius, the contemporary of Catullus, still belongs, by his sometimes rather wearisome meticulousness, to the archaic type, the art of the Alexandrians of Rome,

---

[1] 94-8 ff.   [2] G. Radet, **XXI**, 1907, p. 9.   [3] lxii, 39 ff.

more supple but not yet given over to feeble elegance, already has all the classical qualities. It is an imitative art, no doubt, but by its own qualities, above all by its sincerity and youthful vigour, it will soon far surpass all its models. Just as the talent of Cicero, animated by life and sometimes borne forward by passion, rises far above the rhetoric which has formed it, nourishes it, and often hampers it, so the Roman poetry at the end of the Republic adds real inspiration to the delicate, scholarly art of the Greek craftsmen. The Hellenic world at that time had no poet to match with either Lucretius or Catullus.

CHAPTER IX

GREEK ART IN ROME

I

THE INVASION OF GREEK WORKS OF ART AND ARTISTS

WHILE, during the last century of the Republic, the contact
of life gives the eloquence, the history, and the poetry of
Rome a more robust and passionate quality, that is, an
infinitely more vigorous character than anything that we
can find in the Greek world after Alexander's time, the
plastic arts are far from showing the same originality. No
doubt they display, in a general fashion, the same tendencies
and tastes as literature as a whole, but they do not clothe
Greek inspiration in a Roman form. One might say that
they show without disguise the fundamentally Hellenistic
character of the civilization which Rome and Italy share
with the rest of the Mediterranean world.

When, at the beginning of the IInd century before our
era, Rome found herself drawn towards Greece and the
Hellenized kingdoms of Asia, she already had behind her a
long and fine artistic career, of which we have already tried
to discover certain features. The early art of Rome was that
of Etruria and that of Campania and southern Italy, of which
she assimilated the diverse qualities in the course of her
history and her conquests. As capital of Italy, she had
produced a composite of the genius of the whole peninsula.
In the course of the IInd century Italian traditions gradually
gave place to those of contemporary Greece. In the Ist
century the revolution was complete, and Roman art had
become purely Greek.

There occurred in Rome at this time a phenomenon
similar to that which we see in France in the XVIth century.

The country was suddenly invaded by new artistic principles, which caused the old forms to fall into contempt, completely smothering them, or at least reducing them to a latent existence. The result of the Roman expeditions in Greece and Asia may be compared to that of the French expeditions in Italy which produced the Renaissance in France.

No doubt, all memories of the old art did not utterly vanish. They survived obscurely in popular art, especially in country districts remote from Rome. Long afterwards, under the Empire, we are surprised to find, even in the provinces outside Italy, like Gaul, religious statuettes which recall the ancient Etruscan types, and in the art of the capital itself we see certain tendencies reappearing, such as realism in portraiture, and exact reproduction of historical events ; these tendencies certainly seem to have their roots in the old Italian tradition. They seem to point to the emergence in high art of traditions preserved by craftsmen and popular workshops rather than to a reawakening of faculties innate in the race. It was the old art of Italy which, with the peasant dynasty of the Flavians and the new nobility of provincial origin, rose out of the long lethargy imposed on it, nearly three centuries before, by the general enthusiasm for Hellenistic art.[1]

This stifling of native art is like a vengeance of the Greek world pillaged by conquering Rome. Subjecting Greece and Asia to the same treatment as Italy, the Roman armies regularly laid hands on the works of art accumulated in cities and sanctuaries. To adorn the triumphs of generals, statues and pictures were consigned to Rome wholesale. Most of the statues in Rome, and the best, so Strabo wrote in the reign of Augustus, came from Corinth. The city and the State warehouses were packed with the artistic loot of two centuries of victories.[2]

First the Romans were astounded ; then they came to admire and love all this beauty ravished at the point of the

---

[1] Furtwaengler, **LXXVII,** iii, pp. 266 ff., notes this survival of early Italic art in the engraved stones of the last two centuries of the Republic. He associates with them certain reliefs from rustic shrines like that of Aricia (cf. **XVI,** 1920, xii, p. 169), chiefly terra-cottas and popular ex-voto offerings It will suffice to mention, as links in this chain of popular art, the tomb of the baker M. Vergilius Eurysaces, of the Ist century B.C., and that of the Haterii of the Ist century A.D.

[2] On the plundering of the artistic treasures of Greece, see Colin, **LXXVI,** pp. 563 ff. ; Courbaud, **LII,** pp. 31 ff.

sword.   Pliny dates this change in feeling from the death of Attalos, that is, from the last third of the IInd century.[1] The too easy satisfaction of the love of beauty dulled in them the restless spirit of experiment which strives to obtain new aspects from known elements, and is one of the essential ingredients of artistic feeling.   An ideal which you seem to possess ceases to be an ideal, and loses its virtue as such. Ill-gotten works of art and superabundance of foreign master-pieces killed Roman art.   " The artistic dialect of Italy dies ; " Furtwaengler says, " the artistic language of Greece becomes the universal language of the Roman world." [2]

Not only works of art, but artists poured from the Greek lands into Rome.   From cities and kingdoms impoverished by the passage of the legions, artists made for the new capital where the wealth of the world was collected, and they might hope to find buyers.   No doubt they placed themselves at the orders of these customers, and did the work which they ordered, in the manner which they required.   Thus, the painter Metrodoros, whom Aemilius Paullus went to fetch from Athens, was ordered to turn out the usual pictures which, on the day of the triumph, related the exploits of the armies to the Roman people.   No doubt the demand governed the artist.   But the ideas, tastes, and habits of the artist also imposed themselves on the customers, especially when these latter, like the Roman élite of the time of Flamininus and Scipio Aemilianus, were infatuated with Hellenism and recognized all the superiority of the Greek tradition to their own.

Moreover, it was not isolated artists, but whole Greek families and studios that came and settled in Rome.   Such was the family of Timarchides, Polycles, and Dionysios, whom Metellus Macedonicus brought home with him.[3]   Such, later, were the gem-engraver Dioscurides and his three sons, Eutychos, Herophilos, and Hyllos, under Augustus.[4]   At the beginning of the Imperial age, a certain number of signatures tell us the names of artists working in Rome ; they were almost all Greeks, and far the most of them Athenians, Apollonios, Antiochos, Criton and Nicolaos, Glycon, Cleomenes, Menophantos, etc.

[1] N.H., xxxiii. 149   [2] LXXVII, iii, p. 300
[3] Collignon, XLVII, ii, pp. 622-3.   [4] Furtwaengler, LXXVII, iii, p. 305.

So Greek art took root in Rome with them, Greek art with its motives, its style, and also its theories. In art, as in science, as in rhetoric, as in poetry, Greek technique, τέχνη, was imposed on the Romans. Since art had no need of the transposition which language made necessary in literature, and since it was not generally practised by Romans, the art of Rome, during the last centuries of the Republic, cannot be distinguished from that of the contemporary Hellenistic world. Not in Rome shall we find its governing tendencies.

In this great Mediterranean civilization which was now invading Italy, the aesthetic schools corresponded to the literary schools. We recognize in art the opposite influences of Asia and Attica, and also that of Alexandria. For the great intellectual centres were also the artistic centres. Their influence was felt in Rome. There the various tendencies ended and mingled. If Roman art has a character of its own, it is just the eclecticism which welcomes the most different styles, with a readiness which perhaps betrays lack of discrimination. Before the flood of new ideas brought to him by the Mediterranean current, the Roman felt a little helpless ; he did not know which to choose, and in his perplexity adopted them all. Circumstances rather than a definite choice or taste decided in favour of the fashions and styles which reigned in succession.

II

ASIATIC ART. PERGAMON

The earliest and deepest current seems to have been that which came from Asia. At the beginning of the IInd century, Asia, which the Roman armies entered almost as soon as Greece, struck the imagination of the Romans far more than Greece Proper.

In Greece the Romans found a municipal life not unlike that of the Italian country towns, and more petty than that of the Greek cities in Italy. The country was poor. Athens, and above all Corinth, were the only exceptions to the general mediocrity. Very few among the Romans were capable of appreciating the noble memories and the greatness of the modest cities which, by the free development of the intelligence and the passion for beauty, had contributed to the progress of Hellenic civilization. Very few, on the other hand, could fail to be impressed by the dazzling wealth of Asia.

Asia was the land of colour and size. Its countries stretched to infinity, being bordered by deserts which prolonged the horizon rather than bounded it. Every kingdom embraced many provinces, each more vast than Greece. The cities were immense, and teemed with an active, industrious, noisy population. In the capitals, the court led its luxurious life around the sovereign. The lesser cities displayed the ambition of the Royal governors, who were lords of the fortune and obedience of abjectly submissive subjects. The power of the master manifested itself in the splendour of his wealth, the size of his palace, and the ostentation of monuments pure in taste but more sumptuous than those of Greece. What an example and what a temptation for the Roman leader, as for the least of his soldiers ! It was in Asia that the Romans acquired the taste for luxury and colossal size, together with habits of despotism.

From the shores of the Mediterranean to those of the Euphrates and the Nile, the triumphs of Alexander had blended two worlds, Greece and the East. The hero's lieutenants had founded in barbarian lands Greek monarchies copied from the Oriental model ; the Macedonian generals and their descendants had developed into successors and emulators of the Great King. They remained Greeks, however, and attracted round them the best Hellenic elements as well as the native aristocracy. The latter became Hellenized, but it neglected what it did not understand of Greek culture, and in exchange introduced, among the Greeks who mingled with it, some of the traditions of its own past and some of its moral, political, and social principles. It was only too easy for the Greek masters of Asia to " go native " and to adopt the material wealth of those whom they ruled together with their vices, the natural consequence of excess. The most admirable thing was the persistence of Hellenism in these more than half Oriental courts and the almost religious reverence which was always paid in them to Greek art and literature.

Moreover, their new wealth enabled the Greek rulers of Asia and Egypt to give artistic and intellectual life a far more ample and brilliant development than was possible in Greece Proper. In the Greek cities architecture had usually been confined to the erection of temples to the gods. In Asia whole cities had to be built. Private dwellings, the vistas and arrangement of streets, public places, official buildings, and, above all, the palaces of princes with their appendages raised an infinity of new problems, the solution of which was entrusted to the artist. The religious art of earlier times had sought beauty in harmony of proportion, simplicity of line, and severe gravity of decoration. The new spirit resorted to gigantic size and piled on ornament. To the sculptor, the painter, the mosaicist, and even the metal-worker, the architect entrusted the decoration of vast surfaces. The huge public squares, the long porticoes, and the gardens required statues, or rather groups, and every device which could attract, occupy, and entertain the eye. Greek art had to fill an Oriental frame.

Three cities had taken the lead in this movement since the IIIrd century—Alexandria, the capital of the Ptolemies, Antioch, the capital of the Seleucids in Syria, and, rather later, Pergamon, the capital of the Attalids in Asia Minor. Of Antioch we know too little to be able to estimate the part which it played in Hellenistic civilization. But one cannot understand Roman art unless one has at least a general notion of the development of Greek art at Pergamon and Alexandria.

Pergamon was a creation of its ruling house, which had built it almost entirely, and had gradually formed a kingdom round it. It began to play a big part in the Hellenistic world with Attalos I (241-197), who had conquered a large part of Asia Minor from the Syrians. The enemy of Philip of Macedon, Attalos displayed his phil-Hellenism in contrast to Macedonian brutality, and, in particular, heaped attentions on Athens. At the same time he was, from the end of the IIIrd century, the friend of the Romans ; it was he who, about the end of the second Punic War, in 204, sent them the sacred baetyl of Pessinus. Homer was treated as a national poet at Pergamon, and the friendship of Attalos probably had something to do with the development of the legend of the Phrygian Aeneas in Rome. The successor of

Attalos, Eumenes II (197-159), definitely sided with the Romans against Macedon and Syria, and shared the spoils of Antiochos with Rome. At the same time he presented himself in Asia as the protector of Hellenism against the barbarians, Galatians or others, and built in Athens the portico whose ruins can still be seen between the Odeion of Herodes Atticus and the Theatre of Dionysos. In the reign of Attalos II (159-138) the Romans found themselves already practically the masters of Pergamon. Intelligent and exceptionally virtuous among the princes of Asia, gallant soldiers and clever diplomats, the kings of Pergamon employed their wealth, which became proverbial, in building fine monuments and attracting artists and scholars to their court. Collignon compares them to the Medici.[1] But in 138 Pergamon fell into the hands of Attalos III, a restless, suspicious lunatic who, having no heir, carried devotion to Rome to the point of bequeathing his treasures and kingdom to her. On his death, in 133, the vast dominion constituted by the Attalids in Asia Minor became the Roman province of Asia.

At Pergamon Hellenism was triumphant, a Hellenism purer of any native mixture than in Syria and Egypt, almost the Hellenism of Athens, but animated by the favour of energetic rulers and the wealth of Asia. Athene reigned in Pergamon. While Athens took on the aspect of a dead town, peopled by idlers among whom rhetors and philosophers declaimed, Pergamon was a hard-working, busy city, with flourishing royal manufactures of gold brocade, where the artist's effort was sustained by a big movement of industry, intense political life, victories to be celebrated, and a very large demand to be satisfied. Its kings tried to vie with those of Egypt. They founded a Library, which they made a centre of as varied studies and teaching as the Museum at Alexandria. Here Crates of Mallos taught, whose mission to Rome about the middle of the IInd century was one of the capital events of the intellectual life of the city. It was at Pergamon, at the feet of Crates, that Panaetios received his education. When the kingdom of the Attalids became a Roman province, Rhodes took up the heritage of the schools and studios of Pergamon. Poseidonios taught at Rhodes.

---

[1] **XLVIII,** p. 190.

The teachers of Pergamon, and later those of Rhodes, were the true intermediaries between Hellenism and Rome.

The Romans received from Pergamon their initiation into Greek artistic life. Attalos and Eumenes had created in their capital a veritable royal museum in forming the collections destined to adorn the palaces and the Library. They had brought together a selection of originals or copies of all the great Hellenic schools of art. They bought the most famous pictures, or had them copied. They gave the impetus to the first history of art. The scholars of the Library, such as Antigonos of Carystos, who was both artist and writer, drew up a canon of the Greek masters, which was the accepted authority in Rome even in Pliny's time.[1]

But not only art criticism flourished at Pergamon. The arts themselves received a fruitful impetus from the phil-Hellenism of the rulers. The artists mostly came from Greece, and from Athens in particular. It is truly Greek art that we find at Pergamon, but Greek art in a new form, due to the new demands made on it by an Asiatic monarchy. At the end of the IIIrd century Attalos I caused his victories over the Galatians to be represented in a series of statues intended to adorn a great triumphal monument. Greek artistic tradition taught that allusions to contemporary events should be concealed in a veil of mythological allegory. At Pergamon, on the contrary, we find genuine Galatians, exactly taken from the living models supplied by prisoners. Roman art, M. Collignon observes, afterwards took it upon itself to follow the consequences of this evolution to their extreme, reproducing with strict accuracy the physical type, costume, and arms of barbarian peoples.[2] The historical sculpture which was to flourish in Rome had its origins, not only in the Italian tradition of representing the exploits of victorious armies naturalistically, but also in the lessons of Pergamon.

About the first quarter of the IInd century, Eumenes II in his turn wished to immortalize by a signal monument the memory of the victories, won in co-operation with the Romans, which finally ensured for Pergamon the rank of a great power.

Allegory was not excluded this time. It is the defeat of the Giants in their war against the gods that we find repre-

---

[1] For all these details cf. Collignon, **XLVIII**, pp. 195 ff.
[2] **XLVIII**, p. 207.

sented on the frieze of the great altar. But even in the allegory one sees the same tendency to realism, and above all to pathos, as in the figures of defeated and dying Gauls. The artist piles on tragic episodes and romantic contrasts. In the agonized writhings of the Giants' bodies he tries to express the intensity of extreme physical pain. His manual skill is astonishing, and his mastery of his art remarkable. His work is full of *bravura* passages, produced according to the studio formulas which were to art what the recipes of rhetoric were to literature. " Asianism," the tendency to the declamatory form, dominates. The conception is powerful, but theatrical. The Hellenistic evolution which started from the pathos of Scopas and the naturalism of Lysippos is now complete. It will not go further. It is in Italy that the influence of this Pergamene art will later be felt.[1]

For Pergamon was the birth-place of the school of Asiatic art, so fond of grandiose forms and exaggerated movements, the most typical and famous specimens of which were produced by the Rhodian studios about the beginning of the Ist century. The Laocoon and the group of the Farnese Bull represent in the domain of art the declamatory Asianism personified in eloquence by the rhetors of Asia Minor. When we find these features reappearing in Rome, we must beware of seeing in them a particularly Roman character. In Rome they are but the representatives of a style which was formed at Pergamon during the IInd century before our era, and expanded, down to the middle of the Ist century before our era, on the soil of Asia.

III

ALEXANDRIA

The influence of Alexandria on the imagination and art of Rome seems to have been less profound than that of Pergamon, and, above all, much later in date. The political relations of Rome with Egypt did not become definite and frequent until the time of Pompey. Caesar, after Pharsalus, was the first Roman general to enter Egypt with an army. This does not mean that before his time the life, science, and art of Alex-

[1] Collignon, **XLVIII**, pp. 214-15.

andria were unknown in Italy. As early as the IInd century, Delos had acted as intermediary between the kingdom of the Ptolemies and the Romans. About the end of that century the Egyptian ships were landing at Puteoli their men and their gods, who easily made their way thence to Rome. Alexandrian science and erudition seem to have been known in Rome no less than those of Pergamon. Nevertheless, the Egyptian current seems to have been for a long time weaker, and, above all, to have been always considered much more foreign, than that which, through Pergamon, brought Hellenism into Italy, tinged with the colour of Asia.

Instead of being an ally, and presently a subject, like Pergamon, Alexandria had the position of an independent capital of Hellenism. Founded by Alexander to be the capital of his empire, the city of the Nile had maintained a kind of pre-eminence over the whole East. It had the busiest port, the largest and most industrious population, and the most celebrated monuments of all. There was nothing in the world to equal the Pharos, which seems to have been the model of the minaret and our steeples, nor the Arsenal with its huge magazines. The monumental tomb of Alexander stood in the centre of the city. The Temple of Neptune and that of Serapis, the Serapeion, had not their like anywhere. The Royal Palace surpassed all others in luxury and size ; it occupied a third of the city, and was a city itself, amid parks and colonnaded gardens. To the Palace the Theatre belonged ; the Palace included the Museum, which was the royal library, the greatest library of antiquity, which came to possess 900,000 volumes.

The Library was the centre of an intense intellectual life, which was the pride of the Ptolemies. All round it, in the gardens, were the Porticoes in which teachers discoursed with their disciples. Lecture-rooms and even dining-halls awaited scholars and students. It was the Prytaneion and the Gardens of Academos in one. "At Alexandria," a satirist said, " they fatten a whole flock of scribes who cackle frantically in the hen-coop of the Muses." By every means the kings strove to attract and keep in the Museum the most renowned scholars. The erudite poet Callimachos (310-240) was one of the first directors of the Library. After him came Eratosthenes, a mathematician and geographer, and then

Q

Aristophanes of Byzantion (265-185) and Aristarchos of Samos (220-145), the greatest masters of poetry, science, and philology. Among the productions of the Museum, catalogues, learned editions, and commentaries alternated with allegorical poems full of both erudition and graceful wit. All this intellectual life gravitated between books and the court.

With its magnificent kings and its wealthy aristocracy of merchants, Alexandria could not fail to be an artistic city. Its style was markedly different from that of Pergamon. At Pergamon Athene reigned, the grave, heroic goddess, who raised majesty to pomp and endeavour to declamation. Alexandria was the city of Dionysos, the joyous, effeminate god of voluptuous ecstasy, surrounded by his jolly, grinning satyrs and light-limbed Maenads, taming the wild beasts and rejoicing in the intertwinings of vine and ivy. Pleasure and flowers, wit carried to parody and caricature, prettiness and grotesqueness with all the intermediate shades—that is the soul of Alexandrian art.

This was the art which produced the many pleasing types of Venus which were disseminated over the ancient world in countless copies—the crouching Aphrodite of Doedalsas and all the greatly humanized daughters of the immortal Cnidian. The charming little Venus of the Esquiline, who belongs to this graceful band, is fairly clearly shown to be Egyptian by the uraeus which coils round the vase at her feet. In this voluptuous city the study of the female nude became the great problem. The Italian museums show how fruitful this vein was in Rome.

In sculpture, as in painting, the Alexandrian school spreads ornament in profusion everywhere. It is especially fond of pliant garlands and gay wreaths, flowers and fruit. Among the roses of Alexandria, mythology becomes pretty and light-hearted. The Loves hold the chief place, passing easily from the legends of the gods to scenes of ordinary life, and displaying on all sides the chubby graces of childhood. Alexandrian are the innumerable Loves of Pompeii, who ply every trade, drive chariots, play with all the animals, wrestle together, or gather the vintage. The spirit of Egypt brings gaiety and light grace into the fertile exuberance of Campanian nature.

But Egypt was also a land of vivid realism, sometimes coarse but never drab, always bringing laughter into ugliness. The court of the Ptolemies welcomed Theocritos and the idyll ; the freshness of the pastoral and the simplicity of popular scenes were a rest after the erudition and affected graces of the courtly spirit. Alexandria was the birth-place of the celebrated types of the drunken old woman, smiling toothlessly at the bottle which she clasps to her withered bosom, the wriggling, grimacing little nigger, the countryman and wench driving their calf or carrying their lamb to market, and probably, also, all the rustic scenes which, on a picturesque background of rocks crowned by a tree, show a lamb sucking its mother or a lioness half rising at the approach of danger to her cubs. (See Plate X.)

All this art has no object but to please and amuse the mind ; it is sheer diversion and dilettantism. It is a part of domestic luxury. Statues, reliefs, paintings, mosaics, chiselled plate, have no other purpose than to lend beauty and gaiety to the house in which the master receives his friends at banquet and entertainment. To Alexandria in particular Rome was indebted for her luxury and the pleasant setting with which her aristocracy endeavoured to surround their life.

Asia taught Roman art its pompous majesty ; Egypt taught it grace. Alexandrian beauty is symbolized by a single figure, that which tradition gives to the last queen of Egypt, Cleopatra, the cultured and amorous, who combined all the refined charm of coquetry with subtle ambition and passionate energy. How many great ladies and Empresses of Rome, consciously or otherwise, copied Cleopatra ? No image gives a better understanding of Alexandrian art than Plutarch's picture of the queen going to Tarsus for the interview to which Antony had summoned her. The scene is reproduced almost word for word by Shakespeare. Here is his translation.

> The barge she sat in, like a burnish'd throne,
> Burn'd on the water. The poop was beaten gold ;
> Purple the sails, and so perfumed that
> The winds were love-sick with them. The oars were silver,
> Which to the tune of flutes kept stroke, and made
> The water which they beat to follow faster,

As amorous of their strokes. For her own person,
It beggar'd all description. She did lie
In her pavilion, cloth-of-gold of tissue,
O'erpicturing that Venus, where we see
The fancy out-work nature. On each side her,
Stood pretty dimpled boys, like smiling Cupids,
With divers-coloured fans, whose wind did seem
To glow the delicate cheeks which they did cool,
And what they undid, did. . . .
Her gentlewomen, like the Nereides,
So many mermaids, tended her i' the eyes,
And made their bends adornings. At the helm,
A seeming mermaid steers. The silken tackle
Swell with the touches of those flower-soft hands,
That yarely frame their office. From the barge
A strange invisible perfume hits the sense
Of the adjacent wharfs. The city cast
Her people out upon her ; and Antony
Enthron'd i' the market-place, did sit alone. . . .

Caesar's passion for Cleopatra marks the triumph of
Alexandrinism in Rome. Cleopatra, with part of her court,
had been living two years in Rome when Caesar was assassinated in 44. We can imagine how much her presence
helped to propagate in high Roman society the fashions and
artistic tastes of Egypt.

This, very clearly, is the date of the beginning of the
Roman busts of Egyptian style which are found in a continuous series from Caesar to the end of the Empire. The
Caesar in the Baracco Collection in Rome is one of the most
typical examples. (Plate XII, 1.) The stone is a black
basalt or some very hard marble, the tone of which brings
out the broad surfaces of light and shade in strong contrast.
The skull is long and sticks out behind as in the ancient
Egyptian type. A marked realism, which spares no wrinkle,
is combined with the conventional treatment of the hair and
beard, which are indicated either by dotting or by arabesques
of minute curls, incised rather than carved. The deliberate
conventionalization gives the whole a pronounced exotic
appearance. It is not merely Alexandrian Hellenism, it is a
gleam of ancient Egypt which here appears in Rome. Still
more must all the elements which made up Greek life, as it
had developed in Egypt since Alexander's day, have at this
time come into favour on the banks of the Tiber.

IV

THE NEO-ATTIC SCHOOL

While Pergamon and Rhodes sought for new colours in emotion and picturesqueness, and Alexandria strove after graceful combinations of Greek beauty and the Egyptian spirit, Athens, on her side, with pious pride in the past which was her especial glory, grew more and more attached to her tradition and endeavoured to make it live again. Attic art had always been marked by certain archaistic features. Henceforward, in deliberate reaction against foreign novelties, it displayed the qualities proper to this archaism. Against Asiatic declamation and Alexandrian prettiness, it maintained

FIG. 13.—Reliefs on the vase of Sosibios.   (Louvre.)

the severity, the strong sobriety, and the purity of line of the early period, carrying this purity to the point of dryness. The virtue which it esteemed above all others was clarity. Marble, in Attic hands, took on the precision and rather hard contrasts of bronze. In other respects the artists of Athens showed the widest eclecticism. They did not choose any one period ; all the schools of the past were equally glorious in their eyes. They copied with equal readiness the ancient models of the most different styles to be found in Athens, often even mixing them in a single work.

This worship of the past was detrimental to their originality. From the middle of the IInd century, and especially during the Ist century B.C., the Attic artists show more interest in perfect execution than in invention. They represent a reaction in art exactly parallel to the literary movement of the young orators who called themselves Attic.

Their influence and their work filled Rome and the rest of

Italy, from the time of Sylla onwards, with the decorative reliefs which are easily recognized as copies, or rather as imitations, more or less free, of the famous works of great artists of the past. We may mention one example—the marble vase, signed by Sosibios, in the Louvre. (Fig. 13.)[1] The belly is adorned with a delicate sculptured frieze. On the two sides of an altar, an archaistic Artemis and Hermes advance. Behind Artemis, a Maenad plays a lyre and a satyr blows a double flute; behind Hermes are a Maenad, whirling in delirium, and a Pyrrhic dancer. Two other Maenads look on. The dancing Maenad is copied from a celebrated original by Scopas. All the other figures reappear, isolated or in groups, on a number of other reliefs, mostly found in Italy. They are transpositions of Attic works of the Vth and IVth centuries. All the motives and all the styles of the past reappear in these Neo-Attic reliefs.

V

The Hellenistic Schools of Art in Rome

These diverse influences of Asia, Alexandria, and Athens mingled not only in the Greek world, but still more in Rome. Ancient Attic art influenced Pergamon, which itself transmitted a number of the artistic elements developed by it, particularly the picturesque element, to Alexandria. Moreover, Alexandria and Athens were in direct relations. The academic reliefs attributed to Alexandria bear distinct traces of Neo-Attic purism, and the Attic artists are not insensible to the variety and versatile fancy of Alexandrian art. The reliefs in which imitation of the past is most conspicuous appear especially Attic; in many picturesque reliefs certain details—ibises, storks, crocodiles, hippopotamuses—clearly betray Egyptian origin; but no one will venture to maintain that nothing but imitations of the past came from the Attic studios, and that the Alexandrians never sculptured anything but picturesque reliefs. The distinctions which I have tried to draw must not be taken too strictly even for the history of art in Hellenistic countries; they must be applied still less

[1] Collignon, **XLVII,** ii, p. 645.

rigidly to Rome, where artists from everywhere worked side by side. Moreover, each one of these artists might have worked in different centres before he settled in Rome. For example, a man might have been first trained in Athens, and then have perfected his talent and enlarged his repertory in Asia, or in Egypt, or in one country after the other. Or, more simply, he might take his inspiration now from a Pergamene model and now from an Alexandrian type. We must be content, therefore, to note the presence in Rome of works belonging to the different artistic currents of the Hellenistic world.

Did Greek art assume in Rome, under the influence of Roman life, any special character which we can regard as peculiarly Roman ?

It would seem that the Roman demand encouraged a tendency, which was already noticeable in Hellenistic art, to the industrial production of works of art.

In Rome, even more than in the royal residences or great commercial cities of the East, the patrons of art were most of them *nouveaux riches* who lacked both ideals and educated taste. Finding no artistic tradition in their own country, they made up for its absence by excessive and undiscriminating enthusiasm for anything that came from the renowned foreign art-centres, and still more for all that bore the hall-mark of an accepted artistic tradition. Hence the rage for foreign things on the one hand and for the antique on the other.

Among Knights enriched by trade, tax-farming, or simple money-lending, and soldiers or provincial governors who owed their magnificence to loot, we see the love of antiquities and the collector's mania developing. The work of art, especially the ancient work of art, takes on a commercial value, and becomes an article of trade. The freedman Chrysogonus fills his house with such things. Scaurus spends the legacy of his mother and his stepfather Sylla on increasing his collections. In Sicily, Verres is not content with stealing works of art ; he goes in for all kinds of speculations in them, fakes them, and has restoring-shops which make forgeries out of portions taken from ancient vases. The veterans whom Caesar established as colonists on the site of Corinth excavate the ancient cemeteries in search of ancient plate with the thoroughness of archaeologists.

In Rome there were dealers in antiquities, experts, commission-agents, and restorers. We hear of C. Avianius Evander, a Greek by origin, a sculptor and metal-chaser, taken from Athens to Alexandria by Antony, brought to Rome, sold as a slave, and then freed, who carried on the trade of sculptor and dealer in works of art of all kinds. Collectors and dealers had their meeting-places, the *atria auctionaria*, like our own auction-rooms.[1] This trade in beauty stifled original experiment and creation.

This was the time when great luxurious villas were springing up in the country near Rome and all over Italy. For their adornment, the activity of the Italian studios was not sufficient. Cicero asks Atticus to buy him reliefs in Greece for his villa at Tusculum, and Atticus, keen broker that he is, at the same time procures for Pompey Greek statues for his theatre. Appius Claudius goes to Greece in person with the sole object of bringing back sculptures and paintings. Works of art were consigned to Italy in ship-loads, as at the time of the conquest.

Some time ago the wreck of a cargo of this kind, dating from this period, was found in the sea near Anticythera. More recently, in 1907, M. Merlin had the good fortune to explore the cargo of an ancient ship, sunk off Mahdia, on the east coast of Tunisia.[2] The bulk of the cargo consisted of about sixty marble columns, destined apparently for a portico. From the sides of the ship were taken works in bronze and marble, colossal heads and torsos, fauns, satyrs, female figures, statuettes, reliefs, Greek inscriptions, triangular candelabra-bases, fragments of monumental craters adorned with Bacchic scenes, and many metal fittings of furniture representing heads of deities, masks, griffins, and heads of animals. Some of these objects are veritable masterpieces— an Eros of Praxitelean type, a herm of a bearded Dionysos, signed by Boethos of Chalcedon (a Rhodian sculptor of the first half of the IInd century), two cornice fittings representing Ariadne and Dionysos, a torch-bearing Hermaphrodite, a satyr on the point of leaping, a charming little Eros with a cithara, and two figurines of grotesque dancing-girls, misshapen dwarfs with huge heads, accompanied by a male

[1] Cf. Rayet and Collignon, **CXXXV**, p. 60 ; Collignon, **XLVII**, ii, p. 611.
[2] A. Merlin, **XV**, xvii (1909) and xviii (1910).

PLATE V

1

2

CAMPANA PLAQUES. TERRA-COTTA RELIEFS
1. Curetes dancing round the infant Zeus. (British Museum)
2. The rising of the Nile. (Rome, Terme)

[face p. 248

PLATE VI

ARTEMIS FROM POMPEII
Marble, archaistic style. (Naples Museum)

[face p. 249

dancing buffoon. The cargo almost certainly came from Attica, to judge from the inscriptions and some of the reliefs, but it includes the most different styles. The columns are new, and had just left the quarry ; but many of the works of art were repaired antiques. The whole must have been consigned by some Athenian art-broker, and have been intended to adorn some Roman villa. M. Merlin holds that the date of the wreck can be fixed about the second half of Ist century before our era. How many other cargoes of the kind must, in the course of centuries, have safely reached the ports of Italy !

The original contribution of Italy at this time seems to have been chiefly the industrialization of the production of works of art. The marble quarries of the Etruscan coast were not yet being worked,[1] and the other native stones were little adapted to sculpture. There remained the material which was so much used by the old native art—terra-cotta. Now, we have a fairly large number of terra-cotta reliefs, which, by their style and dimensions, recall the Alexandrian and Neo-Attic academic reliefs which were set in the walls of rooms and porticoes. Like the reliefs themselves, these terra-cotta plaques were coloured. In the adornment of buildings they served the same purpose as painted panels set in architectural features. These decorative plaques, turned out from a mould, which made multiplication possible, but very delicately retouched, are known as Campana plaques ; they are beyond dispute of Italian manufacture. (Plate V.)

The subjects on them are those of Hellenistic reliefs in general. Most of these compositions are inspired by mythology, and by the Bacchic cycle in particular. The art is vigorous and easy. There is a fine specimen, in the Terme Museum in Rome, representing the dance of the armed Curetes round the infant Zeus,[2] and one in the British Museum showing satyrs and Maenads dancing round the young Bacchus.[3] Another example from the Terme depicts, through two arches of a colonnade or window, an Egyptian landscape, huts threatened by the Nile floods, with storks on the roofs,

---

[1] The marbles of Luni and Carrara seem to have been first used by Mamurra, Caesar's friend, and then only for architectonic facings.

[2] Della Seta, **CXLIX,** fig. 286. Our pl. v reproduces the specimen in the British Museum, which is less beautiful but more complete (Walters, **CLXVI,** pl. lviii).

[3] *Ibid.*, pl. lix.

and men in a boat hunting crocodile and hippopotamus. (Plate V, 2.) So the different inspirations of pictorial art, those which come from Attica and those of Egypt, appear in the Campana plaques.

Thus the motives and styles of Hellenistic art spread in Italian decorative industry. Walls and ceilings, in houses and tombs, were covered with pictures on stucco relief, executed swiftly but with wonderful dexterity and ease. Those found at the Farnesina, on the left bank of the Tiber, which date from about the beginning of our era, may be taken as typical of them. (Plate VII.) In frames of architectural motives, flowers and foliage alternate with Loves, winged Victories, and griffins. Or there are little mythological or rustic pictures, in which human figures appear against a picturesque background, an altar beneath the shade of an old tree, the entrance of a farm, or a bridge boldly thrown over a miniature stream. The style is intermediate between relief and painting ; it calls up a crowd of familiar images, such as we find in a poem of Catullus, Tibullus, or Propertius.

Art appears in even smaller form, but without losing its delicacy, in the graceful reliefs which adorn the walls of the red clay vases from Arretium (Arezzo).[1] Just as the Campana plaques imitate the Hellenistic marble reliefs, so Italian pottery reproduces, cheap and wholesale, the works of toreutic art of Pergamon and Alexandria. We know how wonderfully this pottery developed during the last century of the Republic and at the beginning of the Empire. It was derived from an old Italic tradition, which, through the relief ware made at Cales in Campania in the IIIrd and IInd centuries, was connected with the old Campanian and Etruscan workshops previous to the conquest of the Greek world. But we find the native tradition, in the Ist century B.C., entirely rejuvenated by the influence of the so-called " Samian " ware, of which writers speak ; but it must be admitted that we do not know exactly what this pottery was. Probably the Greek workshops, and those of Samos in particular, were the first to undertake the reproduction for the use of the poorer classes of the precious vases of chased metal which adorned the tables of the rich. The Italian potters hastened to follow their example, and, as they had

[1] Walters, CLXVI, pp. 140 ff.

PLATE VII

1

2

1. Stucco from the Farnesina. (Rome, Terme)
2. Decorative painting from the House of Livia on the Palatine. Second Pompeian
   style. (Naples Museum)

[face p. 250

PLATE VIII

1

2
PAINTINGS OF THE THIRD AND FOURTH POMPEIAN STYLES
1. A Poetess. Painting from Herculaneum
2. Spring. Painting from Stabiae

already succeeded in doing in the IVth century with painted pottery, they were not long in completely cutting out foreign imports. Italian industry in general continued until the beginning of the Empire to be extremely active in all forms of production, and its undiminished versatility proves great vitality. It did not try to resist foreign fashions and to set up against them a style of its own ; on the contrary, it adopted and appropriated the innovations of the various Mediterranean workshops.

The master potters of Arretium were Italians. The earliest of them, who belongs to the Ist century B.C., signs himself Marcus Perennius. His successor, or a later rival, Publius Cornelius, must have worked under Augustus. But both men employed workmen, Greek or Latin, whose names often appear beside theirs. With Perennius, for example, we find Tigranes, Bargates, and Cerdo associated. The relief compositions were produced by stamping in a mould, and were then delicately retouched. The subjects belong to the same cycle as those of the marble and terra-cotta reliefs—mythological persons and episodes and genre scenes, treated in the graceful style, with a slight affectation of archaism suited to the taste of the time.

The vases of Cornelius, which are later, are distinguished by the development of floral decoration treated in the realistic style which appears in sculpture in the time of Augustus. In this they recall certain silver cups in the Boscoreale treasure, girt with a thickly leaved branch of laurel. The figure motives are still those brought into fashion by Hellenistic art. From this repertory the decorative art of the Empire, down to the end of the IIIrd century, was to take its subjects.

Whether it was industrial or not, whether it was exercised by Greeks or Italians, the art which was formed in Italy in the last centuries of the Republic and, in its main lines, would remain that of Imperial Rome, owed its inspiration to the last original efforts of the Hellenic imagination.

VI

PAINTING

As the differences of style between the vases of Perennius and those of Cornelius indicate, this Graeco-Roman art did not remain stationary. It evolved like a living thing. The succession of mural decorations at Pompeii, which extends from the IInd century B.C. to the catastrophe of 79 A.D., allows us to follow the changes in taste, if not in Rome itself, at least in a small town in Campania.

During the Republican period the method known as "incrustation" reduced the painting of walls to a very minor matter. It was confined to panels of coloured stucco, in imitation of the marble slabs which covered the walls of the Eastern palaces. Luxury during this period consisted in splendid mosaics like the *Battle of Issos* in the House of the Faun,[1] the still-life subjects in the same dwelling, or the scene from comedy, signed by Dioscurides of Samos, in the so-called Villa of Cicero. These were Greek works, copied by Greek artists from Greek paintings. Large compositions like the *Battle of Issos* were certainly executed on the spot, but the smaller works may well have been sent ready-made from some Hellenic studio.[2] Painting itself did not rise above the art of the "painter and decorator."

The second style covers the period from Sylla's time to about the end of the reign of Augustus (80 B.C. to 14 A.D.). If we allow for the backwardness of a provincial town, it must correspond roughly to the style which flourished in Rome before the age of Augustus. The cornices and side-pieces of the panels are depicted in perspective. Columns casting a strong shadow give an illusion of depth. The trick of the painting sometimes seems to make a hole in the wall ; in this apparent hole a small landscape, a genre scene, or a mythological subject is set, so as to look as if it was outside the house. The style of these compositions is exactly like that of the Farnesina stuccos. The pictorial motives were usually added later and laid by incrustation in the centre of the

---

[1] Thédenat, **CLVII**, p. 109, fig. 65.
[2] For mosaic, see P. Gauckler, **LVI**, s.v. *Musivum opus*.

monochrome panel, like the *emblemata* of the mosaics in the pavement. They were carefully composed in the studio by quite other artists than those who painted the walls. The illusory architectural setting was the work of skilled crafts-men ; the pictorial subjects belonged to Graeco-Roman art. (Plate VII, 2.)

The third style belongs to the period of the Julian dynasty, from the end of the reign of Augustus to the first destruction of Pompeii in 63 A.D. Its characteristic is fantastic, quite imaginary architecture, without solidity or relief, altogether light and airy. Within this setting in light colours, the panels are bordered with bands of small subjects treated in miniature, and generally on a black ground ; the centre is occupied by a picture of varying size and in a much more realistic style than those of the preceding period.

The fourth style comes between the two catastrophes of 63 and 79. The painted architecture, while still remaining fantastic, is given realistic relief. The pictorial motives are more developed in the framework of mural decoration. The subjects become more and more varied ; marine subject and still life alternate with genre scenes, often very realistic, and mythological themes. Persons or animals seem to come through doors painted on the walls. The style grows more and more complicated, until it is an incoherent jumble of every form and every motive.

Many of the pictures of the third and fourth styles are beautiful works of art, remarkably sure in drawing, pure in line, and harmonious in colour. (Plate VIII.) Italy at this time possessed artists, true artists, even in minor towns like Pompeii. No doubt we cannot tell how far these paintings were original ; at least we can appreciate the great skill which they display.

VII

The First Attempts at a Roman Art. Pasiteles and his School

Art, as practised in Rome in the time of Pompey, Cicero, and Caesar, drew its sap from Hellenistic sources, but it was a vigorous branch of Greek art. It aimed chiefly at imitation; it was still in the apprentice stage, and had not developed a personality distinct from the lessons of its masters; but it was already bearing fruit, and manifested at least some interesting tendencies.

The best-known of these men who tried to realize beauty in emulation of the Greeks is Pasiteles. He was an Italian, perhaps of Greek origin, but a Roman citizen in virtue of being an inhabitant of southern Italy. He settled in Rome, and was at the height of his fame in 62, the year of the death of the great actor Roscius, in memory of whom he made a chased silver vase of which Cicero speaks.[1] Metal-chasing seems to have been the first talent which he displayed, and silver mirrors bearing his signature were admired.[2] From this work he went on to sculpture; he made a statue of Jupiter in gold and ivory.[3] Like many great artists of Pergamon, Pasiteles was a learned man; he had considerable knowledge of the ancient schools of Greek art, and wrote a description in five volumes of the most famous works of the whole world.[4]

An original characteristic was said to be the very great care with which he modelled in clay. He never executed a work without first making an extremely detailed clay sketch, and he maintained that clay-modelling was the mother of sculpture,[5] very probably a memory of the old Italic tradition whose use of terra-cotta I have described. Moreover, work in clay enabled him to make very careful studies from nature. There is a story that one day he was nearly eaten by a panther when he was engrossed in modelling a lion in a harbour where beasts from Africa had just been landed. Accuracy and naturalism were qualities which were, no doubt, highly developed in Hellenistic art, but they were to be still further developed in Roman art, to which they would give its special stamp.

We possess no work by Pasiteles. But his pupil Stephanos, who lived in the second half of the Ist century B.C., signed a fine statue of an Ephebus now in the Villa Albani. " The structure of the body," M. Collignon says of this statue, " recalls the early Peloponnesian works, but the much softer execution somehow gives a conflicting impression, and con-

---

[1] *Div.*, i. 36.
[2] Pliny, *N.H.*, xxxiii. 130.
[3] *Ibid.*, xxxvi. 39.
[4] On Pasiteles, see Collignon, **XLVII**, pp. 658 ff.
[5] Pliny, *N.H.*, xxxv. 155.

trasts with the solidity of the form."[1] Yielding to the archaistic fashion and the love of the antique which prevailed in Rome, the Roman school of Pasiteles sought its ideal in the period before Pheidias, but tempered the stiffness of antiquity by a gleam of Alexandrian grace.

The pupil of Stephanos was Menelaos, who worked under Augustus and Tiberius. Of this Menelaos we have a careful but insipid group representing a woman greeting her son. Is it a scene of farewell or reunion ? It is not certain. In any case, the motive seems to be a not very skilful adaptation of some Attic grave-relief of the IVth century.[2] Menelaos remained faithful to the Neo-Attic tradition. This archaistic school, which may be taken as especially Roman, produced many works in Italy. We may mention the Artemis in the Naples Museum, a copy of a cultus-statue of the beginning of the Vth century, but a very much modernized copy, at least in the expression of the face. (Plate VI.) We may also mention the so-called Harmodios and Aristogeiton, and the other group, known as Orestes and Electra, both in the same museum. The " Orestes " seems to be a copy of the same original as the Ephebus of Stephanos ; it is associated with a female figure of almost masculine mould, animated by all the restrained force of ancient statues. Without doubt, the great abundance of classical and pre-classical Greek works in Rome was partly responsible for the production of all these imitations.

But by the side of these austere works we find the studied coquetry of the Venus Genetrix ordered by Caesar from the sculptor Arcesilas. The goddess inclines her head slightly, gazing with a smile at the apple of Paris, which she holds in her right hand. With a gesture not free from affectation her beautiful left hand lifts the end of her transparent chiton over her shoulder, so that it reveals her right breast and its light folds caressingly follow the graceful curve of her stomach and her round thighs. The whole recalls the classical style of Alcamenes, made languorous by Alexandrian voluptuousness. Without being original, these first productions of Graeco-Roman sculpture bear witness to an active artistic life and a noble taste. The Romans sincerely loved Greek beauty ; their artists strove to reproduce and to rejuvenate its charm.

[1] **XLVII**, ii, p. 661, fig. 346.   [2] Collignon, **XLVII**, ii, fig. 349, pp. 364-5.

VIII

The Altar of Domitius Ahenobarbus

From this period we possess a complete monument which presents the interest of being possible to date exactly, and of illustrating the eclecticism of Roman works of the end of the Republic—namely, the friezes of the altar which stood before the Temple of Neptune built by Cn. Domitius Ahenobarbus, an ancestor of Nero, between the years 35 and 32 B.C. The two friezes are separated, one being in the Louvre [1] and the other at Munich ; they were recognized as belonging to the same monument by Furtwaengler in 1896.[2]

The Munich frieze represents the bridal procession of Poseidon and Amphitrite. In the centre, the divine pair are seated on a chariot drawn by young Tritons, one playing a lyre and the other blowing a conch. They are followed by Nereids riding on sea-monsters and a Triton who idly lets himself be rocked on the waves. All the poetry of the sea, the music of the wind playing in the lyre, the roar of the sea expressed by the conch, the waves which leap with foaming crests like the marine steeds which bear the Nereids, and those which lazily come and die on the beach, form the escort of the gods. In front of the bridal pair, Amphitrite's mother advances, mounted on a sea-horse and carrying the nuptial torches. She is escorted by a nymph and two Nereids, one of whom shows only her back, and supports herself on the crupper of a young Triton. The whole theme is carried out with a wealth of fancy in which, before it was known that the frieze belonged to a Roman monument, scholars in general recognized the style of the classical schools in their later period, still impregnated with the influences of the IVth century, but already heralding the versatile fancy of the Hellenistic age. The frieze seems to be the work of a Greek, but of one who worked in Rome for a great Roman noble some years before Actium.

The relief in the Louvre is quite different in character. The execution is much less skilful ; it is feeble and heavy, and lacks delicacy and decision, but not life. (Plate IX.) The

---

[1] Michon, **XV**, xvii (1909), pp. 145 ff.   [2] **LXXVI**, pp. 33 ff.

PLATE IX

ONE OF THE FRIEZES OF THE ALTAR OF DOMITIUS AHENOBARBUS. (Louvre)

[face p. 256

sculptor is certainly not the man who did the Poseidon frieze, and must have been a Roman. Leaving Greek models alone, he has attempted an original, thoroughly Roman composition. In the centre of the scene is an altar, on which a thanksgiving sacrifice is about to be performed. On one side stands the Imperator, helmeted and leaning on his lance ; on the other, the priest turns his face towards the procession which he awaits. First come the victims, bull, sheep, and pig, driven by servants, and after them two armed legionaries, while a horseman in a plumed helmet prepares to mount his horse. At the opposite end of the frieze is a scene which is supposed to represent the dismissal of legionaries at the end of a campaign. Two soldiers still wear their military kit ; two others have already donned the toga. They stand round two seated personages, one of whom seems to be some clerk, making out a certificate. This regularly arranged composition is a historical relief—sacrifice after victory and demobilization.

So the altar of Domitius combined in its decoration the Greek allegorical tradition, commemorating the naval victories of Ahenobarbus by a scene from mythology, and historical realism, which was doubtless not unknown to Greek artists, especially those of Pergamon, but in this case, where it depicts purely Roman scenes, certainly seems to be derived from the triumphal pictures and other representations of ancient Italy. Under the Empire, we shall see in many examples the procession of the *suovetaurilia* which here forms the central motive. It is in ancient Etruria and Campania that we should look for the prototypes of the procession, at once military and religious, which was the subject of the decoration of so many Imperial monuments.

Roman art at the end of the Republican period no more distinguished between its own inheritance and foreign lessons than it did between the different Hellenistic schools. It carried eclecticism to the point of confusion. This period of passion and dilettantism lacked a directing idea. In art as in politics, it was an age of anarchy.

R

IX

ARCHITECTURE

The dominant art in the Hellenistic world was architecture. Sculpture, painting, mosaic, even metal-engraving, for the metals were much used in architectural decoration, were made much more strictly subordinate to it than sculpture and painting had been in the classical period. In the great sanctuaries of the old days, at Delphi, at Olympia, the statues were set up as they were presented, without reference to the temples, and pictorial compositions, even when they adorned a monument like the Lesche at Delphi, were often more important than the monument itself. But now the idea of the general effect prevailed in art. In the towns private houses, public monuments, temples, streets, squares, were all made subject to a general arrangement, and in every building the decorative motives were thought out with reference to the exact place which they should occupy.[1] In the palaces, which were often as large as a city, the essential object of sculptures and paintings was the adornment of halls, porticoes, and gardens. Splendid monuments were a sign of power. The Roman State could not fail to follow the royal houses of Asia and Egypt on this path. It owed the King-People monuments and a city worthy of its might. Great architectural undertakings were the price which victorious leaders had to pay for the command to which they owed glory and profit.

These generals, whom their education, travels, and campaigns had familiarized with the things of Greece and the East, employed some architect whom they had brought home with them or had found in Rome, having come to seek his fortune in Italy like other artists—sculptors, painters, or metal-workers. This architect came to an arrangement with a contractor, *redemptor*, who was usually the representative of one of the great financial societies which exploited the whole basin of the Mediterranean. The architect had done his apprenticeship and worked in one or more of the great cities

[1] In particular, take the example of a new city like Priene. P. Bonnet, " Observations sur le plan et la construction de Priène," in **XVI**, 1919, ii, *Variétés*.

of the Hellenistic world ; the contractor had built wherever the Romans might have wanted building done, from Spain to Africa and even in Delos. The works-foremen were slaves or freedmen, most of them from Syria, Asia Minor, or Egypt.[1] All these people were thoroughly acquainted with the artistic fashions and technical innovations of the Mediterranean world. Labour was supplied by prisoners of war and slaves bought in the market. It was extremely plentiful, but of very poor quality ; there were few masons and many unskilled labourers. Therefore the simplest processes were employed, such as saved time and money and required only the smallest skill on the part of the workman.

As might be expected in these circumstances, the workmanship of the monuments of the IInd and Ist centuries has no longer anything in common with that of the IVth and IIIrd centuries. The stone is no longer cut exactly for the place where it is to go, but is turned out in uniform blocks by an industrial process. Good quality and careful construction are confined to the essential parts of the building, and hasty rubble-work is good enough for the rest. The walls are cut away ; they vary in thickness, and are no longer continuous, but are composed of arcades, filled with many door and window spaces and recessed niches. Structural mechanics are applied to the wall ; resistances are exactly calculated, and material is economized. By the side of monolithic columns, pilasters, and door-jambs of hewn stone, most of the construction is of mortar-joined masonry. The large, heavy architrave is replaced by the arch for which inferior material can be used. The use of mortar seems to have originated in Syria. From there, too, the various types of the arch appear to have come ; the art of construction at the end of the Republic is definitely Hellenistic.[2]

Just as in literature, so in Roman architecture Greek and Hellenistic influences appear before any direct contact with the East. Even during the greater part of the IInd century, they seem to have reached Rome by way of Sicily. At the eastern end of that island, Syracuse had been, since the beginning of the IIIrd century, a great Hellenistic city.

---

[1] M. Licinius Crassus Dives had 500 architects in his service, in 108 B.C. Plut., *Cras.*, 2.
[2] Delbrueck, **LXI,** ii, pp. 111-14.

Being in constant intercourse not only with Greece and the Greek islands but also with Egypt and the ports of Syria, it received, from then onward, many Oriental elements. The Roman conquest of 212 opened the whole of southern and central Italy to Syracuse. It was there, as I suggested, that Appius Claudius probably found the model for the first Roman aqueduct. From Syracuse, too, the first lessons in the new art of building probably came.

Asia cannot have affected Roman architecture directly until about the end of the IInd or even the beginning of the Ist century B.C. Its influence reached its full development in the time of Sylla, who rebuilt Rome after having partly burned it down. Of the regions of Asia, that from which the most fruitful innovations seem to have come was Syria. It was in Syria that the old technical processes and some of the artistic forms of the Asiatic continent had been adapted to Hellenic art. The arch, mortar, and bricks of baked clay seem to have originated in Syria. So Syracuse in the IInd century and Antioch in the Ist were the great teachers of Roman architecture. We know that the influence of Syrian architecture continued under the Empire, and it was to this country again, chiefly at the end of the IIIrd century and the beginning of the IVth century A.D., that the last transformation of the art of building in the West was due.

The architectural transformation of Rome commenced at the beginning of the IInd century, that is, under the influence of Syracuse. Henceforward the Romans were not content with building temples on some site chosen by the Senate and Pontifices, generally outside the walls or in outlying quarters. Even in the case of temples, attention was paid to the perspective and the setting in which they were to be built. But chiefly civil edifices were erected, intended to adorn the very centre of the city. In 185-4 Cato the Censor built the Basilica Porcia, and in 179 the Basilica Aemilia was erected on the Forum, where its foundations can still be seen.[1] Opposite, on the south side of the Forum, the Basilica Sempronia was erected in 169, on the site afterwards occupied by the Basilica Julia, while on the short west side, against the Capitol, not far from the Temple of Concord, stood the Basilica Opimia. The date of these last two basilicas cannot

[1] It is true that it was rebuilt several times.

be exactly determined, but must certainly be earlier than 150. As we see, there was a perfect efflorescence of basilicas in a space of about thirty years.

We do not know the plan of any of these old Republican basilicas. The name is Greek—Βασιλικὴ στόα, Royal Portico —although the Greek denomination itself only appears late, at least in the texts which we possess.[1] There are very few examples of basilicas in Greece and the whole East. To judge by the later Roman basilicas which have survived, the type was derived from buildings like the hypostyle hall at Delos, studied by Monsieur G. Leroux, which was built about the last third of the IIIrd century B.C. as an Exchange for the Delian merchants.[2] This hall probably recalled Egyptian structures. In any case it appears as a creation of Hellenistic architecture. The special achievement of the Romans, in Leroux's opinion, was the adoption of the great hypostyle hall as the principal edifice of the city, the use of it as a meeting-place and law-court, and the consecration of the name of *basilica*, hitherto little used and doubtless of popular origin. But between Alexandrian Egypt, Delos, and Rome, Syracuse probably served as an intermediary, and in the basilica, as we find it in Rome in the first half of the IInd century B.C., we cannot tell exactly what is Roman and what Syracusan.

To the same period as the basilicas, the Navalia belong, which were built on the banks of the Tiber by the architect Hermodoros of Salamis (149), to serve as warehouses, and so does the great Temple of Jupiter dedicated by Metellus Macedonicus, the work of the same architect. This temple, which was of Pentelic marble, occupied the end of a square surrounded by a colonnade ; it is the first example of a religious building really forming part of a larger architectural plan. The portico, an eminently Hellenistic type of construction, now became one of the essential elements of urban architecture. As early as 193, Aemilius Lepidus built the portico of the Emporium, to shelter goods brought to Rome by the Tiber boats. The porticoes along the two sides of the ramp leading to the Capitol were built in 174, and that of Cn. Octavius in 168. Later, chiefly from Caesar's time onwards, many porticoes were built in Rome ; they became

[1] Leroux, **XCVI** and **XCVII**, pp. 272-3. [2] **XCVI.**

the usual setting of every Forum and public square, the favourite place for meeting and for doing business, and the resort of the *flâneur*.

In the Ist century B.C. the great periods of building were those of Sylla, Pompey, and Caesar.

To Sylla we must ascribe the construction of the Roman Archives, the Tabularium, looking on to the Capitol on one side and on the other dominating the west end of the Forum by the whole height of its front.[1] Sylla also constructed, outside Rome, the great sanctuary of Fortune at Praeneste,[2] the temple at Gabii, and the two temples at Tibur,[3] one of which, the round one, is still almost intact to-day.[4] In construction and in forms, all these monuments in Rome and Latium are derived from Hellenistic architecture. There is nothing peculiarly Latin or even Italian about them. It is true that we hear, at this time, of an architect named Cossutius who, after working in Rome, was summoned by Antiochos IV of Syria and ordered by him to complete the Olympieion in Athens. It is argued that the renown of a Roman architect must therefore have impressed even a Syrian prince. But it is very probable that the Latin name Cossutius merely disguises as a Roman a Syrian artist already celebrated in his own country.[5]

Pompey, in his turn, presented the Roman people with buildings imitated from those of the great Asiatic cities. In 55 he dedicated his theatre, crowned by a sanctuary of Venus Victrix, the first stone theatre constructed in Rome. Beside the theatre, a celebrated portico, adorned with numerous works of art, enclosed gardens which were soon the resort of all the fashion. From there another portico, the Hecatostylon or Hundred Pillars, led towards the Capitol. Near this portico was the Curia, also built by Pompey, in which Caesar was assassinated. All this part of the Campus Martius, between the present Farnese Palace and the Capitol, was transformed by Pompey.

Caesar made it his object to cause the architectural

---

[1] See Delbrueck's detailed study of this monument, **LXI**, i, pp. 23-46.
[2] Fernique and Blondel, **X**, ii (1882), pp. 168-203 ; Delbrueck, *ibid.*, i, pp. 47-90.
[3] *Ibid.*, ii, pp. 5-22.
[4] The round temple by the Tiber, in Rome, seems to date from the period immediately before Sylla, Altmann, **XXVI**, pp. 23 ff.
[5] Delbrueck, **LXI**, p. 179.

munificence of his rival to be forgotten. The booty from Gaul was used to build, north of the old Forum, a new Forum, better arranged and more majestic than the old. With his passion for size and novelty, the Dictator's imagination was thoroughly infected by the East. His Forum was conceived, we are told, on the pattern of those of the Persians.[1] It was completely surrounded by a wall lined with porticoes. In the centre stood the Temple of Venus Genetrix, a peripteral Corinthian building, entirely of marble, adorned with sculptures and " radiating the lustre of gold." [2] The statue of the goddess was the work of Arcesilas. Beside it Caesar placed a figure of Cleopatra in gold—or at least gilt. In front of the temple he dedicated a statue of himself on the marvellous horse with the split hoof, which was supposed to ensure for its master the dominion of the world.[3] In the centre of the Forum were the Appiades, which were fountains, probably with nymphs carved by Stephanos, the pupil of Pasiteles.[4] The ceremony with which this Forum was opened was a kind of Oriental pantomime with a procession of elephants. Egypt at this moment was the rage in Rome, and Caesar's ambition was about to lead him to the conquest of the Parthian kingdom. The artistic ideal of the Romans was merely a reflection of that of the Graeco-Oriental monarchies.

Whether we are considering architecture, sculpture, painting, or the minor arts, it is only exceptionally that we see, in the works of the end of the Republic, any specifically Roman feature. The native tradition is not dead, but it makes a poor show beside the triumphant expansion of Hellenistic art, and has, as it were, fallen from artistic dignity. It has taken refuge in rustic shrines and humble booths, and hardly appears in the art of the capital, except in the survival of clay-modelling preached by Pasiteles and of the craft of the terra-cotta relief. One is almost surprised to find on the altar of Domitius Ahenobarbus the Roman motive of the *suovetaurilia* and the exact representation of contemporary historical events.

In general, the technical methods are Greek, the governing ideas are those reigning all over the Mediterranean world, and subjects and styles are those current in the great intellectual

[1] Thédenat, **CLVI**, p. 169.
[2] Pliny, *N.H.*, xxxv. 45. 2.
[3] Suet., *Caes.*, 61.
[4] Thédenat, **CLVI**, pp. 178-80.

centres of Greece, Asia, and Egypt. The Roman art of the last days of the Republic is only a branch of Hellenistic art, a strong branch, and already fruitful, but one which has not yet felt the influence of the soil into which it has been transplanted.

Conclusion of Part II

From the middle of the IIIrd century to about the last third of the Ist century before our era, we have sought in Roman ideas and works for the general characteristic which might establish the connexion between them and could be interpreted as the expression of the special spirit of the people. We have not found it ; or rather, the dominant faculty which gives its special character to this period of rather confused richness seems to be chiefly, as in the preceding period, a marvellous power of assimilation. We find it both in Cato and in Scipio, both in Naevius and Ennius and in Catullus, both in the people which is infected by the religious unrest of the whole of Italy and in the Senate and Pontifices who admit the Greek gods into Rome, and even the Great Phrygian Mother of Pessinus. We find it in art, which becomes Sicilian, then Pergamene, and then Neo-Attic and Alexandrian, and also in common life, which, from the time of Sylla, completely amalgamates Greek manners with those of Italy, just as it usually combines the Hellenistic peristyle house with the old Roman atrium. Rome, during these two centuries, absorbed the civilization of the conquered Mediterranean world just as, in the preceding centuries, she had assimilated that of Italy. The wealth of this civilization stifled, at least for a time, the native tradition.

Moreover, in whom should we look for a specially Roman spirit ? The only Latin writers who come from Rome itself are Lucretius and Caesar, between whose minds there really does not seem to be the very least kinship. Cicero is a Latin like Cato, Lucilius is an Umbrian like Naevius and Pasiteles, Ennius is a Calabrian, Plautus is an Umbrian, Catullus comes from Verona and Terence comes from Africa. Italy, all Italy, with its infinite variety and its wealth of different aptitudes, had for centuries been making Rome. After the end of the Punic Wars all the countries of the Mediterranean supplied her with her ideas, her technical processes, her science, her art, and even her artists, and, indeed, the mass of her citizens. When a city conquers a world, she can hardly hope to continue to be herself.

PART III

THE AGE OF AUGUSTUS

IN spite of civil wars, in spite of the corruption of the morals of the ruling classes and the bad government of the Senate, the last century of the Republic had been for Rome a period of vigorous life and progress. It was the end of an adolescence full of turbulence and passion but also full of generous exuberance. The greed and brutality of the conquest of the world are partly redeemed by the very energy which this conquest required, and by the ardour with which the Romans proceeded to assimilate the best of the Hellenistic civilization which they plundered. Failing originality, one cannot deny the age of Caesar, Cicero, Lucretius, and Catullus vigour of intelligence and a lively sense of beauty.

Coming after this time of tumult and activity, bringing peace and order, the age of Augustus has the air of a period of rest. The work of the generations who were called to enjoy the fruit of the Republican victories was to order and elaborate the too rapid acquisitions of their elders. Minds were less distracted by repeated new visions of the foreign world ; attention was concentrated on Italy, and on Rome herself and her past. The pride of triumph raised the national tradition from oblivion. Having been educated by Greece and the Hellenistic world, the Roman spirit gradually, during the long reign of Augustus, developed its own personality, and laid the foundations of the new edifice which has transmitted to posterity the memory of Rome.

CHAPTER I

POETRY AND MORALS

I

THE END OF ALEXANDRINISM

THE partition of the Roman world between Octavian and Antony in 42 B.C., even the battle of Actium in 31, and the Principate of Augustus, at first affected the great intellectual currents prevailing in Rome only imperceptibly. Political changes take time to influence the civilization of a people, and even when they force it to turn in new directions they do not cut previous developments short. So we see the literary movement represented by Catullus continuing down to the end of Augustus's reign, and, in spite of the moral campaign of the Sovereign, the manners of the upper classes at the end of the Republican epoch also survive. The conflict between the old spirit and the new order was to produce tragic incidents in the family of Augustus himself, and the last representative of poetical dilettantism, Ovid, was to find his brilliant career pitilessly cut short and to end in the melancholy exile of Tomi.

The Epigoni of the Alexandrian school certainly contributed to the poetical lustre of the age of Augustus. From their ranks, indeed, came the greatest poet of the new era, Virgil. The elegiacs of Tibullus and Propertius and the work of Ovid are no doubt profoundly different from the poetry of Catullus. But the art of all of them, no less than that of Virgil in his earlier works, is derived from Hellenistic inspiration. Propertius owns his debt to Calvus and to the school which was that of Catullus; [1] he asks the shades of Callimachos and Philetas of Cos to admit him to their grove; [2] Gallus once

[1] ii. 34.   [2] iii. 1.

imitated Euphorion, and Virgil himself tried his pipe in the countryside of Theocritos. With one accord, these poets aim, before anything else, at perfection of form, piquant novelty of expression, the elegance of picturesque description, very much conventionalized, and the orthodox colouring of learned mythology. Their delicacy is intensely studied; without excluding sincerity, in Tibullus, or strength, in Propertius, it very often becomes preciosity. It dares not go beyond small themes. Even longer works, like Ovid's *Metamorphoses* and *Fasti*, are merely collections of genre scenes in the manner of the academic reliefs dear to Alexandrian and Neo-Attic art.

In calling up the memories of his youth, Ovid enumerates this pleasant company in the *Tristia*.[1]

"Often Propertius, bound to me by ties of comradeship, would recite to me the story of his passion. Ponticus, master of heroic song, and Bassus, mighty in iambics, were dear members of my circle. And melodious Horace charmed my ears. . . . Virgil I only saw; nor did the envious fates allow time for my friendship with Tibullus. He was your successor, Gallus; Propertius, his; and I was the fourth in time. And as I adored those that went before, so those who came after adored me, and my light Muse soon was famous."

Quintilian passes judgment on each of these poets in authoritative fashion : [2]

"Of our elegiac-writers, Tibullus appears to me to have a polished and extremely elegant style; some prefer Propertius, who is more scholarly but more obscure. The style of Ovid has less restraint than that of these two poets, and that of Gallus is stiffer."

Tibullus (born in 54, died in 19 or 18 B.C.), Propertius (about 50 to 15 B.C.), and Ovid (43 B.C. to 17 A.D.) were younger than Virgil (70 to 19 B.C.) and Horace (65 to 8 B.C.) by nearly a generation. Yet almost all died about the same time, and prematurely; only Horace and Ovid survived. Virgil had been the first to win poetic glory, under the patronage of that precious Alexandrian, Gallus, or rather of Gallus's mistress, the actress Cytheris, who had once been loved by Antony, and was, moreover, about this time preparing to leave her poet for a soldier in the army of the Rhine.

Alpinas, a ! dura nives et frigora Rheni
Me sine sola vides ! [3]

[1] *Trist.*, iv. 10. 41 ff.   [2] *Inst.*, x. 1. 9.   [3] Virg., *Ecl.*, x.

PLATE X

RELIEFS FROM THE GRIMANI PALACE
Marble. (Vienna Museum)

[face p. 270

This was about the year 40. Driven from his family estate by the veterans of Octavian, Virgil had taken refuge in Rome. As the friend of Gallus, he had read him the sixth Eclogue which he had just composed, that in which Silenus sings of the genesis of the world, and the poem had ravished the actress. Cytheris wanted to recite it on the stage. The actress's triumph made the success of the poet.[1] Next day Virgil was celebrated in Rome ; soon he was received by Maecenas, who introduced him to Octavian. Shortly afterwards he gave up bucolic poetry, first paying his debt of gratitude to Gallus and the fair deceiver.

"Grant me this last labour, Muse of Theocritos. I must sing a small song for my Gallus, but one that Lycoris too will read. Who will refuse Gallus a song?"

This song is the tenth and last Eclogue.

But the poetic vein which Virgil deliberately abandoned was not exhausted. It still continued to attract the young writers. Tibullus and Propertius were Knights, enjoying a fortune which made them accessible to the temptations of the Roman world. Like Catullus, they seem to have been diverted by love and easy pleasures from the ambition of making a career for themselves. That is certainly the purport of the prophecy which a soothsayer is said to have made to Propertius.

Militiam Veneris blandis patiere sub armis,
Et Veneris pueris utilis hostis eris ;
Nam tibi victrices quascumque labore parasti,
Eludet palmas una puella tuas.[2]

"You will serve Venus, bearing her sweet arms, and will be an easy enemy for the little sons of Venus ; for whatever victorious palms you may win by hard toil, one girl will snatch them from you."

Moreover, Propertius had accepted the augury readily.

Ut regnem mixtas inter conviva puellas

. . . .

Me juvet hesternis positum languere coronis,
Quem tetigit jactus certus ad ossa deus.[3]

---

[1] This episode is charmingly related by M. Bellessort, **XXX,** pp. 35-6.
[2] iv. 1. [3] ii. 34.

" Let me reign at the banquet with girls all around ! . . . . It is my delight to lie idly on the wreaths of last night, for the god with sure aim has struck me to the bones."

Such a profession of faith might equally well be that of Tibullus or even Ovid, with the difference that, if love struck Propertius and Tibullus to the very marrow, it seems to have given Ovid a fairly superficial wound, and in the head rather than in the heart.

II

TIBULLUS [1]

Like those of Propertius, the elegiacs of Tibullus are, before all, love-poems. Delia is his Muse. The poet sings of the joys and also of the pains which his Delia causes him. This name Delia, corresponding to that of Lesbia which was so dear to Catullus, conceals a person of humbler condition. Delia is married, no doubt, but it is hard to say what was the exact rôle of the husband in this *ménage*. Delia's mother, in any case, whom Tibullus sometimes blesses, when she leads him to his mistress at night, and sometimes curses roundly, when she devises schemes to keep him away, seems to have been of very dubious respectability. Certainly Delia does not belong to the class of long-robed matrons whom Ovid exhorts not to read his verses. Tibullus was able to think himself loved ; he was none the less deserted for a richer lover. After a short absence as Messala's aide-de-camp, a resumption of his liaison with Delia was full of disillusionment and bitterness, and other loves, more completely vulgar, soon succeeded the passion of his youth.

Love seems to have brought Tibullus more grief than pleasure. At least he talks more about his sorrows than his joys. Catullus railed against his rivals and upbraided his faithless mistress ; Propertius even beat his ; Tibullus took refuge in melancholy. Melancholy, to judge by the fatherly encouragement which Horace offers him, was the very foundation of his temperament.[2] Allusions to death are frequent in his work ; funerals, ashes, and the pyre are themes

[1] Ponchont, **CXXXIV.**   Cf. Cartault, **XLIII,** and Plessis, **CXXXIII,** pp. 336 ff.
[2] *Epist.*, i. 4.

on which he often enlarges. With him the elegiac, even when
amorous, walks in long mourning robes. Moreover, these
funereal interests, which are especially strongly marked in
Tibullus, seem to be the result of a fairly widespread tendency
in his generation, since we find them also in Propertius and
in an otherwise unknown poet named Lygdamus, whose works
are mixed with those of Tibullus, forming the third book of
his collection. So the very sincere melancholy of Tibullus
corresponds to a state of mind fairly usual in a tired age.
His morality, on the other hand, is allied to that of Catullus.

> *Interea dum fata sinunt jungamus amores.*
> *Jam veniet tenebris mors adoperta caput.*
> *Jam subrepet iners aetas nec amare decebit*
> *Dicere nec cano blanditias capite.*[1]

"While the fates allow, let us join our loves. Death will soon come,
with her head veiled in shadows; heavy age will soon creep up, and it will
not be seemly to love, nor to say sweet things, with a white head."

Catullus spoke more of kisses; the thoughts of Tibullus
dwell rather on coming decay and death with her veil of
shadows. The passion of love only partly satisfies an over-
refined generation. It no longer fills their souls. It leaves
room for the moral *malaise* which darkens nature and life.
This romantic sadness is always appearing in Tibullus; it
spreads through his work in gentle plaints, without violence,
in lassitude, in a sort of pessimism, one may say, which turns
the mind of the poet from the present to the past, to the
idyllic simplicity of the Golden Age or of a rustic life of
purely conventional idealism.

The elegiacs of Tibullus contain much besides love and
melancholy. They are animated by an amiable spirit,
sometimes a little artificial, but always graceful and often
ironical. They please by the many familiar pictures which
they sketch. Scenes of common life, anecdotes, and frolics
alternate with expressions of feeling, memories, hopes, and
philosophical or didactic passages. He essays all the forms
in favour among the Alexandrians—pastorals, descriptions of
landscape, scenes of magic or sacrifice, a little mythology, and
much morality. There are plenty of points of comparison,
not only with Propertius and Ovid, but with Virgil and Horace.

---

[1] i. 1, end.

S

Tibullus hesitates to go beyond the idyllic style. Occasionally his ventures, which are chiefly checked by his timidity and excessive modesty, take him to the level of the little poem, derived from a model by Callimachos but Latin in substance and wholly personal in sentiment, in which we may recognize a reflection of the new ideas which at this same time were inspiring Horace and Virgil.

III

PROPERTIUS [1]

These new winds which were coming to breathe life into the old aesthetic ideal make themselves felt still more often and more forcibly in Propertius than in Tibullus. Propertius is of more robust and vigorous poetical temperament than Tibullus ; he has more art ; his mind has a greater wealth of images, which he excels in presenting in tiny pictures, always drawn with a clear, almost hard line, lacking depth and atmosphere, and sometimes so abbreviated as to be obscure.

His lady, Cynthia, is an aristocrat like Lesbia, rich, coquettish, and highly cultivated, who recites and even writes poetry, and sings and dances with art. The charming, educated woman now appears in Roman society. Among the elegiacs of Tibullus, we possess those of a poetess named Sulpicia. The funerary inscriptions of this time frequently extol not only the virtue of the deceased lady, *mores*, but her beauty, *forma*, and her wit, *faceta*, *consulta*. The verse epitaph of one blue-stocking alludes to her lyre and her cithara.[2] (See Pl. VIII.)

Love took Propertius into an elegant world steeped in literature. At the same time the poet was a member of the circle of Maecenas. He was a zealous supporter of Augustus, whose praises he sang, although Octavian had been responsible for his father's death in Umbria. He had a deep admiration for Virgil. Nevertheless, his models were the minutely ingenious and refined poets of Alexandria. Fashion, and also, probably, Cynthia's taste and his desire to please her, com-

---

[1] Plessis, **CXXXIII**, pp. 377 ff.
[2] Cf. Focillon, in Plessis, **CXXXII**, pp. xlvii-xlix.

pelled him to adopt the elegiac.[1] But the later part of his work, after his quarrel with his mistress, clearly shows a tendency towards a wider form of poetry, in which ideas shall take the place of sentiment.[2]

Propertius will sing chiefly of his love, and, since the sorrows of love are more poetic than its triumphs, he will not hesitate to give voice to his complaints, against his mistress, against society, against the world and life, all more or less responsible for his sorrows. Why be at pains to seek a subject for a work of art elsewhere? His inspiration is Cynthia. *Ingenium nobis ipsa puella facit.* His friend Ponticus attempts the epic. What use to him is this solemn poem? In love, Mimnermos is better than Homer. Be off, then, and compose the melancholy little poems which every woman in love likes to repeat.[3] He deliberately takes his stand among the poets of the preceding generation, Catullus, Calvus, Gallus. Following their example, he has sung Cynthia. May fame give him a place among them.

But the very protests, which constantly recur in his poems, against the loftier forms show that his mind is haunted by the thought of them. In the second book, the tenth elegy, addressed to Augustus, is an attempt in a graver tone. Elsewhere in the same book [4] we note a tendency to minutely accurate description of things he has seen, particularly works of art, such as the Portico of Apollo just built by Augustus. But he soon returns to Cynthia; the wisdom of Socrates, the science of Lucretius, are too austere for him, and he defers the study of them until later, when Venus shall have fled from his old age, grown heavy, and the white shows among his black hair.[5] In the meantime, let it be enough for him to admire, without following them, those of his friends who have dared more than he, whose talent has been seconded by their wisdom, whom Venus has not stayed in their course to the summits of Parnassus.

Yet, without his seeking it, and almost against his will, great images and a breath of a power beyond that of the elegiac come and raise the tone of his poem.

"Not the cost of Pyramids raised to the stars, nor the house of Olympian Jove, vast as heaven, nor all the wealth of the Mausoleum escapes the final

---

[1] i. 7 ; i. 9 ; ii. 1.　　　　　　　　　　[2] See especially Bk. iv.
[3] i. 9.　　　　　　　[4] ii. 31.　　　　　[5] ii. 34.

law of death. Either their glory is sapped by fire or rain, or they fall beneath the blows of the years, crushed by their weight. But the name which genius seeks does not vanish from time; the glory of genius abides without death." [1]

But it was not in the epic that the very real talent of Propertius would have found its expression, if he had lived. What emerges in his second book, and is still more pronounced in the third, is a tendency to moral disquisition, illustrated, as it were, by plastic and coloured images. What is the good of human ambition and agitation? The essential thing is the soul, the life of the mind. How mad was Prometheus, who, when moulding the human body, forgot the soul!

> *Corpora disponens mentem non vidit in arte ;*
> *Recta animi primum debuit esse via.*

All material distinctions will be effaced by death.

> *Nudus ad infernas, stulte, vehere rates.*
> *Victor cum victis pariter miscebitur umbris,*
> *Consule cum Mario, capte Jugurtha, sedes.* [2]

The same idea, or a very closely related idea, the vanity of human ambition and especially of the pursuit of wealth, is the theme of the beautiful elegy in Book III, in which the poet mourns the death of the young Paetus in a shipwreck, a commonplace idea, but developed with a really powerful sincerity of emotion and wealth of image.

> *Ergo sollicitae tu causa, pecunia, vitae es,*
> *Per te immaturum mortis adimus iter.*
>
> . . . .
>
> *Nam dum te sequitur primo miser excidit aevo*
> *Et nova longinquis piscibus esca natat.*

What Propertius praises in Maecenas is not so much his talents as his moderation : [3]

> *. . . In tenues humilem te colligis umbras,*
> *Velorum plenos subtrahis ipse sinus.*

While all around him are exerting themselves to sing the glory of Rome, he perceives and remarks on the hidden canker

---

[1] iii. 2 ; see, too, the *Dream of Propertius*, iii. 3.
[2] iii. 5. See the whole elegy.   [3] iii. 9.

in her triumph. The greed which has directed conquests
will be the ruin of this empire.

> *Proloquar, atque utinam patriae sim vanus haruspex,*
> *Frangitur ipsa suis Roma superba bonis.*

He preaches the examples of Sparta to his country.

> *Quod si jura fores pugnasque imitata Laconum,*
> *Carior hoc esses tu mihi, Roma, bono.*[1]

Here Propertius is on the same path as the Horace of the
Odes and, still more, of the *Satires*. Cynthia's lover, whose
love, as he himself once said, made all his talent, becomes a
teacher of social morality. Yet he has not altered his art ;
it is no heavier in sound, the images are not diminished, the
mythology is not simplified ; it is still Alexandrian in form.
But the matter is changed. Hellenistic art was essentially
non-utilitarian ; it was art for art's sake. By a tendency
which was natural in Rome, and was strengthened by the
trend of ideas in the age of Augustus, the poetry of Propertius
assumes a moral purpose ; it subordinates beauty to use.

This new tendency, which reduces Alexandrian art to
the function of a gorgeous, precious setting for Roman ideas,
triumphs in the fourth and last book of Propertius.

Hellenistic poetry, that of Callimachos no less than that
of Apollonios of Rhodes, was inspired by erudition even more
than by feeling. One may say that it was often archaeological poetry. This learned Muse, the product of the Museum
and the Libraries, triumphed in Rome with the maturity of
Ovid, in the *Metamorphoses* and, still more, in the *Fasti*.
She had already appeared in Catullus's work, in the *Epithalamium of Thetis and Peleus*, for example, and in *Berenice's
Hair*. She gave a new spirit to the elegiac of Propertius.

But it is not from Greek fables, but from Latin tradition,
that Propertius takes his subjects. So, too, Varro had applied
to the past of Rome the curiosity and the methods of Hellenistic erudition, and so, too, Virgil's epic takes for its theme
the foundation of Rome. In this way Propertius, when he
adopts an original line, departs from his Alexandrian masters
and is carried in the wake of the reviver of the Roman state.
But, while his spirit becomes Roman once more, his talent

----

[1] iii. 14.

has been formed by the study of the Greek poets; he is an Alexandrian, and he remains one. The legendary past of Rome is illustrated in a series of pictures in the Hellenistic style, descriptions which are at once familiar and precious. Everything is too precise and rather dry in this succession of miniatures; there is no general composition, no sustained effort, no width of horizon.

Hoc quodcumque vides, hospes, qua maxima Roma est,
Ante Phrygem Aenean collis et herba fuit.[1]

The masterpiece in this manner is perhaps the poem devoted to the legendary heroine Tarpeia. The painting of violent amorous passion gives soul and life to a poetry which is too purely academic.

The poem most characteristic of the talent of Propertius, that in which his vein of melancholy, morality, and historical memories are found together, is the *Consolation* addressed to Paullus. His young wife Cornelia, who has just died, appears to Paullus as Cynthia once appeared to Propertius.[2]

"Cease, Paullus, to assail my tomb with tears. The dark doors open to no prayer. Once the dead have entered into the law of the underworld, the way is closed with inexorable steel. Even if the god of the dim hall hears your prayer, the soundless shores will drink your tears. The upper gods are moved by prayers; when the Ferryman has taken his fare, the wan door closes on the dead, and the grass grows on their pyres. . . .

"I am now a burden that five fingers could lift. Nights of my doom, and you, slow shallows of the marshes, and waves coiling about my feet, I came here before my time, but not in guilt. . . . Paullus, it is written on my gravestone that I was wedded to you alone. I call on the ashes of my fathers, deserving honour of Rome, beneath whose titles Africa lies broken . . . the gods of our hearths have blushed for no shame of mine; Cornelia has not diminished the glory of these great spoils. . . . Nature gave me laws, inherited with my blood, so that no fear of judges could make me better. Whatever be the sentence of the stern tribunal, no woman will take shame if I sit beside her, not Claudia, who with a rope loosed motionless Cybele, nor she whose veil gave out the living flame when Vesta asked for the fire entrusted to her. . . .

"Now I commend to you our common pledges, our children. Care for them lives, unburnt, even in my ashes. Father, be a mother to them. . . ."

This is indeed the masterpiece of the Latin elegy. Sainte-Beuve recognized Propertius for the most noble of the Latin elegiac-writers; he praised the grandeur of his sentiments,

[1] iv. 1.   [2] iv. 11.

the variety of his inspiration, and the seriousness and force which are not usually found in this type of poetry. He is sometimes compared to André Chenier, and indeed the abundance of the images which he takes from the erudite mythology of Hellenism justifies the comparison. But one must add that, by the ideas which he introduces into the elegiac, Propertius is the most Roman of the Alexandrians.

IV

OVID [1]

Ovid represents the end of this school. In him Alexandrinism has outlived its strength. It is not that Ovid has a less delicate sense of art than his predecessors, but the effects which they used to obtain by reasoned endeavour spring spontaneously, in him, from the application of the stock methods. His inferiority lies chiefly in his facility. The image presents itself to his mind ready-made, with the lines and colours discovered by two generations of poets before him. The result is agreeable, it pleases ; that is all Ovid wants. In this way he was able to turn out a quantity of rather commonplace works, composed of a succession of pieces which are individually charming, but taken all together soon produce an effect of wearisome monotony. Ovid does brilliant exercises, but, until the *Tristia*, he never does anything more.

That his first work, the *Heroides*, written when he was about twenty, should present this character, is not surprising. It is a collection of a score of letters written by famous love-sick heroines of myth to their husbands or lovers. A letter from Penelope to Ulysses opens the correspondence.

> *Hanc tua Penelope lento tibi mittit, Ulixe ;*
> *Nil mihi rescribis, attamen ipse veni.*

"This letter your Penelope sends you, dallying Ulysses. Write no reply, but come yourself."

It is not parody, but wit marked by a smile. This beginning sets the tone. Moreover, the letter is as plaintive

[1] Plessis, **CXXXIII,** pp. 410 ff.

and sentimental as one could wish. Penelope utters suitable curses against the faithless ravisher, the cause of her long widowhood ; she recounts with feeling her anxieties during the war, the joys of home-coming which she envies the other wives, and her own doubt and melancholy. It is a perfect copy of Latin verse, but it inspires only the mildest desire to read the following poems. Yet what pretty pictures they sometimes contain ! Deserted Ariadne writes her reproaches to Theseus (Epistle X).

"It was the hour when the earth is first spread with glassy rime, and the birds hidden in the leafage raise their plaint, Half-waking, still languid with sleep, I put out my hands as I lay, to touch Theseus. There was no one. I drew back my hands, and stretched them out again, and moved my arms over the couch. There was no one. Fear shook off sleep. I rose in terror, and flung myself from the lonely bed. . . ."

These are not stories of metamorphosis, but they are just like the *Metamorphoses*, medleys of wit and fable.

Renouncing the ambitions which his father had conceived for him in the country town of Sulmo, behold young Ovid aspiring only to be a poet. His elders, Tibullus, Propertius, welcomed him into a world where the god Love had taken the place of Apollo. Love must be sung, and, to sing him, the poet must suffer from him, or at least pretend to be touched by his arrows. So Ovid, like the rest, composed the elegiacs which made a poet's success with the young women and would ensure him immortal renown in the future. The *Loves* (*Amores*) appeared between the years 19, when Virgil and Tibullus died, and 15, when Propertius died. Ovid, the last-comer, thus found himself the sole representative of the poetic school of which he possessed all the secrets. He had already been married twice, but conjugal bonds which were soon slackened and presently untied did not hamper the liberty of his social career. He celebrated Corinna as his elders had sung Lesbia, Delia, and Cynthia. But these latter had been very real mistresses of the poets who had loved them. We have good reason for asking whether Corinna ever existed. She was not a particular woman whom Ovid loved ; she was all women. " No one fixed form inflames my love," he says. " There are a hundred causes that I should always be in love." [1] If amorous sentiment is spread so wide it will

[1] *Am.*, ii. 4. 9-10.

obviously lack depth.   Love of this kind, in any case, springs
only from the head, and the sincerity of the poem is accordingly
much diminished.

Still in the light, pleasantly witty tone which is dear to
him, and is perhaps the most original feature of his talent,
Ovid then undertakes to expound the theory of the life of
gallantry of which the *Loves* were, so to speak, a chronicle.
The *Art of Love* appeared between the year 1 B.C. and the year
2 or 3 A.D.[1]   In 3 A.D. the *Remedies of Love* was published,
a kind of palinode which emphasizes the lessons of the *Art of
Love* rather than offers a palliative.   About this date Ovid
had married a third time, and very brilliantly.   His wife
belonged to the Gens Fabia, and was related to Consuls and
on intimate terms with an aunt of Augustus.   Through her
the poet obtained a position in official society.   He was just
over forty.   He had done with light loves and the free-and-
easy world of the *Loves* and the *Art of Love*.   More fortunate
than his predecessors, Ovid was able, after the trifling of his
youth, to attempt a great work.

It was at this time, between 3 and 8 A.D., that he began to
write the *Metamorphoses* and *Fasti*.   The *Metamorphoses*, in
fifteen books of about 800 lines each, were almost finished in
the year 8.   Of the twelve books which were to make up the
Fasti—one for each month of the year—six were drafted, at
any rate provisionally, by the same date ; the other six were
never to see the light.   So these years were for Ovid a period
of steady work.   He had long been the favourite poet of
the highest Roman society.   He wanted to become the
official poet, and to win the favour of Augustus.   It was
with this ambition that he attempted great didactic poems.
The *Metamorphoses*, no doubt, are still only Greek mythology,
turned on the old prescription into pleasant stories, always
of love and often highly erotic.[2]   We find in them the spirit
of the *Heroides* and sometimes even of the *Loves*.   In them
Ovid is still the master of prettiness.   But the *Fasti* show a
wish to do something different.   Ovid sets forth with full sail
on the route which Propertius opened in his fourth book, he
approaches a subject at once Roman and religious, he does
sacrifice to the spirit of the new age.   He hopes in this way to
raise himself to the post left empty since the death of Horace

[1] Bornecque, **XL.**   [2] Cf. Lafaye, **XCII.**

in 8 B.C. Had not the learned Verrius Flaccus, whom
Augustus had chosen as tutor for his grandsons, just started,
in the palace itself, upon erudite investigation of the old
Roman calendar, seconding the efforts of the Sovereign to
restore antique piety and the old national religion ? So
Ovid set out to popularize the gods and festivals of old times
by making them agreeable, lending them all the graces and
pleasant colours of his wit.

Then exile came suddenly, in 8 A.D., and destroyed all
these hopes, cut short his ambitions, and interrupted the work
which he had commenced.

The reasons for this unexpected blow are wrapped in
mystery. It was a personal condemnation. Ovid had
committed some fault or error of conduct, as he admits
himself, but without allowing us to divine in what he had
sinned.[1] But it was also the effect of Augustus's disapproval
of his poetry, since the *Art of Love* was at the same time
excluded from the public libraries. His works, or at least
his early works, were the true cause of the banishment of
Ovid, and the rest was simply the occasion. Such is the
opinion of M. Boissier,[2] and he certainly seems to be right.

For all this poetry, from Catullus to Ovid, is that of a
worldly society, with nothing to do, whose spirit, lacking
ideals, amuses itself with love. In Catullus, in Tibullus, and
in Propertius, love is a deep sentiment which gives birth to
poetry ; it is the god of a temple ; its image is framed in the
columns of a scholarly and graceful architecture and the
groves and vistas of a conventional background. It reigns,
but from far off, and the art which surrounds it often causes
it to be forgotten. But in Ovid it is libertinism pure and
simple, displaying its licence in all the work hitherto published
by him. The poetry seems to be no more than an invitation
to love. This is the theory expressly formulated in the *Art
of Love :* literary attainments are chiefly useful for winning
lovers.[3]

"Song is a charming thing; let girls learn to sing. For many a one
her voice has been as good a go-between as her face. Let them sing, now
what they have heard in the marble theatre, now lyrics played to tunes of
the Nile. . . . Learn, too, to strike the gay psaltery; it suits the play

[1] *Trist.*, ii. 1. 200.
[2] XXXVIII, p. 144.   Cf. Reinach, CXXXVII, iv, pp. 69-79.
[3] iii. 315 ff.

of love. You must know the verses of Callimachos . . . and Sappho—is anything more voluptuous than she? . . . And you can read the songs of tender Propertius, or something of Gallus, or of Tibullus. . . . Perhaps my name, too, will be placed among these great ones some day, . . . and some one will say ' Choose a passage from the three books called the *Loves*, and read it in a voice of cunning softness, or recite an *Epistle of a Heroine* with art.' "

Is it surprising that such poetry incurred the wrath of Augustus, as a procuress ?

He was not only thinking of the success of his social laws against adultery and in favour of marriage and large families. In his own house, two grave incidents, the misconduct of his daughter and granddaughter, the two Julias, one after the other, had touched him to the heart. He might, without injustice, blame this poetry, " set to tunes of the Nile," and the poet himself, who, all through his long reign, had won for this type a more brilliant success than it had ever enjoyed. In spite of Ovid's secrecy about the occasion of his disgrace, there is every reason to think that the poet was more or less directly mixed up in the scandal resulting from the love-affair of the second Julia with Silanus. *Galeotto fu il libro e chi lo scrisse.* The Latin elegiac fell with its last representative by the sentence of Augustus.

The survival throughout the reign of Augustus of a poetry inspired by love corresponded to the continuance, under the Empire, of the liberty of morals which had marked the end of the Republic. In spite of the anecdotes which attributed his show of austerity to hypocrisy, Augustus had given up the debaucheries of Octavian. He strove to revive the ancient severity in his own household. His wife and daughter span wool, and he would wear no toga which had not been entirely made in his house. But the aristocracy which he endeavoured to rally round his power refused to return to the manners of the past. Horace was interpreting the ideal of the Sovereign, rather than writing a true chronicle of things as they were, when he celebrated in advance the success of the moral regeneration of his contemporaries.[1]

" The chaste house is stained by no adultery," he sings. " Manners and law have subjugated foul sin, mothers are praised, for their children are like their fathers, and punishment follows hard on crime."

[1] *Od.*, iv. 5. 21 ff.

Alas, just about the time when Ovid's *Art of Love* was appearing, the scandal of adultery had broken out in Augustus's own house, and pitiless banishment had followed the crimes of Julia, the beloved daughter, the only child, and the pride of the Sovereign.

The Roman chroniclers have left a series of damning accusations against Julia which would degrade her to the level of the fallen Lesbia against whom Catullus rails.

" At night," Seneca relates,[1] "she was seen roving about the city with a following of lovers, parading her shame on the Forum and polluting with her wantonness the speaker's tribune from which her father had promulgated the law against adultery. By day, it was near the Statue of Marsyas that she met her lovers ; there, mingling with the lowest creatures in Rome, she shared their vile pleasures, and gloried in it."

The writer's tone is enough to show that the legend made the worst of the condemned woman.   Seneca is clearly thinking, and wants to make others think, of Messalina, who had driven him into exile.   In Julia's case the facts probably did not go beyond a looseness of morals for which, we must admit, there were many extenuating circumstances.   Julia was a pleasant, frivolous woman who loved luxury, art, and literature. " A sweet culture and a soul far from strict," says Macrobius,[2] " had won her immense popularity, which she did not lose in her misfortune."   The people and her faithful friends interceded for her several times.   Of her guilt there can hardly be any doubt ; letters of hers, it seems, definitely compromised her, and it needed clear proof to convince the tenderness of Augustus, which had so long been blind.   But the fact of her guilt does not confirm all the infamous charges brought against her.

The examination of his own conscience might have inclined the father to indulgence.   A youthful caprice had led him to marry Scribonia, Julia's mother ; another caprice had made him repudiate her, to marry Livia, in circumstances which are well known.   The education which the girl had received in the palace under her stepmother's eye had been strict enough to make her hate virtue for ever after.   She had sat at home and spun wool without other society than Livia, Augustus's sister Octavia, and their children.   At Baiae,

[1] *Ben.*, vi. 32 ; cf. Velleius, ii. 3 ; Pliny, *N.H.*, xxi. 3. 9 ; Dio C., lv. 10 ; Macrob., ii. 5. 6.
[2] ii. 5. 1.

one day, a young man ventured to come and salute her.
Augustus at once wrote to the presumptuous youth, repri-
manding him for his improper conduct.[1] While quite young,
she had been married to Marcellus, Octavia's son, who died
less than a year after the wedding. It was to her that
Augustus wished to leave his Imperial dignity. So, for
reasons of State, he bestowed her hand on all the heirs whom
he destined for the Empire, one after another. When
Marcellus died, the prospective successor was Agrippa, who
was over forty and had to divorce a wife before he could marry
the young widow. He was a hard, energetic plebeian, an
indefatigable worker, with a permanent frown (see Plate
XII, 2)—not, perhaps, the most suitable husband for Julia.
Like a dutiful daughter, Julia at first did her duty to the full.
Five children were born of this marriage—Caius and Lucius
Caesar, the younger Julia, Agrippina, and Agrippa Posthumus.
But the affairs of the State called Agrippa away to all the
ends of the Empire. At first Julia accompanied him to the
East, where she was fêted like a queen. In Rome, all the
brilliant young generation flocked around this charming
woman, the first lady in Rome and one of the most beautiful.
Idle, gallant butterflies, like Appius Claudius, Lollius, Sempronius Gracchus, and Scipio, fluttered about her, and also
the companion of her childhood, Julus, Antony's son, the
friend of poets and a poet himself, to whom Horace dedicated
an ode.[2] At once they became, it seems, so many lovers.
Perhaps grief and dignity were not unconnected with the
perpetual travels of Agrippa and his premature death, at the
age of fifty-two, at the beginning of the year 12 B.C.

Until the sons of Julia should be old enough to govern,
the death of Agrippa raised Livia's son, Tiberius, to the first
rank in the Empire. This fine, gloomy being had once, we
are told,[3] inspired Julia with an inclination, which he brutally
repelled. Tiberius was married ; he was ordered to repudiate
Vipsania, whom he loved, and to marry Julia. " She was
passed on," Boissier observes, " from one to the other with
such speed that she could hardly tell her husbands from her
lovers ; " only she could choose her lovers, whereas her
husbands were forced upon her.

Few marriages have been less reasonable than this last.

---

[1] Suet., *Aug.*, 64.   [2] iv. 2.   [3] Suet., *Tib.*, 7.

Tiberius was one of the Claudii, with all the dark obstinacy of his race, an uncompromising upholder of old tradition, a severe man, who smiled even less than Agrippa, and he hated and despised the age. Julia, gay and frivolous, was quite disposed to believe that the time in which she lived was the true Age of Gold. As soon as they were married, Tiberius took his wife far away from Rome, to Aquileia, where she gave birth to a son who died the next year. But the death of his brother Drusus compelled him to go at once to Germany. In any case, the exile of Aquileia could not last for ever. The incompatibility between the young woman of thirty, with her " sweet culture," and her suspicious husband became still more acute. Tiberius buried himself in melancholy ; he dared not accuse his wife or repudiate her. Besides, he had taken on his brother's command in Germany, and there made himself detested by his sullen severity. Finally, he said that he was ill, abandoned all activity, and asked as a favour for leave to retire to Rhodes.

In Rome, around Julia, the young nobles whose idol she was commenced a stubborn campaign against the dark, sour man whose practical desertion had filled the Emperor with bitterness. As rivals to that austere champion of the past they proceeded to uphold the sons of Julia and Agrippa, delightful young princes, adored by Augustus, who were nominated to the Consulate as soon as they were out of their childhood. Julia triumphed ; she was all-powerful and free. The absent Tiberius imperceptibly fell into the position of a banished man. Being urged to make the most of the few years of comparative youth left her, and already seeing white threads in her beautiful hair, Julia threw off all restraint. The company of old friends was joined by new ones—Murena, Caepio, Lepidus, all the great names of the days before Actium. This was the time when Ovid was polishing the lines of his *Art of Love.*

It is probable that a woman's hate had some share in the explosion of the scandal. The Empress Livia can have felt neither tenderness nor indulgence for the daughter of the first wife of Augustus, the mother of the young Caesars, who were ostensibly intended for the Empire at the cost of her own son Tiberius, and the daughter-in-law who was partly responsible for that son's hypochondria, and by her misconduct had kept him for eight years in the disguised exile of Rhodes. It was she, no doubt, who collected proofs of the rumours which must have been going about, and placed them under the eyes of Augustus. She had been patient, for she was wary. She was, as her grandson Caligula said of her, Ulysses in woman's dress. Her proofs must be irrefutable if they were to conquer the tenderness, so long blind, of the father. She won all along the line. Friends and lovers, without distinction, were struck. Sempronius Gracchus was banished to Africa ; Antony's son killed himself. The freedwoman Phoebe, Julia's confidante, hanged herself. " I would sooner have been Phoebe's father," said Augustus. He wished to put his daughter to death. He contented himself with banishing her to a desert island under strict supervision. Scribonia, the wife whom he had divorced long ago, alone obtained permission to accompany her child. Augustus advised the Senate of his decision in a letter which was read by the Praetor, and for a long time he would not let himself be seen, as if in shame. Shortly afterwards the two sons of Julia, Caius and Lucius Caesar, died, one eighteen months after the other. Suetonius says that Augustus bore the loss of his grandsons, the sole hope of his line, more easily than the dishonour of his daughter. Tiberius had returned to Rome directly after the fall of Julia. The removal of the young Caesars once more opened to him the path to the Empire.[1]

Five years later the assembled people asked for Julia's pardon. " I wish," the Emperor replied, " that you might have such daughters and such wives, so that you could appreciate my feelings and judge my conduct." The unhappy woman lived another fifteen wretched years, long enough to see Tiberius succeed Augustus, and Livia, at the beginning at least, exercise even greater sway over her son than she had over her husband.

This tragedy took place in the year 1 A.D., just about the time when Ovid was publishing the *Art of Love*.

Eight years later Julia's daughter repeated the scandal. This time it seems that Ovid was more or less directly mixed up in her love-affair with Silanus. " My songs were the cause," he confesses, " that all, men and women, wished to

---

[1] Public rumour did not fail to accuse Livia of the death of the two heirs presumptive.

know me, to my cost ; my songs were the cause that Caesar censured me and my ways." [1]   He was probably, as Boissier suggests, one of those confidential friends whom lovers like to call in occasionally, as a change from their *tête-à-têtes*.   No one could have known better than this poet and wit how to brighten up a conversation or to give life to a gay party. And who knows how far the *Art of Love* may have been responsible for the aberrations of the second Julia, who was under twenty-five ?   The two lovers were exiled separately in Italy, and Ovid was sent to Tomi, on the coast of the Euxine, where he died in 17, three years after the accession of Tiberius.

From Ovid's exile we have two collections of elegiacs, the *Tristia* and the *Letters from the Pontus*.   These are no longer school exercises or drawing-room trifles, but sincere poetry. Love themes have given place to a melancholy deeply felt and increasingly marked.   No doubt the wit has not gone, nor the mythology, nor the sense of the picturesque, nor the nice art of polishing a detail.   Ovid's talent remains, in its form, what it had been made by thirty years of Alexandrinism. But for the first time the poet's soul reveals its natural self, without the effort imposed by literary fashion or the attractions of social life.   One may apply to him the words in which Macrobius describes Julia's disposition : *mitis humanitas minimeque severus animus*—" sweet culture and a soul far from strict."   The impressions of his unhappy voyage, his life at Tomi, his descriptions of the Scythian country and of the small frontier garrison, where he sometimes had to don helmet and cuirass himself, are among the most picturesque, original, and living things in Latin poetry.

Art, an entirely Hellenistic art, pleasant and flowery, even in sadness, had really become second nature with Ovid. But the warmth with which he tries to justify himself, and his tenacious hope, down to the death of Augustus, of obtaining leave to return to Italy after his hard penance, sometimes raise his light Muse to the discussion of ideas.   In the light of his misfortune he examines his conscience ; he reflects on his work and, with it, on all the class of poetry to which it belongs, and on the whole of the civilization which he loves and regards as the supreme form of human culture.   How

[1] *Trist.*, ii. 5.

far, he asks himself, is art responsible for the loosening of morals ?

His reply, no doubt, is simply an apology *pro Musa sua*. But it does state, in a much more profound fashion than the lyrical optimism of Horace, the whole problem of the moral reform attempted by Augustus.

" My Art of Love," he admits, " is not a serious work. But it contains nothing contrary to the laws. Besides, it is not addressed to Roman ladies ; it is a light work for light women. ' Oh, but a matron can essay an art intended for others.' Then the matron must read nothing ; for from every poem she can learn something towards sinning. If she is bent on vice every book she takes up will form her character for it. This does not mean that every book is criminal ; there is no good thing but can also do harm. And where should one stop ? If poetry corrupts, plays also offer the seeds of vice. Have all the theatres put down, which have given so many cause for sinning ! Put down the Circus ; there the young girl sits next to a complete stranger ! Why is that portico left open ? Some women walk there to meet their lovers ! And an honest woman should avoid the temples. In the Temple of Jupiter she will at once think how many women the god made mothers. At the Temple of Mars the statue of Venus stands before the door, together with her mate, the Avenger. In Venus she will find Anchises, in Diana, the hero of Latmos. . . . *Everything can corrupt perverse minds.*" [1]

The last sentence is perfect, and the whole argument seems fair. But arguments like this were not calculated to heal the wound done to the paternal heart of Augustus, nor to allay the vexation which he must have felt at his impotence to reform morals. Moreover, Ovid could hardly deal with the very bottom of the question. If corruption was not due to literature, nor to art, nor to society life, what were its real causes ? He could not attribute it to the idleness imposed on an ardent generation of young men, nor to the excessive wealth of a minority for whom pleasure was the sole ideal. Still less could he point out to the Emperor the contradiction between his antiquarian laws and the moral and social condition of the time, and charge him with the example which he had set by all the divorces and marriages on which he had insisted in defiance of every consideration of feeling, infinitely more immoral than the most licentious poem.

Nevertheless, even if it is true, as Ovid well says, that neither Homer, when he describes the escapade of Mars and Venus, nor Menander, who never wrote a play without a

---

[1] *Trist.*, ii. 1. 240 ff.

T

love-story, nor Catullus, nor Tibullus, nor Propertius, can be made responsible for the corruption of hearts, it cannot be denied that all this amorous and often erotic poetry developed in the Hellenistic world, which spread in Rome from Catullus onwards, represents the effect of this corruption. It is like the flower of it, a charming flower, no doubt, but one whose roots are fed on immorality. And Ovid, more than all the rest, Ovid, who, without real passion, from sheer dilettantism and ambition for success, had set himself to flatter the already excessive propensity of his contemporaries to love and everything connected with it, was, if not a corrupter, at least a profiter by corruption.

If Catullus, Tibullus, and Propertius deserve to be forgiven much because they loved much, Ovid, too, has a right to some indulgence, not on account of the sincerity of his feelings, but on account of his ardent love of the art of writing and his talent.

"The lover," he says, "knows the injury he does himself, but he clings to it. I, too, have delight in my poems, though they have ruined me, and love the weapon that wounded me. Perhaps this passion will be thought madness. . . . As the Bacchant does not feel her wound when she howls in delirium on the top of Edon, so, when my heart flames, stirred by the green thyrsus, I am filled with a spirit which is above human ills." [1]

Ovid is a sufficiently great artist to deserve to be judged only as an artist. He did not think about morality ; he wanted to be a poet alone. This was the bottom of Augustus's grievance against him. His banishment was the act of the Emperor in his age and bitterness, of the ruler who wished to be the restorer of the old Rome ; it was the death-sentence of Alexandrian art for art's sake.

[1] *Trist.*, iv. 1. 35 ff.

CHAPTER II

AUGUSTUS AND THE NATIONAL REACTION.
HORACE AND VIRGIL

I

CAESAR AND AUGUSTUS

OCTAVIAN, the nephew of Caesar, presented himself to the
Romans as his heir and avenger.   Indeed, his adoption by
the Dictator was, from the political point of view, the most
definite of his titles.   But from the point of view of character
and ideas the contrast between Caesar and the man who
claimed to succeed him was very great.   It would be hard to
imagine a more absolute opposition than that between the
direction in which Caesar turned Roman civilization and the
tendencies which Augustus caused to triumph.

The influence of Caesar is manifested, in the course of the
few years between his crossing of the Rubicon in 50 and the
Ides of March (15th March, 44) when he was murdered, in
the complete expansion of the cosmopolitanism which, since
the conquest of the East, had taken possession of Rome.
It was the time when Egypt imposed its fashions in art and
in manners.   The fourfold triumph of Caesar in 45 displayed
to the eyes of the astonished Romans the Rhone, the Rhine,
and the Ocean conquered, Vercingetorix a prisoner since
six years, Pharnaces, King of Pontus, and Juba of Mauretania
in chains, Africa and Spain subjugated, and, above all, with
the captive Arsinoe, wife of King Ptolemy, pictures of the
Nile and the island of Pharos.   Cleopatra did not appear in
the triumph, but she must have looked on, as a queen, with
all her exotic court about her.   The Dictator's example
carried Roman imaginations towards the distant unknown
and to foreign lands, those of the still half-barbarous Gauls,

Britons, and Germans no less than those which were sinking under the ripeness of an over-refined civilization.

Caesar was the new Alexander. He had adopted the heroic dream of personal, world-wide dominion conceived by the megalomaniac soul of the great Macedonian. In him, war of conquest and political power were imbued with the mystic intoxication of the Dionysiac *thiasos*. As Dionysos had led his rout as far as India, so Caesar, at the time of his assassination, already saw himself riding, at the head of his legions, to the great Eastern adventure, conquering the Parthians, plundering their treasures, dominating the continent of Asia far and wide, and then traversing the still unknown regions of Europe on his way back to the Rhine, on a triumphal progress strewn with high deeds. Like Alexander and the Oriental despots, Caesar set himself above the level of mankind, identifying himself with Jupiter,[1] declaring himself son of Venus. Seated, like a god, before the temple of his mother, he received the respects of the Senate without rising. In his eyes, which embraced the whole universe, Rome was only a single point, and the Roman people and Roman tradition were something to be conquered, ravished, and thrown away as soon as the good was squeezed out of them. It was said, perhaps truly, that he formed a plan, realized by Constantine three and a half centuries later, of abandoning Italy, as exhausted and too confined, and transferring the seat of his empire to Alexandria, Ilion, or some other site in the East, and there assuming the title of King.[2]

The true heir of Caesar's thought and continuer of his policy was not Octavian, but Antony, the new Dionysos, the husband of Cleopatra whose lover Caesar had been, and the master of the East. To what extent Octavian, the rival and then the declared enemy of Antony, actively caused the protest of the national Roman and Italian spirit against the preponderance of the East, and how far he merely benefited by this trend of ideas, is very difficult to determine. In any case, he managed to espouse the Italian opinion with great skill, and allowed the stream to carry him forward.

The national reaction had begun with erudition. We see its origin in the work of Varro. Little by little, it was pro-

---

[1] Suet., *Caes.*, 76.   [2] *Ibid.*, 79.

pagated in intellectual circles, in the middle classes of the city, and among the people of the country. But poetry, above all, lent its lustre to the new patriotism and ensured its diffusion. The Muse defined Octavian's policy and placed herself at his service. Horace and Virgil were the heralds of this national reaction.

II

HORACE

Horace, the son of a petty official, a freedman, of Venusia in southern Italy, happened to be in Athens, terminating his studies in the company of the sons of the Roman aristocracy, when Brutus and Cassius took refuge there after the murder of Caesar. With his comrades he enlisted in the army which the avengers of Roman liberty and of the Senate were raising. He was at once made Tribune of a legion. The disaster of Philippi was a rude awakening from this heroic dream, and he found himself in Rome, fallen from his ambitions, deserted by all, destitute of fortune, disowned by the young nobles to whose level his education had raised him, and lost in the mass of men without position. To sing of love, as was the fashion, hardly occurred to him. Dissatisfied with himself and others, and feeling that he was better than his lot, he was more inclined to scoff. The old moralizing form of the satire tempted him. Why, he asks, is nobody content with the portion which has fallen to him in life ? What is the good of always wanting more than you have ? [1] Fools can never keep to a happy mean.[2] In whatever world we live, let us have the sense to put up with the failings of our friends.[3] Such are the themes which he develops in his first satires.

But at the same time he seeks a richer and more brilliant form of poetry. Not to Hellenistic forms, but to ancient Greece, he looks for an original type of lyric. In the *Epodes*, in which he is still uncertain, we find here and there definitely political inspirations, mingled with many others. Having suffered from the Civil Wars, he seeks to dissuade the Romans from further mistakes ; [4] he celebrates Octavian's victory over

[1] *Sat.*, i. 1. [2] *Sat.*, i. 2. [3] *Sat.*, i. 3. [4] *Epod.*, 7.

Sextus Pompeius and already reviles Cleopatra;[1] he prophesies the end of the Iron Age.[2] But it is somewhat later, about the time of Actium, that present events take a preponderant place in the *Odes*. With the peace of the gods, Octavian will bring spring-time to the Romans;[3] subject to Jupiter alone, he will give wise laws to the whole earth.[4] Not without a touch of irony, perhaps, he celebrates his own return to piety,[5] and, above all, he sings the triumph of the young Caesar and Italy over the baleful Egyptian.[6]

> *Nunc est bibendum, nunc pede libero*
> *Pulsanda tellus, nunc Saliaribus*
> *Ornare pulvinar deorum*
> *Tempus erat dapibus, sodales.*

"Now is the time to drink, to beat the ground with careless foot, to adorn the table of the gods with feasts of the Salii, my friends!"

Soon, in the second book of the *Odes*, we find the poet rising to social reflections on the invasion of luxury and the large property, and invoking the laws of Romulus and the austere Cato.[7]

> *Jam pauca aratro jugera regiae*
> *Moles relinquent . . .*
> *. . . non ita Romuli*
> *Praescriptum et intonsi Catonis*
> *Auspiciis veterumque norma.*

Neither Maecenas, whose friend he had become, nor his own spirit seems to have been the best possible example to inspire the eulogy of warlike virtue which is the theme of the second ode in Book III.

"Let the lad, stalwart in hard warfare, learn to suffer cramping poverty as his mate. Let him harass the ferocious Parthians, formidable on his horse, with his lance in his hand."

So, with a martial blast, he replies to the maledictions which his gentle friend Tibullus, and the elegiac-writers in general, heaped on military service. He preaches a virtue which Augustus would have liked to see revive in the sons of the too peaceful aristocracy of Rome.

[1] *Epod.*, 8.   [2] *Epod.*, 11.   [3] *Od.*, i. 2.   [4] *Od.*, i. 12.
[5] *Od.*, i. 34.   [6] *Od.*, i. 37.   [7] *Od.*, ii. 15.

The last two books of the *Odes*, which were composed between the return of Augustus to Italy and the year 23 B.C., set forth the whole of the Sovereign's programme of moral and political reform. The prosperity and power of Rome demand before everything else reconciliation with the gods, the rebirth of the old piety, and the restoration of the temples.[1]

> *Delicta majorum immeritus lues,*
> *Romane, donec templa refeceris,*
>
> . . . .
>
> *Dis te minorem quod geris, imperas ;*
> *Hinc omne principium, huc refer exitum.*

Regulus is the hero whom he proposes as a model for his age.[2] He begs Augustus, in order to put an end, once and for all, to the impious murders of civil war, to restrain the licence of morals. With the corruption of Rome he contrasts the virtue of the barbarians and their large families. He already sings the happy consequences of peace.

" Thanks to you, the ox roams in safety over the meadows, and Ceres and kindly Abundance nourish the land, the sailors fly over a peaceful sea, and Honour shrinks from the very breath of blame.[3]

" How shall the love of the Fathers and the people by offices of honour immortalize your virtues, Augustus, for ever, in inscriptions and recording annals ?[4]

" Your age, Caesar, has brought back plenty to the fields, and restored to our Jove the standards torn from the proud doors of the Parthians, and closed the shrine of Janus. . . . It has imposed right restraint on unreined licence, driven out sin, and called back the old virtues by which the Latin name and the might and glory of Italy grew great, and the majesty of our empire reached from the rising of the sun to his bed in the West. . . .

" And we, on working-days and holidays alike, amid the gifts of jovial Bacchus, having first prayed duly to the gods, with our wives and children . . . shall, in the manner of our fathers, sing great heroes, and Troy, and Anchises, and all the sons of Venus."[5]

In the same way Pindar, in ancient Greece, had made himself the mouthpiece of the enthusiasm aroused by Olympic and Pythian victories. Horace chose the light form of the ode, that of Alcaeos and that of Anacreon, not venturing upon the great lyrical poem such as Pindar wrote ; but into this form he poured the poetry which is exhaled by great collective sentiments felt by a whole people.

[1] *Od.*, iii. 6.   [2] *Od.*, iii. 5.   [3] *Od.*, iv. 5.
[4] *Od.*, iv. 14.   [5] *Od.*, iv. 15.

His triumphant joy in calm and order restored after the agonies of civil war, his hymns to an Italy saved from the Eastern danger and henceforth certain of her conquests, his aspirations to old-world virtue, to piety, to an idyllic life in the country which was once more fruitful, all this lyricism is astonishing in a sceptical Epicurean like Horace. As a poet, he made himself the mouthpiece of the great hope of the Roman people. Victorious over deadly Egypt, and rid of all fomenters of faction, Rome was herself again, under the reign of law represented by Augustus. Her trials, the result of the ambition, greed, and vice of the old generations, were over ; peace had come back, and, with peace, fruitful labour and happiness. It really was a new age, following on the Iron Age ; it was the Age of Gold, once announced by Virgil in the mystical transports of the fourth eclogue.

Ultima Cumaei venit jam carminis aetas ;
Magnus ab integro saeclorum nascitur ordo,
Jam redit et Virgo, redeunt Saturnia regna ;
Jam nova progenies caelo demittitur alto.

We at this day can better than ever understand the ecstasy of peoples before the hope of such a change. War, all war, was over for ever ; there were no more enemies to conquer abroad ; within the Empire wisdom, moderation, and piety would ensure harmony. Cruelly though these hopes have been disappointed, this idea of the Roman Peace extending its blessings over the world is truly a great and noble conception. It was only an aspiration, no doubt, only an ideal, but it is all to the honour of the Roman people that they ever conceived it. It roused genuine enthusiasm in a whole generation, and, in that generation, chiefly among humble, simple people, all those who were most helpless in the presence of public calamities and had the most to hope from a social rebirth. Virgil, the poet of shepherds and the son of peasants, gives this ideal a religious and miraculous colour. Earth, of herself, without labour, will offer her gifts to man ; all ills, all perils will fade away ; the lion will no more be the terror of the flocks ; the serpent will die, the poisonous plants will die ; there will be flowers and fruit everywhere. When Horace, in his skilfully chiselled lines, expresses the popular feeling, he tries to make it clear in more realistic pictures. He finds the elements of them in the sights of country life and in the beautified memories of the past of Rome. The peace of Augustus is the ox cutting his furrow, the god Faunus going through the byres and folds and heaping his blessings on the beasts and their young, or the ploughman happily enjoying his supper in the midst of his family. It is also the revival of the glorious days of Romulus, Regulus, Fabius, Cato, the days when everyone, it was thought, had been wise and good, and the gods, content with the piety of the people, had given Rome unmingled glory.

While others were writing elegiacs, tied down by their imitation of Hellenistic works and never daring to rise above paltry love-stories, in the midst of all the lyrics which they turned out of a mould of elegant social convention, affected, artificial, and finical, Horace created a poetry perfect in form and deliberately simple, popular, and Roman in inspiration. His *Odes* were truly the poetry of the new age.

III

THE *GEORGICS*

In the midst of his success, Virgil had given up the artificial form of the pastoral. It is himself that he condemns, with the Alexandrian school, when he renounces all the hackneyed themes which are only fit for occupying idle minds. " Who does not know about cruel Eurystheus, or the altars of Busiris of evil fame ? Who has not sung boy Hylas, and Latona's Delos, and Hippodameia, and Pelops of the ivory shoulder ? " [1] He himself, in the eclogue which had won him his first triumph, had sung Hylas.[2] He resolves henceforward to try a new path, which shall raise him to glory.

Cetera quae vacuas tenuissent carmina mentes
Omnia jam vulgata. . . .
. . . Tentanda via est qua me quoque possim
Tollere humo victorque virum volitare per ora.[3]

The origin of this new inspiration is to be found both in

[1] *Geor.*, iii. 4 ff.   [2] *Ecl.*, vi. 43-4.   [3] *Geor.*, iii. 3 ; vii. 8.

the intellectual and learned life of his time and in the economic
and political circumstances of Italy. There can be no doubt
of the influence of Varro and learned writers of his school on
the origin of the *Georgics*. The *De Re Rustica* had appeared
in 37. In the same year a Greek scholar whom Caesar had on
some former occasion brought from Alexandria, Hyginus, had
published an agricultural treatise of his own, in which an
especially large place was given to bee-breeding. We know
that the whole fourth book of the *Georgics* is devoted to this
subject. The reasons why the Romans were turning their
attention to agriculture at this time have been set forth by
Sig. Ferrero.[1] Sextus Pompeius was blockading the coasts
of Italy and preventing the arrival of foreign corn. Antony,
the master of the East, held back the flow of gold. In order
to live, Italy must return to the principles of the economic
system of the past, which was essentially agricultural. Being
eighty years old, Varro could remember from his own youth
the tradition of the elder Cato. His life-long experience
enabled him to adapt it to the present state of Italian
agriculture.

Virgil, too, who was always a countryman in manner and
tastes, knowing the land and loving it, easily recovered, when
he left the conventional pastoralism of the *Eclogues*, the
country life of Italy. He found it revivified by the science of
Hyginus and Varro. In the *Georgics*, he passes from the
school-room to real life. He receives his inspiration from a
truly living current of ideas.

Here the originality of the poem lies—in the matter still
more than in the form. Poetry abandons mythological
fiction for positive, real facts ; it descends from the clouds of
Ida and sets its feet on the ground, the soil of Italy.

To contemporaries, Virgil's experiment must have seemed
less daring and novel than it does to us. The *Georgics* is a
didactic poem ; now, the didactic form was in great esteem
among the Alexandrians and their Roman imitators. Virgil's
poem recalled to some extent Hesiod's *Works and Days*, and
Roman poets had already translated or imitated Hesiod.
Moreover, Virgil was careful to acknowledge his debt to this
venerable patron. " I embark," he says, " on a matter of
ancient glory and poetry ; I have dared to unseal the sacred

---

[1] Ferrero, **LXXIII,** iv, 85 ff.

springs, and to sing the song of Ascra in the Roman town-ships." [1] But it is in honour of Italy that he resumes the ancient strain ; as a son of Italy he celebrates the land of Saturn, the mighty mother of harvests, beasts, and men. The *Georgics* have in reality very little in common with the *Works and Days*.

Reality, Italian reality, not merely a sentiment or an idea, but what the poet has seen, the exact detail, however humble it may be, that is the great novelty in the *Georgics*. Let us leave on one side the features which are due to the special character of Virgil's mind and his poetic temperament, in particular the sentimental emotion and the sort of tenderness inspired in him not only by men but by beasts and even things, which wraps the clear lines of his pictures as in a soft atmosphere ; let us pass by the very quality of these pictures, the vividness and harmony of their colour. Let us be content to consider what constitutes the art of Virgil in its essence, the composition of the whole poem and of the separate parts. The originality of his art lies, it seems to me, in the profound and unprecedented union of impressions taken direct from reality with the academic traditions of Greek poetry, of Roman realism with Hellenic idealism.

It is hardly necessary to lay stress upon the great part played by realistic details in the *Georgics*. The poem is, first and foremost, a minute, accurate description of rustic toil and life in the country. There are many passages of what may be called a technical character ; they owe their poetry to the picturesque force of the expression.

> . . . *Ergo age, terrae*
> *Pingue solum primis extemplo a mensibus anni*
> *Fortes invertant tauri, glebasque jacentes*
> *Pulverulenta coquat maturis solibus aestas.* [2]

"Up, then ! While the soil is still heavy with the winter damp, in the very first months of the year, let your stout bulls turn it over, that the sods as they lie may be baked by dusty summer with its full suns."

With all his art, like a good, conscientious workman, Virgil is at pains to accomplish the didactic task which he has assumed. So he describes things as they are, quoting many

[1] *Geor.*, ii. 174-6.　　　　　　　　　　　　[2] i. 63 ff.

details observed, just like the writer of a technical treatise. We may quote, as an instance, his description of a good cow.

> . . . *Optima torvae*
> *Forma bovis, cui turpe caput, cui plurima cervix,*
> *Et crurum tenus a mento palearia pendent.*[1]

" The best kind of cow is an ill-looking beast, with an ugly head, a very thick neck, and a dewlap hanging from her chin to her legs."

Holding fast to reality, he seizes its beauty and can express it like an artist. But this naturalism is not continuous. Virgil would be afraid of wearying his reader with it. Sometimes he seems to grow tired of it himself.

" Let us go to the woods of the Dryads and their clearings, where I have not yet ventured, obedient, Maecenas, to your hard command."[2]

The authority of Maecenas does not prevent his imagination from frequently flying off from fields and cattle to the fictions of myth. Sometimes, too, he sets himself to merge the realistic details which he has himself seen into a mythological theme inspired by the schools. The famous eulogy of Italy in the second book affords a remarkable instance of this method.[3]

The idea which first occurs to Virgil's mind is to contrast his own country with the distant lands famous in Hellenistic legend, that of the Medes with its precious forests, those of the Ganges and the Hermus, rich in gold, Bactriana, and Arabia where the frankincense is found. That makes a kind of background to the picture, rather a misty background of exotic colouring, to which the accumulation of well-known names and the mention of gold, rare woods, and perfumes give a note of brilliance. Then come, still in the form of contrasts, mythological allusions. Our land was not ploughed, like Cholcis, by bulls breathing fire, to be sown with the Hydra's teeth ; we do not see crops of spears and helmets growing here. Finally we have, in very broad lines, a picture of the Italian countryside, bearing heavy harvests of corn and the Massic wine dear to Bacchus, olive trees and fat beasts.

" The war-horse gallops over the meadow, with his head high. In thy water, Clitumnus, the white herds and the bull have stood, which are

---

[1] iii. 51 ff.   [2] iii. 40.   [3] ii. 136 ff.

sacrificed on days of triumph before the temples of Rome. Here is eternal spring, only broken by summer. Twice in the year the flocks bear young, twice the tree gives apples. There are no tigers; no scaly serpent drags itself in coils. But there are fine cities, and mighty works, and little towns set on sheer rocks by the hands of men, and rivers flowing under ancient walls."

It is a purple passage, in which the mythology is intended to give a specially majestic impression, and the enthusiasm is not free from exaggeration.[1] But we cannot fail to perceive the accuracy and descriptiveness of certain features.[2]

The composition of each of the books of the poem shows the same skill in combining the real and the ideal and in enhancing the naturalism by the traditional device of allegory and myth.

The first book, for example, treats of ploughing and sowing. Virgil carefully describes the various kinds of attention which must be given to the soil, and says at what moment each task should be done. But he does not refuse to lift his eyes to the sky; science and philosophy often come in and interrupt the farmer's calendar. The work of man is subject to the course of the stars. The signs of the zodiac, the division of the world into habitable zones, the variations of the atmosphere, lead the poet on to discuss the prevision of the future and to recall the presages of the death of Caesar, a brilliant close which must in the eyes of contemporary readers have lent nobility to the vulgar technical details and practical hints which are the real subject of the poem.

The second book is devoted to the fruits of the earth, plants and trees. After detailed advice on grafting, planting, pruning, and the growing of young trees, we get a eulogy of spring. This book, too, ends in a purple passage, philosophic and political, it is true, rather than mythological, in spite of the large place given to mythological reminiscences.

> *O fortunatos nimium, sua si bona norint,*
> *Agricolas! quibus ipsa, procul discordibus armis,*
> *Fundit humo facilem victum justissima tellus!* [3]

The passage should be read through; it is composed

---

[1] *Bis gravidae pecudes, bis pomis utilis arbos* (150).
[2] *Tot congesta manu praeruptis oppida saxis,* | *Fluminaque antiquos subterlabentia muros,* etc. (156 ff).
[3] ii. 458 ff.

entirely of literary memories, or at least reminiscences. It is
the work of a scholarly poet rather than of a countryman.
Nor is Virgil blind to the fact; just like Tibullus and
Propertius, and like Ovid after him, he proclaims his love
for the learned Muses.[1]

> *Me vero primum dulces ante omnia Musae,*
> *Quarum sacra fero, ingenti percussus amore,*
> *Accipiant, caelique vias et sidera monstrent.*

Rustic cares only take the second place, and even then
they are presented under the image of their gods.

> *Felix, qui potuit rerum cognoscere causas*
>
> . . . .
>
> *Fortunatus et ille, deos qui novit agrestes*
> *Panaque Silvanumque senem Nymphasque sorores.*[2]

The last two books present a similar composition. In the
third book it is not only the great white oxen of the Clitumnus
which inspire his Muse. A more ambitious, less Italian
feeling inspires him. The race-horses of the plain of Argos
and the hounds of Laconia call him first.

> . . . *Vocat ingenti clamore Cithaeron*
> *Taygetique canes domitrixque Epidaurus equorum.*[3]

We see Actaeon's hunt dashing through the poem of Italian
agriculture.

What Virgil sees in animals is their form, no doubt, but
also, and chiefly, their passions, their love, their keenness in
fight, their life, their suffering, everything which brings them
near to men. The stock-breeder will find in his lines some
good advice, no doubt; the moralist who has no interest in
stock-breeding will most certainly find in many of them
food for thought and images full of sense. The book ends,
like all the others, with a long purple passage entirely in the
classical tradition, a picture of the plague among animals, a
sort of replica, transferred from men to beasts, of the plague
of Athens described by Thucydides and Lucretius.

Men, again, can be seen in the fourth book under the bees.
Moreover, the whole of the second part of the book is taken

[1] ii. 475 ff.   [2] ii. 490-4.   [3] iii. 43-4.

up with a purely mythological episode, the story of Aristaeus, in which we find, not boy Hylas and Pelops of the ivory shoulder, it is true, but the nymph Cyrene and Nereus and Orpheus and Eurydice. The ancient countryside was peopled with gods. Virgil greets at length all those whom he meets, and he adds many foreign deities and heroes, familiar guests of his imagination, whom he has no difficulty in acclimatizing in the fields of Italy.

The influence of the lessons which formed his mind and trained his poetic eye is to be seen in his new work. Roman poetry could not break away from the Hellenistic form all at once. In their mythology and in the art with which the images are composed, the *Georgics* are still subject to the aesthetic ideas of their time. But their spirit is original, for the inspiration comes straight from the Italian soil, and this inspiration in itself includes accurate observation of the things of the earth and realistic painting of the humblest details. Virgil is thus led to give artistic expression to one of the deep veins of national life. Since the prehistoric age, in the country, far from the towns, off the track of history, millions of men had invented, little by little, and repeated from generation to generation the actions and the labours described by the poet. No less than war and the deliberations of the Senate, their obscure toil made the greatness of Rome. We cannot understand the Augustan renascence if we forget the humble but manifold activity which, in pacified Italy, every day and in every season, was busy drawing from the earth food to keep men alive. This arduous, intelligent work of the fields had recaptured the veterans rewarded for their long years of fighting by a piece of land. Through it, the old Italian tradition took hold of old and new colonists alike. Made up of careful thoroughness, prudence, perseverance, and energy, country life was forming the future aristocracy which was destined to take the place, in the city and in the Empire, of the old, exhausted nobility. The land was the true secret strength of the Roman Empire, the force behind all the unexpected recoveries which, like radiant mornings, followed nights of storm and horror. While a stranger was bringing forth new harvests on his father's farm at the foot of the Alps, in the plain where the Mincius wound in slow curves, Virgil, for the use of all and for his own pleasure in his art, sang of agriculture which gave Rome her bread.

IV

THE *AENEID*

In 29 B.C. Virgil was able to read the completed *Georgics* to Octavian, who had just returned to Italy. After Actium the victor had spent nearly two whole years in organizing the East. Prosperity was reviving everywhere, and concord was achieved by forgetting old rivalries. The Senate unanimously offered supreme power to the pacifier of the world. He refused to accept more than an authority lasting ten years, which he strove to bring within the framework of the ancient constitution. The old Republic seemed to rise again, rejuvenated, better ordered, and simply guided by a new wisdom. A sincere enthusiasm centred on the person of Augustus all the hopes of a Golden Age. The glorious memories of the past of Rome and aspirations to a calmer but still more brilliant future formed a kind of aureole about his recent victory. In these feelings, common to the whole people, Virgil seems first of all to have sought the inspiration of a new poem. He announces this project in the third book of the *Georgics*.

"In a green field I shall build a temple of marble by the waterside . . . where the banks of Mincius are fringed with soft rushes. In the middle Caesar shall stand, lord of the temple. Before him I shall race by the river, victorious and resplendent in Tyrian purple, driving a hundred chariots." [1]

Between his first notion of a poem in honour of Octavian the victor of Actium and the *Aeneid*, a whole succession of reflections must have occurred to Virgil, the trend of which is seen in the work as it has come down to us. What were the ideas which presided over the composition of the national epic of the Romans ?

The first, beyond question, is that of Rome and her grandeur. It is asserted in the first lines of the poem. Through the flames of the last night of Troy, in the wanderings and all the adventures of Aeneas, in councils of gods and battles of men, everywhere and at every moment, the theme of Rome, the future mistress of the world, recurs—*gravidam*

[1] iii. 13 ff.

imperiis belloque frementem—ac totum sub leges mitteret orbem.[1] The *Aeneid* is the epic of the predestination of Rome. Rome, not Augustus, holds the first place ; the city, the people, Italy are substituted for the ruler himself. The inspiration has become infinitely vaster.

Elevating his thought high above present times, Virgil takes his subject from prehistoric ages, and makes Aeneas his hero. The figure of Augustus only appears in two passages, at the end of the sixth book, when Anchises shows Aeneas the line of his descendants,[2] and, more fully developed, in the description of the shield of Aeneas.[3] But do we not constantly see his figure in that of the first founder ? The portrait of his pious forbear is said to lack character. But how alive it becomes if we see in it, as contemporaries cannot have failed to do, a prefigurement of the ruler who had completed the work of Roman greatness ! Aeneas sacrifices himself to the task imposed on him by destiny. Augustus, too, could say " My fate does not allow me to guide my life by my own auspices and to dispose of my cares as I would." [4] His motto had long been that professed by Aeneas : " Wherever the fates may lead, hither and thither, let us follow. Whatever may fall, every fortune must be overcome by bearing it." [5] This dogged patience in difficulty is allied in Aeneas with daring—*Tu ne cede malis, sed contra audentior ito | Qua tua te fortuna sinet* [6]—and love of the glory which must come from great and useful achievement.[7] Was this not Octavian's whole history, and the secret of his triumph in the Civil Wars ? Was not the cold will-power which Aeneas displays the dominant feature in the character of Augustus, and that in which he took most pride ?

" But no tears can move him, no words can turn him. His fate stands in the way, and a god closes his untroubled ears. As the blasts of the storm strive in vain to shake a stout oak," etc. [8]

In the eleventh book, when the Latins, after their first defeat, come to sue for a truce to bury their dead, the reply of Aeneas might come from Octavian : " You ask peace for the dead . . . I would give it to the living." [9] The leader who appeals to the rights conferred on him by destiny, who

---

[1] iv. 229, 231.	[2] vi. 790 ff.	[3] viii. 671-728.
[4] iv. 340.	[5] v. 709.	[6] vi. 95.
[7] vi. 888.	[8] iv. 438 ff.	[9] xi. 110.

desires the submission of his opponents for the good of his country, and is quite ready to welcome those who have just been fighting him, is he not the victor of Actium ? Like Aeneas, too, at the time when Virgil was finishing the *Aeneid*, Augustus in his triumph could say : " My son, learn virtue and real work from me ; others will teach you happiness." [1] The features of the Trojan hero, perhaps intentionally rather vague, and the dim colours of his image were vividly clear in Virgil's mind. Caesar was not completely evicted from the monument raised by the poet ; his is the cold, formal figure enthroned in the middle of the temple, in the ideal form of the legendary hero.

In the same way, all through the poem, Virgil's Roman patriotism perceives living reality in myth. For Virgil, *patria* is not only the Sovereign, the father of the Empire, but the land of Italy and the men who live there, its legends and traditions, familiar pictures and great historical memories. The poet's deep feeling gives life to things, and colour and substance ; it inspires descriptions and makes them true. There is a religious note in the passage in the third book in which Aeneas and his comrades, and even old Anchises, who will lie on the threshold of the promised land, hail from mid-Adriatic the " dim hills and low line of Italy." [2] With the fifth book the *Aeneid* becomes a sort of geographical epic of the land of Italy. Learning is mingled with picturesque description. We see Eryx, famous because of the Punic Wars, and Drepanum, which owes its glory to the tomb of Anchises ; we see Euboean Cumae and its citadel, where Apollo presides high aloft. Cape Misenum and Cape Palinurus take their names from the graves of companions of Aeneas ; Caieta, the old nurse of the hero, by her death brought eternal fame to the city which bears her name. When the Trojans set foot on Latin soil, the poet is affected by a new emotion.

" Say, Erato," he entreats, " who were the kings, what was the story, what was the state of ancient Latium. . . . Greater things are before me ; I take up a greater work." [3] " What men were then the flower of the kindly land of Italy ? Thou dost remember, Goddess, thou canst relate. Barely a faint breath of report has come through to us." [4]

This faint breath is enough for Virgil to animate with precise details the enumeration of the Latins and their allies,

[1] xii. 435.   [2] iii. 523 ff.   [3] vii. 37 ff.   [4] vii. 641 ff.

and later, in the tenth book, that of the Etruscans and Ligurians who come to the aid of Aeneas. These episodes are no doubt inspired by Homer, but, as an admirable judge recognizes, by the value of the pictures and their ethnological value, the imitation surpasses the model.[1]

As Aeneas sets foot on the still unknown land of Latium, he knows it for his home. *Hic domus, haec patria est.*[2] As in the paternal home, the smallest details have their importance, charged as they are with memories and emotions. This sentiment becomes for Virgil the principle of an essentially concrete art which, by a stroke of exact observation, by a single epithet full of precise meaning, calls up a whole picture or aggregate of impressions in brief, just as, among children of one family, a single word is enough to reawaken the dear old days they have spent together. So, for Roman readers, the lines in which Virgil mentions the places or men of Latium, or alludes to their traditions or rites, were charged with impressions of reality, and were like charms which conjured up things they had seen and felt themselves. Such images, such words which awake distant echoes, are surely the very secret of poetry.

Not only in Latium and Italy, but all through the wanderings of Aeneas by land and sea, Virgil's patriotism finds the present realities of Rome. When Aeneas sails the Adriatic, he does not fail to espy the cloudy top of the promontory of Leucas, the abode of Apollo, Apollo of Actium. He lands, sacrifices to Jupiter, and, on the shore of Actium, which will one day finally decide the fortune of Augustus, he holds games and sets up a trophy in advance. By his visits the founder seems to conquer, in anticipation of the Empire, the Mediterranean lands which are destined to become Roman—Thrace, Crete, the shores of Epeiros and Africa, and the rest. The poem thus becomes the common possession of the Romans and their subjects.

The first four books of the poem are placed at Carthage. There Aeneas recounts to Dido the fall of Troy and his long wanderings, and there is laid the love-story which Roman readers must have enjoyed so much. The tragic outcome of the idyll is no doubt a foreshadowing of the fury of the Punic Wars. But another idea also seems to inspire the

---

[1] Bellessort, **XXX**, pp. 204-5.   [2] vii. 122.

pictures which Virgil presents.   We see Aeneas, clad in Tyrian fashion, presiding over the embellishment of the foreign city. This hive of industry, where everyone is hard at work, a harbour being dug here, and the foundations of a theatre laid there, and a temple erected to Juno in the centre, is not only Dido's Carthage, it is that of Augustus.   It is a topical picture.   On the site of the Punic city, cursed and deserted more than a century before, Augustus had ordered a new city to be built, as capital of Roman Africa.   " He found in Virgil," M. Carcopino observes, " a poet who, while the city was rising from its ashes, undertook to embellish it with his verse and to dispel, with the purifying breath of the most popular legends of Latin tradition, the atmosphere of distrust and fear which still stifled it and might arrest its development." [1]   Virgil's imagination constantly takes its stand on Roman realities, on direct knowledge of the land and things of Italy, on national history, and on the political conception of Augustus.   In spite of the transposition of the subject into the realm of myth, the *Aeneid* is truly the epic of Rome as mistress of the world, of Italy and of Latium, the epic of the moral and material restoration for which Augustus strove.

That is why an importance is given to the gods and religion which causes some surprise.   The perpetual intervention of some deity or other is a device which seems to damage the action ;   the piety of Aeneas is occasionally tedious.   The heroes of the *Iliad* and the wily Odysseus show us human activity much more emancipated from divine leading-strings. They help themselves, pending help from Heaven.   Aeneas defers action until Heaven shall have decided the event.

In the *Aeneid* the gods are arranged, as it were, in several planes.   Above all, Destiny reigns ;   then come the great gods, Jupiter, Juno, Venus, Neptune, Vulcan, Diana, Mercury, etc. ;   lastly, there are the innumerable local gods, oracles, Manes, Penates, and all the divine powers of land and water, sky and underworld.   Destiny ordains everything ;   from the beginning of time it has decided to give the dominion of the world to Rome, the heiress of Troy.   The power of Asia and the race of Priam fell when it seemed good to the upper gods ; [2] Aeneas recounts to Dido not his own deeds, but the decrees of the gods.   *Fata renarrabat divum cursusque docebat.*[3]

[1] **XLII,** p. 750.   [2] iii. 1.   [3] iii. 716.

Aeneas abandons himself entirely to this higher power, which leads him by the hand, protects him, if not from difficulties, at least from any unexpected happening, has arranged even the smallest details in advance, and will ensure the future of his posterity with equal care. The interest of the action owes nothing to the element of surprise. The whole epic is dominated by a majestic finality, as flattering to Roman pride as it was consoling to the conquered. But this Destiny answers to a philosophic rather than religious conception. It expresses an idea closely allied to the " plan of Fortune " imagined by Polybius and is hardly distinguishable from the Providence beloved of Bossuet. Destiny, master of the very gods, is only a pious image symbolizing the philosophy of history generally accepted in Rome.

The great gods of the family of Jupiter hardly appear except as a conventional epic device. The resentment of Juno, the motherly care of Venus, the frown of Jupiter which causes Olympus and earth to tremble, to no apparent purpose, are simply the inheritance of Homer. These miraculous interventions are the correct thing in an epic. Very different is the rôle of the modest deities of the lowest plane. They are the chief object of the awe, the scruples, and the cares of the founder. They represent the true religious element in the *Aeneid*.

It has been possible to maintain that the true hero of the poem is not Aeneas, but the Penates. During the tragic night of the burning of Troy, Hector's shade entrusts them to Aeneas.[1] But the hero dares not touch them with his blood-stained hands. Anchises, who is in any case the head of the race, shall take charge of them for the time being.

> *Tu, genitor, cape sacra manu patriosque Penates.*
> *Me, bello e tanto digressum et caede recenti,*
> *Attrectare nefas, donec me flumine vivo*
> *Abluero.*[2]

It is for his Penates that Aeneas seeks a favourable land and conquers Latium. The Trojan name will vanish, the speech and manners of the comrades of Aeneas will become those of Italy,[3] the blood of men will mingle, but the Penates will pass from the Trojan camp to the city of Latinus, thence to

[1] ii. 293. [2] ii. 716. [3] xii. 791 ff.

Alba, and from Alba to Rome ; they will ensure the continuity of the people.   The essential element of the Roman fatherland is its gods.

The piety of Aeneas consists in the absolute submission of his mind to the bidding of the gods ; it chiefly shows itself in constant attention to all the signs by which the gods are believed to manifest their will.   Portents accompany his footsteps ; he is not at all surprised, and indeed he looks for them as a natural thing.   His wanderings to Delos, Crete, Epeiros, Sicily, and Cumae are simply a round of oracles.   At every approach of danger the Trojan leader—Anchises, while he lives, and after him Aeneas—lifts his hands, palm upwards, to the sky and prays :

> Di, prohibete minas, Di, talem avertite casum,
> Et placidi servate pios.[1]

The last phrase, placidi servate pios, perfectly expresses the spirit of Roman religion.   Aeneas and his companions are pious in that they scrupulously perform, each on his own account, their duty to the gods.   Gods, ward off adversity from them, for you owe your peace to them !

Destiny has, no doubt, determined the foundation of Rome.   But what an amount of divine assistance is needed everywhere and on every occasion to ensure the accomplishment of its orders !   A god dictates every decision and inspires every thought, both of the Trojans and of their adversaries ; a god guides every step and directs every act.   It is the god that wins the fight and kills, or at least decides the fated moment by abandoning the man whom Destiny has doomed.   After all these episodes in which the gods play a more important part than the men, it is in heaven that the conclusion of the epic is arranged and Jupiter and Juno discuss the terms of a solemn alliance between Trojans and Latins.[2]   From the mixture of the two races a people shall be born which will surpass the gods themselves in piety.   Once this pact is concluded, there is nothing left for the nymph Juturna but to desert the chariot of her brother Turnus, who feels himself lost ; and with a groan his soul flies raging to the shades.

Profoundly religious thought dominates the whole action

[1] iii. 266-7.   [2] xii. 791 ff.

of the epic ; it combines with patriotism to gather up the tradition of the Roman cults with pious care and to sing their praise. There is hardly a rite which is not illustrated by an episode. Already in the third book we find Aeneas rendering funeral honours to Polydorus.[1] The theme reappears several times, and is fully developed in the eleventh book in the detailed description of the funeral of the hapless Pallas.[2] The fifth book is almost entirely devoted to the worship of the Manes.

In the sixth book we have the temple at Cumae and ample information about the oracles of the Sibyl. " Your prophecies and secret fates," Aeneas announces, " I shall impose on my people, and I shall devote chosen priests to them." [3] At the beginning of the following book, after all the portents which greet Aeneas on Latin soil, Latinus on his side goes to Albunea, to consult the oracle of Faunus,[4] then comes the description of the temple of Picus,[5] and soon after we have the outbreak of orgiastic frenzy which drives Amata into the forests of Lavinium.[6] All through the eighth book, while war is threatening, Aeneas dallies with Evander on an archaeological excursion over the holy places of the future city of Rome. On the Aventine he is told the story of Cacus, and all about the rites of the great altar dedicated to Hercules,[7] and the legends of the Porta Carmentalis, the Tarpeian Rock, the Capitol, and so on. At the end of the book, he comes with his horsemen to the ancient shrine of Silvanus on the territory of Caere, near the river enclosed among hills with many caves (doubtless old Etruscan tombs) in their sides and black firs on their crests.[8] There he receives the divine arms which Venus brings to him. At every spot, and about every people, Virgil does not fail to mention its gods, myths, and sacred associations.[9]

The part played by religion in the *Aeneid* is further increased by the descent of Aeneas into Hades. The episode occupies almost the whole sixth book, in the very centre of the poem. The idea, no doubt, comes from Homer, who, in the eleventh book of the *Odyssey*, shows Odysseus raising from a pit filled with blood the souls of his mother Anticleia and

---

[1] iii. 62 ff.   [2] xi. 29 ff.   [3] vi. 72 ff.   [4] vii. 81 ff.
[5] vii. 170 ff.   [6] vii. 341-405.   [7] viii. 309 ff.   [8] viii. 597 ff.
[9] E.g., the legend of Hippolytus Virbius (vii. 761 ff.). The episode of Camilla is full of memories of the nature-worship of Diana.

the soothsayer Teiresias.   But how Virgil has developed it !
Under the guidance of the Sibyl, Aeneas goes all through the
underworld and learns its secrets.   This journey through
mysteries is a kind of initiation for him, which consecrates
his sanctity and, by infusing a new virtue into him, prepares
him to vanquish the last difficulties which await him on
Latin soil.

Virgil seems to have set himself the twofold task of
embracing the whole Graeco-Latin religious tradition and of
replying to the theological questionings of his time.   The sixth
book of the *Aeneid* fills a gap in the old Roman religion.   To
earth and heaven, already filled with gods, he adds the underworld and, in the voice of Anchises presenting to Aeneas the
souls of his descendants, he shows even Hades big with all
the future glory of Rome.

Rome and the gods—these seem to be the two great ideas
inspiring the *Aeneid*, the two Muses who have furnished the
matter of the poem, have given it its form, and have even
determined the art of Virgil down to details.   They make the
originality of the Roman epic.

Yet Virgil had his models, from whom he openly took not
only the very type of his work, but many individual elements.
Homer is his master, but he is not his source.   In the *Iliad*
Aeneas appears only as quite a minor character.   His rôle
was developed by the imagination of later ages, though we
cannot say exactly how his legend began.   The historians
of Sicily seem to have transmitted it ready-made to the
first Latin poets.   Virgil found in them all that was essential
to his theme.   The choice of Aeneas as a hero connected him
with the tradition of the Roman epic.   The old poets, brought
into fashion by the archaistic vogue of which the severe
Asinius Pollio was the centre, stand as intermediaries between
the inspiration of Homer and the epic of the age of Augustus.
" At the beginning," Norden says, " was Homer ; then came
Naevius ; then Ennius ; and finally Virgil." [1]

The few fragments of the *Annals* which remain enable us
to recognize in the *Aeneid* not only expressions, half-lines,
and even whole lines of Ennius, though they are never reproduced word for word, but also episodes from the same source.
Instances are the opening of the gates of the temple of Janus

[1] Norden, **CXVII,** p. 170.

in the seventh book [1] and the council of the gods with which the tenth book opens. The picture of the fall of Troy in the second book is taken, according to Servius, from Ennius's account of the destruction of Alba.[2] The combats in the *Aeneid* no doubt recall those of the *Iliad*, but they also owe many touches to the numerous descriptions of battles in Ennius. *Premitur pede pes*, the old poet said ; [3] *haeret pede pes densusque viro vir*, we read in Virgil.[4] Virgil seems to be almost equally indebted to Naevius. The storm in the first book of the *Aeneid* and Venus's complaints to Jupiter come straight from the *Bellum Punicum*, according to Macrobius.[5] The ancients, possessing Ennius and Naevius, could judge better than we how much Virgil took from them.

"If Virgil," says Aulus Gellius, "sometimes writes harsh lines, and excessive lines, something beyond measure, it is in order that the people of Ennius may easily recognize the traces of antiquity in the new poem." [6]

So, by the side of Homeric models, Virgil gives a large place to the Roman epic tradition. In it he found his hero and his subject ; he borrowed much from it. Moreover, he profits by all the virtuosity which Hellenistic education had developed in Roman poetry since Ennius's time. Alexandrian art taught him to see the picturesque and to express it in a few words, in a kind of epitome. His poetry often calls up plastic and coloured images. In the description of Hades Monsieur S. Reinach quotes several scenes which he considers directly inspired by paintings or reliefs.[7] The whole *Aeneid* abounds in passages of the kind, not to mention those in which Virgil takes pleasure in describing works of art, such as the subjects adorning the doors of the temple of Apollo at Cumae,[8] or the scenes portrayed on the shield of Aeneas.[9] Thus, the apparition of Neptune and his retinue in Book V recalls the frieze of the altar of Domitius Ahenobarbus.[10] Vulcan's forge in the eighth book is quite a pictorial subject.[11] But if Virgil introduces all the art of his time into the epic, it

---

[1] 601-23.   [2] *Ad Aen.*, ii. 469.   [3] Frag., 572.
[4] x. 361.   [5] vi. 2. 31.
[6] Aul. Gel., xii. 2, quoting a passage in Seneca's *Epistulae Morales*, now lost. What is the exact meaning of *enormes et aliquid supra mensuram habentes ?* Norden himself admits that he is not certain. He suggests that it may refer to lines made abnormally long by an accumulation of elisions, e.g., vii. 311 : *Magna satis, dubitem haud equidem implorare quod usquam est*, CXVII, p. 153.
[7] Sisyphus and some other sufferers in Hades. CXXXVII, ii, 159-205.
[8] vi. 14 ff.   [9] viii. 626 ff.   [10] v. 814 ff. ; cf. above, p. 256.   [11] viii. 626.

is to subordinate it to the ideas of patriotism and piety which the age of Augustus had reawakened in Rome, and he perhaps found the tradition of these ideas in the old Roman epic poets.

So the *Aeneid* created a new art which came down to the realities of the land and the soul of Italy and sought to seize their beauty. In this art there are no trifling fancies, intended to amuse by surprises, wit, and prettiness. Its gravity sometimes seems a little cold, but beneath it is sincerely passionate and profoundly living—passionate for all that concerns the Roman fatherland, its past history and its present glory, and profoundly living with a religious thought whose roots go down to the earliest ages. These great sentiments animate the myth with the life of the poet's own day, they attach his descriptions to actual things the sight of which stirs his heart. Through them a legendary epic, cast in the Homeric mould, becomes an original poem truly expressing the spirit of Augustan Rome.

With right, the *Aeneid* became the great national work, not only for Rome itself, but for the whole Roman world. Here was a poem in which the whole of the Graeco-Roman artistic tradition was gathered up in a new and living form, the memories of the old Republic were united with the noblest aspirations of the new Empire, the purest Latin patriotism was allied with a generous philosophy of Mediterranean history, Latium and Italy were extolled but reconciled with Africa while the origins of their glory were linked with Asia, and the practices of the old worship were associated with the mystical aspirations of contemporary religious feeling. In details of workmanship, the idealism and conventionalizing methods of great classical poetry were enhanced by realistic touches and minute accuracy, while the myth was studded with pictures of present-day life and localized in a fundamentally true landscape. By its very complexity, Virgil's epic answered to the most diverse tendencies of the individuals and peoples pacified and brought together by the Empire. It was truly the poem of Imperial Rome, the epic of the world and the new age.

Its fame and influence outlived even the civilization which had given it birth. After the downfall of the ancient world, Virgil and the *Aeneid* continued to live in the imaginations of the Middle Ages, and, even to men for whom the poem and the ideas which inspired it had become dead letters, Virgil assumed the figure of a hero, the greatest of romancers, the great prophet, the great magician.[1] The poet's name and the memory of his work were indissolubly bound up with the memory of Rome itself and of all antiquity, with the haunting vision of a past which, even when it was dim and mysterious, never ceased to appear to humanity as the image of its greatness, its nobility, and its beauty.

V

THE SECULAR GAMES

The literary work of Virgil and Horace is the expression of a veritable national renascence, a deliberate, conscious rebirth which was solemnized by the Secular Games organized by Augustus.

Virgil died in the year 19 B.C., on his return from a voyage in Greece and Asia which he had taken in order to make the descriptions in the first books of the *Aeneid* more definite by seeing the places for himself. At the end of his sixth book he already announces the great symbolic festival which was to celebrate the new era.[2]

> *Augustus Caesar, divi genus, aurea condet*
> *Saecula.*

This was a thought which had long been in the mind of the sovereign, and had haunted the Roman imagination since the time of Caesar. It was based on one of the oldest traditions of Etruscan religious speculation, and had been restored to prominence by some of the portents which had always made such a strong impression on the imagination of the people. The religious inauguration of his age, therefore, was for Augustus an effective act of political propaganda, and at the same time an application of his programme of religious restoration. The Secular Games were to be like an ideal triumphal arch, marking the passing of Rome from old times to new.

[1] Comparetti, **XLIX.**   [2] vi. 792.

It was the will of the gods, the Etruscans taught, that marked the divisions between the epochs of mankind. For them, a *saeculum* was not a fixed period of a hundred years ; it was a cycle of varying length, which expired on the death of the longest-lived man who was born at its beginning. Since men were not in a position to observe this event, the gods undertook to reveal it to them by portents. These beliefs had been adopted by the Romans in ancient times together with the whole of the Etruscan augural discipline. Secular Games had been held, according to Pontifical tradition, in 449, on the fall of the Decemvirs, in 346, in 249, at the end of the first Punic War, and, lastly, in 149 or 146, about the time of the reduction of Greece to a Roman province. In 43, shortly after the death of Caesar, a comet had appeared and a haruspex had declared that this portent indicated the end of the ninth *saeculum* of the Etruscans.

Circumstances at that moment were not at all propitious for the celebration of Secular Games. But the appearance of the comet, combined with the general weariness and desire for better times, raised great hopes in the people, apparently the very hopes expressed poetically in Virgil's fourth eclogue. Years went by ; Actium had accomplished the unification of the Empire, and the Senate had renewed for another ten years the exceptional powers of Augustus, when, in 17 B.C., a fresh portent, the reappearance of the comet of Caesar, seemed to announce that the Golden Age for which all hoped had come at last. This was the moment to hold the traditional Games. Augustus did not miss the opportunity.

We know all the details of the festival particularly well, thanks to numerous fragments of an inscription found by the Tiber in 1890, which bore the official account of the ceremonies.[1]

On the apparition of the comet, the Quindecimvirs were, in accordance with ancient usage, instructed to consult the Sibylline Books. On their report, the Senate decreed that the Secular Games should be held. Heralds were sent all about the town, dressed in the ancient fashion, with high-plumed helmet, small round shield, and great staff, to summon the people to the unique festival which no living man had seen

---

[1] Barnabei and Mommsen, " I Commentarii dei Ludi Secolari di Augusto," in **XIV,** i (1891), coll. 608 ff.

and no one would see again. The details were arranged by Augustus himself, with the assistance of the Quindecimvirs. It was to last three consecutive nights and days. As a preliminary, the whole people must be subjected to rites of fumigation, intended to purify it of all the stains contracted during the previous age. It was a new and virgin generation, pure of all the ancient sins, that would be admitted to the enjoyment of the new time.

The feast began on the night between the 31st May and the 1st June, at the Tarentum, on the left bank of the Tiber, a place long sacred to the infernal deities. Crowded on the two banks, the people of Rome silently contemplated the fires on the altars and the illuminations which the officiating priests were lighting. On the first night the Greek Moerae, the goddesses of fate, were invoked, and nine black sheep and nine goats were sacrificed to them. On the second night sacrifice and prayer were offered up to Eileithyia, the goddess of child-birth, and on the third to Mother Earth. In each case Augustus himself uttered the prayer in the traditional form.

" As it is prescribed in the Sibylline Books, for this reason and for the greater good of the Roman people of the Quirites, receive this sacrifice of nine ewe-lambs and nine she-kids and grant my prayer.

" Increase the dominion and the majesty of the Roman people of the Quirites in war and in peace.

" Protect the Latin name always, and grant eternal integrity, victory, and health to the Roman people of the Quirites.

" Be favourable to the Roman people of the Quirites.

" Keep safe and sound the State of the Roman people of the Quirites.

" I beseech you to be propitious to the Roman people of the Quirites, to the College of Quindecimvirs, to myself, and to my family, and to my house.

" I beseech you to accept this sacrifice of nine ewe-lambs and nine she-kids which are dedicated to you and will be immolated to you."

In restoring the ancient solemnities, Augustus had brought them into line with the fashion of the day ; he had substituted the Greek ritual, *Achivus ritus*, and Greek deities, the Moerae and Eileithyia, for the Etruscan rites and the dark underground deities Dis Pater and Proserpine. To them he had further added the great shining gods of heaven, in whose honour the feasts by day were held.

On the first day the citizens went up to the Capitol in

procession and offered sacrifice to Jupiter. The second day was reserved for the matrons ; one hundred and ten of them sang in chorus while, again on the Capitol, Augustus and Agrippa sacrificed a white heifer to Juno. The third day was the day of the young, who did honour to Apollo and his sister Diana. This time the ceremony took place on the Palatine, the hill consecrated by Romulus long ago, which Augustus once more made a sacred centre of the new Rome, before the Temple of Apollo of Actium, erected about ten years before hard by the Imperial Palace.

Here, by a last innovation of the imperial patron of letters, the feast terminated with a kind of recital of lyric poetry. Twenty-seven young men and as many maidens sang the new poem which Augustus had ordered from Horace, as once the Senate had ordered from Livius Andronicus the hymn of thanksgiving for the victory over Hannibal's brother. If Virgil had lived, he would certainly have been chosen for the honour of composing this Secular Hymn, as an epilogue, so to speak, to his epic of the destiny of Rome. Horace made it a sort of repetition of the prayers of the preceding nights and days, substituting the charm of poetry for the magical potency of the old litanies and adding an allusion to the moral and social renovation accomplished by Augustus.

"Bountiful Sun, in thy shining car, dispensing and hiding the light, born another yet the same, mayest thou see nothing greater than Rome !

"Thou whose care is to give easy child-birth in due time, Eileithyia, guard all mothers, whether thou will be called Lucina or Genitalis,

"Goddess, make our children grow up, and prosper the decrees of the Fathers on the marriage of women and the law of wedlock which shall bring forth a new generation abundantly ;

"That the circle of one hundred and ten years may bring back the games and hymns which fill three glorious days, three joyful nights.

"And you, Parcae, true prophetesses, whose words, once spoken, are fulfilled by the inevitable event, add happy destinies to those which have been accomplished.

"May the earth, fertile in fruits and beasts, give a crown of wheat-ears to Ceres ; and may the healthful rain and winds of Jove nurture the seed in her bosom."

Nor did Horace omit to recall on this day of rejoicing the memory of the national epic, the masterpiece of his friend who had died too soon.

"If Rome is your work, and by your command the Ilian band made the Etruscan shore, having changed Lares and city and come safe through thei wanderings,

"When through the flames of innocent Troy pious Aeneas, outliving his home, made a free road for his comrades, to whom he would give greater things than they left behind,

"Gods, give upright manners to heedful youth ; give rest to peaceful age ; and to the race of Romulus give wealth and offspring and all glory ! . . .

"And the Prophet, glorious with the gleaming bow, Phoebus the darling of the nine Muses, who raises weary limbs with his healing art,

"If he looks kindly on the altars of the Palatine, and the State of Rome, and happy Latium, may he continue our age into another and ever better cycle of years !"

CHAPTER III

KNOWLEDGE AND THE IMPERIAL IDEA.
GEOGRAPHY AND HISTORY IN ROME

WHILE Rome was conquering the Mediterranean provinces, she had been content to take over the acquisitions of Greek science as she found them, and as well as she could. We have seen in Rome disseminators of popular knowledge and writers of didactic treatises, but no true science. Neither the Augustan age nor the Empire brought any progress in the knowledge of nature.

But, while neither the universe nor life nor things roused the Romans to any personal effort, this was not the case with ideas which affected themselves, their national life, and their past. Varro and his emulators had tried, by applying Greek methods to Roman traditions, to form a notion of the intellectual, moral, social, and political activity of ancient Italy. Failing scientists, the Republic had at least possessed learned men and historians. Man interested it more than nature.

World-dominion necessarily widened the intellectual horizon of the Romans. Even practical requirements obliged them to look beyond their city and the shores of the peninsula. It was indispensable that they should know the very various peoples which obeyed them, the distant countries which they administered, and even those regions outside their sway, from which some danger to themselves might come. An exact knowledge of itself and of the world was indispensable to the people which governed the world. It might be expected that the age of Augustus would have seen considerable progress in geography and history.

Let us first see how it understood geography, and what it made of it.

320

I

GEOGRAPHY

Geography was a science cultivated with brilliance in the Hellenistic world. The conquests of Alexander had laid the whole inhabited earth, the οἰκουμένη, open to the curiosity of scientists. Knowledge, guided by logic, had rapidly gone beyond the bounds of experience and embraced both earth and heaven, of which it tried to give a precise and concrete image. Scientists like Eratosthenes, Hipparchos, and Artemidoros had turned geography into a veritable cosmography. Not only had they determined by calculation the extent of the continental regions between the known coasts of the Mediterranean and the still mysterious shores of the Northern Ocean, between the coasts of Asia and the Eastern empires of India and even of the Seres, that is, of China, but they had tried to do the same for Africa. What was more, astronomy had led them to conceive the true shape of the earth. They knew that it was a globe. Eratosthenes taught that, if the vast size of the Atlantic had not been an obstacle, it would have been possible to sail along the same parallel from Spain to India.[1] The Roman compilers did not fail to note this theory. It was through them that it came down to the learned men of the Renaissance and determined enterprises like that of Columbus. " How far is it," Seneca asks, " from the outermost coast of Spain to the Indians ? " " A very few days' sailing, with a following wind." [2]

The Roman world seems hardly to have known this Greek science except through abridgments and popular works. Strabo, at the beginning of the Empire, was the great geographer ; he had abandoned all the mathematical and deductive side of Alexandrian geography. In the IInd century of our era Ptolemy wrote a summary of Greek geographical knowledge. To these two Greek writers we owe the best part of our knowledge of ancient geography. In addition to them, Pliny made a compilation, without much

---

[1] Quoted by Strabo, i. 4. 6 (c. 64).
[2] *Q.N.*, i. fr. 13. Cf. Pliny, *N.H.*, vi. 57.

discrimination and without method, of information obtained from Greek sources.

The application of mathematical reasoning to a small amount of information of bookish origin and very inferior value, or to the few indications supplied by too infrequent explorers or traders—that was the method of Hellenistic geography. It was above all rational; its empirical foundation was glaringly inadequate. The Greek students and the princes of Pergamon and Alexandria who took an interest in their efforts lacked the means necessary to organize the exploration of the world. In short, the information on which scientists worked was supplied by chance.

We might have expected that the Roman Empire, having all material means at its disposal, would have undertaken to provide geographical science with the experimental foundation which it had hitherto lacked. But it was content with a knowledge which was purely utilitarian and consequently imperfect and limited. With a thousand opportunities to make infinitely better observations than the Greeks, the Romans could not even do as well as they.

Having to describe Spain, Strabo remarks on the uncertainty and vagueness prevailing about all regions in which the Greeks have not worked themselves. " Roman writers," he says, " follow the Greeks; everything they say, they take from the Greeks; they do not contribute any true curiosity of their own. The result is, that where the Greek writers fail us, the Romans do not do much to fill the gap." [1] It may be urged that Strabo was a Greek, and prone to exaggerate the virtues of his fellow-countrymen at the expense of the Romans. But his geographical descriptions, taken as a whole, bear out this remark only too well. Take the course of the Rhine. The Greeks had no opportunity for studying it. But since the invasion of Caesar, that is, for half a century, Roman armies had been up and down the shores of the great western river, policing it. Augustus himself had stayed on its banks, founding cities, deciding the site of camps, and tracing roads. Thousands of officers, engineers, and administrators had passed along its valley. Yet Strabo cannot find out whether the total length of the river is 6,000 stades (over 600 miles), as Asinius Pollio asserts, or only half the figure, nor whether it

[1] iii. 4. 19 (c. 166).

flows into the sea through two mouths or more.[1] Beyond the Rhine, Roman armies had advanced as far as the Elbe. For three years, from 12 to 9 B.C., Drusus had fought all over western Germany. Between the two rivers, there were Roman camps at intervals all along the road. The will of Augustus declares that all Germany is subdued as far as the Elbe. Strabo reckons the distance between the two rivers at 3,000 stades (332 miles) ; Velleius, rather later, after the defeat of Varus and Germanicus's campaigns of reprisals, makes it 400 *millia* (360 miles). The two figures agree well enough, but are double the real distance.

II

THE MAP OF AGRIPPA

Augustus himself, however, and still more his collaborator Agrippa, were anxious to have a detailed geographical inventory of the Empire. They caused the official map of it to be painted on the wall of the Porticus Vipsania on the Campus Martius, near the present Piazza Colonna. Agrippa having died before it was complete, the map was executed under the personal direction of Augustus, from the *Commentaria,* or notes, left by Agrippa.[2]

A hard worker and an indefatigable traveller, Agrippa had been the great organizer of Roman rule over the world. The establishment of the survey seems to have been his work, and public works—especially roads, the system of which he planned—were his domain. A plebeian by birth, Praetor at the age of twenty-two or twenty-three in 40 B.C., Consul for the first time in 37, and from then onwards the right hand of Octavian, whose fleet he commanded at Actium, Agrippa was an administrator and not a student. He cared for nothing but practical results. He had presented the people of Rome with the Pantheon and baths. Pliny tells us that he would have liked all works of art, pictures and statues, to be exhibited to the public instead of hidden away in villas.[3] His map, likewise, must have been designed for the benefit of the people of Rome. It was intended to show the Romans a

---

[1] iv. 3. 3 (c. 193).   [2] Detlefsen, **LXIII.**   [3] *N.H.*, xxxv. 26.

picture of the vast world, most of which obeyed them. His object was not to further science, but to edify the public.

In what form must we imagine this map ? It was painted on the wall of a portico. Unlike the Greek maps, which, rationally, represented the earth as a circle, *orbis*, it must have been in a long band. This is exactly the form which we find in our great document for Roman cartography, what is known as the Peutinger Map, from the name of the Augsburg banker in whose possession it was discovered at the end of the XVth century.[1] On a long band of parchment, intended to form a roll, we find the whole of the world known to the ancients depicted. The western end is missing. Therefore we have not the British Isles or Spain ; but, following the map from left to right, we see, in succession, Gaul above and Africa below, separated by the Mediterranean, then northern Italy, Noricum, Pannonia, and Macedon, with the Italian peninsula and Sicily underneath, and then Asia, with Egypt below it, followed by Arabia, Mesopotamia, and, lastly, India. It is quite a conventional diagram, which has nothing in common with our maps, but one can more or less recognize the outline of the coasts. Moreover, the names of places, which are clearly marked, prevent uncertainty.

The Peutinger Map is only a mediaeval copy ; it is taken from an original which, to judge from the names, was apparently produced in the IVth century A.D. The first model which it reproduces certainly seems to have been no other than the map of Agrippa. This map, we know, was copied many times, either on parchment [2] or on the walls of schools, for example at Augustodunum (Autun) in Gaul.[3] We may, therefore, take it that we possess a revised, corrected, and probably simplified version of the map of the world prepared by Agrippa and painted in the Roman portico under the direction of Augustus.

As is proved by the lists of names in Ptolemy's *Geography*, the Greeks were careful to give the position of places as exactly as possible by their longitude and latitude. These abstract indications meant nothing to the Romans. We find no trace of them on the Peutinger Map. Moreover, they

---

[1] Now in the Library in Vienna. Cf. Desjardins, **LXII**, and Miller, **CXI**.
[2] Suet., *Domit.*, 10.
[3] Eumen., *Pro Restaur. Scholis*, xx, ed. Baehrens, p. 130.

could not appear on such a distorted picture of the earth as the map of Agrippa. Even topographical features, mountain ranges and river valleys, are represented in a very summary and entirely conventional fashion. The important things are the roads and the stages marked by cities, with distances. The map is merely a painted road-book. The Greeks, in a happy phrase, guided themselves by the stars to determine the surface of the earth ; the Romans looked at the milestones along the roads.[1]

So the great geographical work of Agrippa and Augustus was no more than a diagram of the system of roads by which Roman life moved from one end of the Empire to the other. These roads were an inestimable boon for the world and an indispensable means of government for Rome. The Sovereign and his henchman might be justly proud of having laid them. The representation of them which they caused to be painted seems to have been inspired, not by Greek science, but rather by the memory of the pictures which the victorious general used to display on the day of his triumph to the eyes of the people, in which the shape and topography of the conquered regions were shown in rather diagrammatic form. Agrippa's map was only intended to instruct the masses. The mistake of the Romans was to invest it, partly from respect for its makers, with an authority which it did not possess, and not to try to represent the world more correctly. One of their weaknesses was that they always lacked curiosity.

III

TACITUS AND HIS *GERMANIA*

To see the effect of taking an interest in foreign countries on a Roman, we have to come down to Tacitus and his little treatise on the *Manners of the Germans*. It is hard to say exactly how much in this essay is really original. Geographical and ethnographical descriptions had been a tradition of Greek historians since Herodotos.[2] The Romans had conformed to it. Caesar had not omitted to illustrate his

[1] Schanz, **CXLIII**, ii, 1, p. 460.
[2] Cf. Norden, **CXVIII**, pp. 26 ff.

Commentaries with some passages of this kind, behind which we recognize the influence of the Greek writer Poseidonios. Since Caesar's time the wars with the Germans had held such an important place in the life of Rome that historians turned their attention to the people and the land where they dwelt. Livy, as we can gather from the epitomes we have of his lost books, had devoted several chapters to Germany and the Germans. He did not follow Caesar exactly, but he had only second-hand information about them. His authorities were probably Asinius Pollio, who had served on the Rhine, and, above all, a Greek historian, only known to us by name, who seems to have enjoyed great authority, Timagenes. Later, Pliny the Elder, whose military and administrative duties had taken him to Germany, had devoted a large work to the wars against the Germans. Tacitus himself had in his youth held a command in the country. Not having any of the works written between Caesar's and his, we cannot say exactly how much he owes to his predecessors and how much to personal observation.

The first part of the treatise, the description of the manners of the Germans, certainly is indebted in large part to all these sources which are unknown to us. The second part is more especially geographical. It gives us a list of the different German tribes, with the districts which they occupy. A mere examination of the text is enough to show that Tacitus is following a map. " As I just now followed the Rhine, so I shall now follow the Danube." [1] " Beyond the So-and-so," " In the neighbourhood of the So-and-so," " Behind them," " Before them," " By the side of them," are the usual beginnings of his chapters. This map was of the most indifferent kind. Topographical details are almost wholly lacking ; we hear hardly anything of the mountains and rivers, and nothing of the nature and the products of the soil. It is quite possible that Tacitus was simply guided by Agrippa's map. That map, as we know from Pliny, extended as far as the Vistula.[2] In 98 A.D., in Trajan's reign, when Tacitus wrote the *Germania*, a document of this kind might have been regarded as obsolete, or might at least have received copious corrections and additions. Nothing of the kind was done. Tacitus himself notes that since the time of Augustus geo-

[1] *Germ.*, 41.   [2] *N.H.*, iv. 87.

graphical knowledge had fallen back rather than advanced. The Elbe, he says, was " once a famous and well-known river ; now we only know its name." Compare the work of Tacitus with the few pages which Strabo gives to Germany ; the latter are less detailed, no doubt, but they produce a more definite impression.

Tacitus is a psychologist and an artist, but not a scientist goaded on by a passionate desire to ascertain the truth. Pliny the Elder, an older contemporary, perished in the eruption of Vesuvius of 79, no doubt the victim of his curiosity. His passion for knowledge was unparalleled. He did not lose a moment. All the time that he was not attending to his duties, he read or made others read to him. He took notes and made extracts from everything. There is no book so bad, he used to say, but one may find profit in it somewhere. His nephew inherited from him over one hundred and fifty note-books of choice morsels, written in a very fine hand. Plenty of diligence, but no ideas, as a critic said of the elder Cato. Books, chiefly Greek books, instead of waking his mind up, smothered it. They hid real life. The Roman student had eyes to read but not to see.

Moreover, a human mind, however exceptional, cannot create science by itself. It needs material means, instruments, preparatory work. Above all, it needs a current of scientific thought, public interest, contradiction. Now, science in Rome was not distinguished from erudition. Compilation was its triumph. And presently compilations like Pliny's were to be succeeded by abridgments and résumés. Attention to a long work was beyond the capacity of the reader. The rhetor took possession of geography, as he had taken possession of history. The *Chorography* of Pomponius Mela, in the reign of Claudius, and the *Epitome* of Roman history of Julius Florus, in Hadrian's, are the least bad examples of the invasion of verbal futility and the progressive falling-off of intellectual effort. There never was a scientific circle in Rome.

IV

THE *HISTORY* OF LIVY

It is as a work of art, not of science, that we must regard the great historical monument of the Augustan age, namely, Livy's *History*. It belongs to the same stream of ideas as Virgil's epic, to which it forms a kind of pendant. The *Aeneid* gave a kind of prefigurement of Rome, it proclaimed her dominion over land and sea, it glorified the power of Augustus as the reward bestowed by destiny on all her wisdom and heroism. Livy, tracing the fulfilment of her destiny, step by step, and usually year by year, composes a series of majestic pictures of Roman piety and virtue. The poet sang Rome outside time ; the historian tells of her greatness in the course of the centuries.

We must not underestimate the active movement of erudition marked by the publication of the *Annals* of the Pontifices and, still more, by the researches of Varro. This movement went on under Augustus, in the immediate circle of the Sovereign and under his encouragement. Verrius Flaccus, the tutor of his grandsons, studied the ancient Roman calendar. Augustus himself caused the archives of the Capitol to be put in order. When the Regia on the Forum was restored, he caused a new edition of the Consular *Fasti* to be engraved on it. Knowledge of the past of the city was made public property, as it were. We see it in the poetry of Propertius. Ovid looks to the *Fasti* for the inspiration of a great poem. This knowledge also assumed a political character. Augustus, and with him the great body of public opinion, saw in it a means of establishing the new political conditions for ever and of consolidating the Republic by its ancient traditions. This is how Horace understands it, making Romulus, Regulus, and Cato appear as models of social virtue. History became a sort of militant morality, or even policy.

This practical preoccupation is revealed by the exercise of greater diligence than discrimination. In the Forum which he built, Augustus set up statues of all the great men of the past, beginning with Romulus, and for each he had an inscription composed, recording their virtues. Aeneas, Lavinia, and their son Sylvius had their statues and inscriptions no less than Fabius Cunctator. The object was glorification, not truth. It was felt that legend might, from the political point of view, have as beneficial effects as true history.

It was the fashion to resuscitate the past for the education of the present. Augustus carried this passion for useful history to the point of pedantry.

" He constantly read the Greek and Latin historians," Suetonius relates,[1] "looking especially for useful precepts and examples for private and public conduct. These he copied out verbatim and sent in quantities to his own household, to the army commanders, to the governors of provinces, or to the city magistrates, according as they needed advice. He even read whole books to the Senate, and had them made known to the people by decree, such as the speech of Q. Metellus on raising the birth-rate and that of Rutilius against luxurious buildings, in order to impress on people that he was not the first to deal with these matters, but that they had already been a matter of concern to former statesmen."

These extracts from historians which were honoured with sittings of the Senate and public posting were very probably passages from Livy. The historian could support the cause of Pompey against Caesar and sing the praises of the old Republic without offending the Sovereign who posed as the restorer of the ancient state of things. In itself, history was regarded as being of public usefulness.

As a philosopher and rhetor, Livy did not for a moment think of diverging from the ideas of the Emperor and his contemporaries on the moral and political purpose of historical work.[2]

"My wish," he says in his Preface, "is that everyone should strive to know for himself what the life and manners of Rome were, and by what men, and by what means, the Empire was founded and increased at home and in foreign warfare. Then he should trace how, with the gradual

---

[1] *Aug.*, 89.
[2] Born in 58 B.C., Livy seems to have devoted to writing his *History* the whole time between the battle of Actium (31 B.C.) and the death of Drusus (9 B.C.), i.e., twenty-one or twenty-two years. He published each part as it was completed. The whole work, in 140 or 142 books, covered Roman history from its beginning to the death of Drusus. We only possess 35 books, barely a quarter, viz., i-x, from the beginning to the third Samnite War, covering 461 years, a sort of introduction to the modern and contemporary history which was the main part of the work, and xxi-xlv, from the second Punic War to the triumph of Aemilius Paullus (167 B.C.). Of the rest, we have only short summaries (*Periochae*). The division into "decades" (sets of ten books) is ancient, but does not seem to come from Livy himself.

relaxation of discipline, morals declined from their first elevation, then fell more and more, and at last began to rush downhill, until our own day, when we find our ills and their cure equally unbearable.

"That is what is especially salutary and profitable in the knowledge of history—you can study the lesson of every kind of action or circumstances in illustrious examples. In history you will find models to imitate for your own good and that of your country, and errors to avoid because their outcome was as shameful as their inception.

"Moreover, if my love of my subject does not deceive me, no common-wealth was ever greater or holier or richer in good examples, or was invaded by avarice or debauchery so late, or honoured poverty and thrift so much and so long. For the less men had, the less they desired. Only lately have riches infected the State with avarice, and abundance of pleasures with a passion to perish and to destroy everything through luxury and debauchery."

His object, therefore, is not to obtain, determine, and expound the truth, a final acquisition which will hold good for all time, but to show his contemporaries a picture of ancient manners, and that with a twofold intention—first, to provide a lesson, and secondly, to glorify ancient Rome. His attitude is simply that of a moralist.

Livy thereby comes into line with the tradition of Roman history-writing. The elder Cato, we are told, wrote his *Origins* in large letters for the instruction of his son. Another writer, Fabius Pictor, composed a history of Rome for the glory of the Gens Fabia. Caesar's *Commentaries* were a personal vindication. Sallust in all his works pleads the cause of his party against the pride of the aristocracy. Livy's ambition is higher and nobler; he has no thought of parties, of the interests of the Senate or of the plebs. The whole of Rome and her whole past are what he means to bring back to life. The picture which he wishes to show to his con-temporaries for their political education and moral improve-ment is one of a city guided by the best and wisest men, a city in which the people, after attempts at resistance, always ends by understanding the idea of its aristocracy and devoting itself to the same cause, in the higher interest of the Republic. This was the civic and national ideal which the Roman people conceived at the end of the Civil Wars and Augustus was striving to realize. Nothing is more sincere than the en-thusiasm with which Livy is inspired by his subject. " From writing of ancient things," he says himself, " I have acquired an antique mind." [1] The Roman spirit at its highest presides over this great historical work, not the historical spirit.

The historical spirit we find in Greece in Thucydides and Polybius. It excludes any moral, political, national, or other bias ; it demands scrupulous investigation of evidence and severe criticism ; it conceives its essential task to be the attainment of truth, and subordinates art of exposition and style to this austere duty. Livy, on the contrary, in order to impose his own ideal on his readers, is at pains to charm them by the colour of skilfully composed pictures, and to carry them with him by the warmth of his eloquence. If history is intended to be useful it must necessarily be, above all, a work of art. The dry accuracy of erudition does not suit it. The style must be in harmony with the subject ; sometimes majestic, sometimes familiar, it must always be worthy of the greatness of Rome. In this point, too, Livy remains faithful to the Roman tradition which treated history as essentially an oratorical form,[2] or, as we should say now, a literary form.

His education had been that of a rhetor.[3] A declared Ciceronian, he does not think of applying in his work any principles but those formulated by Cicero himself.

"Is not history a work worthy of an orator ? I believe that it requires more flow of oratory and more variety than any other. . . . The historian must not only set forth the deeds of men, but also, in the case of those especially famous, the life and character of each. The style should be fluent and level, pouring in a kind of equable stream, without the sharpness of the law-courts and the stinging sentences of the forensic pleader." [4]

Cicero would certainly have had nothing but admiration for the way in which Livy's work follows the programme which he laid down for historians. We must not ask Livy for more than he has meant to give us—a fine work of moralizing art, with scenes and portraits intended to inspire love and admiration for ancient Rome.

The problem of truth which dominates our thought when we consider a historical narrative does not present itself to Livy in the same terms as to us.

[1] xliii. 13.   [2] Cic., Leg., i. 2. 5.
[3] In addition to his History, he wrote, according to Quintilian, a short treatise on the Studies of Youth, in which he recommended the study of Demosthenes and Cicero, and, according to Seneca the Rhetorician, various philosophical or philosophico-historical works. We know that his daughter married a rhetor.
[4] Cic., De Or., ii. 15. 62-4.

In his first book, which relates the foundation of Rome and the period of the Kings, Livy finds himself in the presence of legends. These legends perhaps contain some portion of truth, but in any case they give a very incorrect version of it. His contemporary Dionysius of Halicarnassus, likewise a professional rhetor, but a Greek, studies these legends with care. He tries to understand and to interpret them, to extract the nucleus of truth which they are supposed to contain. He does so in a puerile manner which inspires only very small esteem for his intellect. But he treats them, as a student should, as a subject of knowledge. Livy, on the other hand, treats them with a light-hearted mixture of scepticism and pride. He explains his attitude in his Preface.

"The things which happened before the city was founded or contemplated have been handed down in an adornment of poetic fables more than in untainted records of events, and I do not propose to confirm or to deny them. Let us allow antiquity the right of making the beginnings of cities more august by mingling human things with divine. And, if any people has a right to sanctify its origin and to take gods for its founders, the Roman people has won such glory in war that, when it chooses Mars as father of itself and of its founder, the races of mankind accept this pretension as willingly as they accept its dominion. But, however these stories are regarded and judged, I do not attach great importance to them."

Accordingly, he relates the substance of these fables, without laying stress on them or lingering long over them. He is content to compose an orderly narrative of the legend, a sort of poetical fairy-tale, toning down its miraculous character with a smile.

"The Vestal Rhea Silvia, having become through violence the mother of two sons, attributed the uncertain paternity to Mars, either in good faith or because a god was a more respectable author of her guilt. But neither gods nor men could save mother or children from the cruelty of the king."

In general, as is natural in a keen rhetorician, verisimilitude is for Livy the measure of truth. Moreover, he is not very exacting in the matter of verisimilitude.

Later on, he comes to the earliest records, which are very doubtful and, as he admits, mostly tainted with mistakes and lies. But he makes use of them, as of the legends, while maintaining towards them a superior attitude of genial rationalism.

"The matters which I have related so far are obscure because of their great antiquity, like objects barely seen at a great distance, and because written documents, the only faithful guardians of the memory of past deeds, were brief and few in those days, and also because the records preserved in the registers of the Pontifices and in public and private papers were mostly destroyed when the city was burned by the Gauls. From now onwards I shall describe events at home and abroad more clearly and with more confidence."[1]

He is well aware that the Greek writers who first treated of Roman history, the Latin poets who sang the achievements of the Republic, and the pride of the great families had exaggerated the number of triumphs and Consulships. He notes the fact, but he does not trouble to seek in his predecessors for the effects of these many sources of error. Citizens and foreigners had to accept the Roman tradition as it had been formed by the generations which had made the Roman Empire.

To obtain acceptance of this tradition, he is content to give it verisimilitude, and with this object he arranges it in the most adroit fashion. He passes it all through his reason, suppressing at least apparent contradictions, diligently selecting from the details supplied by his sources, harmonizing them, and establishing logical relations between them. He combines them all into a single narrative, great in its conception, in which everything fits together and one must accept or reject everything bodily.

The conduct of the narrative is perfect. The historian treats the information furnished by his sources as an orator does the facts of a case. He brings them out, slurs them over, or rejects them, according as they harmonize or conflict with the thesis which he is maintaining and the general picture which he wishes to present. He does not judge a piece of information in itself, he does not analyse its intrinsic value. He is content with appearances, and appraises a fact with reference to his story. His sole guide is, not a critical method, of which he has not even an idea, but his artistic instinct and literary sense.

All through his history, as at the beginning, verisimilitude is the measure of truth and oratorical suitability the rule of selection.

To-day we chiefly look to Livy for evidence. It is a

[1] vi. 1.

mistake ; in the mind of the author facts do not hold the first place, but are subordinated to the idea.

" In great events, worthy of record," Cicero taught, "we want to know, first, the counsels which prepared them, then the action taken, and, lastly, the issue. Regarding the counsels, the writer must tell us what he approves, about events, he should say, not only what was done or said, but how, and when he speaks of the issue he should unfold all the causes—chance, wisdom, and folly." [1]

So the historian's thought comes first, before the account of what was said or done ; the conclusion consists in a moral judgment of the result. This is the method of Livy. His personal conception first supplies the woof ; it is a political idea, the assurance of which gives colour to the uncertain facts. The facts are set forth with the object of justifying this idea and preparing the moral lesson which will emerge from the conclusion. Being based on a superficial study of the evidence, these guiding ideas can have only a slight historical value. Yet they look thoroughly reasonable ; above all, they are presented in such a coherent fashion that they have been accepted by most of the writers who have sought to discern the chain of causes and effects in Roman history. As it stands, the picture does not inspire us with great confidence, but we must admit that its conception is powerful, its development fine, and its construction deserving of all admiration.

It goes without saying that an artist as accomplished as Livy takes good care not to present the incidents of his narrative always in the same order. He is careful to avoid monotony. The idea is sometimes only implied, and emerges from the arrangement of the facts. More often it is developed at length in the speeches which, in accordance with the old tradition, the historian places in the mouth of his characters. In other cases it is shown in action, as it were ; it is expressed by some particularly dramatic episode, as artificial and as carefully worked up as the speeches themselves. Is an example required ? As early as the second book, that is to say, in the Royal period, Livy feels that he should mention the exhaustion of the rural classes in consequence of continual wars, while showing the union of all classes before foreign danger. He accordingly invents, or transfers into this

[1] *De Or.*, ii. 15. 63.

primitive time, a minor incident which he regards as significant.

"An old man, bearing the marks of every misfortune, ran into the Forum. His garments were thick with filth, and his pale, wasted body was even fouler. His long beard and hair gave him the look of a beast. Yet he was recognized, in his disfigured state, and people said that he had been a centurion, and, as they pitied him, spoke loudly of his military honours. When they asked him how he came to be in that plight, and a great crowd collected round, almost like the Assembly, he said that he had served in the Sabine War ; that he had not only lost his harvest, through the ravaging of the country, but his farm had been burned down, all his things had been looted, his cattle had been driven off, and he had been ordered to pay tax in his destitution. He had had to borrow ; the debt, swollen by interest, had stripped him first of the land of his father and grandfather, and then of the rest of his fortune. Finally disease had taken hold of his body. In his creditor he had found, not a master, but a jailer and torturer. And he showed his back, scored with the marks of recent flogging." [1]

Angry murmurs went up from the crowd, riot was brewing, the abolition of debts was demanded, there was a rush on the Senate, and the magistrates were powerless to restrain the people, when suddenly it was reported that the enemy were attacking ; everyone ran to arms and took his place in the ranks.

Shall we quibble with Livy over the authenticity of his story and ask him for his source ? He would reply with a smile, as Atticus did to Cicero, that a historian surely has the right to twist the facts a little to make a good story.

"His chief concern being to make his characters talk and to praise noble deeds," says Taine,[2] "Livy only happens upon causes by the way. He omits many, he arranges the facts badly, he does not know how to select among them. . . . He happens upon all the general ideas which one can find when one is not looking for them." Yet even in his oratorical spirit and moralizing tendency Taine recognizes something of the philosophic and scientific intelligence which he demands of a historian. Let us not ask for so much. Let us be content to note that his whole narrative is animated by thought which is always calm and generally lofty, and at least presents, in its perfect proportion, every appearance of fullness and truth. This thought is not the result of original speculation, nor is it what we should consider particularly profound. It simply expresses the point of view of the aristocratic tradition

---

[1] ii. 23 ff.　　　　　　　　　　　　　　[2] **CLV**, p. 127.

and of almost all Roman historians, which Augustus used as a basis in his attempt at political and moral renovation.

It is, therefore, the spirit of Augustan Rome much more than a correct picture of the old Republic that Livy's history gives us—the ideal picture of the national past formed by a generation which had not yet lost all interest in public affairs, but was no longer agitated by political passions, by a cultivated élite steeped in rhetoric and the recent memory of the oratorical contests of the Forum, by a new class of men of good will who transferred into past ages the aspirations by which they themselves were animated.

We must not judge this majestic literary composition as a work of science or even of erudition. It is first and foremost a work of art. Facts are to the historian what reality is to the poet. From his store of impressions, the poet chooses those which shall go to make his work, as his fancy dictates ; he elaborates and combines them with a view to the whole which is in his mind. Livy does the same with his sources, of whatever kind they be. Legends, *Annals* of the Pontifices, *Fasti*, epics, earlier histories, all supply him with elements for his work. He subjects them to the formula prescribed by rhetoric. One great idea dominates the whole work and gives it a soul, the idea of Rome justifying the glory of her destiny by her virtues. This may not be " history," in the strict sense which we give the word to-day, but it is a picture of what the best Romans of the time of Augustus wished their past to have been, and at the same time, in a way, the ideal which they set up for their future.

By the literary qualities of the narrative, Livy's history is fully in accordance with the Romans' idea of a historical masterpiece. This perfection ensured for the work the practical effect which its author desired. We hear of the enthusiasm which it inspired, not only in the capital, but perhaps even more in the provinces. Pliny the Younger tells the story of a Cadiz man who travelled to Rome with the sole object of seeing the great writer who had so eloquently told the history of the City. Having merely seen him, he went home content. Livy gave the Roman tradition its final form. Generations of citizens learned from him to know their country. True or false, the picture drawn by the great writer became their ideal. More than any other book, **Livy's** history contributed to the education of the new aristocracy which, after the tyranny of the Caesars, appeared under the Flavians and Antonines, the heirs of the wisdom, virtue, and manly qualities with which the noble imagination of the writer had endowed ancient Rome.

To the conquered peoples Livy, like Virgil, presented the conquering Republic in a guise worthy of respect and admiration. Both made the vanquished love their new country. One may apply to these two great artists in words the fine line which the poet Rutilius Namatianus addressed to Rome herself : *Patriam fecisti diversis e gentibus unam*—" Of the diverse nations you have made a single fatherland." In minds and hearts they achieved the Roman Peace.

Chapter IV

AUGUSTAN ART

I

The Augustan Ideal and Official Art

The new ideal which animated literature under Augustus was intellectual rather than aesthetic, and even more moral and political than purely intellectual. Horace is separated from Tibullus, Virgil from Propertius, not by a difference of artistic principles, but by a new purpose of usefulness, a sort of political ambition. The elegiac is always art for art's sake, and its inspiration is individual. The ode, on the other hand, aims at expressing collective sentiments; Virgil, in singing of the soil of Italy and the Roman fatherland, assists Augustus in his work of restoration. But the social purpose which the poet sets before him acts on his art indirectly. First, the idea of a reformation detaches men's minds from fashions and formulas now regarded as obsolete; it restores art to liberty. Secondly, new subjects and new ideas lead the poet to new forms. The Alexandrian trifle and the elegiac couplet are not sufficient for the more ambitious lyricism of Horace. The poet turns to the stanzas of the ancient Greek lyric, and with the stanzas a new spirit is breathed into Latin poetry. So, too, love of the earth, interest in humble rustic occupations, and the desire to bring the farmer pleasure and profit fill the *Georgics* with a realism quite unlike that of the *Eclogues* and the Hellenistic pastoral. To sing the predestination of Rome, Virgil goes back to Homer and to the old Latin epic poets. The Augustan ideal, by taking the Muse out of the little literary schools and *salons*, changed her appearance and her instrument.

On the plastic arts its influence was similar, but slower, less clearly marked, and less completely successful. Painting, sculpture, and the arts in general were less susceptible than literature to abstract ideas; in any case, they were not penetrated by them so directly and rapidly. Technique and studio tradition kept them more firmly bound to the accepted formulas. Nor must it be forgotten that under the Empire the majority of artists were still Greeks, and, being in a lower social position than the prose-writers and poets, they remained more outside the new currents of thought. The age of Augustus did not find its great innovating artist, as it had its poets and its historian.

So the mass of artistic production in the Augustan age continued the same rather confused tendencies of the preceding period. Light elegance, episodes of common life, mythological subjects, Alexandrinism, and Neo-Attic art, to which should be added the experiments of the school of Pasiteles, still enjoyed the favour of the Roman aristocracy, with which, in literature likewise, Ovid was still as popular as Catullus had been with the previous generation. All through the reign of Augustus and into that of Tiberius, the old styles continued a fairly monotonous existence, in which development is barely perceptible.

Yet in the midst of all this commonplace work there were some new tendencies which, later in the course of the centuries of the Empire, would give Roman art its special physiognomy. They only manifested themselves in a few works closely connected with the Emperor himself and with certain great events of his reign. They were born of the Imperial atmosphere, so to speak, of the historical facts, the ideas, and the sentiments which had already transformed literature. Their origin was intellectual rather than artistic; the conception of the work of art was changed rather than the method of execution. New motives were due to the new idea; it inspired the composition and obliged the artist to break away from the traditional models and to invent modes of expression suited to his purpose. The most original art at this time was official art.

I shall therefore speak here only of official Augustan art, and especially of two signal monuments of sculpture—the statue of Augustus found at Prima Porta, now in the Braccio Nuovo of the Vatican, and some of the surviving fragments of the Altar of Peace.

II

THE STATUE OF AUGUSTUS

Some miles from Rome, a little above the Tiber valley, on the territory of Veii, near the Flaminian Way, Livia had caused to be built for herself, shortly after her marriage with Octavian, a villa of moderate size. This was the Villa of the Hens, *ad Gallinas*, the ruins of which were excavated about the middle of the last century. The modern village is called Prima Porta. This villa, the quiet country-house of the sovereign and his wife, had its legend, which connected it symbolically with the destiny, if not of the Empire, at least of the family of the Julii. The story was that one day an eagle had dropped, right into Livia's lap, a white hen with a laurel-branch in her beak. This hen had produced such a quantity of chickens that the estate had taken its name from the poultry-yard. As for the laurel-branch, it had developed into such a magnificent shrubbery that all the Caesars took to picking there the branches required for their triumphs. Under Nero, the laurels withered and all the hens died, a melancholy presage for the line of Augustus.[1] From the ruins of this Villa of the Hens comes the most celebrated of the statues of Augustus ; [2] it must have stood in the place of honour. (See Plate XI.)

The Emperor is represented standing, bare-headed but dressed as a military chief, with the cuirass. The sceptre in the left hand is a modern restoration ; he must have held a spear, or perhaps a standard, one of the standards lost by Crassus, which the Parthians had just returned to the Romans. The right arm, raised horizontally, also seems modern, but must reproduce the original gesture fairly exactly. The attitude is that of one who speaks with authority and calmness ; we have before us the Imperator addressing his troops after a victory. In this pose Trajan and Marcus Aurelius were represented in later years on the reliefs of the columns consecrated to their exploits ; so, in the past, many Roman

[1] Cf. Suet., *Galba*, 1 ; Pliny, *N.H.*, xv. 30 (41).
[2] Martha, in Rayet, **CXXXVI**, ii, 6, 1 ; also Studniczka, **XIII**, xxv (1910), 7, 27-55.

PLATE XI

1

2

3

1. Terra-cotta statue from the pediment of a Roman temple. (Rome, Conservatori)
2. Augustus from Prima Porta. Marble. (Rome, Vatican)
3. The Orator. Bronze. (Florence, Archæological Museum)

[face p. 340

PLATE XII

1

2

3

4

1. Cæsar. Basalt. (Rome, Baracco Collection)
2. Agrippa. Marble. (Louvre)
3. Octavian as a youth. Marble. (Vatican Library)
4. Augustus. Bronze. (Vatican Library)

[face p 341

leaders, soldiers or statesmen, must have been portrayed, beginning with the Etrusco-Roman Orator in the Florence Museum, who presents in his toga the same attitude and gesture as Augustus in his armour. (See Plate XI.) So the motive is thoroughly Roman; it expresses something real from Roman life, and reproduces a type traditional in Rome.

But when we compare the Augustus of Prima Porta with the Orator of Florence we cannot fail to be struck by the superior ease, the more restful assurance, the less rigid majesty of the Imperial portrait. The reason is that the attitude and movement of the body, and even the proportions, are inspired, in part at least, by the Doryphoros of Polycleitos. No doubt, it is not an imitation, nor even a new rendering, of that famous statue, but, as Wickhoff [1] very aptly says, the structure of Augustus's body is the work of an artist obviously well acquainted with the statue of Polycleitos. In short, Latin and Greek traditions are blended in a new whole.

Purely Greek inspiration would have presented the Emperor in heroic nudity. So, for example, two Greek sculptors had once portrayed the Roman C. Ofellius Ferus at Delos, in almost exactly the same attitude, but stark naked except for a mantle thrown over the shoulder and left arm. [2] Here, on the contrary, all the details of the costume, the fastenings of the cuirass, the folds of the tunic, the fringes hanging from the belt, are treated with scrupulous accuracy. We find the same care for correct detail on the grave-stones of soldiers of the Rhine army; one can count and identify their decorations and the smallest peculiarities of their uniform. The statue of Augustus has kept only one reminiscence of the heroic convention—the bare feet. This part alone escapes from reality. As a whole, the Prima Porta statue gives an impression of reality, not of an idealized portrait.

Livia wanted a good likeness of her illustrious spouse, and the artist obeyed. This is doubtless the explanation of the heaviness of the lower part of the statue, and the tendency to shortness in the legs. The heaviness is further accentuated by the very crowded folds of the chlamys below the belt and the voluminous mass of drapery hanging from the left arm. The stature is that of a man, not of a god; the folds are those

---

[1] **CLXX,** p. 17.
[2] Homolle, **II,** 1881, pl. xii; Collignon, **XLVII,** ii, fig. 328, p. 624.

of a real, warm material, a genuine Imperator's *paludamentum*, and not of the conventional drapery of an inhabitant of Olympus. This statue rests solidly on the ground ; it glorifies but does not deify.

The face is certainly that of Augustus ; we recognize not only the features of the ruler as described by Suetonius [1] and represented in many other portraits (see Plate XII. 3, 4),[2] but even his age, which is about forty. The number and the arrangement of the locks of hair on the forehead are those shown in portraits of Augustus from his early days onwards, and we recognize his large eyes, set deep in the shadow of their sockets but lit by the cold light of a very clear gaze, his lean cheeks, his long, fine nose, the fairly full lips, the upper being short, and, above all, the prominent, almost heavy chin, casting its shadow over the strong, thick neck. These very individual features are, as it were, frozen in an immobile expression of calm majesty. They are broadly treated, in large planes, without superfluous or over-minute detail. The workmanship is that of an ideal head, but idealization is strictly subordinated to resemblance.

Certainly the Greeks of the Hellenistic period also made portraits which were likenesses, and sometimes even produced works of intense realism. Among them realism was definitely opposed to idealism ; they sought to render nothing but the individual, and in the individual, as far as possible, an episodic peculiarity, a salient feature, almost a touch of caricature, which should dominate the whole countenance. Realism became a game in virtuosity, and was carried almost to the pitch of freakishness. In Roman portraiture, in the time of Augustus, at least, and in serious art, realism and idealism were allied, and were blended in a whole of a quite special character. Scrupulous fidelity to the model was the instinctive foundation of all work. The artist must have begun by reproducing all the details, and then toned them down, wrapping the whole in a convention intended to raise the individual face to the nobility and universality of a type

---

[1] *Aug.*, 79.
[2] See especially the admirable portrait of the young Octavian, from Ostia, in the Gallery of Busts in the Vatican ; the bronze head, more markedly realistic, in the Vatican Library, recently published by Nogara (**XIII,** 1914, pp. 186-99) ; and the statue of Augustus in the toga found near Rome in 1910 (Pasqui, **XVIII,** 1910).

conceived by the imagination.[1] Is this the old tradition of the Italic portrait, reappearing in the Imperial epoch in a more highly developed art, or are we in the presence of an eclectic combination of the two opposite tendencies found in Hellenistic art ? It seems rather to be an alliance of the Latin spirit and its love of the real with the Greek classical culture which seeks in nature for a more perfect beauty than that of the individual and a higher truth than that of the senses alone. But there are absolutely no arguments, we must admit, to exclude the influence of Hellenistic realism, which may have been the very thing which revived the old Etrusco-Latin realism and restored it to favour.

What strikes one in the statue of Augustus, as in the art of Virgil, is the intimate union of a deep sense of reality with scholarly idealism. Augustus is shown as a man, but he has something heroic in him. The features of the face are individual, but the immobile gravity of the expression breathes a nobility which is more than human.

The reliefs which adorn the cuirass are conceived in the same spirit. The central motive is a representation of a real historical event, exact in its smallest details. It is surrounded by allegories which also contain realistic elements, mingled with convention, while other figures are pure mythological symbols. Thus the meaning of the whole is widened and raised above the mere interest of an episode.

These reliefs have often been described and have been the subject of ample discussion. Some have maintained their connexion with purely Alexandrian art, while others have endeavoured to bring out their originality.[2] The technique is evidently quite Hellenistic—Alexandrian if you will—and the effect is that of the hammered and chased metal-work which was developed with especial brilliance at Alexandria. The motives seem to be Hellenistic, at least in part. But the idea by which they are brought together is thoroughly Roman.[3] It is to the idea that this decoration owes its originality.

[1] I am thinking particularly of the charming portraits of Roman ladies of the first century of the Empire, such as that found near the Farnesina, published by Rayet in **CXXXVI**, ii, 6, 2.

[2] In particular, Courbaud (against Schreiber), **LII**, pp. 66 ff.

[3] In general, I follow the interpretation, particularly well supported by evidence, given by Studniczka in **XIII**, xxv (1910), pp. 27-55.

On the confined surface of the breast-plate of Augustus, the artist has sought to represent the whole world, governed by the power of Rome. Above, over the pectorals, the Sky spreads out his veil, and the Sun advances in his chariot, preceded by Aurora, who sheds her dew, while the Moon is already vanishing with her paling torch. It is the morning

FIG. 14.—Reliefs on the breast-plate of Augustus.

of a radiant day which rises for the world. At the bottom of the breast-plate lies the maternal Earth, softly reclining in peace ; she seems to contemplate her horn of plenty, full of flowers and fruit, and two children cling to her. On either side are the two patron gods of the Empire, Apollo, the god of Actium, mounted on his griffin, and Diana riding a stag. None of these motives is in itself new ; but their association on the breast-plate of Augustus assumes an original significance.

In the centre of the universe thus symbolized, the historical scene which marked the triumph of Rome and made peace secure is enacted by two persons. A barbarian, a king, shown by his diadem and costume to be Phraates, King of the Parthians, presents the eagle of a legion to a figure dressed as a Roman officer, who extends his two hands to receive it. A dog is represented sitting at the feet of the Roman. It is quite clearly a dog and not a wolf or she-wolf. Nothing authorizes the identification of the figure in helmet and cuirass who faces Phraates with Mars. We must see in him, not a god, nor yet a mere typical Roman, but Tiberius himself, the Emperor's young stepson, who had been delegated to receive the trophies, taken from Crassus in the past, which the King of the Parthians restored to Rome the peace-maker as a sign of friendship. This occurred in 20 B.C. As is confirmed by the age which the statue gives the Emperor, the work must have been executed about this time. The principal scene of the decoration of the breast-plate therefore represents, no doubt, in concentrated fashion, but with the most perfect precision possible and scrupulous realism in all the details of costume and armour, one of the most glorious episodes of the reign, one which, without bloodshed and by the mere prestige of the new power of Rome, seemed to ensure for the civilized world the respect of the barbarians of the East for ever.

Nor is the West forgotten in this glorification of a very definite date in the reign of Augustus. Right and left of the group formed by Tiberius and Phraates, we see two figures seated in the weary attitude of the vanquished. That on the right holds an empty sheath in one hand and a Gallic trumpet with a monster's head in the other ; before it is a standard representing a boar. This is evidently Gaul. The other figure holds a sword, which it seems to be handing to a conqueror. This must be Spain. There Agrippa had dis-armed the Celtiberians in 21 B.C. So these allegorical figures of conquered provinces also represent definite events ; every detail, the empty sheath, the surrendered sword, the Gallic trumpet and boar, has its meaning. The personification of provinces, rivers, and continents is very usual in Hellenistic art. Here the originality perhaps lies in the expression of history by the attitude, action, and attributes of these geographical symbols.

In any case, it is clearly seen in the composition of the whole, at once harmonious and full of ideas. The central motive stands out from its allegorical setting by its greater dimensions and stronger relief. The historical event is very clearly shown as the essential thing. The air moves about the figures. These very various motives, collected in a small space, give no impression of overloading or incoherence. Whether taken from the repertory of Hellenistic art or not, they are impregnated with Roman thought ; the Imperial idea has given them their value and their place.

To complete our understanding of this art, we must not forget the colour which made these representations more living still. The finders of the statue have managed to discover traces of it.[1] The Emperor's tunic and chlamys were scarlet, the true colour of the Imperator's *paludamentum*. The fringes of the cuirass were yellow, imitating natural leather ; on the shoulders, the clasps of the cuirass, supposed to be of bronze, were brown. On the flesh and on the ground of the breast-plate no traces of colour could be seen. The vault of the Sky was pink like a sunrise, and the chariot of the Sun was purple. In the centre, light blues dominated in the garments of the seated figures. Diana's stag was tawny. The Parthian king wore bluish trousers and a red tunic. The bluish steel of Tiberius's helmet and cuirass set off the brilliance of his red cloak. The colours were true, like the details. But it is difficult for us to judge from what remains how they harmonized.

This statue, intended not for a public monument but for the peaceful seclusion of Livia's villa, gives a general impression of rather cold nobility, which is gradually redeemed, as one examines it more closely, by the wealth and life of the details. It is indeed an image of the Augustan ideal—determined will, solemn majesty, and conventional heroic pose, which filled even family life with the preaching tedium of morality perpetually on the war-path. When we look at the Prima Porta statue, we can understand, and almost excuse, Julia's revolt against the suffocating atmosphere of grandiloquent vanity and sermonizing and rather hypocritical virtue which Augustus, with Livia and Octavia, must have caused to reign about her. But once we overcome this first impression

[1] Kohler, **VI,** 1863, 432-52.

we see, beneath the solemnity of the pose and the coldness of the features, a vigorous life of disciplined passion, imposing calm and subordinating caprice and fancy to realities. The greatness of these realities excuses the pride and grandiloquence, for they were nothing less than Rome restored to order and, through her, peace and all her blessings given to the world, and even independent nations made respectful— truly a new day, radiant with hope, rising for mankind. " When authors," writes one who knows the Hellenistic world well,[1] " show us the spirit of the West appearing in the Greek world in the person of Scipio Aemilianus, one is truly grateful to these collectors of anecdotes for bringing a breath of fresh air into the ghastly charnel-house." One may say the same of the figure of Augustus, appearing in the midst of the world of the Civil Wars.

Even if Roman virtue was no more than an ideal, even if it was reduced to a half-hypocritical convention, to ineffectual aspirations towards an antiquity that never was, was it not better for the world than intellectual dilettantism or the fancies of some brilliant despot ? If Augustus had wished, and as might have been feared from his beginnings, he could have become a frightful tyrant, overcoming the opposition and difficulties which he never ceased to encounter by wholesale executions. Yet, as soon as he was master, he set himself the duty of winning over minds and hearts to an ideal of moderation, reason, and justice. The moral effort which he imposed on himself and on others can be seen in his face as in the spirit and the works of his time. It bridled imagination, and substituted the rule of social utility for the caprices of individualism. Yet this severity did not stifle beauty. On the contrary, it bore fruit in poetry nobler and richer than the unrestrained fancies of Alexandria, in history which owed to it, if not its literary perfection, at least its majesty and ample sweep, and in art truer and deeper than that of the Hellenistic schools.

Augustan art makes up for its coldness by the life of the complete work and the expressive value of the details. Its realistic accuracy often seems a little dry. The blame rests with the artists, who were not endowed with genius equal to that of the poets. But it is bathed in an atmosphere of

[1] G. Radet, **XXI,** 1907, p. 9.

nobly humane ideas and feelings. In the finer works—
scenes from religion, mythology, or history, or portraits—we
find in Rome, from the time of Augustus, a new spirit. Art
loses none of the sure workmanship and skill in composition
which were brought to perfection by Greece. It renounces
the commonplace and the excesses of fantasy without foundation or sincere idea ; it applies itself to reality ; it seeks to
extract beauty from truth.

III

The Altar of Peace

We remember the line in which Propertius condemns
Prometheus for forgetting to give a soul to the being he had
fashioned with his hands : *Corpora disponens mentem non
vidit in arte.* The criticism might be applied to the art of
Hellenism in its last days. The technique is perfect and the
elegance beyond reproach, but the soul is lacking. Take, for
example, the celebrated reliefs from the Grimani Palace, now
in the Vienna Museum—the lioness threatened in her cave
and half rising to protect her cubs, or the sheep suckling her
lamb, both excellent specimens of the many Hellenistic
reliefs published by Herr Schreiber.[1] (See Plate X.) These
are charming little pictures. But it would be idle to look in
them for an idea, and still idler to expect feeling. All this
art is merely play ; it is done for the amusement of idle
minds. Roman art tries to mean something, to call up an
idea, to perpetuate a memory and recall the emotion of it,
to hand on to the future an impression of greatness and
beauty. It is inspired by Roman life, and seeks to express
the soul of the city.

We have noted, at the end of the Republican period, the
originality of the frieze round the altar of Domitius Ahenobarbus, representing the triumphal sacrifice and the dismissal
of the veterans.[2] It was no novelty for Roman pride to
entrust art with the celebration of historical events. We
remember the paintings which by old tradition figured in
the triumphal procession. This tradition had not expired.

---

[1] **CXLV.**   [2] Above, pp. 256-7.

With it the great plastic epics of the Triumphal Arch of Titus and the Columns of Trajan and Marcus Aurelius are connected. For it was consecrated by the official art of the beginning of the Empire. Its development in the future was due to the deserved celebrity of the reliefs of the Altar of Peace.

This monument has been the subject of many studies since Herr von Duhn identified the scattered fragments of it in his first masterly article in 1879. Recent excavations have brought to light further portions, and have made it possible to form an almost complete idea of the whole. As it can be reconstructed to-day, the Ara Pacis truly stands as the most characteristic example of great art in the Augustan age.[1]

The altar was built between 13 and 9 B.C. After a long absence, in the East in 17 and in Gaul and on the Rhine since 16, Augustus was impatiently awaited in 13 by the people of Rome.

"Come back, good Chief," Horace sang.[2] "Give your light to your country again. When your countenance shines on the people, like spring, the days go by more gladly and the suns have a fairer light. As a mother sighs for her son . . . so the country, smitten by loyal yearning, wants its Caesar."

Being entrusted with the organization of the rejoicings with which this much-desired home-coming was to be celebrated, Julus Antonius, the Triumvir's son, the lover of Julia, had first turned to Horace. He seems to have asked him for a pendant to the *Carmen Saeculare* which had been written before the Emperor's departure. But Horace had excused himself.

I write, not without difficulty, the poor songs of which I am capable. "A poet like you will sing Caesar in a nobler strain. . . . You will sing the days of rejoicing and the merriment of the city over the return of brave Augustus, vouchsafed to our prayers."[3]

The popular festivities and rejoicing which Horace declined to celebrate, Antonius decided to commemorate by a work of art. It is not known who was the artist to whom he gave the commission.

Two games were organized by the Consuls.[4] The Senate decided that the whole people should go to meet the Emperor

---

[1] Cf. Courbaud, **LII**, pp. 77 ff. ; Strong, **CLI**, pp. 40 ff. ; also Studniczka, **CLIV**.
[2] *Od.*, iv. 5.   [3] *Od.*, iv. 2.   [4] **LI**, vi, 386.

at the city gate—the present Porta del Popolo—and accompany him in procession to an altar which should be set up on the Campus Martius for the thanksgiving sacrifice. Their beautiful programme was upset by Augustus, who returned to Rome incognito the night before he was expected. On the day itself, the 4th July, the people, having been advised,

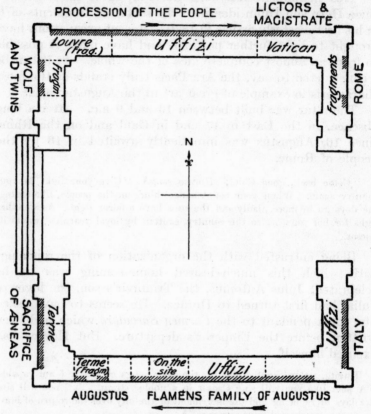

Fig. 15.—Plan of the Altar of Peace.

went to greet him on the Palatine, and organized a procession to the Capitol and the Forum, where the Senate had assembled. The permanent altar which was to perpetuate the memory of his return was not completed and inaugurated until four years later, in 9 B.C.

The monument consisted of a marble wall surrounding the altar itself. Its foundations have been discovered on the

Corso, beneath the Fiano Palace. The whole was a square
with a side of 38 ft., 3 in., and the surrounding wall must have
been 10 or 13 feet high. The inside was carved with heavy
garlands of foliage and fruit attached to bucrania. (See
Plate XV.) The sculptured field outside was divided into
two bands, the lower part being merely adorned with conventional foliage (see Plate XV.) and the friezes of figures
occupying the upper part and running all round. We
possess part of these friezes. They rendered the essence of
the programme described by Horace and translated the
sentiments expressed by him into images—Italy made happy
and fruitful by Augustus, and the rejoicing people forming a
procession on his return to Rome.

There were two wide openings, in the east and west sides
of the enclosure. That on the west was preceded by a few
steps ; that on the east, which was no doubt reserved for the
sacrificial beasts, had only a slightly raised sill. On these
two sides, therefore, we have four bits of wall which, being
further reduced by the pilasters of the corners and the
entrances, were less than 10 feet long. These short sides were
decorated with allegorical reliefs, only one of which has been
preserved intact. From coins representing the altar we
gather that the figure of Italy (Plate XIII. 1) was placed
left (south) of the eastern entrance and that of Rome on the
right, while the western entrance had on its right (south)
the relief of Aeneas sacrificing to the Penates, the right half
of which, representing Aeneas, was found in 1903 (Plate XIII.
2), and on its left (north) very probably a figure of the She-
Wolf suckling Romulus and Remus under the Ruminal
Fig-tree.[1]

Along the continuous sides the procession was depicted,
a kind of Roman replica of the Panathenaea on the Parthenon.
On the south was the head of the procession, in the persons
of Augustus and his family, moving towards the left ; on the
north was the people, moving to the right, and thus seeming
to follow the Imperial family.

The intact relief of Italy, which stood by the eastern entry,
and is generally called Tellus, is in the Uffizi at Florence, with
the portions of the large friezes representing the family of

---

[1] I follow the indications of Studniczka, which seem to me to preclude any
uncertainty.

Augustus and about half of the procession of the people. Two other fragments of this procession are in the Vatican and the Louvre. The Terme Museum in Rome possesses, in addition to various fragments, the two halves, almost complete, of the sacrifice of Aeneas to the Penates. The part of the southern frieze which went immediately in front of the Florence portions is still in its place under the Fiano Palace. The reliefs set in the wall of the Villa Medici, on the garden side, which were formerly believed to come from the Altar of Peace, seem really to have belonged to a monument of the time of Claudius.[1]

Let us be content with examining some of the fragments of this great work of sculpture.

The best known is the allegorical relief in the Uffizi which adorned the small wall left of the east entrance. (Plate XIII. 1.) Formerly it was supposed to be a figure of Fruitfulness; others interpreted it as Mother Earth. With Mr van Buren, I believe that it has a more precise significance; it is Italy, and formed a pendant to the figure of Rome on the right of the same entrance.[2]

On a rock a woman sits, holding two babies, one of whom seeks her breast while the other seems to be playing. Her lap is full of flowers, fruit, and grapes. Behind her are a bush on the left and a tuft of flowers on the right. In the bottom left-hand corner of the relief, an overturned urn represents a spring; the water flows through luxuriant vegetation, a bird comes to drink, and on the grassy bank of the river born of this spring, at the bottom of the relief, a great ox lies, chewing the cud, while a sheep browses at the feet of the central figure. Two smaller female figures complete the picture; their breasts are bare, their mantles belly above their heads like sails, and their feet do not touch the ground; that on the right has a dolphin by her, and the other sits on a swan which is flying away.

The principle of a representation of this kind, the personification of an abstract idea, Fruitfulness, Mother Earth, or a river, is certainly Greek. But let us consider the face of the

---

[1] Sieveking, in *Oest. Jahreshefte*, x (1907), pp. 175 ff., who is followed by Studniczka. Claudius, not Augustus, can be identified on one of these reliefs. The head of Augustus appears on one of the fragments of the Altar of Peace now in the Terme.

[2] A. W. van Buren, **VIII**, 1913, pp. 134-41.

PLATE XIII

1

2

THE ALTAR OF PEACE.

1. Italy as foster-mother. (Florence, Uffizi)
2. Sacrifice of Aeneas to the Penates. (Rome, Terme)

[face p. 352

principal figure, the beautiful woman with the babies, sitting on the rock. There is nothing Greek in the type; the features are lean and almost hard, and the countenance is severe, even in the smile with which she seems to watch the play of one of the children. The small round head, the big nose, sharply detached from the forehead, the strong mouth, set very high in the face, and the long chin suggest a portrait rather than an ideal head, and an Italian portrait much rather than a Greek one. A woman certainly sat for that face, and the artist has reproduced her very individual beauty.

This foster-mother with the mighty breasts which stand out beneath the pliant folds of the *peplum* is the land of Italy, *magna parens frugum, magna virum.* In the details of the carving Mr van Buren finds all the essential features of the famous eulogy of Italy in the second book of the *Georgics;* they are not mere fancies of the artist. In her lap are the fruit and grapes, *gravidae fruges et Massicus humor* (l. 143); behind her, the flowers and greenery, *ver assiduum* (l. 149); at her feet, the river and the beasts, *armenta laeta* (l. 144),

> . . . *albi, Clitumne, greges et maxima taurus*
> *Victima, saepe tuo perfusi flumine sacro* (ll. 146-7).

The maternal figure is seated on a rock, like so many old towns of Italy, while beneath her the meadows stretch, with the stream winding over them,

> *Tot congesta manu praeruptis oppida saxis*
> *Fluminaque antiquos subterlabentia muros* (ll. 156-7).

The airy figures on either side which make a sort of frame about Italy are *Jovis aurae,* the kindly breezes of Jupiter on which Horace calls in the *Carmen Saeculare.*

> *Fertilis frugum pecorisque tellus*
> *Spicea donet Cererem corona.*
> *Nutriant foetus et aquae salubres*
> *Et Jovis aurae* (ll. 29-33).

"May the earth, fertile in fruits and beasts, give a crown of wheat-ears to Ceres; and may the healthful rain and winds of Jove nurture the seed in her bosom."

On the right, clearly indicated by the presence of the

z

dolphin, is the air of the sea ; on the left the land breeze takes flight on her swan ; these are the two winds which, on hot days, come in turn to bring coolness to the Italian country. No Roman who, about the hour when the sun sinks towards the horizon, has waited for the relief of the wind from the Apennines, succeeding the sea-breeze which has given freshness to the morning, could have any doubt of the aptness and meaning of these symbolic figures.

The inspiration of the whole allegory is too definitely Italian for it to be possible to accept Herr Schreiber's hypothesis, which would see in it nothing but an Alexandrian motive. Herr Schreiber argues from the discovery at Carthage of a relief almost exactly the same as that of the Ara Pacis, at least in respect of the central figure.[1] The subsidiary figures, on the other hand, have been modified so as to represent, apparently, the stormy Syrtes and the African coast. It seems very likely that the Carthaginian relief was an imitation of that in Rome. Like many other provincial capitals, Carthage may have wanted to have its own Altar of Peace, or even its Altar of Rome and Augustus, and may have been content to adapt to its own purposes the models furnished by the famous Roman altar.[2] On the other hand, it is hardly likely that a copy of a commonplace figure would have been allowed into the decoration of the monument erected in honour of the return of Augustus.

While the relief of Italy may have been inspired by the *Georgics* and a stanza of the *Carmen Saeculare*, it is the *Aeneid* that we find recalled in the two fragments in the Terme, which adorned the south side of the western entry of the Ara Pacis. The scene represents Aeneas sacrificing to the Penates. (Plate XIII. 2.)

A figure of purely ideal type, like some Jupiter or Aesculapius, stands with his breast bare and his head veiled in his cloak. Behind him, to the right, the arm of a companion can be seen, resting on a stout staff. These must be, not a personification of the Senate, as has been suggested, but Aeneas followed by the faithful Achates. Aeneas stretches out his hand towards a basket of fruit or cakes which a

---

[1] In the Louvre. Cf. Michon, **XV**, xvii (1911), pp. 156 ff. ; **XII**, x (1896), pp. 89-96.
[2] Among the fragments of the Altar of Rome and Augustus at Lyons, preserved in the town museum, garlands may be seen very like those on the Ara Pacis.

camillus, or choir-boy, is offering to him ; a servant drives a sow towards him. At the back, on an eminence, is a small temple, inside which two seated figures appear. This is the Temple of the Penates, which Augustus had just restored. The scene represents the first sacrifice offered by the mythical ancestor of the Roman people to the national gods of Troy, whom he had just established on Italian soil. The figure of Aeneas with the full beard is quite Greek, an idealized hero in the style of Pergamon. The little temple at the back and the hollow rock on which it stands are just like the picturesque backgrounds of the so-called Alexandrian reliefs, but it conveys at the same time a definite allusion to a recent Roman event, the rebuilding of the Temple of the Penates.

By the side of these conventional motives, the group of the two *camilli*, the dish of offerings, the vase of lustral water, and the sow, with her snout to the ground, being driven towards the altar add a living, realistic note.[1] The picture is composed, like an episode in the *Aeneid*, of motives taken from Hellenistic art, heroic idealism, topical events, and things seen every day. The whole presents a new meaning, and is inspired by the national legend, of which imaginations were full at the time. The memory of Troy and the thought of Rome hover about the scene and animate the composition.

We can only guess, from the scanty fragments picked up and from the indications of certain coins, the subjects of the two other reliefs which adorned the short walls near the entrances. Fruitful Italy had a counterpart in Rome seated in her glory ; the sacrifice of Aeneas was matched by the She-wolf feeding Romulus and Remus. The conception, we see, was the same as in the reliefs which have survived.

On the two great continuous friezes on the north and south sides reality is presented, pure of any conventional or mythical alloy. We see the procession of the Roman people, escorting its ruler whose return it is celebrating. (Plate XIV.) This long line of figures, all animated by the same movement but infinitely varied in their attitudes, is a veritable series of portraits. It is sufficient to look at the leading group on the slab in the Vatican, two old Lictors, one in

---

[1] It is found again all through the Empire in innumerable scenes of sacrifice to the Lares and *suovetaurilia*. It is an old motive of popular religious art, which appears in official art as early as the altar of Domitius Ahenobarbus.

profile and the other looking towards you, going before a magistrate. The individual character of the faces, the intensity and variety of the expressions, the full countenance of the first Lictor, the wrinkles of the second, the marked profile of the magistrate, all indicate the most exact portrayal of living models.

Men of the time must have been able to give a name to every figure on the friezes. It is not an ideal people, like that of the Panathenaea, going by in beauty and glory, but the Roman people, walking, quietly but solidly, on their own soil. The artistic problem before the sculptor was in the composition of this crowd ; he had to avoid both monotony and a scattered effect, to combine the individuals in a compact crowd, yet to make the spectator feel the special movement, the life, and even the thought of each. He has succeeded. By varying costumes, by mingling men, women, and children, by showing them full-face, in profile, or three-quarter-face, distributed generally in two planes and sometimes conversing together, and, above all, by making very skilful use of the different ways in which his figures are looking, so as to connect them with one another, the artist has shown incomparable virtuosity in the portrayal of this procession. His work has been justly compared to the Dutch masters' pictures of corporations. There is the same realistic inspiration supported by perfect technique and animated by a spirit full of understanding and subtlety.

It will suffice here to examine one part of the south frieze, and to try to recognize at least some of the members of the Emperor's family.

At the head of the procession walked Augustus, surrounded by Lictors and doubtless accompanied by Livia. Of this slab we have only a few fragments.[1] Then came the block which is still in its place under the Fiano Palace, on which, among other persons, two flamens can be recognized by the *apex*, a pointed thing on the top of their cap. Immediately after this part came the section now in Florence, the first two figures on which are also flamens. (Plate XIV. 2.) Thus these priests are represented as numbering four. Now, the college had not this number before 11 B.C. From this it has been inferred that the procession shown on the frieze

[1] In the Terme Museum.

was not that of the reception which failed to come off in 13, but that of the inauguration of the altar in the January of the year 9. It has been observed, in support of this hypothesis, that the figures are represented warmly wrapped up in their cloaks, as they would be in January, even in Rome, whereas it would be very uncomfortable in July. For all the careful accuracy shown in the frieze, it is perhaps a mistake to take such very small points into consideration. The people are in ceremonial dress, which meant the toga for men and the cloak for women, and they might wrap themselves up in it against the sun as well as against the tramontana. The frieze was carved between the end of 13 and the beginning of 9. It must have required many sketches and perhaps some alterations. The artist would naturally bring it up to date, but it is very unlikely that he thought of distinguishing between the procession of 13, which never took place, and that of the inauguration, which, since his work had to be ready for it, had not yet taken place. We may say simply that we have in the frieze a solemn procession of the Roman people celebrating the return of its ruler and, at the same time, the peace which he had given to the world.

We may therefore expect to see in it the figures of the family of Augustus as it was about the year 10, when the sculptor must have put the last touches to his work.

Who is the person who, in the middle of the Florence slab, is shown with his body facing us and his face in profile, slightly inclined to his right ? He is tall, and stands in a very noble attitude, veiling his head with the end of his toga, like a priest in the act of doing sacrifice. He walks behind a Lictor ; on his left a young boy clings to the corner of his garment. His features are already sharpened by age. It has been suggested that he is Agrippa. But Agrippa had died in 12. Besides, the rather tired, dreamy countenance of this figure is not like the well-known energetic features of the fellow-worker of Augustus. (See Plate XII. 2.) The place occupied by this figure would suit Agrippa perfectly well ; but it is not Agrippa ; it cannot be Agrippa. We do not know who it is. Perhaps the face was retouched so as to change its identity and to obliterate the likeness of the good administrator and heir-presumptive of the Empire.

On the left of this mysterious figure, separated from it, or rather connected with it by the young boy between them, is a woman with her mantle gracefully draped about her. She also stands facing the spectator, almost outside the procession ; her face, seen in three quarters, is slightly inclined to her right ; her gaze seems to be bent on the boy, who looks up at her, but it is really absent and wandering, while her mouth wears an enigmatic smile. The unknown man with the veiled head, the child, and this graceful young woman obviously form one group. The beautiful, charming matron, with her rather bored expression, is not Livia. Livia would be older, and must have walked at the head of the procession with Augustus. This is Julia, the daughter of Augustus. The boy by her must be Lucius Caesar, the second of her sons. The elder, Gaius, must have accompanied Augustus. In 13 Julia was the wife of Agrippa. The group of three which stands out so clearly from the rest of the procession must have formed a pretty family picture at that time. The unknown man was evidently Agrippa.

But in the year 11 Julia, after being a widow for some months, had been compelled by her father's command to marry the suspicious, jealous Tiberius. It is certainly the hard profile of Tiberius which we see on the frieze behind her, looking at her fixedly as she turns her head away. Without doubt, the figure of Tiberius was brought into closer connexion with that of Julia, with which it is really coupled, and, without doubt, the direction of his gaze was made to unite them at the same time as a few strokes of the chisel destroyed the likeness of the dead Agrippa, perhaps substituting the portrait of some priestly official unknown to us.

What a contrast there is between the group of Julia and Tiberius and that immediately following it ! Turning towards each other, and apparently not troubling much about the ceremony, a young woman and a young man are talking gaily together, so gaily that a severe lady behind them, rolled up tight in her veil, puts her finger to her lips to call them to seemly silence. The man, tall, well set up, with his military cloak thrown over his shoulder, has a pleasant profile, which is not, however, unlike that of Tiberius. It is his brother Drusus. Since the year 12 he had been occupied in conquering Germany ; he came back to hold his triumph in Rome at the end of 10. He was about to return to the Rhine for a

PLATE XIV

1

2

3

THE ALTAR OF PEACE.
1. Procession of the people. Fragment. (Vatican
2, 3. The family of Augustus. (Florence, Uffizi)

[face p. 358

fresh campaign, which he hoped to carry even farther into unknown country than his previous campaigns. And in the autumn of 9, across an Italy stricken with grief, Tiberius would bring back to Rome the ashes of the young general who died at the age of thirty from a fall from his horse on the banks of the Elbe. The woman in front of him on the frieze is Antonia, his wife ; he holds the hand of their son, a baby of about two, rather overwhelmed by his little toga, Germanicus, who was to avenge Varus and to follow in the footsteps of his father beyond the Rhine. Having been born in 15 B.C., he must have looked something like this in July 13.

A pretty childish scene follows this picture of married happiness. A little boy of about five has caught hold of the corner of Drusus's *paludamentum*, just as young Lucius Caesar clutches the garment of the unknown priest in front. His mother, a lady with a very pure profile in the second plane, holds him in an absent-minded way, while his elder sister, behind him, smilingly makes some remark which he receives very solemnly. The mother can only be the elder Antonia, the wife of L. Domitius Ahenobarbus, who walks behind her and their children. The old man whose profile appears between the husband and wife in the background is probably the father of Domitius. We have here the whole line of Nero grouped together.

The frieze goes on in the same way, in a succession of individuals and groups full of life. Every figure seems to have been copied from life with attentive, minute care ; costume, features, and attitude are true ; each portrait and each group is a work of close psychological observation, which one feels to be true. Touches of sentiment, such as the look of Tiberius at Julia and the conversation of Drusus and Antonia, and pretty childish interludes give colour to the historical scene. It is animated by a great religious idea, indicated by the ritual dress of the flamens and the attitude of the priests walking with veiled heads, and now and again recalled by some detail, the silent lady stopping chatter and the open hand of Domitius raised in prayer. This art is full of meaning, and therein lies its originality. The thought is essentially concrete and positive ; it does not lose itself in an ideal above the senses. These men, women, and children do not float like the horsemen of the Parthenon in an ethereal region between heaven and earth. Their feet rest on the ground, they are beings of flesh and blood, their forms are true likenesses of living human individuals, their sentiments are those of their everyday life and are revealed in their features, and the whole idea is a Roman idea, the idea of the moment which the frieze represents, piety towards the gods of the city, to whom solemn thanksgiving is being made for the return of the ruler.

The Roman artist has eyes to see ; his mind analyses sensation, selecting elements from it and arranging them ; he does not rise above the senses and soar to a higher world in which the individual is merged in the idea, accident in law. Material reality is his domain.

This is not the place to dwell on the technical mastery of these reliefs and the art of the composition, which is very carefully thought out and extremely skilful, under its apparent simplicity. Using only two planes, the artist has managed to give an impression of depth. He makes harmonious combinations of lines and masses. He distributes the various folds of white woollen togas, softer robes, and light veils over the whole composition. He excels in bringing the features and expressions of faces into the light beneath the shadow of hair crowned with laurels. All this virtuosity is the heritage of Greece ; Roman art makes a new use of it.

We must not leave the Altar of Peace without glancing at the floral decoration which adorned the pilasters and filled all the lower field of the surrounding wall, under the friezes, and embellished the inside with garlands. (Plate XV. 2, 3.) It is magnificent decoration, at once very rich and gracefully pliant.

Outside, the ornament is more conventional ; its fantastic arabesques contrast with the realism of the friezes. (Plate XV. 2.) From heavy clusters of acanthus, whose lower leaves fall back towards the earth, an airy tracery of conventional foliage rises in wide spirals. From the main stems spring tendrils, folioles, flowers, and cinquefoils, every one of different design, which here and there strike a naturalistic note amid the unreal pattern of the stems. The whole is conceived in a very broad decorative style ; yet the details are executed with minute care. Aquatic birds with sinuous necks stand on buds, spreading out their wings, sparrows peck at flowers,

PLATE XV

1

2   3

1. Marble Altar. (Rome, Terme)
2, 3. Outside and inside decoration of the Altar of Peace. (Terme)

lizards run along the stems ; we even see mosquitoes flitting beneath the leaves. Just as in the allegorical and mythological scenes, the ideal is animated by the real. The artificial, conventional setting is filled with a solid substance of things seen and felt ; a homely breeze blows among this foliage of fancy, a living sap feeds the pliant grace of the arabesques.

Much stress has been laid, with rather exaggerated enthusiasm but not without a foundation of justice, on the delicate observation of nature to which Roman art bears witness. People have talked of impressionism, illusionism, and Japanese art.[1] We need not concern ourselves with these ambitious generalizations, which perhaps betray a lack of sufficient attention to the very various antecedents of Augustan art. The decorative naturalism which we see in Roman monuments of the Imperial age may well have its origins in Alexandria, the city of flowers and fruit, quite as well as in the realistic vein of the Latin spirit. We see it in the painted garlands which adorn series of Hellenistic vases of terra-cotta.[2] It is triumphant in the chiselling of vases of precious metal. No doubt we have no proof that all the examples furnished by the treasures of Boscoreale and Hildesheim come from Alexandria. Many of them are certainly Italian. But it is none the less true that the floral decoration with which they are adorned seems inspired by Alexandrian models. The Romans understood the beauty of flowers and foliage, conventional or copied from nature, but they did not discover it.

Let us, therefore, be content to note the development of realistic plant decoration in the age of Augustus. In painting, the most typical example of this style is the panel in Livia's Villa at Prima Porta, which represents the shrubbery of a garden, with its different kinds of trees, its fruit, and its birds. (Plate XVI. 1.) In sculpture, we may mention first of all the heavy garlands on the inner faces of the Altar of Peace. (Plate XV. 3.) Each leaf, each flower, each fruit, pear, fig, laurel-berry, pine-cone, grape, and ear of corn, is carved with delicate care for its own sake, and can be recognized at a glance, without this accuracy of detail spoiling the decorative effect. We may also examine the

---

[1] Wickhoff, **CLXX**, pp. 21 ff.   [2] G. Leroux, **XCVIII**.

plane-branches which adorn an altar of the same period in the Terme Museum. (Plate XV. 1.) They are treated like real branches laid on the marble. Every leaf has its own folds, and even the veins are clearly visible. If colour were added, as it was in ancient times, the illusion would be complete.

Pliny tells us that there was in Rome, in the time of Augustus, an artist named Possis, who specialized in thus reproducing fruit in marble, so as to deceive the eye.[1] But was this Possis an Italian ? His gift, which, of course, does not represent the highest form of art, might be no more than an imitation of what was done elsewhere, somewhere in the Hellenized East, at Antioch or Alexandria. Essays of this kind may lie at the bottom of the strictly naturalistic plant decoration which appears in Roman sculpture in the age of Augustus and supplied the adornment of the inside walls of the Ara Pacis. Nor should we forget that on the outer face of these same walls realistic ornament was only scattered here and there amid a highly conventional decoration.

Neither in decoration, nor in historical scenes, nor in portraiture did the Romans invent realism. They were content to make use of it and they gave it a new development.

For this tendency of Hellenistic art coincided with one of the traditions of popular art in the form in which it survived among the lower classes and in the country districts of Italy. In Italy, as in most countries of simple, not highly educated minds, there had always been a fondness for portraits which were " like," scenes representing real things, and ornament so close to the ornament of nature as to deceive. The sound sense of the people generally likes to understand what it sees and to see what it understands. Like the national literature of Virgil and Livy, Augustan art looks beyond little intellectual circles and cultivated connoisseurs, and speaks to a larger public, to the new strata of the population which were coming to take the place of the old aristocracy, decimated by the Civil Wars. This art, therefore, adopts for preference a less sophisticated, less abstract style, one which retains the most elements appreciable to the senses and can therefore be most immediately and most generally understood. By its realism, Roman art leaves its school-days and the atmosphere of the schools behind, and becomes an

[1] *N.H.*, xxxv. 155.

art for the whole people. As against the dilettantism and preciosities of the last years of the Republic, it presents a more robust, fuller, and healthier appearance. It comes as a reaction of the national taste against the exoticism which prevailed before. It thus becomes the form most habitually adopted by the official art of the Empire.

Examples like that of the friezes of the Altar of Peace must have done more than anything else to foster the diffusion of these new artistic tendencies. This style gained some reflected glory from the halo attaching to the memory of the founder of the Empire, and was regarded as that most adequate to the political and religious ideal of the time. But in reality the Augustan ideal did not in itself comprise any aesthetic theory. Augustus showed equal favour to all the various forms of art which Rome picked up on the shores of the Mediterranean. We see all forms pursuing their normal evolution in his reign, often under his protection. When we study the great cameos, the Triumph of Augustus in Vienna and the Triumph of Tiberius in the Bibliothèque Nationale in Paris (Plate XVI. 2), we find, in the heroized figures of the princes, a fairly definite reminiscence of Alexandrian art and, in the composition of the scenes, the clear trace of Asiatic, Pergamene reminiscences. Even on the Altar of Peace, by the side of the great realistic friezes, the panels flanking the doors give us allegories and mythological compositions of quite a different style. In the statue of Augustus, too, and among the reliefs which adorn the breastplate, the idealism and conventional motives of Hellenistic art are mingled with details of realistic accuracy.

But in all these works, from the cameos to the breastplate of Augustus, the allegories and figments of the imagination express purely Roman ideas and sentiments. In them we see the motives and formulas of Hellenistic art adapted to the glorification of the Emperor and his family, of Rome, and of Italy, together with the representation of the national Roman legends or the expression of the hopes raised by the Roman Peace which was dawning on the world.

Augustan art, in short, is not one particular style ; it is only in a limited measure a new creation or a resurrection of the old traditions of Italian art. It is neither pure realism nor idealism. It is the permanent adoption by Rome of the various aesthetic tendencies going on all over the Mediterranean world. The motives, the forms, the technique, all the outward aspect of this art simply represents the heritage of the Hellenistic world. But the Imperial idea imbues this tradition with a specially Roman soul, which becomes the principle of a new life.

Chapter V

THE IMPERIAL RELIGION

St Augustine has preserved for us a profound saying of Mucius Scaevola, the Pontifex Maximus, whom Cicero had known in his youth. " There are," this official representative of Roman religion declared, " three kinds of religion : the poet's, the philosopher's, and the statesman's. The two first are futile or superfluous or positively harmful ; only the third can be accepted." [1] Here we have a perfect expression of the Roman political tradition in respect of religion. The gods were made to serve the State. This was certainly how Augustus understood it. The religious restoration which he strove to bring about was essentially political.

The poet's religion was nothing but imagination and Greek fancy. Never did it flower in such profusion as at the end of the Republic, in the literature and art inspired by the Hellenistic world. It lasted all through the Empire, until after the triumph of Christianity. But it contained neither belief nor feeling, and furnished nothing which could be of practical interest.

The religion of the philosopher, that of Lucretius, that of Cicero,[2] must have had a more profound influence. It addressed itself to the intelligence ; its importance grew as intellectual culture developed. It tended to rationalistic interpretation of old mythical conceptions, it adapted itself to individual opinions, it varied in the same man according to the circumstances of life.[3] As a fact, it generally ended, with regard to the gods of the city, if not in absolute negation, at least in scepticism and indifference. " How I wish," Cassius confided to Brutus, just before Philippi, " that there were gods, that we might have confidence not only in our

---

[1] *Civ. Dei*, iv. 27.   [2] Boissier, **XXXVII**, i, pp. 54 ff.
[3] In Cicero, for example. Cf. Warde Fowler, **CLXVIII**, pp. 278 ff. ; **CLXVII**, pp. 381 ff.

arms but in the justice of our cause." [1] Neither Cassius nor any of his contemporaries was really convinced of the existence of the gods, or at least their conviction was too irresolute to influence their action.

But the official religion still existed. Its priests continued to perform their offices regularly, when they were not taken from them by political life. There was no interruption of the rites. The very spirit of the Pontifical College did not change or grow broader. There were even unexpected reawakenings of the old exclusiveness of which the affair of the Bacchanalia had furnished a tragic example. Four times, between the years 58 and 48, the Senate prohibited the worship of Isis in Rome.[2] These were vain efforts; the soul of the people turned away from the cults practised in its name by the State; the ancient gods and the old temples kept no worshippers. Varro expresses the fear that all the Roman gods will perish, not by the act of the enemy, but by the neglect of the citizens.[3]

True to the aristocratic tradition of the Pontifices, Scaevola forgets just one thing—the religious needs of the people. Poets, philosophers, and even statesmen only represent the small minority who can express their thoughts and try to suit their acts and attitudes to them. The people, in respect of religion, was not only the illiterate mass of the plebeians, but also all the half-educated classes and all for whom abstract speculation was not more than an accessory in life, from the slave to the Knight who did business all over the Mediterranean, from the private soldier to the general, from the peasant to the Senator who looked after his property and was engaged in politics. All had henceforward other interests than those of the State, interests for which they felt the need of divine protection. No doubt they prayed to the gods from abroad, who were so full of promises. But they also had at home, in their houses and in their fields, gods whom they knew, invoked, feared, or loved. Between the individual religion of the thinkers and the official worship there was a popular religion made up of the simple fancies, the pious traditions, the earnestness, and the emotion natural to man in the presence of the unknown. It formed the deep

---

[1] Plut., *Brut.*, 42. [2] Lafaye, **XCI**, pp. 44 ff.
[3] Aug., *Civ. Dei*, vi. 2; *Antiq. Div.* (Aghad), 141.

stratum which, even among the most highly cultivated, was always cropping up at some point.   On this popular religion Augustus based, at least in part, his national restoration.

I

THE POPULAR RELIGION

The form and the vitality of this religious sentiment are chiefly revealed to us by the recent discovery at Delos of a number of monuments of family worship belonging to the Roman colony which settled in the island in the first half of the Ist century B.C.   These modest monuments agree, in general, with the information supplied by many paintings from Pompeii, most of which date only from the Ist century A.D., and are therefore later than the Augustan restoration. They thus form a link in the chain which connects the religion of the Imperial epoch with that of the early centuries of Rome, and, as such, are of quite especial interest.

In most of the houses occupied by Romans at Delos we find, as at Pompeii, the family altar adorned with or surrounded by paintings representing a worship which is not Greek, and gives us every reason for connecting it with the earliest religious conceptions of Italy.[1]   At Delos the altar stands before the door, whereas at Pompeii it is only found inside the house.   Above, in the wall, there is often a small arched niche to protect the sacrificial fire.   On the coating with which the altar is covered, or on the house wall on either side of the altar, are paintings depicting the rites performed in honour of the Genius of the paterfamilias and of the Lares and Penates.   These perpetuate the sacrifice, as it were, and, by making it permanent, give it a virtue which continues to be efficacious.   When the colour fades and tends to disappear, it is carefully restored.   The many superimposed layers of paint, which it has sometimes been possible to detach from one another, show what pains were taken to keep these ritual pictures always fresh.

Between the painted garlands which frame the scene we

[1] M. Bulard, " Peintures murales et mosaïques de Délos," in **XV,** xiv (1908), pp. 11-84.   Cf. Plassart, **II,** xl (1916), pp. 175-217.

see, in the midst of his family, the father, who, with the end
of his toga drawn over his head, pours out a libation before
the altar.   Opposite him a man accompanies the prayer on
a flute.   Sometimes at Delos, and more often at Pompeii,
two snakes are painted beneath the scene, and seem to crawl
towards the altar as if to take the offerings.   One of the two
generally has a crest on its head and a kind of little beard on
its chin ; the other lacks these attributes.   We recognize these
as a naïve figuration of the Genius of the paterfamilias and
the Juno of the materfamilias, blended with the spirits of
the ancestors which watch over the house.   These paintings
of the Ist centuries B.C. and A.D. represent the celebration
of the very ancient family cult which was born of the
divinization of the various parts of the house, the hearth
where the fire burns and the *penus* or store-closet over which
the Penates watch, and of the head who commands it and,
as heir of the forbears gone below the ground, ensures the
perpetuity of the race.[1]   So this household religion was still
a living thing in the Roman family.

With the gods of the hearth, the paintings at Delos and
Pompeii commonly associate those of the ground on which
the house stands, the Lares.   The Lares are outdoor gods,
whereas the Penates belong inside.   Their domain is the
street and the public place in the city, and the fields, roads,
and crossways in the country.   There their altars or modest
shrines stand.   They protect servants, slaves, and all who,
being strangers by blood and therefore excluded from the
worship of the hearth, none the less form part of the *familia*.

Beside the sacrifice to the Penates, on the lateral faces of
the altars at Delos or on the house wall by the side of the
entrance, we find pictures of the rites of worship of the Lares.
A pig is sacrificed to them, while the common people give
themselves up to merriment and horse-play, boxing and
wrestling, the prizes for which will be the hams of the victim
and jars of wine.[2]

The Lares are friendly gods, without prejudices.   About
their altars on the cross-roads they collect all the vagabonds,
all those who have no family, no hearth, no worship of their

---

[1] Cf. above, pp. 87 ff.
[2] Bulard, *op. cit.*, 41 ff. ; Plassart, *op. cit.*, pp. 184 ff.   See also R. Vallois,
" Observations sur le culte des Lares," in **XVI,** ii (1924), pp. 21-36.

own. Their humble devotees combine to celebrate their feasts as best they can, forming Colleges of the Cross-roads, *collegia compitalicia*. Several inscriptions from Delos mention " Competaliasts," doubtless presidents or dignitaries of these joyous brotherhoods. During the Civil Wars, the fomenters of disorder found these pious worshippers of the street and the public place to their hand, ready to be converted into paid gangs. So the Colleges of the Cross-roads appear, just for a moment, in the light of history. They were forbidden in 64, and restored legally a few years later by the Tribune Clodius, Cicero's enemy. Caesar abolished them again. We shall find them once more, more full of life than ever, under the Empire.[1]

Yet other deities appear associated with family worship at Delos and Pompeii. First, there is Fortune, very often combined with Mercury, who carries the caduceus and purse and is accompanied by animals, such as the cock, the dog, or the tortoise. Then there is Hercules. Mercury, god of trade, and Hercules, god of physical strength and all beneficial work, are the professional patrons of the small tradesmen, shopkeepers, and craftsmen who form the population of the towns. All pray also to Fortune, that she may see that their business prospers. Several inscriptions at Delos introduce us to colleges of free men or freedmen grouped under the patronage of gods like Hermes, Apollo, or Poseidon—Hermaistae, Apolloniastae, Poseidoniastae, clearly professional associations of traders, craftsmen, and sailors. These inscriptions are found collected in certain public places where the college seems to have had an altar or a small shrine. In ancient cities, as in those of the Middle Ages, the guilds of the various crafts were apparently settled in a particular quarter, which was under the protection of the patron god of the trade. A paterfamilias who belonged to one of these colleges would bring the god of his livelihood into his home, associating him with his Penates. In addition, he joined the other members of his guild in public worship of the professional god in the shrine of his quarter. These gods, whose rôle we gather from the Delian inscriptions and paintings as early as the Ist century B.C., Mercury, Hercules, Apollo, Fortune, are those whom we find still receiving the most

---

[1] **LVI**, s.v. *Vicomagistri*, pp. 829-30.

2 A

honour under the Empire, both in Italy and in the provinces. We chiefly find them on altars in streets and public places, and they seem often to have given their name to streets and city quarters.[1]

So the worships of the home, the street, and the fields, the gods of the family, of agriculture, and of the crafts, the simple protectors of daily life and labour, continued to live. They had no theology, their horizon was limited, they did not trouble about what might have been before life or what might follow, nor about the phenomena of the world, and still less about those of heaven. They owed their existence and nature to simple, primitive thoughts ; they protected man in his activity, however humble, and gave him health, prosperity, a roof to cover him, offspring to make him happy, and feast-days on which he could enjoy himself.

They were kindly, familiar, and gay. They were the gods of a pleasant land, of a practical people, without soaring ideals, but hard-working and essentially healthy-minded. Their worshippers hardly feared them, but they loved them and remained true to them. They offered a more effective resistance to Christianity than did Jupiter. They are the special object of the fulminations of an article in the Theodosian Code which forbids men " to keep up the fire in honour of the Lares, to make libations of wine to the Genius, to offer perfumes to the Penates, to light lamps, to burn incense, or to hang garlands round their altars." [2]

The early city had grown until it embraced the whole Mediterranean world, but in extending his empire Jupiter of the Capitol, the greatest and best of all the Jupiters, had lost his power over souls and even his personality. He had become a mere symbol of pride and dominion, to whom the magistrates mechanically paid official honour. He was confounded, even in Rome, with the great foreign gods, Greek Zeus, Egyptian Serapis, Asiatic Sabazios, but all in vain ; these contaminations and transfusions did not bring back life. His figure, made for a single city and its neighbourhood, was

---

[1] **LVI,** s.v. *Vicomagistri*, p. 829, and *Vicus*, p. 863. Cf. the Vicus Apollinensis and Vicus Salutis at Mainz. See, too, the fine altar of Fortune on which Fortune and Apollo are represented in Espérandieu, *Recueil des bas-reliefs de la Gaule romaine*, vii, no. 5727, pp. 270-1.

[2] *Cod. Theod.*, xvi. 10. 20.

lost in the immensity of the Mediterranean and its distant shores, and in the dazzle of ideas with which they were filled.

As the capital of a great state, Rome had its philosophers and poets who diffused among the ruling class, to whom conquest brought wealth and leisure, the ideas and fancies born of the reflections or imaginations of all mankind. At the same time men and priests of the most different nations taught the half-educated, especially the women, to feel the mystery of life and to care for their personal happiness after life. For the anguish which they thus created they offered the balm of childish stories and rites which attracted by their mystery and exaltation of the senses. But outside schools and social gatherings, outside little temples and retreats where the initiates of the mystery gods assembled, in the houses and streets of the city and in the broad countrysides, the life of the people went on in the old way. It remained almost unaffected by political changes, which hardly altered economic conditions or the state of society. The old constitution of the family lasted. In order to live, men tilled the earth as they had always done, worked with their hands, and sold their wares from humble stalls. The old gods who protected their unchanged activities were as necessary as ever. So great was their vitality that, far from yielding before foreign cults, they followed their worshippers into the new lands where they settled, and, with Italian craftsmen and traders, their altars abounded even on the sacred island of Delian Apollo.

Beneath the brilliant but superficial facing of cosmopolitan intellectual life, beneath the more vulgar stratum of Graeco-Oriental mysticism complicated by magic and astrology, we must not forget the profound, vigorous life of the mass of the Italian people. History, being wholly aristocratic and political, hardly noticed them. For they lived outside history, so to speak, content to be alive under a sunny sky, on a land which they loved. They needed no more than a few very simple ideas inherited from their forefathers and a few homely rites to give them confidence and joy. A loyal, courageous race, feeling no dread in the presence of the unknown and, at bottom, not caring much about it, when the thoughts and fancies of the Mediterranean came pouring in they kept alive the original conceptions and religious acts of the first masters of the Italian soil. At the unextinguished fire of their humble altars the religion of Imperial Rome was rekindled.

II

THE RELIGIOUS THOUGHT AND WORK OF AUGUSTUS

In temperament Augustus seems to have been fundamentally religious. Nervous and impressionable to excess, he carried fear of the gods to the point of superstition. He had a morbid fear of lightning. To protect himself against it, he always wore an amulet of seal's skin, and at the smallest storm he took refuge in a vaulted shelter.[1] Auspices and omens of all kinds were sacred to him and he took them scrupulously into account ; in this respect he had exactly the same ideas as the humblest citizen of the little town of Velitrae, the home of his family. Suetonius dwells on this trait in his character at length, and relates many instances. Portents and their observation played a considerable part in his life.

A mystical tendency led him to adopt all beliefs which passed the understanding of man. He took a keen interest in astrology and professed the greatest respect for Nigidius Figulus, a philosopher and mage, who since the time of Cicero had done more than anyone to spread these doctrines in high Roman society. Had not Nigidius cast his horoscope and foretold his future greatness on the day of his birth ? This horoscope Augustus caused to be published officially, no doubt in order to put an end to the false prophecies which were being circulated about him. In so doing he only showed what importance he attached to all such fancies. Suetonius also tells us that he had a silver coinage struck with the sign of the Goat, under which he was born. This is the Goat which we see above his head on the great Vienna cameo which depicts him enthroned beside Rome in heroic glory.

Nigidius Figulus was not only an astrologer ; he was a Pythagorean. Now, since the time of Cicero, and especially in the reign of Augustus, there had been a revival of the

---

[1] Suet., *Aug.*, 90.

Pythagorean doctrine, mingled with Platonism, which gave a mystic tinge to Stoic pantheism. Pythagorean teaching was what propagated the belief in a future life, and, above all, gave a form to this belief.[1] The soul lives in Hades, awaiting its reincarnation. There it undergoes various purifications. Its returns to earth are new trials ; the quality of the matter which it is called to animate, vegetable, animal, or human, and the fortunes of the individual which it helps to form depend on its purity. So life is only a preparation for other existences. It represents only one moment in being ; in this moment everything should be sacrificed to the infinite future which awaits us.[2] The teaching abounds in ascetic precepts tending to ensure the constant purity of the soul. In the reign of Augustus the Pythagorean school was represented especially by two philosophers, Sextius and his son of the same name. They held a practical school of virtue and preached sincerity, temperance, frugality, and vegetarianism with brilliant success.[3] Through them mysticism became the principle of a powerful movement towards purity which came to win the whole-hearted favour of the ruler.

That the religious tendencies of Augustus were profoundly sincere cannot be doubted. That they were reinforced by a political purpose also appears evident. Augustus saw in religion one of the essential elements of Roman tradition, and he deliberately modelled his attitude on that of the old Roman magistrates. Like them, for example, he made a fundamental distinction between the official worships consecrated by Roman usage and innovations. He evinced profound respect for the former and disdained the latter. In Athens he had been initiated into the Eleusinian Mysteries, but in Egypt he had refused to look at the ox Apis, and when his grandson travelled in Judea he congratulated him on having refrained from offering prayer in the Temple of Jerusalem.[4]

Nothing, therefore, could be more natural than that he should think of restoring the peace of the gods and by it

---

[1] Book vi of the *Aeneid* is impregnated with Pythagorean doctrines. Cf. espy. Reinach, **CXXXVII**, iii, pp. 66-84 ; F. Cumont, " Lucrèce et le symbolisme pythagoricien des Enfers," in **XXI**, 1920, pp. 220-40.
[2] Ov., *Met.*, xv. 75 ff. ; in general, cf. Delatte, **LVIII**.
[3] Sen., *Epist.*, lxxiii. 15 ; cviii. 17 ; *Q.N.*, vii. 32. 2.
[4] Suet., *Aug.*, 93.

ensuring his own power and the prosperity of Rome. Horace seems, like a good courtier, to express his master's idea rather than his own when he warns the Romans that they will suffer for the impiety of their fathers so long as they do not restore the altars of the gods, their temples which are falling into ruin, and their images disfigured by black smoke. Augustus set himself the task of putting the dilapidated temples of Rome into good condition. In his will he glories in having repaired eighty-two.[1] Livy calls him the " founder and restorer of all the temples." [2] To enforce respect for religion, he also proceeded to raise the dignity of the priestly offices, which were henceforward to be reserved to Senators and Knights. He declared that if he had himself had a daughter fulfilling the required conditions he would have been proud to make her a Vestal. After rebuilding the Temple of Vesta he installed her priestesses in the Regia. He esteemed it an honour to be himself a member of the old Arval Brotherhood, which he caused the princes of his family to enter. The very old procession of the Luperci had fallen into disuse ; he restored the custom. Every year he repeated, in their most ancient form, the ceremonies of the alliance with the Latins. In short, he combined the archaistic traditionalism of his policy with fear of the gods. As in the celebration of the Secular Games, he tried to stir the hearts of the people by the splendour of the official religious ceremonies and to associate it bodily with the rebirth of the old religion.

Own the gods for your masters, Horace proclaims, and you establish the dominion of Rome—*Dis te minorem quod geris, imperas.*[3] The same reverence will establish the power of their restorer. So Augustus was careful to consecrate every stage in his political career by a gift to the gods. As avenger of Caesar, he built a temple to Mars Ultor. After the victory of Actium, he placed the new order of things under the protection of Apollo, who was given a temple on the Palatine beside the palace which the ruler was building for himself. Thus, opposite the Capitol, the hill of Romulus became like a new acropolis of Imperial Rome. It always remained the hill of the Emperors.

Respect for forms, especially in religious matters, made

[1] *Mon. Anc.*, iv. 17.   [2] iv. 20.   [3] *Od.*, iii. 6.

Augustus wait for Lepidus to die, in 12 B.C., before assuming the office of Pontifex Maximus. But once he held this office he revived the tradition of the College in all its rigour. In restoring the official religion, he wanted to free it from the superstition which stifled it. With this intent, he hunted down all collections of prophecies and books of ritual not authorized by the State, as had been done after the Punic Wars. We are told that he collected over twenty thousand, which he caused to be solemnly burned. But he carefully saved the Sibylline Books, making, it is true, a selection from their oracles. Those which he preserved, he had deposited in the pedestal of the statue of Palatine Apollo.[1] He thus had them in his keeping, almost under his hand. With the help of the College of Quindecimvirs, of which he was president, he could be sure of finding in them a satisfactory solution of any difficulty which might present itself.

The influence and example of the head of the State certainly brought about a return to the old practices of the national worship, at least in the middle classes, who as a rule hardly pretended to liberty of religious thought, and were more or less disposed to follow the prevailing fashion in this matter. To do so was a manifestation of loyalty to the political system which ensured peace and prosperity. This new piety was also a reaction against rationalism and philosophical conceptions regarding the gods. Horace shows this very clearly : [2] " I was a niggardly and infrequent worshipper of the gods while I strayed, learned in insane wisdom. Now I must turn about and sail once more in courses which I had left." So Jupiter and Mars and Apollo and all the gods, great and small, again had worshippers, whom the ruler brought to them in his train. How long would they keep them ?

It was a paradoxical undertaking on the part of Augustus, to revive piety towards an essentially political religion in the people which he excluded from political life. He was astute enough to see this. So it was not only in the past that he sought his means of action. He was careful not to neglect the forms of religious sentiment still living. By the side of the official cults, he strove to give an official constitution to the popular cults and to associate them with the

---

[1] Suet., *Aug.*, 32 ; Tac., *Ann.*, vi. 12.   [2] *Od.*, i. 34.

State religion. His restoration was accompanied by innovations intended to bring tradition into harmony with the present.

Thus, in particular, he brought back to life the religious associations of the cross-roads, which had been broken up as factors of disorder. With his passion for order and organization he wanted to concentrate their scattered forces and make use of them. He made their old independence subject to the favours and obligations of a regular institution.

This important reform came as a consequence of the municipal reorganization of Rome. In 7 B.C. Augustus divided the city into fourteen districts, *regiones*, and each district into wards, *vici*. He gave each ward, for a centre, an altar of the Lares, round which he reorganized one of the colleges which in old days had formed spontaneously. But to the Lares of the *vicus* he added the Genius of the sovereign, the common head and father of the whole people of the city. This official admission of the Genius of a man, and of a living man, among the Lares was in no way new or alien to Roman religious conceptions. At Delos and Pompeii we commonly find the Genius of the paterfamilias and the Juno of the mistress of the house associated with the Penates and Lares about the family altar. It was the usual expression of the devotion and gratitude of the members of the family, servants, and clients to the patron who kept them alive. It was natural that outside the house, in the streets of the city, the craftsmen, whether freedmen or slaves, should honour as the father of that immense family, the people, the ruler who gave them their prosperity, and, moreover, heaped gifts on their associations. The idea was no doubt suggested to them officially ; there was no reason why they should not adopt it with enthusiasm. Long before the year 7 Horace had shown the Italian peasant placing the image of Augustus beside those of his household gods.

"He plies you with many a prayer, with wine poured from bowls, and mingles your name with the Lares, as the Greeks honour the memory of Castor and great Hercules." [1]

The worship of the Genius of Augustus at the altar of the

[1] *Od.*, iv. 5. 32 ff.

Lares was simply the religious form of the people's affection for the person of the Emperor.

The popular worship of the Lares thus became an administrative institution. The presidents of the colleges henceforward appeared with the prerogatives and costume of priestly and municipal officials ; they were the official heads of their wards and were very proud of it. Their office consisted not only in organizing religious feasts at the altar of the *vicus*, but also in helping with the census, doing police work, and putting out fires. The many monuments, in the form of carved altars and inscriptions, which remain of the cult of the *Lares Augustales* or of the Lares and of the Genius of Augustus show us how flourishing it was.

III

THE WORSHIP OF ROME AND AUGUSTUS

Not only in Rome and Italy, but all over the Empire, the Imperial religion found the inspiration for new worships. Greece the maker of myths and, above all, Asia, where the religious form dominated ideas, took active part in the moral and intellectual life of Rome. In spite of Roman pride and the scornful aloofness of Augustus towards foreign cults, it was inevitable that Oriental thought, which had such an influence on private religion, should also have some effect on the religion of the State. It was, indeed, the East which furnished the original idea with which Augustus crowned his restoration. The temple, designed on the traditional plan and carefully rebuilt of the old materials, received on its pediment the deified images of Rome and Augustus. The capital and the master of the world were conceived as gods, and this myth, so contrary to the old Latin spirit, became the new symbol of the Imperial religion.

The personification of an abstract idea like Honour, Virtue, or Victory was one of the usual processes of the Greek mind. The endowment of an entity like a province or a city with human form was only one of the manifestations of the anthropomorphism which made Greek religion. The Romans adopted this type of representation as soon as they found themselves, in Campania, in direct contact with the Hellenized regions of Italy. As early as the first half of the IIIrd century B.C. Rome appears on Romano-Campanian *denarii* in the form of a heroized female figure.[1] When the Greeks were liberated in 196, in their enthusiasm they associated Rome with Zeus himself, and in the very next year Smyrna raised the first temple to the new goddess. The idea of viewing the conquering city as a deity and honouring her as such spread rapidly in Asia. Several cities instituted games in her honour, as was done in honour of the gods. The Romans made no objection ; their pride was hardly surprised at the flattery. A statue of Rome at Delos appears to go back to the Ist century B.C. One may ask if, on this island where East and West met at this time, Rome figured as a goddess or if her image was a mere personification. But the whole of Asia and even Athens became accustomed to regard as a deity the city whose power overthrew kingdoms and ruled over nations far and wide.

The East deifies all its masters. Alexander allowed himself to be turned into a god. His successors copied him. When Caesar was in Alexandria he saw no objection to letting himself be proclaimed a god and son of a god, and Antony after him was a new Dionysos for his Eastern subjects. Even Octavian, when, after Actium, he stayed in Egypt and travelled through Asia, assumed quite another character than in Rome. Having become the master by his victory, he appeared to the peoples as a god mightier than all those whom he had conquered. The portraits of him executed in the East at this time show him as the successor of the Diadochi, wearing, like them, either the jewelled circlet or the rayed diadem, both insignia of divine kingship. These attributes, circlet and diadem, do not appear on any of his Roman portraits. In the East he was king and god ; in Rome he refused to be more than the first magistrate of the Republic and the Imperator or victorious general. In Asia his subjects built temples to him ; a refusal would not have been understood. He was content to make it a condition that his worship should be associated with that of the goddess Rome and that no Roman should be admitted to take part in it.[2] The

[1] E. Maynial, **LVI,** s.v. *Roma,* pp. 875 ff.　　　　[2] Dio C., li. 20.

provinces of the West eagerly vied with those of the East. Their zeal, the spontaneous homage of the conquered to the conqueror, was to become for Rome an instrument of domination.

An altar of Rome and Augustus was erected first at Tarraco (Tarragona). In 12 B.C. that of Lyons was inaugurated, which was the centre of an association of representatives of all the peoples of Gaul. A Gaul was the high-priest of this religion, which was alien to Rome, yet symbolized Roman power and the new form of the empire of the world. When Augustus thought that Germany might be considered as conquered as far as the Elbe, and wanted to make a Roman province of it, the sign of the union was the erection in the country of the Ubii of an altar of Rome and Augustus, served by the most noble of the Germans won over to the Roman cause. The altar of the Ubii, beside which Cologne arose, was to be the capital of Roman Germany. This was the real political worship of the new empire, the religious bond between the capital and the provinces, the sign of spiritual communion between the diverse peoples blended together in the Roman Peace.

But in Rome neither Rome nor Augustus was a deity. Roman tradition was opposed to ideas of the kind. The surname " Augustus," which came to be used as the sovereign's own name, brought him nearer to the gods, but did not assimilate him to them. " He shares his name with supreme Jupiter," says Ovid. " Our fathers called holy things ' august ' ; ' august ' was the word for the temples, duly consecrated by the priests." [1] The person and power of the sovereign were holy things, that is, consecrated to the gods and approved by them, but they were not divine things. Flattery and the influence of Eastern ways of thought tended, from the reign of Augustus onwards, to obliterate this distinction. The Imperial power, as it really was, namely, the concentration of supreme authority in the hands of one man, was the Roman version of Eastern kingship, of which divinity was the attribute. The spirit which developed round this monarchy was that of the East. Augustus lent himself to it, being only too glad of the authority and prestige conferred on him by this undue homage.

[1] *Fasti,* i. 609 ff.

Only after his death was he officially deified, as Caesar had been. Apotheosis was a more or less spontaneous expression of gratitude, which the Romans did not bestow on the Emperor until he had left them. The supposition was that he could not have failed to take a place among the gods. At the time of the funeral of Augustus, a retired Praetor was found who declared on oath that he had seen the Emperor's image fly from the pyre towards the sky.[1] A story was current, later, that an eagle had escaped from the pyre and borne his soul to Olympus.[2] Livia dedicated a temple to her husband

FIG. 16.—The Apotheosis of Antoninus and Faustina.[3] Base of the *Pigna*, in the garden of the Vatican.

on the Palatine.[4] In his own good time Tiberius built another near the Forum, which was only inaugurated by Caligula.[5] Except when he had discredited himself with his successor in advance, the late Emperor received the title of *divus* as a matter of course. "I feel I am becoming a god," was Vespasian's joke, when he felt the first symptoms of the malady which was to carry him off.[6]

Uncertain and extremely various as were Roman beliefs

[1] Suet., *Aug.*, 100. [2] Dio C., lvi. 34 ; lxxi. 5.
[3] On the ground are the Campus Martius with its obelisk and the goddess Rome, seated. A winged Genius and two eagles bear the Imperial couple heavenwards. The Genius holds in his left hand a globe, round which a serpent coils, the ancient symbol of immortality bound to the earth. Cf. p. 368 and Virg., *Aen.*, v. 84 ff.
[4] Pliny, *N.H.*, xii. 19. 42. [5] Dio C., lvi. 46 ; lix. 9.
[6] Suet., *Vesp.*, 23.

PLATE XVI

1. Garden. Wall-painting from the Villa of Livia at Prima Porta.
2. The Great Cameo of France. (Paris, Bibl. Nat.)

[face p. 380

regarding the next world, the idea of making a man into a god, even after his death, was not Roman. For the Romans, the Manes of their ancestors were divine, without doubt, no less than the Genius which animated every man during his life. It was lawful to offer sacrifice and prayer to Manes and Genii. But neither Manes nor Genii were upper gods. They were tied either to the body or to the earth ; they might have altars, but not temples ; they dwelt here below, not in heaven. It was the East which conceived of the flight of souls to heaven and confounded the Genii of the earth and the true gods.[1] Immediately after the death of Augustus, Roman opinion blamed him for having usurped the honours reserved to the upper gods and for having accepted, like them, temples, cult-statues, priests, and flamens.[2] In the same way Cicero, soon after Caesar's death, had protested against the confusion of the honours rendered to a man with the worship of the true gods.

"How can one address supplications to a dead man, who has his tomb at which to receive funeral honours ? . . . May the immortal gods forgive the people and the Senate for this sacrilege, of which they are innocent ! "[3]

The apotheosis decreed to Caesar and his successors is, Lucan declares, a punishment of the gods who allowed the Republic to perish.[4] Seneca, too, makes fun of it all through the *Apocolocyntosis*, and his mocking is simply the echo of Western common-sense against the fancies brought in by the East.

"Who has given me all the details which follow about the manner in which Claudius was received among the gods? If I must quote my authority, go and ask the man who saw Drusilla rise to the sky ; he will also tell you how he saw Claudius take flight thither. Whether he wishes or not, this individual cannot fail to see everything that goes on in heaven ; he is the custodian of the Appian Way, by which, as you know well, Augustus and Tiberius went up to the gods."

[1] The eagle which bears them away is Syrian. Cf. F. Cumont, " L'Aigle funéraire des Syriens et l'apothéose des empereurs," in *Rev. Hist. Relig.*, lxii (1910), pp. 119 ff. The Great Cameo of France, in the Bibliothèque Nationale, represents the apotheosis of Augustus. (Pl. XVI. 2.) This cameo, cut in 17 A.D., must be the work of a son of the Dioscurides whom Augustus had brought from Asia Minor. At the top, above Tiberius enthroned with Livia, we see the deified Aeneas in Phrygian dress and, immediately behind him, Augustus crowned with the Oriental diadem. On his right is Drusus. The fourth inhabitant of heaven, riding a winged horse led by a Love, is, according to Furtwaengler, Marcellus. Is it not rather Caesar, son of Venus, to whom Aeneas brings the empire of the world ?

[2] Tac., *Ann.*, i. 10.   [3] *Phil.*, i. 6. 13.
[4] *Phars.*, vii. 756.

The memory of the apotheosis of Caesar made the apotheosis of Augustus a necessity, and the example of the first Emperor became a law for his successors.[1] It was flattery pure and simple, and was not taken seriously by anybody. As for the deification of Rome and Augustus, it was not accepted in the capital of the Empire until long afterwards, in the IInd century, when the fashions, ideas, and religious feelings of the East finally triumphed in Rome. Hadrian was the first to give official recognition and sanction to the worship of the deified State, by having the Temple of Rome and Venus built on the Sacred Way, near the Arch of Titus. Venus, the mother of the line of Aeneas, and not the Emperor himself, was associated with Rome. Not until the end of the IIIrd century, when the Empire was transformed into a completely Oriental monarchy, was the person of the living sovereign considered as a god.[2] By that time Roman religion was no more than a faded tradition, on the point of disappearing altogether.

IV

THE RESULTS OF THE AUGUSTAN RESTORATION

Reinstated by Augustus in its honours and its official forms, Roman religion would pursue its pompous way for centuries yet. The personal authority of Augustus, the example of his piety, and the genuine enthusiasm aroused in the greater part of the people by his work as a whole, imposed it not only on the generation which had suffered from the Civil Wars and had at one moment dreaded the collapse of Rome before the East, but on all the later generations which came to regard the Augustan age as the ideal and the rule of the new political state of the world. Religion was more closely bound to the State than ever ; it was not so much a means of government as the very expression and symbol of the authority of Rome over the earth. The Roman gods really appeared as the soul of the Empire.

---

[1] On this subject and the many works of art which it inspired, see Strong, **CLII.** See also the short article by G. Boissier, **LVI,** s.v. *Apotheosis*, pp. 325-6.
[2] On this subject see Toutain, **CLXII,** i (1907), espy. pp. 19, 37, 62.

From the political point of view, the conception was perfect and altogether met the circumstances. But it is not enough for a religion to be purely political; it needs a mythological or philosophical legend, and, above all, it needs an emotional, sentimental atmosphere. The legend of the Augustan religion was pale and its philosophy weak, and emotion and sentiment were altogether lacking. On every side its artificiality was too apparent.

Like its poet Virgil, Augustan religion definitely renounced any pretension to penetrate the principle of things. No doubt this was not its purpose. But by this renunciation it also renounced the adherence of anyone in Rome who had learnt to think. Once enthusiasm for the work of the restorer of the Empire and of its gods had passed, the " insane wisdom " of which Horace speaks inevitably came into its own again. Nor was it long in doing so. The successor of Augustus, Tiberius, for all his love of the old Roman tradition, professed utter indifference about the gods and their worship because, Suetonius says, " he was given to mathematics, and was convinced that everything was governed by necessary laws." [1]

As for those who, without being mathematicians or philosophers, did not find complete satisfaction of their religious needs at the fire of the household altar or in the rejoicings of the cross-roads, they gathered very little comfort from the solemn sacrifices on the Capitol. The great gods of the national religion, being occupied in watching over the safety of the Empire, were too remote from their daily thoughts to stir their feelings. In the country the rustic gods were still sufficient for the peasant, and would long continue to be. But in the towns the mystery religions, that of Bacchus and those of the East, had a stronger attraction than ever. They were the very thing to fill the gap which was left by the too purely political restoration of the founder of the Empire.

These religions represented a principle exactly opposite to that of the national Roman religion. The Roman gods were gods of the city; man approached them chiefly as a citizen. In the beliefs of the East, on the other hand, as M. Cumont

---

[1] *Tib.*, 69: *Circa deos et religiones negligentior, quippe addictus mathematicae, persuasioneque plenus cuncta fato agi.*

says,[1] " religion ceases to be bound to the State and becomes universal. It is conceived, not as a public duty, but as a personal obligation. It does not subordinate the individual to the city, but claims, above all, to ensure his particular safety in this world and, still more, in the next. The Oriental mysteries all revealed to their initiates radiant prospects of eternal bliss. Thus the axis of morality was shifted. The supreme good was no longer sought on this earth, as by the old Greek philosophers, but after death. Men no longer acted with a view to tangible realities, but in order to attain ideal hopes. Earthly existence was conceived as a preparation for a blessed life, an ordeal the result of which must be infinite felicity or pain. The whole notion of ethical values was thus overthrown." The triumph of these ideas meant the ruin of the Roman religion and State alike, whose kingdom was of this world and not of the next.

Yet the care expended by Augustus on religious restoration was not altogether vain.

The Roman gods perished, but the fabric of the official administration of religious matters survived. Whether they believed or not, the Emperors after Augustus all clung equally to the office of Pontifex Maximus and performed its functions as one of their chief duties. The history of Roman religion under the Empire is bound up in a way with that of the religious conceptions of each Emperor. It became Stoic with Marcus Aurelius and completely Oriental with the Severi. By the side of the Emperors and under their authority, the College of Pontifices, flamens, Quindecimvirs, augurs, continued to manage the details of official worship, maintaining on traditional lines priestly bodies like the Vestals and religious colleges like the Salii, Luperci, and Arval Brothers. Even when the Romans had ceased in their hearts to revere their gods, the cult went its way imperturbably. When all religious sentiment was dead, the rites of the national gods and the divine honours paid to Rome and the Emperor were more than ever regarded as the symbol and sign of Roman patriotism. Religion had become nationality.

The official administration of the cult even survived the cult itself. When Christianity was triumphant, the Emperors persisted in regarding the direction of religious matters as

[1] LV, p. xix.

one of the essential functions of their power. We find Constantine interfering in a council of theologians. Shorn of her Empire, Rome kept her Sovereign Pontiff who, surrounded by his priestly colleges, has the same authority over rites and worship as the Emperor in old times and, before him, the religious magistrates of the Republic.

Augustus was not able to renovate the old national religion of Rome, because he could not give it back a soul. But he restored all the external fabric indestructibly.

The temple which he built has remained empty. The gods, great and small, have vanished from his Pantheon, but its masonry has conquered the centuries.

THE IMPERIAL RELIGION

CONCLUSION

THE ROMAN SPIRIT

THE religion, literature, and art of the age of Augustus appear as the most perfect expression of that Roman spirit of which we have followed the formation and progress from the beginnings of the city. By the end of the Republic it had reached its full maturity. After assimilating the elements of civilization of all ancient Italy, it had sat at the feet of Greece with passionate enthusiasm and had entered into full possession of the knowledge and crafts of the Hellenistic world. The age of Augustus, the half-century of his reign, shows us the complete mastery of the Romans in every branch of intellectual activity. Rome did not equal Greece in every domain ; in some she surpassed Greece, and by far, at least the Greece of that time ; in all she sought a new path and attained a perfection which she never surpassed or even reached afterwards. This period indeed marks the apogee of her spirit.

When we speak of a " Roman spirit," there is no question, one must repeat, of an unchangeable force, a coherent aggregate of faculties supposed to belong peculiarly to the people, let alone the race. If there is a people which lacks unity of origin and affords no possibility of really determining its ethnic substance, it is the Roman people. What is it ? The Romans themselves attached only minor importance to the question, and they were right. I have tried at the beginning of this work to show how it was gradually formed of a mixture of autochthons, called Siculians, of Aborigines, who were wandering tribes, probably of European origin, and, later, of Latins, Sabines, and Etruscans, themselves the result of very undetermined mixtures. I have shown how Rome had steadily increased her store by elements of varying importance taken from the conquered nations of Italy and the whole

Mediterranean basin—ideas, arts, and men. The population of the city itself, which gave Roman civilization its tone, was constantly being renewed. The ruling aristocracy was doubtless more stable ; yet, in the course of the centuries of Roman history, it was completely reconstituted several times. How many of the old patrician families of the Republic still existed in the time of Augustus ? Mommsen reckoned no more than about thirty. In population as in the world of ideas, the chief faculty of the Roman people was power of assimilation.

We need not, therefore, join those who look to heredity for the explanation of the fortunes of individuals and peoples. We may even renounce any attempt to see in their history the continuous development of qualities and defects ascribed— hypothetically, of course—to the alleged primitive nucleus. " A people of peasants and soldiers," someone will say of the Romans. They possibly were, but they were much more besides, and that from the beginning. Nor have we any reason for supposing that the later periods of a people's history have less influence on its spirit than its origins and early periods ; they may even have more. The Roman spirit never *was ;* it gradually grew ; it was made up of the very vicissitudes of Roman development, of the work and efforts of Rome, of her successive acquisitions, of her troubles no less than of her triumphs.

If, in spite of the renewing of the population and the increase of ideas, which was very rapid at certain periods, we observe a certain consistency in the evolution of Roman civilization, we may attribute it chiefly to the intellectual and moral atmosphere which surrounded the Romans, old and new, to the social tradition handed down from generation to generation by the family, by groups of every kind, and above all by the State. But this tradition was created by history, by the economic and political conditions of life, by neighbourhood and contact, by events, sometimes even by chance circumstances, and often by individuals. The great men who set famous examples and, still more, the great writers whose works influenced the thought and imagination of their fellow-citizens, played an effective part in determining the spirit of the people. They were both agents and reagents ; they felt the influence of their surroundings and of events, and they reflected it, like a " resonant echo," for their contemporaries and the generations to come. Thus it was that religion, literature, and art were the highest expressions of the Roman spirit and were at the same time among the primordial forces which made it.

So the Roman spirit shows itself to us as the succession of different aspects which it presented. First of all it was religious ; at the beginning we shall place the *Gods*. Then the Roman State, once it was constituted, exercised a stronger, more effective, and more lasting influence on the soul of the people than anything else. The second aspect of the Roman spirit will be the *City*. When it became a great state, the City was invaded by the Mediterranean life over which it ruled. The mythology, politics, arts, and letters of Hellas taught it *Play*. But Greek thought was also philosophy and science. The Roman mind learned from it to study and to know man. This knowledge was developed remarkably in the literature and art of Rome. *Humanity* seems also to be a characteristic feature of the Roman spirit.

I

THE GODS

Fustel de Coulanges once noted the primordial importance of the gods in the ancient city, and modern scholarship, only limiting the range of some of his statements, confirms the fundamental justice of his contention. At the beginning the Romans lived with the gods, moving among them, for the whole world seemed to them divine. The gods dominated all their primitive civilization. There was as yet no speculative thought, nor politics, nor law, nor art properly so called ; religion expressed the whole ideal, and everything was merged in it. From religion the different forms of intellectual activity proceeded, and for a long time they continued to bear the mark of the gods. We know hardly anything of this early period, but later ages have preserved traces of it. In the classical epoch we find the old gods still powerful at the domestic hearth, in the country, and at the street crossings in the towns where the common people met. The official religion kept in its calendar and rites the memory of the ancient omnipresence of the gods. Historical tradition, born of the altar, enables us to recover the essential features of these outworn conceptions.

Godhead, in Rome, never seems to have been sullen or ill-natured ; it showed itself modest, friendly, obliging and helpful, and sedulous in its duty of protection. It was content with the sacrifice of the fruits of the earth and libations of milk. It was reasonable and, above all, just ; it expected its due, but was entirely without caprice. Let every man pay his due share to the gods, and every god will do his duty and all will give their peace to men. These gods did not ask to be known, still less loved. They had no myths ; they taught nothing ; they demanded no sentiment. They only responded to perfect regularity in formulas and rites. They clearly lacked breadth of view, and were not in any way cut out for the empire of the world ; they were the gods of a matter-of-fact, hard-working people, lacking in sensibility and free from spiritual unrest.

Moreover, they did not reign alone in Rome—far from it. By their side we see, at the very beginning, gods with more extensive power, apparently inherited from the prehistoric past of Italy. Such, in particular, were Saturn and Mother Earth. As men mingled, they mingled their gods, among whom mutual contamination and imitation took place. Then came the Etruscan gods, likewise born of the fusion of the native deities with others belonging to a more advanced but darker civilization. In the Hellenic manner, Etruria conceived its gods in human form, imagined ties of kinship between them, gave them adventures, and associated them in groups. An Etruscan trias was the first to reign on the Capitol. Etruscan religion possessed a theology and even, it seems, a cosmogony ; it knew the dwelling of the gods in heaven, the details of their influence on earth, and the law of the underworld where they reigned over death. It had colleges of specialist priests, schools, books of doctrine, and books of ritual. Everything was regulated exactly and methodically. The Romans adopted all the essentials of this scientific organization and in particular, it seems, the priestly colleges. This Etruscan organization presided over the birth of an intellectual life in Rome. The laws of the

Kings, which were the beginning of Roman law, the computation of the years, the reckoning of the *saecula*, the calendar, the *Fasti*, the registers and, later, the *Annals* of the Pontifices, which were the beginning of history, the images of the gods, the music and the rhythm of the words which accompanied sacrifice, perhaps, too, the freer lays in which the adventures of men were mingled with those of gods, the ceremonial of religious feasts, the plays with their dancing and comic dialogue, all these deep roots of literature and art first grew about the altar and were fertilized by its ashes. Not the adventures of warriors and mariners awoke the life of the intellect in Rome, as in Greece, but the wisdom of priests.

Soon there came to join the company of the Etruscan gods some of the freer, brighter deities of Magna Graecia and Sicily. With Castor and Pollux, the divine Horsemen, and Apollo, and the great deities of skilful agriculture and the vine, there appeared in Rome a gleam of Pythagorean mysticism and the oracles of Cumae, laden with Hellenic mythology and ritual. Roman religion was disposed to welcome foreign gods, but the Pontifices who watched over it subjected the new-comers to the minute laws of a tradition already established, selecting among them, prescribing where their sanctuaries should stand, and cautiously acclimatizing cults and ceremonies.

This work went on for centuries, according to circumstances, which brought into Rome most of the gods of Italy and then of Greece, and some of those of the East. In the classical period there were a Graeco-Roman official religion and, beneath it, a popular religion which was still Italic. As the Roman mind advanced, religious thought grew weaker and, as it were, became empty of content. The divine figures survived, shut up in their temples, as the symbols of abstract conceptions in which there was no longer anything religious. The externals of religion, the worship and its administration, remained intact, but they were no longer sustained by piety, but by a more recent idea, that of the City.

II

THE CITY

Constituted under the aegis of the gods, the City gradually emancipated itself from their control and lived its own life. This evolution must have begun in the period of the Kings. The Wolf of the Capitol was already a political rather than a religious symbol. The Republican revolution, or whatever the event was which separated Rome from Etruria, committed the city to a principle of national autonomy in which reason seems already to have played more part than religious sentiment. The constitution of the Decemvirs, the Laws of the Twelve Tables, the imitation of the legislative effort of Pythagorean Magna Graecia, mark the appearance of the secular State ; the reign of the gods is followed by that of the City.

This phase in Roman history stamped the Roman spirit with one of its most characteristic aspects. In every branch of activity and in every age we find in Rome the civic idea. The State, its life, its interest, hold first place in the soul of the Roman. The spirit of the people seems to have been fashioned by the State itself.

For nearly three centuries, down to the end of the second Punic War, life seems to have been hard for the young city of Rome, between her former Etruscan masters and her neighbours, Latins, Sabines, Aequi, Volsci, and others. For Rome to emerge victorious from this continual struggle, all had to be strictly subordinate to the ruling aristocracy. Hence arose habits of strict discipline, complete self-sacrifice to the common good, and patriotism always on the alert. Hence, too, came the ruling concern for utility, the contempt of imagination, the hardness of heart, the fear of novelty. Thus was formed the spirit, at once energetic and unenterprising, fiercely combative and prompt to obey, ardent and routine-ridden, ready to give up everything for the City and full of hostile distrust of the foreigner, which is embodied in the elder Cato and stands as the ideal of Roman virtue.

The City, represented by the authoritative, meticulous Senate, made everything serve itself, its gods first of all.

The gods were identified with the City; they were the servants of its interests. This was certainly how Augustus conceived them when he resuscitated the old tradition.

In the life of every man the State came first. For the City he had to marry and have children, for the City he must live, for the City it was glorious to die. He served the City when he tilled his fields, and he served it when he used his mind or his gift of words, either to defend his fellow-citizens or to attack those whose acts or tendencies seemed contrary to the common good. The struggles of parties were one of the forms taken by patriotism. All watched and criticized one another in the public interest. The Roman people was an army in which the efforts of each were constantly bent on the safety of all and the glory of the City.

Art, born of the reign of the gods, was brought into the service of the State, like religion itself and the life of the citizen. It still, no doubt, served to build and adorn temples, and gave the gods their form, but it was also used to commemorate good citizens, those who had deserved well of the City. From the early ages of the Republic, we hear of numbers of honorary statues, glorious examples exhibited for the citizens to emulate. This was another tradition which Augustus restored to honour. In a family, the portraits of ancestors and the inscriptions recording their names and careers were similarly a constant exhortation to civic virtue. Art also served to glorify the City by honouring the triumphs of victorious leaders. In the procession, which reproduced the religious pomp of the Games, among the choirs of singers and *histriones* and the waggons laden with spoil, paintings were borne, representing the great deeds of the campaign and the appearance of the conquered provinces. Chance has given us a single funerary painting in Rome, the fresco of the Esquiline. It depicts various incidents of war, and not, like the Etruscan pictures, religious ceremonies in honour of the dead or scenes of the life underground. Honorary statues, portraits, and historical pictures were the products of an art subordinated to the interest of the State. We find the same vein in the official art of the age of Augustus and of the whole Empire. Beauty had a public function, as it were. This is the cause of the solemn, formal appearance of art, its too reasonable coldness, its tendency to slavish accuracy in detail, its pedestrian realism.   The artist was too obviously doing a task which had been imposed on him.

Given utility as the end and reason as the means, we understand why, under the Empire, architecture became the Roman art above all others.   In Imperial architecture the Imperial idea triumphed.   Temples, palaces, and public monuments manifested the power and munificence of the sovereign.   Pride gave them their colossal dimensions.   The richness of their decoration displayed the wealth of the Roman people.   Their lines and forms generally seem to have been chosen with a view to embellishing Rome with all the styles flourishing in the provinces which were brought into fashion by their prosperity or by the favour of the Emperor.   A history of this architecture would be the best illustration of the history of the Empire and of the Emperors themselves.

It seems almost superfluous to lay emphasis once again on the important part played by the civic and political idea in Roman literature as a whole.   At the very beginning of the literary period, national feeling and patriotism give the epics of Naevius and Ennius their originality.   In composing his songs, the poet remains a soldier, a citizen, and a Roman. It is for the greater glory of Rome that he endeavours to bring the Muses within her walls.   The patriotic inspiration of the old Roman epic is what animates the *Aeneid* under Augustus ; the wholly Roman concern for social utility is what takes Virgil from the *Eclogues* to the *Georgics*.   To preach morality, to correct folly, to enjoin sense and moderation for the good of the City, is the task undertaken by the satirists, from Lucilius to Horace and even to Juvenal and Persius.   In them, the poet turns censor.   In prose, the life of the City inspires eloquence.   The proof of it is, that under the Empire oratory, once it is excluded from the Forum, loses all its character, and becomes, as in Greece, mere academic declamation.   As for history, I have tried to show how its interest and its weakness lie in the fact that it always subordinated the investigation and exposition of facts to political passion or to a moralizing ideal of patriotism.   So the purpose of some Roman poetry and all Roman prose was action for the greater advantage of the City.   The ever-present thought of the State was one of the essential features of the Roman spirit, in religion and in life, in art and in literature.

III

PLAY

But Rome was not only a city, solidly planted on the ground, and fighting with all her might for the possession of the soil and material goods. She was also a commercial town, a crossing-point, a bridge, as she has been called, and almost a port. As soon as the Roman left his walls, westward or southward, he encountered Mediterranean life. He could never shut himself off from it. When, victorious by land and sea, he reached first the Hellenic peninsula and soon afterwards Asia, he was already quite prepared for the teaching of Greece. The Greek imagination soon ruled Rome and taught her to play.

In religion, play consists in the divine fables which are related because they are agreeable and present pleasing pictures to the mind, without it being necessary to inquire what reality they represent. Everyone embellishes and interprets them as he fancies ; without asserting their truth, and without taking the pains to deny it, he finds in them the meaning or symbol which pleases him. In art, play is the fancy of line and colour, familiar or heroic scenes representing mythological legends, Bacchus and his rout, the thousand statues of Venus and deified beauty, the sport of the Loves, pastorals, a rustic altar beneath an old garland-laden tree, exotic landscapes, illusions of architecture, arabesques, flowers and foliage, everything that diverts the mind and the eye. It is music, the skilfully modulated human voice and the accompaniment of various stringed instruments which supplanted the flute ; it is song and it is dance. It is the dramatic performances which turn the religious ceremony into an entertainment for men ; it is all tragedy, which shows the spirit of adventure in every deed, and the comedy of Plautus, which pelts the people with jests in their own language, laden with mirth. It is the didactic fancy of Ennius, imagining the dream of Epicharmos, the story of Euhemeros, and the culinary recipes of the *Heduphagetica*. It is the trivial poetry and lyricism of Catullus, Tibullus, Propertius, and Ovid. In language, it is the picturesqueness and music of words, their harmony and breadth, the construction of the period, and the diversity of the Greek metres which drove out the heavily stressed three-time of the Saturnian.

Play is the predominating aspect of art, literature, and even religion in Rome in the last century of the Republic. But its first manifestations are found much earlier, in the IVth century, in the decoration of the Praeneste caskets, and they must go back to the Etruscan period. Play holds its own, in spite of Augustus, all through his reign and down to the end of ancient civilization.

Play was Greek, but in Rome it took on a special aspect, by reason of the previous elements with which it conflicted or was combined. Coming after the utilitarian strictness imposed by the City, it was like an ebullition of adolescence too long kept under. In the time of Scipio it showed a fervour which was unknown in Greece. The new spirit violently threw over the traditional ideal of caution and submission. In the Gracchi it became generous revolutionary audacity. In life and even in art—in Catullus, for example—it was animated with passion, it became violent, it was always a little raw and easily degenerated into brutality. In an aristocracy greedy for wealth, power, and every kind of pleasure, it was expressed in unbounded and often rather vulgar ambition, in excessive luxury in buildings and furniture, and in a mixture of incongruous tastes, ultra-modern exoticism and archaism. It produced corruption and loose morals and was disgraced by gluttony.

In the people, the example of its rulers destroyed the ancient discipline and developed the spirit of faction. In the plebs play took the form of the listlessness which looked to the caprice of the great for food and amusement, of the increase of idleness, and of the coarseness of the shows of the circus and amphitheatre. The social and economic conditions of Roman life were not favourable to the refinement of minds. Moreover, the Hellenistic age was fundamentally aristocratic; intelligence and beauty remained a privilege of the few; and Rome itself had ceased to be a democratic city since the defeat of the Gracchi and the Dictatorship of Sylla.

The plastic arts, remaining in the hands of Greeks, continued to be purely Greek for a long time. But in the arts of the mind it was Romans who adapted Greek play to the taste of their fellow-citizens. Their efforts gave literature its originality. In general, Greek technique was adopted by the Romans in their practice of every order of intellectual activity. The poets accepted the metres, manners, and forms prevailing in the Hellenic world. Greek poetic art held sway in the drama, the lyric, and the didactic form. Even the subject-matter, at least in dramatic and lyric poetry, seems to have been Greek, being taken from heroic and mythical fable, images and treatment were usually imitations, and the very language was translated from Greek models. Yet in the elegiac, the most Greek of all the Roman forms, we see a tendency, growing more marked from Catullus to Tibullus and Propertius, to use the Hellenic form to express Roman subjects, ideas, and sentiments. The sons of a people made by fighting, the Roman elegiac-writers took even play seriously. They were not content to amuse themselves with it ; it was part of their life, they actually felt emotions which were often mere fiction to their masters, and they consequently expressed them with the more power.

So, too, the orators took all their technique from Greece. Their subject-matter was naturally Roman ; and so were the spirit and passion which animated their eloquence. The Romans went in for Greek play in the serious spirit inherited from their past, treating it almost as a duty. They brought into it an ardour not yet cooled by sceptical dilettantism, and applied its rules with the professional conscientiousness of men habituated to the practical tasks of life.

Above all, they usually blended play with the traditional interests of the Roman mind. Ennius set the example when he made use of all the resources of the Greek epic to glorify the history of Rome and to compose a national poem for his country. Virgil, the perfect disciple of the Greek Muses, the accomplished artist, who combines Greek legend with religious inspiration, patriotism, and a conscientiousness which is fundamentally Roman, represents in its living complexity the Roman spirit which adopted play to employ it for the good and glory of the City.

IV

THE KNOWLEDGE OF MAN

But Greek thought was not only artistic play ; it had also set itself to conceive the reality of the world and to understand universal life. As early as the Vth century B.C. the rational effort of Greece, in its Pythagorean form, seems to have had an influence on the infant Republic. This influence inevitably became stronger when Rome came into direct contact with Campania, Magna Graecia, and Sicily. But it was not until the IInd century that Greece Proper, Pergamon, and Alexandria began to teach the Romans philosophy and science. From the time of the second Scipio to that of Cicero, the Romans evinced equal enthusiasm for the teaching of Panaetios and of Poseidonios. Reflection and love of knowledge were also an aspect of their spirit.

In philosophy and science, however, they never rose beyond the rank of disciples. They were kept back by the principle of social utility which had become so powerful among them. I have tried to show how the cult of the city led to a pragmatism, not in the sense in which Polybius understood the word, but in its most modern acceptation. Doubtless pragmatism does not necessarily stifle the desire for knowledge. We find in Rome scholars full of passionate curiosity, from Varro to Pliny the Elder. But it subjects the life of the mind to laws which are not of the mind. It deprives it of its independence, and is prematurely concerned with the practical results of thought. It looks in science for possibilities of action and subordinates the search for the unknown to respect for what exists. Now, knowledge demands complete liberty. Reality is for it a starting-point, not a goal. From particular facts and series it rises by abstraction to general ideas. The idea, at least among the Greeks, had become the supreme reality. In the world of ideas nothing should arrest the course of logical reasoning. Science cares only for truth, heedless of the breaches which truth may make in the city. The Roman, on the contrary, feared such consequences ; he adhered to the objects of sense, to the concrete, he felt ill at ease among abstractions, he faltered in his reasoning, and changed his course as soon as his conclusions seemed likely to conflict with tradition. He did not allow pure reason ; he always held fast to practical reason.

It is therefore exceptional to find a Roman accepting a system of philosophy or a scientific method in its logical entirety. His eclecticism, his constant desire for the compromise of a happy mean, was simply care for practical considerations and fear of being taken by reasoning too far from the concrete. In philosophy, the New Academy, which tempered the idealism of Aristotle, received the most followers. By its side, Stoicism attracted by the strictness of its morality and the indulgence displayed in its metaphysics for traditional religious conceptions, but its dialectic was left alone. In the reign of Augustus, the religious tendencies of Stoicism were accentuated by being mingled with Pythagoreanism and Platonism. Later, Seneca made a sort of amalgamation of the moralities of Zeno and Epicurus ; it was true that one proceeded from idealism and the other from materialism, but what did it matter, if their precepts came to much the same thing in practice ? Public opinion, which was whole-heartedly espoused by such a distinguished thinker as Tacitus, evinced but little sympathy for those who strictly observed the Stoic tenets, in spite of the loftiness of their character and although they stood as champions against odious despotism. Their uncompromising attitude was too unpractical.

Only one Roman writer possessed sufficient intellectual energy to follow the logic of a system to its extreme conclusions, and that was Lucretius. Accordingly the legend transmitted by St Jerome presents him as a lunatic. Yet even in Lucretius what a thoroughly Roman interest in practical usefulness we find ! It is to cure his contemporaries of the fears and evils caused by ignorance that he has undertaken his arduous labour. With passionate devotion he sets himself to present the hard wisdom of his master in attractive form. Epicurus inspired his enthusiasm by his morality far more than by his natural science.

In science as in philosophy, we have found the Roman incapable of taking sides among the various theories and methods. Rationalism in medicine and analogy in grammar seemed to him perilous paths, which took him too far from reality. Empiricism and anomaly, on the other hand, did not at all satisfy his need of order. The Greeks had not succeeded in obtaining a doctrine of experimental science from the observation of facts. This would have been a fine task for the Roman mind, with its love of the concrete, to achieve. But it would have required too much patience, self-sacrifice, and faith in the power of reason and argument. The Roman, ever in a hurry to act, would not spend time over principles and methods ; between the two opposite ways, he adopted a middle course which gave him a general view but did not take him too high above facts. In his eyes, science was at bottom in no way different from a craft, it was a practical instrument, a means of action. Consequently he devoted himself to adapting, disseminating, and making use of the scientific activity of the Greeks. He became a compiler, but he would never be a great scientist, because he never wished to be a scientist and nothing more. Science does not owe the Roman spirit one idea or one method.

While they left the exploration of the material world to others, the Romans devoted all the efforts of their attention to the moral world. Everything concerning man, his character, and his conduct roused passionate interest in them. When Greek philosophy first made its appearance in Rome a circle of psychologists and moralists collected round Scipio Aemilianus. The comedy of Terence and the satire of Lucilius were the fruit of the first Roman speculations on the nature of man. So far as we can judge from the fragments which remain, tragedy was full of psychological analysis and moral discussion. Under Augustus, the mime, a degenerate and often licentious comedy, owed its literary value and at least part of its success to the strokes of true observation and the moral maxims which adorned it. Horace found subjects for his satires in the moral theory of Greek philosophy as much as in the follies of Rome. The study of man, in general, was regarded in Rome as the essential purpose of intellectual activity ; the knowledge of characters, sentiments, and passions was held to be the highest degree of mental culture. Literature, as a whole, had become " the humanities."

This knowledge of man was one of the characteristic

features which mingled in the Roman spirit with those which we have considered above. It made the Roman conscious of himself and of mankind in himself; all Roman works are deeply impregnated with this sense of human reality.

We recognize it in Lucretius, in the importance attached to psychological analysis, the exact description of impressions, and the picturesque indication of sentiment by action and attitude. It animates the *Georgics* of Virgil, in which man is seen through nature, and, far more still, the *Aeneid*, which is indebted to this feeling for the life of its characters and the vigour of its most striking episodes. So, too, in the play of the elegiac, we find, in Catullus, in Tibullus, and, above all, in Propertius, delicate analysis of all the sentiments attendant on love and moral discourses in a didactic spirit. Even in the plastic arts this scrupulous attention to moral life makes the originality of the Roman portrait and the interest of great compositions like the friezes of the Altar of Peace. The characters of men are revealed in their facial features and the whole attitude of their bodies. There is really a soul, giving its living truth to the image.

One can hardly insist too much on the place occupied by the study and knowledge of man in all Roman prose. Sallust's chief aim is to appear a profound psychologist and an austere moralist. Cicero reveals in all his writings his subtle knowledge of men and the character of man. The attention which he pays to moral truth appears not only in the essays which treat of morality, the *De Senectute* or the *De Amicitia*, but in all his other treatises. Whether they discuss eloquence or philosophy or law or any other subject, his speakers never talk in the abstract; beneath the theory borrowed from Greece the Latin writer sees the mankind to whom it must be applied, he does not lose sight of the effects it will produce in reality, and he is chiefly interested in sentiments and morals. In his speeches and letters, how he loves to linger over fine distinctions of ideas and passions! How surely, and often how delicately, he draws the portraits of his people, friends and opponents alike! Cicero saw almost too clearly into men's characters; that was one reason of the indecision of his acts and the uncertainty of his political opinions.

In history, above all, the constant care for human reality

gives Latin works a colour of their own. The idea of the city dominates the whole thought of Livy, but in the city he shows us men, or rather the Roman who in all times remains the same as the man whom Livy finds in himself or may have seen about him. The material elements of civilization and the aspect of past ages awake no curiosity in the Roman historian. Nowhere do we see a picture like that, for example, of early Greece, which Thucydides conjures up at the beginning of his work. Neither the economic interests nor even the political ideas, however rudimentary, which must have underlain the efforts of the early peoples of Italy are considered at all. The drama of history is played chiefly in the spirits of men, through their characters, their passions, and the acts to which these drive them. It may be said that this is abstract history. This is true in a measure, for it takes very little account of realities exterior to man. But it is also eminently concrete history, in virtue of all the humanity which it contains, the vividness of the portraits, the life and colour of the narrative, and the swing of the speeches. All this practical demonstration of psychology leads to lessons in morality. In the history of the people Livy chiefly sees individuals, he sees them absolutely clearly, as if they were alive before him, and what he first sees is, so to speak, the texture of their soul and the motive forces of their character.

This essentially psychological character of Roman history is found in still higher degree in Tacitus. The narrative is made to follow the play of sentiments in men's minds which gradually determines events. This inward life is painted in strokes of such vigour and reality that the picture impresses itself on the imagination. The moral truth is so intense that the critical effort and care for evidence which would make it historical truth seem superfluous. Even the soul of a crowd is analysed with the same delicate precision as that of an individual. Man is always in the foreground, in the full light. The interest is concentrated, not on his exterior, which is usually hardly suggested, but on qualities of character, which are scrutinized with severe perspicacity. The minds of men, which the study of the past of Rome has accustomed to this strict observation of the human heart, have not been able to forget it. Rightly or wrongly, they find it difficult not to place man in the foreground in history, and, in any

2 c

case, can no longer be content with portraits which are no more than rough sketches or conventional figures.

The epigrams of Martial and all the philosophical works of Seneca show the same attention to conduct and moral life. The knowledge of man and the regulation of the smallest details of the life of his soul became the supreme aim of philosophy. Even religion, which had formerly concerned itself little with the conduct of men, became morality. Man is as much as God the object of the pious meditation of Marcus Aurelius. The "Know thyself" of Socrates had become, as it were, the motto of Roman thought. The qualities and even the defects developed by centuries of history combined to ensure for the Roman, in the knowledge of man, a mastery which, it seems to me, had not been equalled before, and in any case has had a profound influence on the modern world and, in particular, on the classical age of France.

V

THE ORIGINALITY OF THE ROMAN SPIRIT

So the gods, the City, play, and the knowledge of man were the essential concerns of the Roman mind. Coming one upon another, and constantly acting on one another, they gradually built up the spirit of the people. The deep sediment left by earlier ideas bore the later strata superimposed on them. Generally they were hidden, but it was they which determined the form of the surface. If a fault occurs, if a revolution overturns the soil formed by centuries, we see, as in the age of Augustus, the primitive conceptions cropping out once more, according to which the gods are the lords of all human thought and the city and its interest are the chief object of the citizen's activity. Play is subordinated to utility; religion, patriotism, and art seek a new interest in the knowledge of man.

The Roman spirit owes its aspect in the course of each of the different periods of its history to a variously proportioned mixture of the elements which we seem to have been able to discern. Its originality lay not in these elements, but in their mixture and the reactions which they caused, not in the components, but in the composite. All peoples have begun by giving the gods chief importance in their life. Roman religion was first formed by the fusion of the different gods established in Italy by centuries of prehistory and migrations; then it received Etruscan and Greek gods, and even admitted some of Eastern origin; but it was the city which impressed upon it a semi-legal, administrative, and fundamentally political form.

The Roman city itself seems to have been the result of the Mediterranean tendency to collect the villages of a country-side into a single stronger unit and to sow colonies on every coast; it owed its birth to Etruscan expansion; when it became autonomous it looked for models as far as Magna Graecia; when it conquered, it became a state of the Hellenistic type and then a monarchy inspired by Oriental examples. But the soul of the city still remained what centuries of obscure, stubborn fighting had made it—cautious, orderly, passionately devoted to the public interest, and closely attached to the Capitoline rock which was its cradle. Its solid but narrow virtues dominated all its intellectual and moral life.

From Greece Rome learned play, first through Etruria, and then through Hellenized Italy and, still more, Sicily. Later, Athens, Pergamon, and Alexandria completed her artistic education. Into play the Roman brought an application, a care for detail and reality, a seriousness, and a passion which preserved the memory of a long past of austerity and the habits of an activity which had formerly been directed exclusively at the useful.

The whole of intellectual life was Greek in origin, but the Roman mind was content with the scientific results obtained by Greece; its own curiosity was bent on Rome herself and her past or else on man and morality.

Like all other peoples, the Roman people never at any period of its history ceased to borrow the elements of its civilization from its neighbours. Its attachment to old customs hardly curbed its ardour in appropriating all fruits that its conquests brought within reach of its hands. The amount which it borrowed, at certain moments at least, was so beyond measure that it could only assimilate them little by little. The interest of the age of Augustus is just that it shows us in the full light of history the religious and political ideas of the past of Rome acting on the latest acquisitions, selecting from them, developing some and trying to eliminate others, and appropriating play and knowledge to utilize them and bringing them into the national tradition.

Thus was constituted by a slow progress, by the effect of events and by the efforts of men, the mighty personality of the Roman people. The Roman spirit gradually gathered up the substance of the whole ancient world and gave it a new form. In this form, imposed by Rome, the legacy of antiquity has come down to the modern world, at least to that of the West and to the Latin nations in particular.

BIBLIOGRAPHY

A. PERIODICALS

Annuaire de l'École pratique des Hautes Études, Section des Sciences historiques et philologiques, Paris	I
Bulletin de correspondance hellénique, French School in Athens, Paris, 1876, etc.	II
Bulletino della Commissione archeologica municipale di Roma, 1872-3, etc.	III
Dissertazioni della Pontificia Accademia romana di Archeologia, Rome	IV
Istituto di Corrispondenza archeologica, Rome. *Bullettino*, 1830, etc.	V
—— *Annali*, 1829, etc.	VI
—— *Monumenti*, 1829, etc.	VIa
Journal des Savants, Institut de France, Paris	VII
Journal of Roman Studies, London, 1911, etc.	VIII
Klio : Beiträge zur alten Geschichte, Leipzig, 1900, etc.	IX
Mélanges d'archéologie et d'histoire, French School in Rome, 1881, etc.	X
Mélanges de Rossi. Supplement to the *Mélanges d'arch. et d'hist.* above, xii, 1892	Xa
Mémoires de la Société de linguistique de Paris, Paris, 1885, etc.	XI
Jahrbuch des Deutschen Archaeologischen Instituts, Berlin, 1886, etc.	XII
Mitteilungen des Deutschen Archaeologischen Instituts, Römische Abteilung, Rome, 1886, etc.	XIII
Monumenti antichi, pubblicati per cura della Reale Accademia dei Lincei, Milan, 1892, etc.	XIV
Monuments Piot : monuments et mémoires publiés par l'Académie des Inscriptions et Belles-lettres, Paris, 1894, etc.	XV
Revue archéologique, Paris	XVI
Neue Jahrbücher für das klassische Altertum, Geschichte, und deutsche Literatur, Berlin and Leipzig, 1898, etc.	XVII
Notizie degli scavi di antichità : atti della Reale Accademia dei Lincei, Series v, Rome, 1876, etc.	XVIII
Papers of the British School at Rome, Rome, 1906, etc.	XIX
Revue de philologie, de littérature, et d'histoire anciennes, Paris, 1877, etc.	XX
Revue des études anciennes : annales de la Faculté des Lettres de Bordeaux et des Universités du Midi, Bordeaux and Paris, 1876, etc.	XXI
Rivista di filologia e di istruzione classica, Turin, 1872, etc.	XXII
Studi storici per l'antichità classica, diretti da Ettore Pais, Pisa, 1908, etc.	XXIII
Revue des études latines, publiée par la Société des Études latines, Paris, 1923, etc.	XXIV
Bulletin de l'Association Guillaume Budé, Paris, 1923, etc.	XXV

BIBLIOGRAPHY

B. WORKS

Note.—Certain English editions are mentioned in square brackets ; but the
references in the text do not refer to these editions.

Altmann (W.), *Die italischen Rundbauten*, Berlin, 1906   **XXVI**

Appel (G.), *De Romanorum Precationibus* (Religionsgeschichtliche
Versuche und Vorarbeiten, vii, 2), Giessen, 1909   **XXVII**

Babelon (E.), *Description historique et chronologique des monnaies de la
République romaine*, 2 vols., Paris, 1885-6   **XXVIII**

Behn (F.), *Die Ficorinische Cista*, thesis, Rostock, 1907   **XXIX**

Bellessort (A.), *Virgile : son oeuvre et son temps*, Paris, 1920   **XXX**

Bieber (Margarete), *Die Denkmäler zum Theaterwesen im Altertum*,
Berlin and Leipzig, 1920   **XXXI**

Blanchère (R. de la), *Un Chapitre d'histoire pontine : état ancien et
décadence d'une partie du Latium* (Mémoires présentés par divers
savants de l'Académie des Inscriptions et Belles-lettres, vol. x),
Paris, 1893   **XXXII**

Blecher (G.), *De Extispicio capita tria* (Religionsgeschichtliche
Versuche u. Vorarbeiten, ii, 4), Giessen, 1905   **XXXIII**

Bloch (G.), *La République romaine. Les conflits politiques et sociaux*
(Bibliothèque de philosophie scientifique), Paris, 1919   **XXXIV**

Boissier (G.), *Étude sur la vie et les ouvrages de M. Terentius Varron*,
thesis, Paris, 1861   **XXXV**

—— *Cicéron et ses amis*, Paris, 1877. [English translation by A. D.
Jones : *Cicero and his Friends*, London, 1897]   **XXXVI**

—— *La Religion romaine d'Auguste aux Antonins*, 2 vols., Paris, 1884   **XXXVII**

—— *L'Opposition sous les Césars*, Paris, 1906   **XXXVIII**

Bornecque (H.), *Cicéron : l'Orateur*, text and translation (Collection
Guillaume Budé), Paris, 1921   **XXXIX**

—— *Ovide : l'Art d'aimer*, text and translation (Coll. G. Budé), Paris, 1924   **XL**

Buck (C. D.), *A Grammar of Oscan and Umbrian*, Boston, 1904   **XLI**

Carcopino (J.), *Virgile et les origines d'Ostie* (Bibl. des Écoles fr.
d'Athènes et de Rome, 116), Paris, 1919   **XLII**

Cartault (A.), *À propos du Corpus Tibullianum : un siècle de philo-
logie latine classique* (Bibl. de la Fac. des Lettres de l'Univ. de
Paris, 23), Paris, 1906   **XLIII**

Chapot (V.), *La Province romaine proconsulaire d'Asie depuis ses
origines jusqu'à la fin de la Haute-Empire* (Bibl. de l'École des
Hautes Études, sect. des Sciences hist. et philol., 157), Paris, 1904   **XLIV**

Choisy (A.), *Vitruve*, text, translation, and plates, 4 vols., Paris, 1909   **XLV**

Colin (G.), *Rome et la Grèce* (Bibl. des Écoles fr. d'Athènes et de Rome,
94), Paris, 1904   **XLVI**

Collignon (M.), *Histoire de la sculpture grecque*, 2 vols., Paris, 1897   **XLVII**

—— and Pontremoli (E.), *Pergame*, Paris, 1900   **XLVIII**

Comparetti (D.), *Vergilio nel medio evo*, Florence, 1872   **XLIX**

—— *Iscrizione arcaica del Foro*, Florence and Rome, 1900   **L**

Corpus Inscriptionum Latinarum, published by the Berlin Academy,
15 vols.   **L I**

Corpus Inscriptionum Etruscarum, published by the Berlin Academy, 2 vols. **LIa**

COURBAUD (E.), *Le Bas-relief romain à représentations historiques* (Bibl. des Écoles fr. d'Athènes et de Rome, 81), Paris, 1899. **LII**

—— *Cicéron : De l'Orateur*, Bk. i, text and translation (Coll. G. Budé), Paris, 1922 **LIII**

CROISET (A. and M.), *Histoire de la littérature grecque*, 5 vols., 2nd ed., Paris, 1901 **LIV**

CUMONT (F.), *Les Religions orientales dans le paganisme romain* (Ann. du Musée Guimet, vol. xxiv), Paris, 1907 **LV**

DAREMBERG, SAGLIO, and POTTIER, *Dictionnaire des antiquités grecques et romaines*, Paris, 1878-1918 **LVI**

DÉCHELETTE (J.), *Manuel d'archéologie préhistorique celtique et gallo-romaine*, 4 vols., Paris, 1908-14 **LVII**

DELATTE (A.), *Études sur la littérature pythagoricienne* (Bibl. de l'École des Hautes Études, sect. des Sciences hist. et philol., 217), Paris, 1915 **LVIII**

DELBRUECK (R.), *Das Capitolium von Signia. Der Apollo-Tempel auf dem Marsfelde in Rom.*, Rome, 1903 **LIX**

—— *Die drei Tempel am Forum Holitorium in Rom*, Rome, 1903 **LX**

—— *Hellenistische Bauten in Latium : i. Baubeschreibung. ii. Geschichtliche Erläuterung*, Strasburg, 1907-12 **LXI**

DESJARDINS (E.), *La Table de Peutinger*, text and plates, 2 vols, Paris, 1869 **LXII**

DETLEFSEN (D.), *Ursprung, Einrichtung, und Bedeutung der Erdkarte von Agrippa* (Quellen und Forschungen zur alten Geschichte und Geographie, 13), Berlin, 1906 **LXIII**

DUBOIS (C.), *Pouzzoles antique* (Bibl. des Écoles fr. d'Athènes et de Rome, 98), Paris, 1907 **LXIV**

DUCATI (P.), *L'Arte classica*, Turin, 1920 **LXV**

—— *Storia della ceramica greca*, 2 vols., Florence, 1922-3 **LXVI**

DURCKHEIM (E.), *Les Règles de la méthode sociologique*, 7th ed., Paris, 1919 **LXVII**

DURM (J.), *Die Baukunst der Etrusker. Die Baukunst der Römer*, 2nd ed., Berlin, 1905 **LXVIII**

DURUY (V.), *Histoire des Romains*, 6 vols., Paris, 1879 **LXIX**

ERNOUT (A.), *Recueil des textes latins archaïques*, Paris, 1916 **LXX**

—— *Lucrèce : De la Nature*, text and translation (Coll. G. Budé), 2 vols., Paris, 1920 **LXXI**

FABIA (P.), *Les Prologues de Térence*, thesis, Paris, 1888 **LXXII**

FERRERO (G.), *Grandeur et décadence de Rome*, translated into French by U. MANGIN, 6 vols., Paris, 1914-18. [English translation, *The Greatness and Decline of Rome*, by A. E. ZIMMERN and H. J. CHAYTOR, 5 vols., London, 1907-8] **LXXIII**

FISCHER (T.), *La Penisola italiana : saggio di corografia scientifica*, translated into Italian by V. NOVARESE and F. M. PASANISI, Turin, 1902 **LXXIV**

FRAZER (Sir J.), *The Golden Bough*, abridged, 1 vol., London, 1922. (French translation, Paris, 1924) **LXXV**

FURTWAENGLER (A.), *Intermezzi : kunstgeschichtliche Studien*, Leipzig and Berlin, 1896   **LXXVI**

—— *Die antiken Gemmen*, 3 vols. : i. Plates ; ii. Explanation ; iii. History, Berlin and Leipzig, 1900   **LXXVII**

FUSTEL DE COULANGES, *La Cité antique*, Paris, 1865   **LXXVIII**

GRAILLOT (H.), *Le Culte de Cybèle Mère des Dieux à Rome et dans l'empire romain* (Bibl. des Écoles fr. d'Athènes et de Rome, 107), Paris, 1912   **LXXIX**

GRENIER (A.), *Étude sur la formation et l'emploi des composés nominaux dans le latin archaïque* (Annales de l'Est, published by the Fac. des Lettres at Nancy), Paris thesis, 1912, Nancy, 1912   **LXXX**

—— *Bologne villanovienne et étrusque, VIIIe-IVe siècles avant notre ère* (Bibl. des Écoles fr. d'Athènes et de Rome, 106), Paris, 1912   **LXXXI**

HAEBERLIN (E.-I.), *Aes Grave : das Schwergeld Roms und Mittelitaliens*, 2 vols., plates and text, Frankfort, 1910   **LXXXII**

HATZFELD (I.), *Les Trafiquants italiens dans l'Orient hellénique* (Bibl. des Écoles fr. d'Athènes et de Rome, 115), Paris, 1919.   **LXXXIII**

HOLLEAUX (M.), *Rome, la Grèce, et les monarchies hellénistiques au IIIe siècle avant J.-C.* (273-205). (Bibl. des Écoles fr. d'Athènes et de Rome, 124), Paris, 1921   **LXXXIV**

HOMO (L.), *La Rome antique. Historique. Guide des monuments de Rome*, Paris, 1921   **LXXXV**

—— *L'Italie primitive et les débuts de l'impérialisme romain* (L'Évolution de l'humanité, vol. xvi), Paris, 1925. [English translation : *Ancient Italy* (History of Civilization)]   **LXXXVI**

JARDÉ (A.), *La Formation du peuple grec* (L'Évolution de l'humanité, vol. x), Paris, 1923. [English translation : *The Formation of the Greek People* (History of Civilization)]   **LXXXVII**

JORDAN (H.), *M. Porci Catonis praeter librum De Re Rustica quae exstant*, Leipzig, 1860   **LXXXVIII**

KIRCHHOFF (A.), *Studien zur Geschichte des griechischen Alphabets*, 4th ed., Berlin, 1887   **LXXXIX**

KOCH (H.), *Dachterrakotten aus Campanien*, Berlin, 1912   **XC**

LAFAYE (G.), *Histoire de culte des divinités d'Alexandrie hors de l'Égypte* (Bibl. des Écoles fr. d'Athènes et de Rome, 33), Paris, 1883   **XCI**

—— *Les Métamorphoses d'Ovide et leurs modèles grecs* (Bibl. de la Fac. des Lettres de l'Univ. de Paris, 19), Paris, 1912   **XCII**

—— *Catulle : Poésies*, text and translation (Coll. G. Budé), Paris, 1923   **XCIII**

LECÈNE (P.), *L'Évolution de la chirurgie* (Bibl. de philosophie scientifique), Paris, 1923   **XCIV**

LEJAY (Abbé) and PLESSIS (F.), *Q. Horati Flacci Opera*, vol. ii : *Satires*, published by Father Lejay, Paris, 1911   **XCV**

LEROUX (G.), *La Salle hypostyle* (Exploration archéologique de Délos faite par l'École française d'Athènes, 2), Paris, 1909   **XCVI**

—— *Les Origines de l'édifice hypostyle* (Bibl. des Écoles fr. d'Athènes et de Rome, 108), Paris, 1913   **XCVII**

—— *Lagynos : recherches sur la céramique et l'art ornemental hellénistiques*, thesis, Paris, 1913   **XCVIII**

Levy-Bruhl (L.), *Les Fonctions mentales dans les sociétés inférieures*, Paris, 1910 — XCIX

—— *La Mentalité primitive*, Paris, 1922 — C

Lindsay (W. M.), *T. Macci Plauti Comoediae* (Scriptorum Classicorum Bibliotheca Oxoniensis), 2 vols., 2nd ed., Oxford, 1910 — CI

Loisy (A.), *Les Mystères païens et le mystère chrétien*, Paris, 1919 — CII

Martha (C.), *Lucrèce*, Paris, 1867 — CIII

Martha (J.), *L'Art étrusque*, Paris, 1889 — CIV

—— *Cicéron : Brutus*, text and translation (Coll. G. Budé) — CV

Marx (F.), *A. Cornelii Celsi quae supersunt* (Corpus Medicorum Latinorum, i), Leipzig, 1915 — CVI

Matthies (G.), *Die praenestinischen Spiegel : ein Beitrag zur italischen Kunst- und Kulturgeschichte* (Zur Kunstgeschichte des Auslandes, 95), Strasburg, 1912 — CVII

Meillet (A.), *Aperçu d'une histoire de la langue grecque*, Paris, 1st ed., 1913, 2nd ed., 1920 — CVIII

Merlin (A.), *L'Aventin dans l'antiquité* (Bibl. des Écoles fr. d'Athènes et de Rome, 97), Paris, 1906 — CIX

Michaut (G.), *Histoire de la comédie romaine : i. Sur les tréteaux latins ; ii. Plaute*, Paris, 1912-20 — CX

Miller (K.), *Itineraria Romana*, Stuttgart, 1916 — CXI

Minto (A.), *Marsiliana d'Albegna*, Florence, 1921 — CXII

Mommsen (T.), *Römische Forschungen*, 2 vols., Berlin, 1864-79 — CXIII

Mueller (K.-O.), *Die Etrusker*, 2nd ed., edited by W. Deecke, 2 vols., Stuttgart, 1877 — CXIV

Nissen (H.), *Italische Landeskunde*, 3 vols., Berlin, 1883-1902 — CXV

—— *Orientation*, Berlin, 1906 — CXVI

Norden (E.), *Ennius und Vergilius*, Leipzig and Berlin, 1915 — CXVII

—— *Die germanische Urgeschichte in Tacitus Germania*, Leipzig and Berlin, 1922 — CXVIII

Pagenstecher (R.), *Die calenische Relief-Keramik* (Jahrb. des Deutschen Arch. Instituts, Erganzungsheft 8), Berlin, 1909 — CXIX

—— *Unteritalische Grabdenkmäler*, Strasburg, 1912 — CXX

Pais (E.), *Storia di Roma*, 2 vols., Turin, 1898 — CXXI

—— *Ancient Italy*, translated by C. D. Curtius, Chicago and London, 1908 — CXXII

—— *Ricerche sulla storia e sul diritto pubblico di Roma*, 3 vols., Rome, 1915-18 — CXXIII

—— *Storia critica di Roma durante i primi cinque secoli*, 4 vols., Rome, 1913-20 — CXXIV

—— *Fasti Triumphales Populi Romani : i. Text and critical commentary*, Rome, 1920 — CXXV

Pareti (L.), *Studi siciliani e italioti* (Contributi alla scienza dell' antichità, published by G. de Sanctis and L. Pareti, vol. i), Florence, 1914 — CXXVI

Pauly and Wissowa, *Real-Encyclopaedie der klassischen Altertumswissenschaft*, Stuttgart, 1893, etc. (In progress.) — CXXVII

PERDRIZET (P.), *Negotium perambulans in tenebris : études de démono-logie gréco-orientale* (Publ. de la Fac. des Lettres de Strasbourg, 6), Strasburg, 1922   CXXVIII

PICHON (R.), *De Sermone Amatorio apud Latinos Elegiarum Scriptores*, thesis, Paris, 1902   CXXIX

PIGANIOL (A.), *Essais sur les origines de Rome* (Bibl. des Écoles fr. d'Athènes et de Rome, 110), Paris, 1917   CXXX

—— *Recherches sur les jeux romains* (Publ. de la Fac. des Lettres de Strasbourg, 13), Strasburg, 1923   CXXXI

PLESSIS (F.) and others, *Épitaphes*, selected texts and commentaries, Paris, 1905   CXXXII

—— *La Poésie latine, de Livius Andronicus à Rutilius Namatianus*, Paris, 1909   CXXXIII

PONCHONT (M.), *Tibulle et les auteurs du Corpus Tibullianum*, text and translation (Coll. G. Budé), Paris, 1924   CXXXIV

RAYET (O.) and COLLIGNON (M.), *Histoire de la céramique grecque*, Paris, 1894   CXXXV

RAYET (O.), *Monuments de l'art antique*, text and plates, 2 vols., Paris, 1884   CXXXVI

REINACH (S.), *Cultes, mythes, et religions*, 5 vols., Paris, 1902-23   CXXXVII

ROBIN (L.), *La Pensée grecque et les origines de l'esprit scientifique* (L'Évolution de l'humanité, vol. xiii), Paris, 1923. [English translation : *Greek Thought and the Scientific Spirit* (History of Civilization)]   CXXXVIII

RODOCANACHI (E.), *Le Capitole romain antique et moderne*, Paris, 1904   CXXXIX

ROUSSEL (P.), *Délos colonie athénienne* (Bibl. des Écoles fr. d'Athènes et de Rome, 111), Paris, 1916   CXL

—— *Les Cultes égyptiens à Délos du IIIe au Ier siècle av. J.-C.* (Ann. de l'Est, published by the Fac. des Lettres at Nancy), thesis, Paris, 1916   CXLI

SANCTIS (G. de), *Storia dei Romani*, 4 vols., Turin, 1907-23   CXLII

SCHANZ (M.), *Geschichte der römischen Literatur* (I. VON MÜLLER : Handbuch der klassischen Altertumswissenschaft, viii), 3rd ed., Munich, 1907   CXLIII

SCHREIBER (T.), *Die Wiener Brunnenreliefs aus Palazzo Grimani*, Leipzig, 1888   CXLIV

—— *Die hellenistische Reliefbilder*, plates, Leipzig, 1894   CXLV

SCHULZE (W.), *Zur Geschichte der lateinischen Eigennamen* (Abh. der Kgl. Ges. der Wissenschaften zu Göttingen, Phil. Hist. Klass., N.F., v, 2), 1904   CXLVI

SCHUMACHER (K.), *Eine praenestinische Ciste im Museum zu Karlsruhe : Beiträge zur italischen Kultur- und Kunstgeschichte*, Heidelberg, 1891   CXLVII

SETA (A. Della), *Museo di Villa Giulia*, Rome, 1918   CXLVIII

—— *Italia antica, dalla caverna preistorica al Palazzo imperiale*, Bergamo, 1922   CXLIX

SOMMER (F.), *Handbuch der lateinischen Laut- und Formenlehre*, Heidelberg, 1902   CL

STRONG (E.), *Roman Sculpture from Augustus to Constantine*, London, 1907 — **CLI**

—— *Apotheosis and After Life*, London, 1915 — **CLII**

STUART JONES (W. H.), ROSS (R.), and ELLET (L.), *Malaria : a neglected factor in the history of Greece and Rome*, Cambridge, 1907 — **CLIII**

STUDNICZKA (F.), *Zur Ara Pacis* (Abh. der Sächs. Ges. der Wissenschaften, *Phil. Hist. Klasse*, 27, 1909, pp. 901-44) — **CLIV**

TAINE (H.), *Essai sur Tite-Live*, Paris, 1856 — **CLV**

·THÉDENAT (H.), *Le Forum romain et les Forums impériaux*, Paris, 1904 — **CLVI**

—— *Pompei*, Paris, 1910 — **CLVII**

THULIN (C.-O.), *Die etruskische Disciplin* (Göteborgs Högskolas Arsskrift), 1905-6-9 — **CLVIII**

—— *Italische sakrale Poesie und Prosa : eine metrische Untersuchung*, thesis, Berlin, 1906 — **CLIX**

—— *Die Götter des Martianus Capella und die Bronzeleber von Piacenza* (Religionsgeschichtliche Versuche und Vorarbeiten, iii, 1), Giessen, 1906 — **CLX**

TOMASETTI (G.), *La Campagna romana antica, medioevale, e moderna*, 3 vols., Rome, 1910-13 — **CLXI**

TOUTAIN (I.), *Les Cultes païens dans l'empire romain* (Bibl. de l'École des Hautes Études, Sciences religieuses, 25 and 31), 3 vols., Paris, 1907-17 — **CLXII**

VEDRÈNES (A.), *Le Traité de médecine de Celse*, translated with a preface by P. BROCA, 14 plates, and 110 illustrations of ancient surgical instruments, Paris, 1876 — **CLXIII**

VILLE DE MIRMONT (H. de la), *Études sur l'ancienne poésie latine*, Paris, 1903 — **CLXIV**

WALDE (A.), *Lateinisches etymologisches Wörterbuch*, 2nd ed., Heidelberg, 1910 — **CLXV**

WALTERS (H. B.), *The Art of the Romans*, London, 1911 — **CLXVI**

WARDE FOWLER (W.), *The Religious Experience of the Roman People, from the earliest times to the age of Augustus*, London, 1911 — **CLXVII**

—— [*Social Life at Rome in the Age of Cicero*, London, 1908.] French translation by A. BIAUDET : *La Vie sociale à Rome au temps de Cicéron*, Lausanne and Paris, 1917 — **CLXVIII**

WEEGE (F.), *Etruskische Malerei*, Halle, 1921 — **CLXIX**

WICKHOFF (F.), and VON HARTEL (W.), *Die Wiener Genesis*, Vienna and Leipzig, 1895 — **CLXX**

WISSOWA (G.), *Religion und Kultus der Römer* (I. VON MUELLER : Handbuch der klassischen Altertumswissenscha t, v, 4), 2nd ed., 1912 — **CLXXI**

VON DUHN, *Italische Gräberkunde*, Leipzig, 1924 — **CLXXII**

INDEX

Roman men are indexed under their cognomen except those generally known by their gentile name.

Deities and festivals mentioned only in Pt. i, ch. iv, §1, are not indexed separately.

A

Aborigines, 6, 89

Academy : philosophy of, 150, 177, 398 ; and rhetoric, 213

Accius (L.), 128

Aediles of the Plebs, 54

Aeneas : legend, 121, 151, 237, 278, 312 ; in Virgil, 305-6, 308-10, 312 ; on Altar of Peace, 354-5

Aequi, 50

Africa : oil from, 144 ; conquest, 291

Agis IV, K. of Sparta, 181-2

Agram mummy, 107

Agrippa (M. Vipsanius), 20, 285, 323, 345 ; map, 323-5, 327 ; on Altar of Peace, 357-8

Agrippa Posthumus, 285

Agrippina the Elder, 285

Agrippina the Younger, 199

Ahenobarbus (Cn. Domitius), altar of, 256-7, 313, 348

Ahenobarbus (L. Domitius), 359

Alba Longa, 5, 46

Alban Hills, Mount of Alba, 4-6, 46

Albano, Lake, 5-6

Albinus (Sp. Posthumius), see Posthumius

Albunea, 311

Alcibiades, statue, 66-7

Alexander, K. of Macedon, 61-2, 236, 241 ; example of, 141-2, 292, 378

Alexander Severus, Emp., 199

Alexandria : civilization and influence on Rome, 237, 240-4, 263, 291-2 ; art in general, 242-3, 247, 339 ; architecture, 241, 258, 261 ; deification of kings, 378 ; painting, 242-3 ; poetry, 223, 230, 243, 269-70, 273-4, 277-9, 283, 288, 290, 297-9, 303, 313 ; science and erudition, 195-7, 199-201, 204-5, 207-8, 241-2, 321-2 ; sculpture, 242-4, 246, 249-50, 255, 343, 361-2 ; toreutic art, 250, 343, 361 ; woman, importance of, 225

Alimentus (L. Cincius), 124

Ambarvalia, 91, 100

Ambracia, drama on fall of, 125

Andronicus (Livius), 110, 116, 119-21

Annales Maximi, see under Pontifices

Antemnae, terra-cottas, 64

Anticythera, find, 248

Antigonos of Carystos, 239

Antioch, 237, 260 ; *see also* Asia

Antiochos III the Great, K. of Syria, 148

Antiochos IV, 262

Antiochos of Ascalon, philosopher, 205

Antium, 9 n., 50 n.

Antonia, Elder and Younger, 359

Antoninus and Faustina, Apotheosis of, 380

Antonius (Julus), 285, 287, 349

Antony (Mark), 243-4, 248, 269, 292, 298

Aphrodite, *see* Venus

Apollo : worship in Rome, 51, 92, 318-19 ; temples, 63, 318, 344, 374 ; statue from Veii, 24-5 ; statue on Palatine, 375 ; Games, 157-8 ; popular worships, 369-70 ; divination, 104 ; *see also* Delphi

Apollodoros of Carystos, poet, 169

Apollonios of Rhodes, 277

Apotheosis, 378-82

Appiades, 263

Apulia, 55-7

Aqueducts, 80

Ara Pacis, *see* Peace, Altar of

Arcesilas, sculptor, 255

Archagathos, physician, 198

Architecture : Etruscan, 19-26 ; Samnite, 57 ; early Republic, 63-4 ; Hellenistic and late, 237, 258-63, 393 ; domestic, 38, 265 ; Vitruvius on, 196-7

Ardea, terra-cottas and paintings, 64-5

Arezzo, *see* Arretium

Argei, 98 n.

Aricia, shrine, 233 n.

Aristarchos of Samos, 242

Aristophanes of Byzantium, 242

PRINTED IN GREAT BRITAIN BY
THE EDINBURGH PRESS, 9 AND II YOUNG STREET, EDINBURGH

THE HISTORY OF CIVILIZATION

A COMPLETE HISTORY OF MANKIND FROM
PREHISTORIC TIMES TO THE PRESENT DAY
IN NUMEROUS VOLUMES DESIGNED
TO FORM A COMPLETE
LIBRARY OF SOCIAL
EVOLUTION

Edited by

C. K. OGDEN

of Magdalene College, Cambridge

Published by

KEGAN PAUL, TRENCH, TRUBNER & CO., Ltd.

BROADWAY HOUSE: 68-74, CARTER LANE, LONDON

THE HISTORY OF CIVILIZATION

THIS series marks one of the most ambitious adventures in the annals of book publishing. Its aim is to present in accessible form the results of modern research and modern scholarship throughout the whole range of the Social Sciences—to summarize in one comprehensive synthesis the most recent findings and theories of historians, anthropologists, archæologists, sociologists, and all conscientious students of civilization.

To achieve success in this stupendous undertaking, the arrangement of the series, has been entrusted to the experienced editorship of C K. Ogden, M.A., of Magdalene College, Cambridge. The new French series, *L'Evolution de l'Humanité*, in which the leading savants of France are collaborating with the Director of the Bibliothèque de Synthèse Historique, M. Henri Berr, is being incorporated. Distinguished historians, both European and American, are contributing volumes in their several departments. Above all, while detailed and very special monographs have been avoided, no attempt to " write down " to a low level has been made.

The field has been carefully mapped out, as regards both subjects and periods ; and, though the instalments will be published as they are ready, the necessary chronological sequence will be secured by the fact that the volumes of the French collection will be used as a nucleus. Each work will be entirely independent and complete in itself, but the volumes in a given group will be found to supplement one another when considered in relation to a particular subject or period.

The volumes are uniformly bound in a fine art-cambric cloth, with specially designed gold lettering and emblem, royal octavo in size, and usually illustrated.

THE TIMES LITERARY SUPPLEMENT devoted a leading article to the first four volumes, in which the series was described as being " composed by all the talents ".

THE MANCHESTER GUARDIAN wrote that " the experiment is one of great interest. Its difficulty is also great. The intention is to provide something more than an encyclopædia or a series of monographs. The aim is to preserve a certain community of plan while giving a free hand to each author in his own section. It is an heroic attempt, which will be sympathetically watched, to bring some light into the vast mass of ill-organized knowledge which we owe to modern research and so make it available in the end for the guidance of the world ".

NATURE, the leading scientific journal, in a six-column review, provides a striking summary of the aims and objects of the series : " The History of Civilization promises to be perhaps the most important contribution so far undertaken towards the task of organization and systematization of the social studies. A glance at the prospectus makes us anticipate a library of masterpieces, for the best workers of France, Great Britain, and some other countries are contributing from their own speciality and are attempting to bring it into line with the contributions from neighbouring fields and with the results of general sociology. Including all the volumes of the important French collection, *L'Evolution de l'Humanité*, the English library contains additions and improvements which will place it above its continental counterpart. The volumes already issued bear out our best hopes. Arranged so as to include all manifestations of human culture, the series follows roughly a combined historical and geographical plan. Starting from the most comprehensive picture, the empty earth in the midst of the empty universe awaiting the arrival of man, it passes then to the gradual development of organic life and the early history of mankind, accompanied by a series of introductory works which give an account of the various aspects of human culture : social organization, language, geographical and racial factors, man's political evolution and primeval domesticity. The story then begins at the traditional cradle of culture, the ancient East, on the holy banks of the Nile, the Euphrates and Tigris, and on the shores of the Mediterranean, where the origins and history of the early Empires and their civilizations are described. .
After having been shown the growth of the Ægean civilization and the formation of the Greek people we study the history of Greece in all its wonderful cultural achievements. Next, hegemony has to be surrendered to Rome with its laws, politics, and economic organization. This brings us to the vast areas occupied by the Teutonic peoples to the North, the Persian, Indian and Chinese civilization to the East, and the Mongol cultures of Central Asia. These will be studied in a series of monographs. . . . The second division will contain volumes on Christian religion, on the break-up of the Roman Empire, on the religious imperialisms of Christianity and Islam, on the political, social,

4

economic, and intellectual evolution in the Middle Ages and modern times. The English library contains, besides, several special sections, one on the histories of various subjects, such as medicine, money, costume, witchcraft, etc. ; a section on Oriental culture ; on historical ethnology ; and a few more sections not yet exhaustively announced, dealing with modern history. This summary does not do full justice to the merits of the plan and of the achievements of the series, so far as they have been laid before us   . "

*The following plan, comprising upwards of eighty titles, though not definitive, will serve to convey a general notion of the nature and scope of the enterprise :**

A   PRE-HISTORY AND ANTIQUITY

I   Introduction and Pre-History

*Social Organization	W. H. R. Rivers
The Earth Before History	E. Perrier
Prehistoric Man	J. de Morgan
*The Dawn of European Civilization	V. Gordon Childe
A Linguistic Introduction to History	J. Vendryes
A Geographical Introduction to History	L. Febvre
Race and History	E. Pittard
*The Aryans	V. Gordon Childe
From Tribe to Empire	A. Moret
*Woman's Place in Simple Societies	J. L. Myers
*Cycles in History	J. L. Myers
*The Diffusion of Culture	G. Elliot Smith
*The Migration of Symbols	D. A. Mackenzie

II   The Early Empires

The Nile and Egyptian Civilization	A. Moret
*Colour Symbolism of Ancient Egypt	D. A. Mackenzie
The Mesopotamian Civilization	L. Delaporte
The Ægean Civilization	G. Glotz

III   Greece

The Formation of the Greek People	A. Jardé
*Ancient Greece at Work	G. Glotz
The Religious Thought of Greece	C. Sourdille
The Art of Greece	W. Deonna and A. de Ridder
Greek Thought and the Scientific Spirit	L. Robin
The Greek City and its Institutions	G. Glotz
Macedonian Imperialism	P. Jouguet

* An asterisk denotes that the volume does *not* form part of the French collection, *L'Evolution de l'Humanité.*

5

6

7

In the Sections devoted to MODERN HISTORY the majority of titles will be announced later. Many volumes are, however, in active preparation, and of these the first to be published will be

*The Restoration Stage	*M. Summers*
*London Life in the Eighteenth Century	*M. Dorothy George*
*China and Europe in the Eighteenth Century	*A. Reichwein*

The following volumes have already been issued. They are arranged roughly in the order in which they were published. But their place in the scheme of the whole series may be discovered from the above list :

THE EARTH BEFORE HISTORY : *Man's Origin and the Origin of Life*

By EDMOND PERRIER, *late Hon. Director of the Natural History Museum of France.*

With 4 maps, 15s. net.

" It goes back to the birth of the world and the transformations of land and water, and takes us through the growth of life on the planet, the primitive animal forms, the peopling of the seas, and the forms of life in the primary, secondary, and tertiary periods, to the growth of the human form. Thus, starting from the origin of matter, it leads us in easy stages to *homo sapiens* himself."
Daily News.

" A remarkable volume."—*Yorkshire Post.*

PREHISTORIC MAN : *A General Outline of Prehistory*
By JACQUES DE MORGAN, *late Director of Antiquities in Egypt.*
With 190 illustrations and maps, 12s. 6d. net.

" A notable and eminently readable study in the early history of civilization, and one well worth its place in the great series now being issued by the publishers. It bears on every page the impress of the personality of its author, who strives to give the reader a clear, composite picture of early civilization, taking one topic after another."—*Nation.*

" A masterly summary of our present knowledge at a low price. As a full survey the book has no rival, and its value is enhanced by the lavish illustrations."
New Leader.

SOCIAL ORGANIZATION
By W. H. R. RIVERS, LL.D., F.R.S. *Preface by* PROFESSOR G. ELLIOTT SMITH.

10s. 6d. net.

" *Social Organization* is the first volume of the series of historical works on the whole range of human activity. May the present book be of good augury for the rest ! To maintain so high a standard of originality and thoroughness will be no easy task."—JANE HARRISON, in *Nation.*

" The book is a great contribution to the sum of human knowledge in the region of pure sociology."—*Daily News.*

THE THRESHOLD OF THE PACIFIC: *an Account of the Social Organization, Magic, and Religion of the People of San Cristoval in the Solomon Islands*

By C. E. FOX, LITT.D. *Preface by* PROFESSOR G. ELLIOT SMITH.
With 14 plates and 40 text illustrations, 18s. net.

" A masterpiece. One of the very best contributions to ethnology we possess. It has, besides its intrinsic value as a masterly record of savage life, also an indirect one ; it is a remarkable testimony to the indispensable need of scientific method for the observer. His account of magical ritual and spells will become a classical source for students. The account of the life-history of the individual is depicted with a clearness and fulness unrivalled in ethnographic literature . . . " *Times Literary Supplement.*

LANGUAGE : *a Linguistic Introduction to History*

By J. VENDRYES, *Professor in the University of Paris.*
16s. net.

" A book remarkable for its erudition and equally remarkable for originality and independence of thought."—*Sunday Times.*

" As an introduction to philology this volume is a splendid piece of *haute vulgarisation*, for which anyone who at all loves words or who is at all curious about language, must be grateful. It covers nearly all the ground from every useful angle. A wide, level-headed, and erudite study."—*Nation.*

A GEOGRAPHICAL INTRODUCTION TO HISTORY

By LUCIEN FEBVRE, *Professor in the University of Strasburg.*
With 7 maps, 16s. net.

" A masterpiece of criticism, as witty as it is well-informed, and teeming with nice observations and delicate turns of argument and phrase."
Times Literary Supplement.

" A broad, clear-headed introduction to the fascinating study of human geography. It is much more than a text-book for the student : it is a work that anyone with no knowledge of geography can read with avidity, for it is the greatest of pleasures to watch the clear logical thought of the writer rapidly treating with masterly power these great and important topics."—*Nation.*

THE HISTORY AND LITERATURE OF CHRISTIANITY : *from Tertullian to Boethius*

By PIERRE DE LABRIOLLE, *Professor of Literature at the University of Poitiers. Foreword by* CARDINAL GASQUET.
25s. net.

" A masterly volume. A scholar of the finest accomplishment, an enthusiast for his subject, and himself an artist in letters, he has produced a book comprehensive and authoritative, and also a joy to read from the first page to the last."
Universe.

" This interesting and valuable book."—W. L. COURTNEY, in *Daily Telegraph.*

LONDON LIFE IN THE EIGHTEENTH CENTURY
By M. DOROTHY GEORGE.
With 8 plates, 21s. net.

" Mrs. George, by her cumulative method, imparts a shuddering impression of the brutalised life led by the masses under the first two Georges. Her work is full of eloquent detail. All who like to get at close quarters with history will feel immensely debtors to her industrious research and faculty of clear statement. And she will have the satisfaction of restoring faith to many minds in the reality of progress."—*Observer*.

" One of the best pieces of research in social and economic history which have appeared for many years."—*Nation*.

" An admirable study."—J. L. HAMMOND, in *The New Statesman*.

A THOUSAND YEARS OF THE TARTARS
By E. H. PARKER, *Professor of Chinese in the Victoria University of Manchester*.
With 5 illustrations and maps, 12s. 6d. net.

" Professor Parker takes us back to a period roughly contemporaneous with that of the foundation of the Roman empire, and shows their history to be, like that of the Northern barbarians and Rome, a constant struggle with China. With an unfamiliar subject the book is not an easy one to read, but the author has done all that was possible to enliven his subject and has certainly succeeded in giving us a most valuable text-book."—*Saturday Review*.

CHINA AND EUROPE : *their Intellectual and Artistic Relations in the Eighteenth Century*
By ADOLPH REICHWEIN.
With 24 plates, 12s. 6d. net.

" Among the volumes of the monumental History of Civilization, this study of the influence of Chinese art and thought on the European art and thought of the eighteenth century will find not the least popular and distinguished place. The chapter headed ' Rococo ' will be of especial interest to connoisseurs. . . The illustrations are numerous and beautiful."—*Sunday Times*.

" A fascinating subject. The references to literature are admirably full and complete."—*Times Literary Supplement*.

THE DAWN OF EUROPEAN CIVILIZATION
By V. GORDON CHILDE, B.LITT.
With 198 illustrations and 4 maps, 16s. net.

" Higher praise of Mr. Childe's book, which forms a volume of the monumental History of Civilization could scarcely be given than to say that it is in all respects worthy of the volumes which preceded it."—*Sunday Times*.

" He has done a very great service to learning, and given a clear and reliable outline of the earliest civilization of Europe. His book ' fills a gap ' indeed." —*Nation*.

" A very fine piece of work."—*Manchester Guardian*.

" A work of supreme importance . . . places the writer in the very front rank of European archæologists."—*Glasgow Herald*.

MESOPOTAMIA : *the Babylonian and Assyrian Civilization*

By L. DELAPORTE, *Professor in the Catholic Institute of Paris.*

With 60 illustrations and maps, 16s. net.

" This book is for the most part very good. The author has handled his difficult material cleverly. Where he succeeds is in his admirably written description of the social life, of which he makes a fascinating story. Here is presented an entertaining picture of the inhabitants in 2000 B.C. Then from the earlier Babylonians he passes to the Assyrians, dealing with them in a similar excellent way. This is one of the best books of its kind which we have seen for some time."—*Times Literary Supplement*.

" A highly-detailed picture of that orderly and highly-coloured civilization which once assembled libraries, tried divorce cases, and contrived an intricate irrigation system."—*Daily News*.

THE AEGEAN CIVILIZATION

By G. GLOTZ, *Professor of Greek History in the University of Paris.*

With 4 plates, 87 text illustrations, and 3 maps, 16s. net.

" This is a marvellous summary, divided into four books, describing in detail the material, social, religious, artistic and intellectual life of the people. Every one of these sections is full of interesting and new knowledge. A wonderful book, thoroughly scholarly and attractive in presentation."—*Birmingham Post*.

" Reads like a romance . . . presents a very vivid picture of this marvellous civilization."—*Times Literary Supplement*.

THE PEOPLES OF ASIA

By L. H. DUDLEY BUXTON, M.A., F.S.A., *Lecturer in Physical Anthropology in the University of Oxford.*

With 8 plates, 12s. 6d. net.

" Although the physical characters of the principal racial strains are described in some detail, the author keeps before his readers the bearing of these data upon the broader problems of racial distribution, as well as the intensely interesting question of the interaction of race, environment, and modification by contact due to migration. The exposition of anthropological method given in an ntroductory chapter is admirably lucid."—*Manchester Guardian*.

" The student will gain much information presented in an orderly manner. The style is both lucid and concise, and not the least remarkable feature of the work is its compactness."—*Times Literary Supplement*.

LIFE AND WORK IN MODERN EUROPE, *from the Fifteenth to Eighteenth Century*

By G. RENARD, *Professor at the College of France, and* G. WEULERSSE, *Professor at the Lycée Carnot. Introduction by* EILEEN POWER, *D. Lit., Reader in Medieval Economic History in the University of London.*

With 8 plates, 16s. net.

" In a way as attractive as possible they deal with social conditions and economic changes, with the history of labour in all the important European countries, with the gradual disappearance of medieval survivals, and the increasing influence of Governments on economic life. A well-balanced and valuable picture of Europe as a whole during a period of the greatest importance in the history of the world."—*Westminster Gazette.*

" This can certainly be pronounced a most useful book. There is nothing in English that covers anything like the same ground. It is interestingly written and is a storehouse of valuable information."—*New Statesman.*

THE MIGRATION OF SYMBOLS, *and their Relations to Beliefs and Customs*

By DONALD A. MACKENZIE, *author of* " *Ancient Man in Britain* ".

With 16 plates and 53 text illustrations, 12s. 6d. net.

" He certainly abolishes once for all the widely current idea that such forms as the Spiral and the Swastika were created as manifestations of the decorative instinct. Generously illustrated, and written in a most clear and fascinating style devoid of unnecessary technicalities, this most suggestive volume should ensure the suffrages of all intelligent readers interested in the early religions and æsthetic developments of our race."—*Sunday Times.*

" A highly instructive volume."—*Daily News.*

" A volume of extraordinary interest."—*Glasgow Herald.*

TRAVEL AND TRAVELLERS IN THE MIDDLE AGES: *a series of Essays*

Edited by A. P. NEWTON, *Rhodes Professor of Imperial History in the University of London.*

With 8 plates and maps, 12s. 6d. net.

The contributions include : The Conception of the World in the Middle Ages, by Prof. A. P. Newton ; the Decay of Geographical Knowledge, by Prof. M. L. W. Laistner ; Christian Pilgrimages, by Prof. Claude Jenkins ; the Viking Age, by Prof. Alan Mawer ; Arab Travellers and Merchants, by Prof. Sir T. W. Arnold ; Land Routes to Cathay, by Eileen Power, Lit.D. ; Communication in Eastern Europe, by Baron A. F. Meyendorff ; Travellers' Tales, by Prof. A. P. Newton ; Prester John, by Prof. Sir E. Denison Ross ; Ocean Routes to the Indies, by Prof. Edgar Prestage ; etc.

ANCIENT GREECE AT WORK : *an Economic History of Greece from the Homeric Period to the Roman Conquest*
By G. GLOTZ, *Professor of Greek History in the University of Paris.*
With 49 illustrations, 16s. net.

An account of the Greek in the workaday life which lay behind the political, religious, intellectual, and artistic development, described in other volumes of the series. In a succession of lively pictures of fields, markets, workshops, mines, banks, harbours, and building yards, the author traces the progress of Greek trade, industry, and labour from the simple household economy, the farming, the barter, and the piracy of Homeric times, to the extensive business life of the Hellenistic age, with its " world market," elaborate industries, crowded cities and busy trade routes.

RACE AND HISTORY : *an Ethnological Introduction to History*
By E. PITTARD, *Professor of Anthropology in the University of Geneva.*
With 9 illustrations and maps, 21s. net.

This volume is intended to serve as a companion to Febvre's *Geographical Introduction to History*, which estimated the value of "environment " as a factor in history. The present volume considers the " racial " factor, the anthropological reality which depends on somatic characters, build, height, colour of hair and eyes, craniological and facial form, etc. This the author carefully distinguishes from such artificial entities as peoples, nations, civilizations, or language groups.

THE ARYANS : *a Study of Indo-European Origins*
By V. GORDON CHILDE, *B.Litt.*
With 8 plates, 28 text illustrations, and a map, 10s. 6d. net.

The startling discoveries of the Ancient East and the great progress made in the study of the prehistoric civilizations of Europe (and especially of Greece) seem to make the moment propitious for a fresh survey of the fascinating question as to the origin and diffusion of those languages to which we, in common with the Ancient Greeks, Romans, and Hindus, are heirs. In fact, no full discussion of the Aryan question has appeared in English for the last twenty-five years.

FROM TRIBE TO EMPIRE : *Social Organization among the Primitives and in the Ancient East*
By A. MORET, *Professor in the University of Paris, and* G. DAVY, *of the University of Dijon.*
With 47 illustrations and 7 maps, 16s. net.

A study of political organization in the Near East, showing how the claims of social life encroached on the freedom of the individual, so that by degrees totemic groupings gave way to tribes, kingdoms and empires. This view is carefully exemplified in the history of ancient Egypt, Babylonia, and the Near East, whose organization is compared and contrasted with that of primitive Australian Bushmen and North American Indians.

The following publications are nearing publication. They are arranged roughly in the order in which they will appear. Their place in the scheme of the whole series may be discovered from the list :

THE FORMATION OF THE GREEK PEOPLE

By A. JARDÉ, *Professor of History at the Lycée Lakanal.*

With 7 maps, about 16s. net.

Based on the latest findings of archæology, geography, anthropology, and philology, this volume gives a clear outline of the nature of the Greek spirit and the influences which led to its formation. Attention is paid to political and social life, colonial expansion, and intellectual and moral character, in order to show the unity of the Greek spirit in its disunion.

THE HISTORY OF WITCHCRAFT AND DEMONOLOGY

By MONTAGUE SUMMERS, *editor of Congreve, Wycherley, Otway, etc.*

With 8 full-page plates, about 15s. net.

The author includes in his definition of Witchcraft, sorcery, black magic, necromancy, divination, satanism, and every kind of malign occult art. In a volume of supreme interest to the theologian, the psychologist, the historian, and the general reader, the dark and terrible aspects of witchcraft and the immodesty of the witch-cult are not shunned. The witch is revealed in her true colours as a social pest, the devotee of an obscene creed, an adept at creeping crimes, a blasphemer, charlatan, bawd, and abortionist.

THE HISTORY OF MEDICINE, *from the time of the Pharaohs to the end of the Eighteenth Century*

By C. G. CUMSTON, M.D., *Lecturer on the History of Medicine in the University of Geneva. With a chapter on the Study of the History of Medicine, by* F. G. CROOKSHANK, M.D., F.R.C.P.

With 22 plates, about 12s. 6d. net.

This book has been written for the general reader and, as an introduction to the history of his chosen profession, for the student of medicine. It contains an account of the chief medical schools, theories, and discoveries, and will contain much material not to be found in other works. While all unnecessary details have been excluded, the book gives a clear and comprehensive history of the evolution of the healing art.

PRIMITIVE ITALY, *and the Beginnings of Roman Imperialism*

By LEON HOMO, *Professor in the University of Lyons.*

With 13 maps and plans, about 16s. net.

The situation in primitive Italy, the birth of Rome, its growth, the extension of its early conquests, the gradual assimilation of the whole of the Italian peninsular, its spread over the Mediterranean, until finally the Roman empire is complete, these are the themes of this volume. Here one may see the methods by which one of the greatest empires in history attained to the height of its power.

THE ROMAN SPIRIT *in Religion, Thought and Art*
By A. GRENIER, *Professor in the University of Strasburg.*
With 16 plates and 16 text illustrations, about 16s. net.

A full account of the development of Roman civilization from its Latin and Etruscan beginnings to the cosmopolitan maturity of the Augustan age, with a detailed survey of works of art and of the writings of classical authors. We see the old hard morality breaking down before personal ambition, and luxury, and religion passing through all its stages from the countless little gods of house and field to the deified emperor. Vivid character sketches of individuals and pictures of social, literary, and artistic circles in Rome are a prominent feature of the book.

THE CIVILIZATION OF THE SOUTH AMERICAN INDIANS, *with special reference to their Magic and Religion*
By RAFAEL KARSTEN. *Preface by* PROFESSOR E. WESTERMARCK.
About 21s. net.

Based on close personal contact with the natives of South America for five years, the book gives a detailed account of their life, in which, of course, magic and religion play a dominant part. Chapters are devoted to Ceremonial Body-Painting ; Customs relating to Hair, Nails, Head, and Skin ; Feather and other Ornaments ; Mutilation ; Psychology of Ornamental Art ; Animal and Plant Spirits ; Spirits of Inanimate Objects ; Ideas of Generation and Conception ; the Male Child-bed ; Magical Sacrifice ; Taboo and Mana ; etc.

LIFE AND WORK IN MEDIEVAL EUROPE, *from the Fifth to Fifteenth Centuries*
By P. BOISSONNADE, *Professor in the University of Poitiers.*
Translated with an Introduction by EILEEN POWER, *D.Lit., Reader in Medieval Economic History in the University of London.*
With 8 plates, about 16s. net.

This volume, with its companion, *Life and Work in Modern Europe* (see above), together provide an accurate and vivid picture of the social conditions and economic movements throughout Europe from the downfall of the Roman Empire to the beginning of the Industrial Revolution. The early period, covered by the present volume, includes the stupendous work of the colonization and population of Europe, traces the rise of vast labouring classes from conditions of dependence to those of comparative freedom, and demonstrates the early development of such " modern " phenomena as the capitalist entrepreneur, strikes, unions, and the other symptoms of war between rich and poor.

ROMAN LAW
By J. DECLAREUIL, *Professor in the University of Toulouse.*

While the Greeks created art and speculation, it was left to those born realists, the Romans, to produce jurists. So anxious were they to maintain just relations between living beings that they early adopted a legal attitude towards the gods themselves. This volume sets forth in a luminous fashion the sources and the formation of Roman law ; its evolution ; the establishment of a public order where the rights of the individual are reconciled with social interests ; finally the loss of equilibrium due to exaggerated individualism on the one hand and on the other the establishment of State Socialism.

ANCIENT PERSIA, *and Iranian Civilization*

By CLEMENT HUART, *Professor at the National School of Living Oriental Languages.*

With 4 plates, 35 text illustrations, and a map, about 16s. net.

The rôle played by Persia in the history of civilization was one of paramount importance. Not only did she herself make original contributions to the world of moral and religious thought, but she was in a great degree responsible for the fusion of races. Professor Huart traces her history under the great dynasties, the Achaemenid, the Arsacid, and the Sassanid, shows the birth of Mithraism from Mazdaism, and estimates its effect in producing the great world religions.

ANCIENT ROME AT WORK : *an Economic History of Rome from the Origins to the Empire*
By PAUL LOUIS.

Illustrated, about 12s. 6d. net.

Other early volumes, of which details will be announced later, include :

THE NILE, *and Egyptian Civilization*

By A. MORET, *Professor in the University of Paris.*

ART IN GREECE

By A. DE RIDDER, *Director of the Louvre Museum.*

GREEK THOUGHT, *and the Origins of the Scientific Spirit*

By L. ROBIN, *Professor in the University of Paris.*

MACEDONIAN IMPERIALISM, *and the Hellenization of the East*

P. JOUGUET, *Professor in the University of Paris.*

THE LIFE OF BUDDHA, *in Legend and History*

By E. H. THOMAS, D.Litt., *Assistant-Librarian in the University Library, Cambridge.*

THE GEOGRAPHY OF WITCHCRAFT

By MONTAGUE SUMMERS